Two Aspirins and a Comedy

Two Aspirins and a Comedy

How Television Can Enhance Health and Society

Metta Spencer

Paradigm Publishers

Boulder • London

Copyright © 2006 by Paradigm Publishers

Excerpts from *The Power of Film Propaganda: Myth or Reality* by Nicholas Reeves copyright © 1999 by Nicholas Reeves. Reprinted by permission of the Continuum International Publishing Group. Excerpts from "Robert Warshow: Life and Works" by David Denby in *The Immediate Experience: Movies, Comics, Theatre, and Other Aspects of Popular Culture* by Robert Warshow, p. ix, Cambridge, Mass.: Harvard University Press, copyright © 2001 by the President and Fellows of Harvard College. Reprinted by permission of the publisher. Excerpts from *Love and Limerence* by Dorothy Tennov copyright © 1999 by Scarborough House. Reprinted by permission of the publisher. Excerpts from "The Triumph of the Prime-Time Novel," by Charles McGrath from *New York Times Magazine* (October 22, 1995) copyright © 1995 by the New York Times Company. Reprinted by permission of the publisher. Excerpts from *How Things Come Together* by Hanna Newcombe copyright © 1998 by Hanna Newcombe. Reprinted by permission of the author. Two stills from *Street Time* copyright Sony Pictures Television. Reprinted by permission of Sony Pictures Television. Still from *Northern Exposure* copyright © 1990 Universal Television Enterprises, Inc. Reprinted courtesy of Universal Studios Licensing LLLP. Photograph of Richard Stratton by Wayne Maser. Reprinted by permission.

Published in the United States by Paradigm Publishers, 3360 Mitchell Lane Suite E, Boulder, CO 80301 USA.

Paradigm Publishers is the trade name of Birkenkamp & Company, LLC, Dean Birkenkamp, President and Publisher.

Library of Congress Cataloging-in-Publication Data

Spencer, Metta, 1931–
 Two aspirins and a comedy : how television can enhance health and society / by Metta Spencer.
  p. cm.
 Includes bibliographical references and index.
 ISBN 1-59451-154-3 (hardcover : alk. paper) — ISBN 1-59451-155-1 (pbk. : alk. paper)
 1. Television—Psychological aspects.   2. Television broadcasting—Social aspects.   I. Title.
 PN1992.6.S662 2006
 302.23'45—dc22

2005030750

ISBN-13: 978-1-59451-154-7 (hc)-—ISBN 978-1-59451-155-4 (pbk.)

Printed and bound in the United States of America on acid free paper that meets the standards of the American National Standard for Permanence of Paper for Printed Library Materials.

Designed and Typeset by Straight Creek Bookmakers.

10 09 08 07 06   1 2 3 4 5

*With gratitude for the virtual worlds created by
the Fourteenth Dalai Lama, Mikhail Gorbachev,
Garrison Keillor, and Rob Morrow*

Contents

Acknowledgments

Nobody writes a book single-handedly. In one way or another, hundreds of people are involved in the creation, though the numbers vary from one book to another. In this case, I owe thanks to a huge number, including television producers, writers, and actors; interviewees and participants in several e-mail lists; friends who came to my home every week to watch and discuss two television shows; two medical students who fact-checked my physiological reports; friends who read my work critically; and several wonderfully helpful assistants over a period of seven years. You've given me enough material for five or six books! Thanks especially to Erika Alexander, David Assael, John Bacher, Elizabeth Barger, Simon Baron-Cohen, Aaron Bates, Rosanna Bencoach, Liliana Bezjak, Christopher Bolton, Sara Boyles, Joshua Brand, Michelle Bylow, Richard Cefola, Matthew Cloner, Scott Cohen, Silvia Colomines, Barry Corbin, Lee Creal, Rose Dyson, Paul Ekman, Lisa Ferguson, Robert Ferguson, Sonny Fox, Michael Fresco, Joseph Gonda, Patricia Hluchy, Walter Hammontree, Louise Harlow, Jason Hartley, Miro Harven, Greg Hillegas, Jennifer Jewell, Niliema Karkhanis, Diane Katz, Joe Lazarov, Marc Levin, Alexander Likhotal, Jamie Marie Lynaugh, Jeffrey Marcon, Graeme MacQueen, Jeff Melvoin, Kelly McDowell, Amber McNair, Rob Morrow, Michelle Nolden, Aimee Parrott, Wilson Perkowski, Julie Berg Raymond, Rheta Rosen, Bill Ryerson, Joanna Santa Barbara, Morgan Savage, Thomas Scheff, Len Schlichting, Edward Silva, Ken Simons, Ann Sorenson, Roselyn Stone, Richard Stratton, Aparna Swaminathan, Ann Swidler, Jeff Vlaming, John Vreeke, David Wahl, Eric Walberg, Dinesh Xavier, and Dolf Zillmann.

I'm particularly grateful for the good ideas contributed by Arlie Hochschild and Jonathan Spencer, for the helpful support of Melissa Weiner, and the superb, intelligent support at Paradigm Publishers from Beth Davis, Dianne Ewing, Julie Kirsch, and Alison Sullenberger. It has been fun! Dean Birkenkamp helped me through the difficult but necessary process of trimming the book down to a manageable size. Readers who want more information can visit the book's Web site, www.twoaspirinsandacomedy.com.

Chapter 1

Introduction

Suppose you seek professional advice about a problem, and this is what you're told:

By your family physician: "Say, 'Ah.' ... Well, it's just a nasty cold—which isn't surprising. Your immunoglobulin A count is far too low. Take these two aspirins. And we need to boost your immune system. I want you to watch *Ferris Bueller's Day Off* and *Annie Hall* tonight. And after your cold's gone, consider making more time for lovemaking. A little romance every day or two will improve your health. If your wife isn't in the mood often enough, try writing poetry for her. If that fails, just improvise on your own."

By your career counselor: "I don't think you should quit nursing school just yet. Yes, the training is stressful, but nursing fits your personality. Besides, your school has a program in recreational music. You play keyboards, so join the group. Making music is one of the best cures for stress. But don't watch *ER* or any crime or suspense shows for a while. *Seinfeld* would be okay or—even better—inspiring films such as *It's a Wonderful Life.*"

By your marriage counselor: "Clearly, you two still love each other and you don't fight. Your problem is existential. You're bored. Your life together lacks meaning. Both of you are thrill-seeking idealists, but you're stuck in hum-drum jobs that you don't dare quit. You need a joint project bigger than yourselves. I recommend two new TV shows: *Civilian Peacekeepers* and *A Green Cross Team.* They're funny and adventurous, but not violent. The characters are preventing a war and saving the environment. Then check out their Web sites for groups you can join and work together on such issues. Joseph Campbell advised, 'Follow your bliss.' Your bliss will come from doing something valuable for the world."

In order to keep this book to a reasonable length, some of the material originally planned for the book had to be cut. This material is available on the book's Web site, www.twoaspirinsandacomedy.com.

If these proposals seem wacky, just stay with me. By the end of the book, you'll consider them quite reasonable. We're going to explore the potential of entertainment to enhance the quality of your life—your emotions, your physical health, your moral and spiritual worldview, and the significance of your contributions to society. And among all the forms of entertainment, we'll find that television drama offers the greatest potential value.

But perhaps you think that entertainment doesn't *have* any value—that it's just a leisurely waste of time? That it doesn't *do* anything?

Ah, but it does! And you can use it far more effectively.

Entertainment has several obvious uses. First, *it seizes and holds our attention.* It presents us with a situation that takes our mind off our own concerns. We enjoy a diversion that psychologically requires some resolution. (What kind of pitch is he going to throw now? Is Rhett Butler actually going to walk out on Scarlett? Does this hockey strike mean the season will be cancelled? Who altered the murdered billionaire's will?)

People differ in their liking for surprise and physiological arousal. Today, the key attraction of movies and TV may simply be *engagement* with swiftly moving, eye-catching events. You have to pay close attention just to figure out what's going on. Indeed, this intense engagement with complex entertainment probably stimulates your brain and makes you smarter.

Second, *entertainment helps us manage our moods.* Even if your life is satisfying, you may run short of certain passions and begin to feel "beige-colored" if you go without entertainment for a while. We all have emotional holes that we fill up with rodeos, casinos, Ferris wheels, sidewalk art shows, and other forms of entertainment. (I call art a *kind* of entertainment instead of something different from, and necessarily better than, entertainment.)

Think of the shivers of fear you get from Edgar Allan Poe's short stories. Or the exaltation of Handel's "Hallelujah Chorus." Or the triumphant joy of winning a Scrabble tournament. Or the serene, loving sorrow of Michelangelo's *Pietà* sculpture. Or your laughter at *Don Juan De Marco* or *Harold and Maude.* Those moments of intense emotion may have been stronger than anything you had felt within a month of everyday living. Most lives are not very emotional. For example, if you are an average adult, you laugh about fifteen times per day—a sharp decrease from hundreds of times a day in your childhood.

But you need laughter. It's protects your health and replenishes your zest. If you laugh when nothing is funny, you will appear goofy and people may not entrust you with serious responsibilities, but if you rent a comedy, you can laugh twenty times an hour and still be considered normal. Imaginative fiction, whatever the genre may be, stimulates vicarious feelings that you can replay mentally later as you take a shower or drive around town. The average TV show is far from inspiring. Nevertheless, in a study of 909 Texas women, researchers found that watching TV improved their mood more than several other activities, including shopping, taking care of children, and housework.[1]

When you are stressed, you will probably choose a comedy instead of a heavy drama, but other times you may want a tragedy or an intergalactic laser war. You have different emotional needs to fill at different times. One objective of this book is to suggest how to elevate your overall emotional well-being and even your health by selectively using resources from your cultural environment.

Third, *entertainment helps us hone our ethical sensibilities.* Stories and dramas, in particular, can function as a kind of therapy or "soul work," much as the ancient Greeks used the theater and moral philosophy to explore one crucial question: How should human beings live? Greek entertainment was not meant to cure neurotic individuals but rather to show normal people how to live better. This is one aspect of entertainment that I particularly address in this book—the potentially therapeutic effects of stories. For example, as Stanford philosopher Richard Rorty notes, "the novels of Proust and James help us achieve spiritual growth, and thereby help many of us do what devotional reading helped our ancestors to do."[2]

Emotions and ethics are interdependent. If evil triumphs in the plot, you feel bad. Emotions are quivering internal sense organs for perceiving human virtues, desires, and relationships. If yours don't quiver anymore, maybe you've been desensitized by overexposure to pain. But sometimes, even if you are still sensitive to human misery, you may choose a story about wrongdoing anyway, knowing that it will make you feel worse. We'll consider why.

Fourth, entertainment illustrates and critiques social theories and practices. A novelist may draw our attention to a social problem, for example, and spur us to invent ways of overcoming it. As Rorty suggests, fiction makes us rethink our judgments and break with our own pasts. "The resulting liberation may, of course, lead one to try to change the political or economic or religious or philosophical status quo. Such an attempt may begin a lifetime of effort to break through the received ideas that serve to justify present-day institutions."[3]

Some entertainers actually avoid this aspect of showbiz. For example, the movie magnate Samuel Goldwyn told his writers, "If you want to send a message, use Western Union!" But in fact, writers can't help sending a worldview, even if they try. The message of Goldwyn's cotton-candy song-and-dance films was exactly his own philosophy: Avoid thinking about the implications of what you're doing. (Yes, there's room in the world for cotton candy, too, but not every day.)

The Harms and Benefits of Entertainment

Sometimes entertainment does more harm than good—or it can just be a waste of time. Indeed, people often assume that it is almost invariably useless. For example, a few years ago I found myself reproaching my son by saying, "You don't seem to think television is important."

"Exactly. In fact, I think TV is *bad,*" he replied. "It rots the brain. We got rid of our cable recently, and suddenly I started doing all kinds of useful things, such as working in the garden."

Most television programs *are* bad, of course, and none of them pulls your weeds, but my son meant more than that. He was saying that watching TV is inherently harmful. I don't agree, but I wasn't surprised by his remark. Since Plato's day, people have criticized all kinds of entertainment. For example, more than once the Christian church banned theatrical performances, and for hundreds of years, no plays were performed before audiences in Europe.[4]

Nor are other fictional products always more acceptable. Flaubert was prosecuted for publishing his novel *Madame Bovary* though it too implied a criticism of fiction by depicting a silly woman whose judgment had been ruined by romantic novels.

But in contrast to such censoriousness, some societies have encouraged forms of entertainment marked by actual (not just play-acted) violence and excess. For example, the Greeks allowed for a period of sexual revelry every year when devotees of the wine god Dionysus went on an alcoholic binge. The Romans adopted the idea, calling their holiday a *bacchanalia*. When Christianity became the official religion of the Roman Empire, the custom evolved into Carnival, just before Lent, when wild sexuality and other kinds of indulgence were accepted that were prohibited at other times.

And for a truly ghastly form of entertainment, consider the ancient circuses. The Romans enjoyed displays of mortal combat for the last two centuries before Christ and the first three centuries thereafter. Slaves and convicts were thrown to lions and killed before cheering crowds. Hosts would even invite people in to dine and provide two or three gladiatorial fights to the death for their guests to watch while reclining after their meal. Everyone applauded with delight when each of the contestants was killed.[5]

You and I consider this a horrible cultural tradition. But what about other degrees of abuse? Where do we draw the line between acceptable and deplorable? How about dueling? Prize fights? Cockfights to the death? Play-acted fights in which no one is really injured? Video games with spaceship battles? *Batman* comic books? (Say when.) If we search for moral standards by which to appraise leisure time amusements, we can find no consensus whatsoever. We must each think the issue through for ourselves, but we won't reach any agreement. Individuals differ markedly—and always will.

The effects of entertainment can be good, bad, or mixed. If Greek dramas, gladiator fights, television shows, novels, orgies in celebration of Dionysus, auto-theft video games, or soap operas are harmful, that poses a problem. And if a type of entertainment enlightens, delights, and inspires, as some of them do, that poses an opportunity. Indeed, of all conceivable ways of fostering a global florescence of civilization, I think the most promising approach is to improve entertainment.

Of the many consequences of entertainment, I discuss mainly its effects on *emotional well-being, health,* and *moral/spiritual sensibilities.* We will find complex causal interactions among these three factors. Vicarious wrongdoing can make you miserable, and misery can make you sick. I ask what makes a form of entertainment *exciting and interesting,* which nowadays matters greatly to many people. Fast-paced action, ambiguous plots, and puzzling mysteries are more popular today than stories exploring characters' inner struggles, beliefs, and relationships—about which I personally care more.

Some literary critics deny that their own emotional responses and ethical judgments are fair grounds for evaluating a work. I believe, on the contrary, that you should always notice both your emotional response to a story and its deeper messages. Throughout part I of this book, I discuss the psychological factors that link culture, emotions, and physical health. In part II, I demonstrate an ethical/emotional approach to cultural criticism. That method requires critics to express their feelings about the works they review. Hence in the chapters discussing two television series, *Northern Exposure* and *Street Time,* my comments will become more subjective.

Enhancing Global Culture

We need to enhance the excellence of culture on a global scale. Such a goal has been proposed by the Dalai Lama and the United Nations, who are promoting cultures of "compassion" and of "peace," respectively. Indeed, their concerns about culture prompted me to write this book.

In a meeting with Western scholars in 1991, the Dalai Lama discussed how to teach compassion through nonreligious approaches. He said, "I think it's very important to try to present moral principles without any religious involvement. It is a reality now that out of five people, only one or two are religious believers.

So, we must be seriously concerned with the remaining majority.... [As for those nonbelievers who] are quite neutral about compassion, you must still find some way to reach those people."[6] Psychologist Daniel Goleman replied:

> Your Holiness, you raised the point that three to four billion people on the planet have no religious belief. The question is, what kind of ethics can appeal to those four billion? I'm going to present experimental scientific evidence suggesting a completely new path for approaching that question: that the body's own mind, the immune system, provides a basis for a de facto ethical system in the difference between emotional states that help one stay healthy and live longer, and those that promote disease.... [These scientific findings will suggest how to] convince people to live ethically who have no religious belief but only the individualistic ethic, "Whatever I want is what I should get." Perhaps you can say it is in their self-interest to be loving, not to be angry.[7]

The Dalai Lama jovially thanked Goleman for reporting on this biological research, which provided the secular rationale for which he had been searching. He adopted Goleman's suggestions. For example, when he received an honorary degree at the University of Toronto in April 2004, he spoke about this research linking health to emotions and ethics, and he urged academics to foster a culture of compassion.

It may sound contradictory to practice altruism for such a self-centered reason as concern for one's own health and happiness. If one gains from experiencing loving-kindness, perhaps the health benefits should be only a nice side effect, not one's primary motivation. Still, I tend to take Goleman's and the Dalai Lama's side on this. If scientific research can influence people to cultivate loving-kindness, let's use it.

But if four billion human beings are nonreligious these days, what are they doing instead of worshipping? How do they spend their time? When do they reflect on their deeper values or examine their own souls? Where can we find them and communicate with them? When it comes to moral reflection, the secular substitutes for religion are psychotherapy and personal growth programs. I devote little attention to such approaches but a lot of attention to entertainment—especially fiction and drama, which may affect our hearts and minds just as deeply.

Before the Altar or the Screen?

The four billion people who are absent from worship services are spending their time at movie theaters, soccer stadiums, and magazine shops, and with iPods, cell-phone games, and DVD-playing laptops. The entertainment indus-try is booming. During a seventeen-year period in the 1980s and 1990s when household spending increased 4 percent in Canada, recreational spending there increased 40 percent. Spending for such items as athletic fees hardly changed, but home recreational equipment—especially cable TV—increased by 253 percent. In the United States and Canada, spending for entertainment is higher than for health care and clothing.[8] Many of these cultural activities are shallow or harmful, but fiction has the potential to inspire and enhance the quality of entire cultures. Stories on the screen shape global culture, teaching terrible or wonderful lessons.

Novels and dramas arouse emotions—such as religious awe, laughter, love, fear, anger, disgust, and grief—that may influence our hearts and minds in a lasting way. Passions make us recall events more clearly than usual. An example is the so-called flashbulb effect, which sears a powerful emotional experience into your memory. You probably recall exactly where you were when you heard about the terrorist attacks on September 11, 2001, but not where you were at the same time on September 10. You also remember best the messages of highly emotional discussions or dramas. The United Nations has dedicated the first decade of this millennium to developing a *culture of peace*. They call on us to contribute to the creation of such a culture. I had been a peace studies professor and peace journalist for two decades before this proclamation demanded a response from me. Peace workers generally address *structural* problems, not cultural ones. For example, we seek to eliminate nuclear weapons and land mines. We seek to end the use of children as soldiers. We call for spending on democratic institutions and economic development instead of weapons. We promote an International Criminal Court with jurisdiction over rulers who perpetrate crimes against humanity. And so on. Such reforms are structural changes.

Culture, on the other hand, is the symbolic currency of hearts and minds. The preamble to UNESCO's mandate states, "Since wars begin in the minds of men, it is in the minds of men that the defenses of peace must be constructed." Nevertheless, few peace researchers believe that war will be ended by changes in the minds of men and women. Instead, they expect that structural reforms of our political, economic, and legal systems will gradually enable us to manage discord without bloodshed.

To reshape a culture sounds harder, but it is just as necessary as institutional change. Structural innovation can't outrun cultural innovation, just as a dog's front legs can't outrun its back legs. Fortunately, large-scale cultural changes are increasingly feasible—and not by heavy-handed methods such as censorship, preaching, brainwashing, or didactic teaching. Instead, a culture of peace can be stimulated by depicting warm, likable characters in TV dramas handling wisely the same difficult conflicts that trouble us all. Audiences around the world will *choose* such dramas if they are entertaining and challenging instead of bland. This is the answer to the challenge issued by the United Nations. Entertainment already holds the attention of five billion people. In the hands of brilliant storytellers, it can teach them compassion and loving-kindness, heroism, the thrill of discovery, and ethical courage in the face of adversity. Alas, few of us imagine such plots by ourselves; we have to be given stories to experience vicariously. That is the task of entertainers. Fortunately, we have technological ways now of recording, preserving, and disseminating superb ones widely in durable, portable form.

Culture Kits

Culture originates in the imagination, but it must also become objectively physical, so as to move from one mind to another. A writer puts words onto a page; years later, a reader harvests them. A television crew puts a tender relationship onto tape; years later, a viewer's tears and hormones flow while watching and recreating it vicariously.

Sometimes culture kits contain ideas that, though no longer alive in any mind, remain physically present, ready to be absorbed as secondhand notions by another mind. Take the Egyptian hieroglyphs, for example. As part of Egypt's culture, their meaning was forgotten until the Rosetta Stone was discovered in 1799. On it was a text engraved in three languages: hieroglyphic, Greek, and Demotic. Since Greek and the Demotic were still understood, the Frenchman Champollion compared the texts and worked out which words were represented by which hieroglyphs. Since then, much of ancient Egyptian culture has become accessible again and the ideas can once more be discussed. But for many centuries, the ideas encoded in hieroglyphs existed objectively, but not subjectively, since no one could read them.[9]

An immense accumulation of culture exists as objectively concretized records—in pharaohs' tombs, encyclopedias, databases, DVD shops, and cookbooks. This is humanity's cultural storehouse, and while it is vastly important to you, it is a mistake to suppose that your own mind is simply a passive recipient of it, or that culture forces us to act as we do. It is a resource that we may draw upon or forget about. To enhance culture globally will involve both creating excellence and reorganizing the display of the world's cultural resources so as to make superb works conspicuously available for everyone who wants to experience them.

But what is most *worth* preserving and sharing? In reflecting on that question, we become cultural critics. The objective of the second part of this book is to teach such criticism by example.

This book is a meditation on the optimum use of entertainment. It's my answer to the Dalai Lama's and the UN General Assembly's call to support a culture of peace and compassion. What changes in actual entertainment would make such refreshing results possible? In this book, I promote two changes in literary and dramatic practice.

First, I encourage the adoption of *ethical/emotional criteria in evaluating entertainment.* Such standards don't apply to all types of entertainment (garage sale hunting, jazz bands, and quiz shows come to mind as exceptions), but many works of fiction and drama suggest answers to this question: How should human beings live? That's the core question in ethical criticism. Audiences look for answers from cultural producers. Instead of going to temples and chapels to reflect on the quality and emotional wholeness of their lives, people nowadays buy DVDs. The "industry," as showbiz calls itself, already informs audiences on spiritual and social issues, but its representatives could do far better in supporting human flourishing if they recognized their own impact. Ethical/emotional criticism puts those concerns foremost.

Second, I suggest *the amplification of one factor in scripts and novels: reflective thought.* Entertainment has gradually become more complex and less understandable. The maxim "Show, don't tell!" prevails among writers. Fictional characters today don't talk much about the meaning of their situations or the lessons they learn from their experiences. We are supposed to infer their subjective experiences only from their actions, if at all. Writers may hope that audiences mull over the plots afterward and find the implicit messages, but I doubt that this happens very often. Often the action is too quick to comprehend, so we just move on to the next story unless the author makes us stop and think.

Do TV and Video Games Make Us Smarter?

Some people do try to figure out such stories, and for them, grappling with the increasingly complex plots may be intellectually beneficial. Just when this manuscript was ready to go into production, an important book was published: Steven Johnson's *Everything Bad Is Good for You.*[10] In it he argues that video games and television dramas confer valuable cognitive skills on the players and viewers. Instead of expressing the usual opinion that popular culture dumbs us down, Johnson shows that it is becoming increasingly sophisticated and intellectually challenging. For example, instead of having a single plot, today's best TV shows require us follow as many as a dozen distinct plot threads in a single episode, some of them continuing from previous or into subsequent episodes. Each script contains numerous allusions that the audience is not expected to understand, plus a few that are subtly explained to us. There are "in-jokes" and references to events that happened several seasons earlier—or even to unrelated novels, stories, and songs with which only a few viewers will be familiar. Close attention is necessary just to figure out what is going on, moment by moment, and this effort makes us smarter, says Johnson.

Johnson has evidence, too. IQ tests are designed so that the average is set at 100. However, for many years, people have been doing better year by year when taking the tests—though this is not usually recognized because the designers simply keep setting the bar higher, to keep the average IQ at 100.[11] Entertainment deserves some of the credit for the advances.

Television syndication now earns more money than the original runs of TV shows. An episode today is usually written for multiple viewings. Fans will watch it eight or ten times and expect to discover something new each time—so the writers have to produce increasingly clever scripts. People don't *use* television to improve their IQ, but that is an important side effect, of which researchers had previously been unaware.

Johnson has definitely discovered something important. (In chapter 2, I also suggest that TV makes us smarter, though I don't try to prove it, as he did.) However, his main argument needs to be qualified—and to some extent he qualifies it himself. Though it is true that IQ levels have been rising steadily for many years, those increases have been limited to certain *types* or *aspects* of intelligence—especially the capacity to visualize and recall spatial relationships and to strategize in pursuing a given goal. (Video games are especially good at training for strategizing.)

For the most part, Johnson treats intelligence as a single entity, but actually it is a combination of different capacities. For example, Oxford psychologist Simon Baron-Cohen distinguishes between "systemizing" ability (at which males usually excel) and "empathizing" ability (at which females tend to be superior). He says there are corresponding structural differences between typical female and male brains—though many perfectly normal persons have brains like those of the opposite sex. The typical male brain, he says, "systemizes"—it's hard-wired to focus predominantly on *how things work* rather than what other people are experiencing subjectively. Typical male thinking, according to Baron-Cohen, involves fascination with systems, such as science, baseball statistics, mathematics, train schedules, maps, and machinery.[12]

Harvard psychologist Howard Gardner has identified, not one or even two, but about nine distinct intelligences: (1) linguistic, (2) logical-mathematical, (3) musical, (4) spatial, (5) bodily-kinesthetic, (6) naturalist, (7) interpersonal, (8) intrapersonal, and (9) existential. (He is uncertain that the "existential" aptitude is a full-fledged intelligence, since its connection to a particular area of the brain has not been established. It is an attunement to spiritual/religious/ philosophical questions, such as "Why are we here? What's it all about, in the end?")[13] Gardner's inter- and intrapersonal intelligences evidently correspond to Baron-Cohen's "empathizing" skill.

If, say, you're low in bodily-kinesthetic intelligence, you shouldn't become a surgeon. But, fortunately, if you score high in only a few types of intelligence, you can often rely on those enough to get by and avoid using the rest. For example, I have good linguistic, interpersonal, intrapersonal, and existential capacities, but I am seriously subnormal on mathematical, musical, and spatial skills, which I dislike having to use. In fact, I avoid precisely the kinds of TV shows and video games that supposedly would make me smarter.

As Johnson has shown, by exercising a particular mental capacity, you can strengthen it and even alter the corresponding part of your brain. He argues that today's complex television and video games make us smarter—but doesn't say which of these nine types of intelligence they boost. I think they are tailor-made for systemizers with high spatial and logical-mathematical intelligence. People who are already good at those skills are probably attracted to them, which strengthens those aptitudes even more. However, those of us who excel more at empathy will not even try to figure out the kind of puzzles that Johnson enjoys and cannot, therefore, benefit from them.

Johnson's notions and mine are different but complementary. The difference is that he explicitly does not consider the impact of television's *content* at all. He views the message of a show as irrelevant; what counts to him instead are the mental calisthenics it gives the audience and the way it alters their brain structure.

I think the *content* of entertainment is exactly what matters most. That's what I focus on here—the meaning of stories and the empathy involved in following characters as they handle their dilemmas. It's not only intelligence—and definitely not only visual spatial memory or strategic rationality—that we should gain from stories but *wisdom, emotional insight,* and *a capacity for addressing societal problems.*

The improvements Johnson sees in television (the new complexities and ambiguities that make us "smarter") may actually coincide with a *decline* in the aspects of stories that make us "wiser." For example, in modern novels there has been a steady decline in the exploration of character.[14] Readers in earlier periods encountered unique fictional personalities such as Leopold Bloom, Gatsby, and Don Quixote, but today characters with such full inner lives are rare in fiction, especially in films. I think this is because of the dominance of fast-moving, puzzling, multiple-threaded plots. To show us characters going through deep experiences, an author must reflect discursively about their spiritual or intellectual quandaries. We don't expect profound insights from swift-moving crime shows, video games, or *American Idol*. I'm not criticizing people who enjoy video games and TV plots with surprising twists and snappy dialogue. It's just that individuals enjoy very different kinds of experiences. A fast-paced, complex video game or TV cop series that stimulates a systemizer's brain may leave others cold unless it also calls for empathy and reflection (using interpersonal, intrapersonal, and existential intelligence). Stories that boost systemizing and strategizing intelligence do not usually pose questions about the value of what the characters are doing. Those that do so exercise our existential and empathizing intelligence. This cultural imbalance needs to be corrected. Without discussing inner experiences, motivations, or social theories, stories teach nothing about how human beings should live. I'm claiming a bigger share of our culture's products for empathizers.

Johnson is probably right: Television can make you smarter. Can it also make you wiser? Or is entertainment the worst possible way of gaining philosophical insight?

Plato held the latter view. We must reckon even today with his arguments. Since this book will appraise the value of entertainment versus other ways of gaining insight and pleasure, I begin by reviewing the ancient quarrel between philosophers and dramatists. I believe that philosophy and storytelling actually stimulate us in complementary ways, but we must explore *how* they can complement each other. And thereby hangs a tale—an old, old tale.

Popular Culture in the Axial Age: Aristotle vs. Plato

Recall the cultural environment in Athens 2,500 years ago, when the fight began between philosophy and drama. That period resembled the ferment, uncertainty, and social contagion of our own day. If you worry about today's "cultural globalization"—the spread of ideas from one civilization to another—then you would have been shocked by the globalization of the so-called Axial Age between 700 and 200 B.C.E.[15] Within about five hundred years, the great world religions and philosophies—including Buddhism, Jainism, and Hinduism in India; Taoism and Confucianism in China; monotheism in the Middle East; and rational philosophy in Greece—were invented and spread around the Eastern Hemisphere, all the way to Europe.

Everyone traded ideas. Dissatisfied with their old religions, people were adopting new teachings that emphasized universal compassion and transcendence.[16] There was high population growth, capital accumulation, commerce, and urbanization throughout a huge part of the world. Merchants traveled across Southwest Asia, the Middle East, Greece, and North Africa,[17] hawking their wares and spreading ideas throughout a vast area.[18]

For hundreds of years, the stars of Greek popular culture had been professional storytellers who recited mythic poems of Homer and Hesiod about their gods, the Trojan War, and the legendary dysfunctional families of Agamemnon and Oedipus. Lively performances and frequent drama competitions were the Greeks' main religious practice, their way of educating youth, and everybody's favorite entertainment—the showbiz of their day.

But in the seventh century B.C.E., the Greek alphabet was invented. Writing encouraged a more critical and rational way of thinking. The old oral myths had been unverifiable stories, but now historians began writing down eyewitness accounts, and philosophy became recognized as a new way of thinking, based on argumentation rather than storytelling. Fact-based, logical reasoning began rivaling mythology as a way of making sense of life.

Can You Get Wisdom Vicariously? Philosophy versus Showbiz

The cultural transition of the Axial Age did not go smoothly. Indeed, the leading Athenian philosopher, Socrates, was executed for impiety against the gods and for corrupting young Athenian guys by teaching them critical thinking. The accusations against him were led partly by the poets, who wanted to buttress the old traditions. This fight was deadly serious.

Socrates had not been impious, but he had disputed some of the poets' accounts of the gods' behavior. Take, for example, the myth about Zeus transforming himself into a feathery swan and raping a young girl, Leda. Since gods are moral, this story must have been false, Socrates argued. Naturally, the poets and devout Athenians responded angrily. After a trial, they gave Socrates a cup of poison to drink. He did not mind much, for he believed that a god had ordered him to provoke the Athenians, and he had obeyed. Besides, he expected to be reincarnated. He had learned about rebirth from a Greek mystery cult, Orphism, which had originated in an Indian religion, Jainism.[19] (Both Jainism and Buddhism, flourishing in India, had adopted the idea from earlier Hindu teachings, the Upanishads.)

Though Socrates never wrote down his own ideas, his students—especially Plato (427–347 B.C.E.)—wrote on his behalf. Plato wrote in the form of scripts: dialogues between Socrates and friends. Initially Plato started by reporting what Socrates had actually said or what he might well have said. Still, having started putting words into his mouth, Plato continued almost until his death at age eighty.

After the death of Socrates, Plato visited the followers of the late mystical mathematician Pythagoras before returning to Athens and establishing a school of philosophy. His greatest student, Aristotle (384–322 B.C.E.), in turn would tutor the handsome, short-lived military genius Alexander the Great.

Aristotle differed from Plato in many respects, but they did agree in two ways: First, they both appraised the popular culture of their day (notably drama) in terms of *ethical and emotional criteria,* as we'll do, too. Second, they both were *supremely logical,* rational thinkers. Their approach became the basis for the scientific method, which tries to get closer to the truth by a process of elimination. Scholars and scientists look for contradictory explanations and successively eliminate the false ones until, ideally, only one possibility is left standing. In Plato's dialogues, Socrates is forever trapping some poor fellow into contradicting himself and making him admit that his original belief must have been wrong. (This rigorous kind of reasoning—called *logos*—is immensely valuable. Still, as we'll see, its either/or logic does not always yield the wisest solution. Sometimes contradictions can be worth *retaining* instead of eliminating. For example, ambiguity in stories can sometimes be more enlightening than clarity.)

But it is two *dis*agreements between Plato and Aristotle that will haunt us throughout this book, for nobody has yet settled them. First, they disagreed about *whether it is better to pursue spirituality or mastery of this empirical world.* Second, they disagreed about a key question of this book: *the social value (if any) of popular entertainment,* which in their day was the performance of Homeric myths and dramas. Plato considered such "secondhand wisdom" useless, for only philosophizing had value. Aristotle, on the other hand, believed that dramatists sometimes taught profound lessons to audiences, and he tried to identify the principles for doing so. For now I'll deal only with the latter controversy.

What Is the Value, If Any, of Popular Entertainment?

This second disagreement between Plato and Aristotle concerns the value of drama and poetry. (Actually, the two men may never have debated it face-to-face.[20] Long after Plato had expressed his views, attributing them to Socrates, Aristotle wrote on the subject without acknowledging that he was criticizing his teacher's opinions.)

Plato worried about the evil effects that supposedly would result from the proliferation of art and drama in Athens. Secondhand, vicarious wisdom was, to him, an oxymoron. He even mistrusted the process (called *mimesis*) of copying, representing, or reproducing things—even as paintings and sculptures—because it gave only "secondhand" experiences and ideas. He particularly disliked drama because he believed that young people would imitate the immoral acts shown onstage. One could not attain excellence by imitating others—even good models—for only rational philosophizing yields true understanding.

Plato certainly had a point; people (even adults) often do imitate others—including gross acts from popular entertainment. Youths are especially susceptible. Still, it is astonishing that the trashy popular entertainment to which Plato objected included Greek tragedies that today we count among the highest works of art ever created! (Will some television shows of our day be considered great art 2,500 years from now?)

Aristotle was more optimistic. He did not worry that Athenians might copy the immorality depicted in plays. Indeed, he considered the theater therapeutic; audiences could actually benefit by vicariously experiencing terrible situations. It would purify their souls through catharsis[21] and make them into better citizens. His wonderful essay on dramatic criticism, *The Poetics,* offers technical and ethical advice for playwrights. Aristotle recognized the theater's powerful influence on the moral and spiritual development of the public. Yet I still take Plato's concerns seriously and must reckon with them.[22] Enormous harm certainly has been done to society by bad storytelling—whether or not we accept his verdict that all or most myths are harmful.

Conclusion

The United Nations named this the decade for creating a culture of peace. The most promising way is through entertainment, which is far more than merely a diversion from "reality." Yes, entertainment is sometimes worthless, but at other times it's inspiring. It influences our moods, our moral and spiritual values, and our commitment to social reform—for better or worse. It can make us healthy or sick; it can teach us or corrupt us. It can make us smarter or wiser—and sometimes both, and at other times neither. Here we'll consider which kinds of entertainment are worthwhile and how to foster them. As cultural critics, our evaluations must be anchored in our private emotional and ethical responses.

Steven Johnson maintains that popular culture is increasingly challenging and complex. He attributes to that trend another, well-documented finding: that people are becoming more intelligent, generation by generation. However, not all aptitudes are improving. He discusses the skills learned by mentally mastering this increasing complexity, but he does not discuss the content of the entertainment products, as I shall do.

When we explore the *content* of entertainment products, we find that the most influential ones are stories and dramas. Increasingly nowadays, popular culture reaches people who do not belong to formal religions, and it can have as much moral or spiritual impact as the devotional stories our ancestors used to read. I want storytellers—writers, producers, actors, publishers, and critics—to take more seriously their role as creators of a global culture of peace.

But my proposal would appall Plato. He opposed drama and poetry, which induce us to live vicariously through characters and to imitate them. He considered that the worst way of imparting wisdom. He insisted that people should reason critically together rather than emulating fictional persons.

Aristotle, on the other hand, considered the popular entertainment of his day mainly beneficial. A good tragedy would purify our emotions. Accordingly, he developed ethical guidelines for playwrights. We'll consider his arguments later, along with Plato's entirely legitimate warnings about the dangers of imitating.

Can Plato and Aristotle be reconciled? Can storytelling lend emotional power to objective, rational modes of discourse? And can storytellers provide the kind of fast-paced, multi-threaded complexity that supposedly trains our brains, yet also stimulate us to empathize with characters and think seriously about societal and philosophical issues? These questions form our agenda.

Part I

Stories can make you sick or healthy, depending on the feelings they evoke. Your emotional responses depend on the degree of your empathy, as well as on the characters: their morality and emotional appropriateness, whether they receive their just deserts, and the nature of their conflicts.

You need an optimum degree of arousal, which will differ among individuals according to their hereditary need for thrills. Because every gripping story requires conflict, it also requires some negative emotions—which, however, ideally arise in combination with other emotions that offset their harmful effects. For example, pity softens our blaming of a character. Stories that transcend blame help build a culture of peace.

Many popular plots hold our interest by engaging us in the exciting pursuit of blameworthy characters. Other writers, however, give us more valuable stories involving deeper characters who are working on significant societal issues. By following their adventures, we gain knowledge and insight into this vital question: How should human beings live?

Chapter 2

The Power of Stories

Suzanne says a television show saved her life. Before her problems overtook her, she had been a young Boston wife with a great job. She gave birth to a son who, at age two, was diagnosed with autism. She accepted the challenge courageously, but then she had a second son, who also is autistic. That was too much! On the day she got the second boy's diagnosis, she decided to commit suicide. However, someone turned on the TV, and the show *Northern Exposure* caught her attention. She was soon laughing. As she watched the show, she felt her spirits lift. She would live.

That was six years ago. Since then Suzanne has kept videotapes of *Northern Exposure* playing eighteen hours a day. She doesn't watch it now, but hearing it in the background buoys her up. Her boys are doing well, and her marriage is fine.

Suzanne's story is special but not unique. I have come across many other situations that demonstrate the remarkable power of stories—both true and fictional ones—to influence our lives profoundly. In this chapter, I review some of the astonishing effects of the entertainment that surrounds us, almost unnoticed, as cultural environment.

We hardly notice how powerfully imagined events shape reality. By *reality* I mean here empirical *physical* facts (e.g., that Suzanne is alive today), *historical* facts (e.g., a reduction in the world's population growth rate), and even *medical* facts (e.g., the likelihood that a Tanzanian will catch AIDS, or how much my arthritis will hurt today).

That last effect of the imagination on reality—the puzzling medical impact of a TV show on my own body—prompted me to pursue this research. Eight years ago when I retired from my university career, I had pain in my joints. Osteoarthritis, the doctors said. (Eventually I had both hips replaced.) For almost the first time in my life, I turned on a daytime television show—the same one Suzanne was watching. *Northern Exposure* was already running in syndication. The characters were wacky, smart, and kind. There was great music and no laugh track. I fell in love with the inhabitants of "Cicely, Alaska," and I watched them twice a day, experiencing analgesia and joy. My pain was generally reduced for hours.

But I didn't know what to make of my strange new obsession with a fictional world. Had I gone 'round the bend? No, I finally came to regard it as *good* for me. Apart from arthritis, my life had been terrific, in a calm sort of way. But every day now I would leap to my feet laughing and clapping. Or weep with tenderness as a grouchy young doctor reached a new spiritual insight. Or feel as erotic as a high school girl on a date. This was fun!

I joined two e-mail discussion groups of *Northern Exposure,* where I met Suzanne and numerous others who were feeling comparable effects.[1] One was Janie, a married, thirty-year-old, American literature professor, who recalls that period of her life.

> I did a lot of hugging my pillow after an NX episode, a good deal of dancing around my living room table as the theme song finished things up, a lot of folding my hands over my chest in one of those gestures that seem cliché when you see someone else doing it. I think the gesture is an involuntary response to feeling that your heart could fairly burst at any moment, it's been made so big.... NX's best episodes, especially its best "last fifteen minutes," made me feel so vulnerable.... Toni Morrison has written that "anything coming back to life, hurts."

This called for some research. How can one make sense of this kind of experience?

I thought of Plato, who certainly would have disapproved of all this, since he wanted us to become philosophers instead of fans of popular culture. Myself, I couldn't object to any show that taught upbeat wisdom, as this one did.

But then, entertainment is not always benign. It can influence people in terrible ways. In *The Republic,* Plato was particularly concerned with entertainment's impact on children. Recognizing the difficulties of educating youth, given their inevitable tendency to emulate models, he insisted on carefully censoring their exposure to artistic products. His advice is still relevant today, especially when we consider the harm done to children by television.[2]

Nor are adults exempt. Many serial killers are addicted to horror and violent action shows. In the summer of 2004, for example, my newspaper was full of a story about a man arrested for raping, murdering, and dismembering a little girl. His ex-wife had left him because of his obsession with horror videos and kiddie-porn computer images.[3] The police have come to expect such a pattern.

We need ways to limit such effects without censorship. I wondered, How might Aristotle approach this challenge? Intrigued, I began looking for other effects of the stories people consume as entertainment. There were plenty—and not just effects on individuals but even structural impacts on society.

Social Change and Entertainment

Besides affecting our emotions and moral sensibility, novels, plays, and television dramas potentially can reduce the rates of violent crime, global population growth, and warfare. I'm not joking. For example, I have heard gay people attribute the new acceptability of homosexuality in Western society to movies and television dramas, many of which over the past thirty years or so have been designed to liberalize public opinion.

Other effects are going on, worldwide. One puzzling change is the steady increase of intelligence levels around the world over the past century. Broad-spectrum IQ tests are going up by about three points every decade. This change probably has several different causes, such as the improvement in children's diets and child-rearing practices, but some scholars attribute part of the increase to the influence of television and video games. Reading, writing, and arithmetic have gained less than visual analysis skills, perhaps because kids become more visually oriented by watching TV.[4] The effects on children certainly must depend partly on the content of the programming, and more extensive studies of these specific impacts are needed.

Another extraordinary social change is the rapid decline in birthrates in many poor countries. Indeed, demographers have lowered their projected estimates of the world's population by about one billion people this century. In India alone, there may be six hundred million fewer people than previously had been anticipated. Birthrates are dropping in places where poverty and illiteracy are still widespread, confounding the predictions of the previously accepted "demographic transition theory." There is no definitive explanation, but television plays a part. According to Gelson Fonseca, Brazil's ambassador to the United Nations, people in his country observe small, happy families on television, and this prompts them to consider limiting the size of their own families. Few of these changes are the result of deliberate campaigns to promote family planning but are mostly the suggestive side effects of imitating television.[5]

Many social changes have originated in fiction. I'll cite three examples. One is a novel that was largely responsible for the elimination of slavery in Western society. The second is a movie that showed how to overturn repressive regimes nonviolently. Third are broadcasts that promote family planning, AIDS control, and women's emancipation. Maybe these examples will give you ideas about how to promote other social reforms.

A Novel against Slavery: *Uncle Tom's Cabin*

Harriet Beecher Stowe was the wife of a theology professor in Cincinnati and the mother of seven children. Cincinnati was just across the river from the slave-trading region, and Stowe witnessed several troubling incidents on the river, such as seeing a husband and wife being sold apart. Her family hid runaway slaves, many of whom fled on to Canada, where they were safe from the danger of being returned to their owners.

In 1850, the Stowe family lived in New England, and Stowe began writing a novel illustrating the cruelty of slavery and the moral irresponsibility of the nation for allowing it to continue. This was *Uncle Tom's Cabin*. An antislavery weekly published the novel in forty installments, paying Stowe $300. Families passed their copies on to others, so that the story soon became famous and was a topic of conversation in public all year. Because it was initially a series, the public had a long time to discuss it.

Then in 1852, the whole volume was published[6] and broke all sales records: half a million copies within five years. Foreign publishers also cranked out pirated versions. A reviewer said, "*Uncle Tom's Cabin* is at every railway book-stall in England, and in every third traveler's hand. The book is a decided hit."[7]

Today Stowe's writing style seems lurid for its melodrama. In her day, however, such a style was necessary for her purpose: to shock readers who had always accepted slavery without question. It certainly had that effect. The most sympathetic character, Tom, is an honorable, nonviolent black slave who is sold, abused, and finally killed by a vicious master, Simon Legree. Readers of Stowe's day were overwhelmed emotionally. Historians consider the book a key factor—perhaps *the* key factor—in turning Americans' political culture against slavery.

A Film for Freedom: Attenborough's *Gandhi*

Richard Attenborough made a biographical film, *Gandhi,* in 1982 about India's greatest leader. It was distributed around the world. I'm familiar with some of its effects because I had been doing research for a book about human rights and democracy activists in Eastern Europe and the Soviet Union during the first few years after the film was released. I interviewed a number of activists in Poland, Hungary, Czechoslovakia, and the Soviet Union. Several dissident leaders spontaneously mentioned having seen the film. It became clear to me that the nonviolent actions against Communism that occurred in the late 1980s and early 1990s resulted from "diffusion"—the spread of a cultural trait from one society to another when people learn from, and imitate, the examples of others.

Diffusion in this case was facilitated by travelers who spread ideas in face-to-face discussions. For example, a Filipino Jesuit priest named Edmund Garcia had published Gandhi's writings and formed an organization devoted to Gandhian methods in the 1970s.[8] After traveling in Latin America and visiting states that had liberated themselves from authoritarian rule, such as Portugal and Spain, he went to Poland and discussed nonviolence with the students who were aligned with the Solidarity movement. These discussions stimulated human rights activists to emulate Gandhi. Then Garcia returned home and participated in the nonviolent overthrow of the dictator Ferdinand Marcos.

Diffusion especially resulted from the transmission of Gandhi's ideas by Attenborough's film. The Polish dissidents told me that they had never been able to obtain books by Gandhi (Communist regimes disapproved of his un-Marxist methods of social change), but they saw the film while their campaign for conscientious objection was in full swing. Young Poles, Czechs, and Slovaks were influenced by it. Two researchers, Peter Ackerman and Jack DuVall, later documented some effects of the film, which was changing the course of history in Asia and Latin America.

For example, Marcos was ousted through nonviolent resistance, partly because Catholic leaders invited in foreign trainers in nonviolent resistance[9] and partly because of the influence of Benigno Aquino, an opponent of Marcos. Aquino had become acquainted with Gandhian thought in the mid-1970s, during his imprisonment by Marcos. He had tried to defend his rights as a political prisoner by fasting[10] but was sentenced to death. In 1980, however, the U.S. State Department arranged for Aquino to go to the United States. He remained committed to the struggle for democracy in the Philippines, though he knew it was exceedingly dangerous to return there. Indeed, he was killed moments after arriving back home in 1983. Protests followed, and Marcos had to leave the country himself. Aquino's widow, Corazon, became president. This nonviolence was Benigno Aquino's idea, as Ackerman and DuVall note. "Aquino kept speaking out against Marcos, but seeing the Richard Attenborough film *Gandhi* made him rethink his strategy.... Before leaving Boston on his way back to the Philippines, he told a reporter that he was returning to 'join the ranks of those struggling to restore our rights and freedoms through nonviolence.' Aquino even showed his willingness to reconcile with Marcos if democracy was restored."[11]

Ackerman and DuVall also consider another of the film's effects—this time in Chile. The military dictatorship of General Augusto Pinochet ended largely through the leadership of Rodolfo Seguel, president of the Copper Mine Workers' Confederation, who led a day of protest against the dictatorship in May 1983. They were supported by Catholic leaders and inspired by a secular source, reported Ackerman and DuVall.

"I think it was the film *Gandhi*," Seguel recalled. "It was shown in the public cinemas in 1983, when we began, and we all saw it at least twice. We had to, to really get it in ourselves." Seguel saw parallels between Gandhi and Lech Walesa in Poland. "Both men took up struggles without violence that produced better results than armed confrontation."[12]

Television news coverage also helped spread the nonviolent resistance movements in 1989. Every night viewers could watch people marching peaceably in a Communist regime, and within a day or two could witness the former rulers handing their power over to the opposition. The demonstrations stimulated a tidal wave of protest that moved from the Philippines and Burma to Chile, Poland, the Baltic states, Hungary, East Germany, Czechoslovakia, Bulgaria, Romania, and eventually Moscow itself, where the citizens were able to stop the coup against Gorbachev by emulating the Gandhian methods they had seen in Manila when "people power" had ousted Ferdinand Marcos almost a decade before.

Without the Attenborough film and the television newscasts, much of the world that is democratic today might still be ruled by dictators.[13]

Nor has the wave stopped even yet. Since I first wrote the preceding passage, democratic movements have ousted dictatorial regimes without bloodshed in five more countries: Serbia, Georgia, Ukraine, Lebanon, and Kyrgyzstan. Now the leaders of each successful movement train the next country's leaders, distributing thousands of copies of a manual by nonviolence scholar Gene Sharp.[14] Watch for more cases.

Serial Dramas on Drunk Driving, Feminism, Population, and HIV/AIDS

Many of the world's needs—such as better health and nutrition practices, literacy, family planning, and gender equality—can be met only by radical shifts in public opinion and behavior.

Jay Winsten, a professor of public health at Harvard, has demonstrated the effectiveness of television dramas for influencing viewers. In 1988, he launched a campaign to introduce a new social concept—the "designated driver"—to North America. He met with more than 250 writers, producers, and executives, persuading them to add that term to their scripts here and there to discourage drunk driving. And indeed, by 1991 the term *designated driver* could be found in Webster's dictionary. By 1994, that message had been broadcast on 160 prime-time shows and had been the main topic of 25 drama episodes. Surveys showed that the public was influenced favorably; in 1991, 52 percent of all adults under thirty had served as designated drivers. Within ten years, as a result of this campaign and other measures, drunk driving had decreased markedly, and approximately fifty thousand fewer drinking-related traffic fatalities had occurred. According to the National Highway Traffic and Safety Administration, the only way to explain a decline of that magnitude is the designated driver campaign.[15]

Winsten has applied the same principle to other campaigns, such as the reduction of teenage violence. In private conversations with black inner-city youths, he discovered that tough youths actually respect kids who simply walk away from a looming fight—but that in public, they declare that it is cowardly to do so. Winsten's team created television vignettes demonstrating how to walk away without losing face. In each such scene, an influential role model would swing his open palm down decisively against his fist, saying "squash it," to indicate that fight isn't worth pursuing, and then walk away. In a 1997 survey, some 60 percent of African Americans had used the phrase, and a vast majority were aware of the campaign.[16]

The success of any campaign for social reform depends on how the messages are introduced. Radio or TV soap operas and other episodic dramas can work magic, for example, when the messages appear not as ads but as part of an entertaining storyline. These programs are used most widely in developing countries, where politicians have come to recognize their extraordinary effectiveness, whereas regular advertising does not induce much change. The most successful programs are serial dramas, as opposed to single-episode dramas.[17] These serials resemble the soap operas popular in North America, but they often are broadcast in the evenings in Third World countries to men and women alike. The audience can form intense emotional ties to the characters over time, and such sentimental relationships can be forceful. Moreover, the series gives the characters enough time to evolve in their thinking at a believable pace. The story presents the characters with dilemmas that can be worked through and discussed over a period of months.

Miguel Sabido was a pioneer in developing Mexican television soap operas in 1977 promoting reproductive health. Remarkably, this sensitive topic aroused little opposition. Before launching the programs, Sabido found out how the audiences felt about family planning and introduced characters whose views corresponded to mainstream opinion. The characters then began to change so gradually that the audience could follow along and understand their new, nontraditional ways.

During the decade after Sabido's TV serials began, the country's population growth rate declined by 34 percent. In 1986, the United Nations Population Prize was awarded to Mexico, which was the world's most successful country in curtailing its growth. Travelers reported that, wherever they went, people named the soap operas as the single most important explanation for their changing family planning practices.[18]

Similar results followed in India, Africa, and elsewhere. The most popular Indian television soap opera dealt with the status of women—especially the age of marriage, age of first pregnancy, gender bias in child rearing and educational opportunity, and the right of women to choose their own husbands. It reached 230 million viewers and changed their attitudes significantly.

A Tashkent friend sent me a videotape of a soap opera that UNESCO has produced in Uzbekistan. The series *Womankind* involves the patients of a wise male gynecologist who helps them resist patriarchy.

In Tanzania a radio melodrama was broadcast from 1993 to 1997. It attracted 58 percent of the population aged fifteen to forty-five in the area, with more men than women listeners. The plot involved a truck driver who had many girlfriends along his route. His wife realized that his risks might expose her to AIDS, and she started insisting that he use condoms. Indeed, he did contract HIV/AIDS, but she did not. When she realized that he was going to die and leave her penniless, she enrolled in a training program and got a job. These developments were discussed everywhere. Previously it had been considered improper for Tanzanian women to work outside the home, but the soap opera wife was admired for her reasonable responses to her predicament. A nationwide discussion ensued about the idea that women might have careers.

The show had amazing results in comparison to the area where it was not broadcast. Of the listeners, 82 percent said they had changed their own behavior to avoid HIV infection. There was a 153 percent increase in condom distribution in the broadcast areas during the first year. According to demographer William Ryerson, the effective strategy in any area is to provide people with both entertainment and information together, showing vividly what happens in a character's life as a result of her choices.[19] The world needs more statistical studies of such series, showing before-and-after comparisons. Such evidence would thrill Aristotle.

Score One for Plato

But it wouldn't impress Plato. In fact, I am still troubled by his point about imitation. It may seem fine for people to be influenced in a favorable direction—except that perhaps they shouldn't be unthinkingly influenced in *any* direction. Yet let's admit it: I imitate, and so do you. Advertisers pay big bucks to get us to imitate some actor who smilingly consumes their product. Ads work. We rarely notice ourselves imitating, but much of what we do constitutes mimicry. I'll give three examples.

A Movie

In 1979, my son, then a first-year university student, threw a party. When I got home he and some friends were cleaning mashed fruitcake off the walls and carpet. A food fight had just taken place, and my son had found it necessary to ask certain guests to leave.

I mentioned this astonishing event to a friend, who told me that her own son had just attended a party where the participants had thrown pizza at each other. It seems that the kids had seen the campus film *Animal House,* which includes a hilarious food fight in a cafeteria. No one planned to imitate it, but nevertheless some of them did so, just as adolescents can't help imitating each other's body piercing, tattooing, or smoking. The motivation behind it is as normal as the desire to wear this year's fashions. Did the film *cause* real food fights? The kids would never have thrown food if they had not seen it done.

A Novel

In the mid-1770s all across Europe, young men started wearing yellow pants, blue jackets, and shirts with open collars. They had all been reading a new novel by Johann Wolfgang von Goethe, *The Sorrows of Young Werther,*[20] about a young man desperately in love with a married woman named Charlotte. Werther dressed in a peculiar style and was given to reading poetry and wandering morosely through the countryside. When eventually he had to give up hope of winning Charlotte's love, he committed suicide with his pistol. Just as the European men had adopted Werther's clothing style and his sentimental attitudes, some of them also imitated him by shooting themselves. The authorities in Leipzig actually banned the book to stop the suicide epidemic.

News Reports

In 1974, sociologist David Phillips showed that suicide increases for ten days after a suicide has been widely reported by newspapers and television.[21] Phillips wondered whether publicity about suicides also prompts people to commit so-called accidental suicides in automobile and plane crashes. Indeed, this seems so. On about the third day after a well-publicized suicide, car fatalities increase in single-car accidents.[22] In such cases, the driver kills himself without harming others. There is also a correlation between murder-suicide stories in the newspapers and multiple car crashes involving passenger deaths. The more publicity the suicide story receives, the more the suicides and car accidents increase.

Phillips also found that fiction and sports had the same suggestive effect. Whenever a soap opera character committed suicide[23] or whenever a heavyweight championship boxing match was shown, the suicide or homicide rates rose briefly. Stories reported on the inside pages of the newspaper did not affect subsequent mortality rates.[24] Phillips called this finding "the Werther effect." Further research suggests that it may account for a significant proportion of suicides among young people. This raises the possibility of "quarantines" against suicide by restricting publicity about them, just as Europeans quarantined the Werther effect by banning the novel. Indeed, the U.S. and Australian governments have devised programs to address the suicidal contagion phenomenon.

The psychological mechanism behind suggestion and social contagion remains largely unexplained.[25] Sometimes suggestions seem to take effect without being mediated by emotions. It is empirically obvious that people absorb ideas and behaviors unconsciously. For example, a number of years ago psychologists established the "weapons effect"—the suggestive effect of the mere presence of weapons, including toy guns, which induces people to behave aggressively.[26] For another example, such environmental cues as broken windows, abandoned cars, and graffiti regularly induce some people to engage in further vandalism.

The suggestive effects of violence in entertainment have been demonstrated in several countries and may last indefinitely. My morning paper recently reported research showing that children who watch violent television at age fourteen were unduly likely to engage in aggressive acts at age twenty-two. Researchers studied children in New York State from 1975 to 1993, monitoring their viewing habits, psychiatric disorders, and violence and criminal behavior. The more television the kids watched, the more aggressive were both sexes.[27] For space reasons, I have not included my review of other research on the terrible suggestive effects of violence in entertainment.[28]

Violence is shown in places where no one can escape seeing it. You have probably seen only a few violent or threatening acts in real life, but thousands on television. Even without imitating the behavior shown in entertainment, we may be influenced in other ways. Thus most people greatly overestimate the amount of violence in society because they see so many references to it in the press and on shows.[29] Heavy television viewers are especially likely to fear walking alone at night. Many Americans buy real guns as protection against these exaggerated fictional dangers, creating new *real* dangers themselves. Moreover, people abroad form terrible impressions about Americans from watching Hollywood shows. A study of 1,300 teenagers in 12 different countries found that, because of exposure to television and movies, most foreign youths believe Americans are violent, sexually immoral, and involved in crime.[30]

The word *suggestion* or *imitation* implies influence that occurs without thinking. It was only such thoughtless imitation that appalled Plato, not the reflective discussion of ideas by philosophers and moral exemplars—though even this diffusion could be called imitation.

Consider, for instance, the aforementioned spread of nonviolent protest techniques. Mohandas K. Gandhi developed brilliant methods and freed India from British rule with far less violence than other anticolonial movements, such as the subsequent Algerian independence movement. But Gandhi did not invent nonviolence. He knew of previous campaigns, such as boycotts and strikes, and he borrowed ideas from Henry David Thoreau and Leo Tolstoy. In turn, he influenced vast numbers of other people, including Martin Luther King, Jr., who led the civil rights movement that won improvements for black Americans.

We want such beneficial types of intelligent, thoughtful imitation. But the memory of any particular social innovation recedes unless images are kept before the public to remind us. In the case of Gandhi and King, their nonviolent movements had already ceased to be news items by the mid-1980s. Then the Attenborough film reminded people of Gandhi's accomplishments and stimulated new discussions of his approach. However, King's story has not been brought before the public since his death. Aristotle probably would enthusiastically support having a major Hollywood movie made about King. So would I.

Bonding with Fictional Characters

Plato's main objection to plays and poetic performances was that they induced imitation of characters and actions. Yet he knew that people do not imitate equally everything they see. The influential plays were those that evoked strong emotions, so he criticized emotionality for interfering with rational thought. Next we need to consider how we can feel so intensely about imaginary characters.

It is mistaken to suppose that only overly sensitive, weak-minded persons respond with profound emotions to stories and dramas. At times, almost all of us do so. In one study, 7 percent of the subjects' emotions in daily life arose from dealing with cultural artifacts.[31] Psychologist Keith Oatley has presented evidence that when people read fiction, their emotions are as intense as those about their own personal lives.[32]

Consider, for instance, Charles Dickens's 1841 novel, *The Old Curiosity Shop*. Originally it was published in sentimental installments, as a series of chapters. The story involves Little Nell Trent, a kind and devoted girl who looks after her grandfather in a secondhand shop. When Grandfather's money is wasted by his spendthrift relatives, he gambles to recover some of it for Nell, but this attempt fails. A villain seizes the shop and turns the old man and Nell out to wander the country in poverty and then to die. Nell's death could be foreseen by readers who had read preceding chapters.

Letters flooded in from readers all over England, begging Dickens to save her; indeed he felt "unspeakable anguish" about her fate, though he went through with the story as he felt it to be artistically necessary. One famous actor wrote in his diary, "I have never read printed words that gave me so much pain.... I could not weep for some time. Sensations, sufferings have returned to me, that are terrible to awaken." Another reader, a member of Parliament, threw the book out the window of the train he was riding and wept bitterly. As a ship approached the New York harbor, bringing the new chapter of the series, crowds were waiting on the dock, calling out to the crew, "Is Little Nell dead?"

Could such an emotional outburst occur today? Yes—at least if the story is presented in a series, as Dickens's novel originally was. I know of no current novels that have affected their readers so deeply, but I do know of serial television dramas that have overwhelmed viewers. Indeed, millions of people count fictional television characters among their loved ones. It is not unusual for viewers, young or old, to fall in love with characters in a series.

Oxford University social psychologist Michael Argyle studied happiness and leisure. He identified three blessings that generally make you happy: (1) having a spouse, (2) having a network of close friends, and (3) watching a television soap opera![33] He concluded that soaps make you happy because when you watch you "are making imaginary friends." According to his research, soap operas have beneficial effects that nonfictional TV, such as news, sports, and public affairs programs, generally does not have. (If anything, just the reverse.)

It's essential that the television program be a series with the same characters appearing frequently over a lengthy period. You don't form an "imaginary friendship" with characters in a single two-hour drama, but a series may run several seasons and a soap opera five days a week for thirty years. You may form intense attachments to the characters, vicariously feeling their ups and downs as if they were your real loved ones.[34]

You must expect nasty remarks for caring so much about them. Your golf partner may say, "Get a life!" Still, if you have a fondness for fictional friends, that seems to me harmless or even beneficial—at least as long as your friendship endures. Regrettably, viewers cannot control the duration of their favorite shows.

And if television can give, it can also take away. The loss of friends hurts, whether they are real or fictional. Love is the same, whether directed toward a flesh-and-blood spouse or toward light on a screen. The affection that makes a soap opera viewer happier than the average person also makes her miserable when a beloved character suffers or dies.

This misery is normal. Jonathan Cohen has studied the responses of 381 Israeli adult television viewers to the potential loss of their favorite television characters. He found that emotional attachments did not *substitute* for real life but instead reflected a tendency to form strong emotional ties in real life. Those individuals who were standoffish and made few close friends were also far less likely to form intense bonds with fictive television characters.[35]

In 1999, NBC cancelled its TV soap *Another World* after a run of thirty-five years. The network had already offended older viewers by writing out of the story all characters over forty. I interviewed by e-mail some of the fans, many of whom kept in touch with each other through a user group discussion, mourning their departed fictional friends. All who responded to my query expressed outrage over the cancellation of their program. One woman told me it was one of the most painful experiences of her whole life. It felt as if all her family and everyone in her neighborhood had been killed in a single day. She said she would never get involved with another show again because she didn't want to be hurt so much: "It was like when my dog died and I refused to buy another one. I didn't want to replace it."

In response to my question "How does a soap opera compare with the real relationships in your life?" another woman replied, "I hate to admit it, but it's a much easier way to have friends. No misunderstandings, no real anger, no regrets, no embarrassment, no competition. I can't make up for what I lost. With a soap that old I had a history and understanding of the characters that is impossible to find in a new soap."

About one-fifth of adult Americans watch soaps twice a week or more. And, regrettably, they eventually lose their imaginary friends. Such losses are significant for their emotional well-being and probably for their health as well. As I'll show later, the stress of losing a spouse or other intimate loved one produces physiological consequences that often result in serious illness or death. I know of no studies on the health effects of television dramas, but the loss of beloved fictional characters probably is also medically harmful.[36]

Myths and Messages

Plato was not against all stories. In fact, he made up many tales himself. His dialogues involving Socrates were scripts that could be (but never are) performed as plays, and *The Republic* relates his famous story about people in a cave. However, each of his stories was meant to convey a point, which he and the other philosophers would then discuss. What he opposed were mainly the Homeric myths, whether as narrated by professional storytellers or enacted in dramas. These myths were tall adventure tales involving treacherous warriors, gods, seductive sirens, and other odd creatures such as monsters and nymphs, perfectly suited for animated Disney movies: all action and excitement, no reflection. Some of these yarns were cosmological myths explaining the origin of life on Earth. Others described Hades. They were not produced primarily as moral messages. That, Plato thought, was the problem, for he wanted Athenians to debate ideas and not to be swept along emotionally. In fact, a great ideological struggle of his day was the rivalry for cultural influence between dramatists and philosophers. Philosophers believed that the two modes of thinking were incompatible.

Yet the fanciful Greek adventure stories have lasted until the present day, against much criticism. The French scholar Luc Brisson maintains that it was actually philosophers who *saved* myths. They did so by reinterpreting them as *allegories* to which various new meanings could be attributed, according to changing social circumstances. Even the gods could be viewed in this new light. Thus Zeus represents reason, and Athena represents art. Others saw the gods as the personification of natural substances: Demeter was bread, Dionysus was wine; Poseidon was water, and so on.[37] From a moral perspective, divinities could be reinterpreted as specific virtues; from a psychological perspective, they could be seen as personality traits.

This loose kind of interpretation kept mythology flexible enough to remain relevant as society changed, though never as flexible as it had been during the period of oral communication.[38] Seeing myths as allegories even allowed philosophers to ease their way into monotheism without necessarily appearing impious, as Socrates had seemed. For example, Brisson writes that, according to the Stoics, "the universe is a living being, possessing reason, and arranging all things on the basis of the best aims. This universal intelligence, even while animating the whole of the universe and circulating in all of its parts, becomes self-conscious and concentrated into a divine figure called Zeus, Jupiter, or simply God."[39] Not *gods,* plural, but *God.*

In the first century B.C.E., myths began to be assimilated to mystery cults. This trend suggested that myths and sacred mysteries were complementary ways of revealing hidden religious truths. The poets now were viewed as initiates who had received secrets that they were transmitting in codes with enigmatic symbolic meanings. (One may see similarities between this notion and the mythological interpretations of Carl Jung and Joseph Campbell.)

When Christianity became the new state religion, myths were revised to harmonize with history, philosophy, and church dogma, introducing so many distortions that the Greeks could not have recognized them. Only during the Renaissance did scholars shake off the accretions of allegorical interpretations and restore the myths to what they had originally been: action stories, with or without deep moral meaning.[40]

Stories with Messages

Apart from myths and television sitcoms (e.g., *Seinfeld,* the "show about nothing"), probably the majority of stories are meant to impart messages, whether crass or subtle. The most manipulative, biased stories are considered "propaganda"—a term that sounds pejorative in North America, though not everywhere. (In some countries it just means "advertising.") Propaganda is mainly produced for the explicit purpose of inducing people to behave in a specific way or to favor a particular ideology or political party. It may be benign (e.g., documentaries revealing injustices or environmental destruction) or designed to whip up hatred. In wartime, it tends to become more heavy-handed, though the audience does not necessarily respond as the propagandists had intended. Having studied numerous propaganda films, Nicholas Reeves concluded that

> those that were successful invariably shared a number of important characteristics. Thus, audiences were kept unaware of the extent to which the production of these films was orchestrated by the state, and the films themselves demonstrated all the qualities that had traditionally proved so successful in the mainstream, popular cinema—strong narratives, high production values, popular stars.... [A]ddress to the mass audience was the essential precondition for successful propaganda, but it was always only a precondition. Of the films that did reach that mass audience, those that were positively received were almost always films that confirmed and reinforced existing ideas and attitudes—films that set out to challenge and change those ideas and attitudes proved almost entirely unsuccessful.[41]

These filmmakers evidently could have learned from the influential documentary maker Michael Moore or Miguel Sabido, the Mexican who figured out how to change public opinion on family planning and literacy with episodic TV serials.

Turning to morally instructive stories, it is useful to distinguish between two types: *cautionary* and *exemplary inspirational* stories. A cautionary tale issues warnings about the wretched consequences of unwise behavior. Many fairy tales are of this type: the wolf will blow your house down if you don't build a solid one. Soap operas and even Greek tragedies offer cautions as well. Perhaps they keep us morally on our toes, but they are depressing and sometimes may actually do more harm than good. As Plato emphasized, people sometimes imitate actions that were meant to shock them. Cautionary tales are probably more common than subtle, uplifting plots—for this simple reason: they are easier to write. Every story needs some conflict if it is to hold the reader's attention, and it's hard to invent gripping conflicts involving wonderful characters who overcome their problems with ease.

On the other hand, the notion of an "inspirational" story sounds sickly sweet and off-putting. I don't know why. ("Peace" also has an icky connotation: It's what you rest in when you're dead. That's a pity, for we need all the inspiration and peace we can get, and they require intense, heroic struggle. I know plenty of true stories about peace work that would make your hair stand on end.)

A positive exemplary story shows audiences how to live meaningfully. It may demonstrate wisdom in the face of adversity and perplexity—which can be genuinely inspiring. I'll illustrate how such moral and emotional effects can be therapeutic.

Fiction as Therapy

Drawing upon stories in therapy with patients, psychiatrist Robert Coles describes the emotional effects of great literature in his book *The Call of Stories.*[42] He recalls a relationship he once had, early in his career, with a high school boy, Phil, who had contracted polio and who knew that his legs would be paralyzed for the rest of his life. Phil's main concern was that his immobility would keep him from traveling and experiencing adventures himself; he doubted that he would be able to live a full life or learn firsthand what he needed to know to become fully mature.

But friends brought Phil *The Adventures of Huckleberry Finn* and *The Catcher in the Rye.* Those two books were decisive. In his imagination, he joined his friends Huck, Tom, and Holden Caulfield in their travels and lived vicariously through them. He rejected other books that friends brought—westerns and *Lord of the Flies*—but took courage from the three youthful protagonists with whom he identified. Later, he told Coles, "I've seen a lot, lying here. I think I know more about people, including me, myself—all because I got sick and can't walk. It's hard to figure out how polio can be a good thing. It's not, but I like those books, and I keep reading them, parts of them, over and over."

My friend Joanna Santa Barbara, a child psychiatrist and peace studies professor, told me another story upon returning from a visit to the Afghan refugee camp in Peshawar, Pakistan, early in 2001. The BBC produces radio dramas in Farsi and Pushto, the main languages of Afghanistan. One of the producers told her about a letter he received from one of the refugees, a man who had lost his legs to a landmine. He said he had been occupying a tent with his brothers in the camp, but, having decided that he had no prospect of living a pleasant or normal life, he had resolved to commit suicide. He had obtained a knife with which to perform the final act and was waiting for his brothers to leave the tent so he could proceed. However, the brothers were listening to a BBC drama about a man who, having lost his legs, decided to become a tailor and go on with his life. The legless man listened and was persuaded: he, too, would go on living. He became a bicycle repairman and is now doing well, according to the letter he sent the BBC producer.[43]

Gary Solomon is a clinical psychologist who regularly "prescribes" particular movies for patients to help them deal with specific life problems. In his book *Reel Therapy: How Movies Inspire You to Overcome Life's Problems,*[44] Solomon tells how he came to adopt such an approach. As a child, he was a latchkey child in a dysfunctional family. When he was five or six, he began using movies to escape from the frequent yelling of family arguments. "Since I did not learn to read, write, or spell until I was in the tenth grade, I had nothing to do except become absorbed in the radio and television shows I would listen to.... [T]he emotional range of feelings, such as love, trust, and empathy, were learned through the movies."[45]

Miraculously, Solomon turned out all right. He earned a Ph.D. and became a therapist. One of his patients was a young woman whose fiancé was abusive. Her story reminded Solomon of *The Lost Weekend,* and he suggested that she watch the film before her next session. When she next arrived, she said, "That's exactly what I'm going through. He's always drunk, and I'm always trying to fix him. Is that what you mean when you say 'codependent'?"[46]

Solomon has prescribed films to hundreds of patients who were dealing with alcohol, drug problems, gambling, abuse or abandonment, AIDS, and physical illness. His book is an annotated catalog of films, showing the themes of each one, and its possible therapeutic uses. I can see value in some of the films, but I doubt that all their messages are valid. If stories can suggest good advice, they can also suggest dysfunctional ways of living. We need dramas and novels that *do* teach viewers better ways of living—though to be effective, such messages must be subtle instead of preachy. And, as Plato might insist, their meaning must be clear, and viewers should discuss them afterward with friends.

Several psychotherapists told me that they consider group therapy more effective than individual sessions. Clients sometimes come to their group for years, hardly uttering a word the whole time, but then they show that they have benefited enormously. They have followed vicariously while others worked and have taken to heart what they needed for their own soul work.

But how large can a therapy group be and still be effective? Huge. I once participated in a one-day event in a room holding five thousand people. It was probably the most valuable learning experience of my life, for later, in the middle of that night, I had an epiphany, seeing clearly how my recurring depressions had resulted from false assumptions that no one had ever challenged before. Hundreds, possibly thousands, of others in the audience had also benefited from the day. The leader had interacted with several members of the audience, responding to their most troubling problems, and had given a lecture clarifying misconceptions that commonly cause distress. I knew I would never again experience a depression, and I have not.

This thought occurred to me: If it is possible to hold an effective group therapy session with five thousand people at a time, it should be possible to hold one on television with twenty million people at a time—or at least those who will sit quietly and watch instead of chatting and folding their laundry. Therapy of that magnitude might significantly influence a whole population. With technology, we could enhance the quality of culture on a global scale by inspiring a significant proportion of humankind.

And we can think of other types of televised therapy. For example, a program might be more effective if, instead of having the participants discuss their problems with the workshop leader, short plays were to portray their issues as dramas. Each predicament could be discussed later by the workshop leader, who might resemble some kind of Greek chorus—a wise, kindly figure whose commentaries could dispel the misconceptions that had caused the personal problems. The television show might include, say, three different plots in each episode, all with different protagonists, whose various difficulties arise from the same false assumption. The Greek chorus (who might even be a character inside the drama—say, a teacher or a next-door neighbor) could clear up their shared error for the millions of viewers participating vicariously in these experiences. Such a production would return theater to its original therapeutic purpose in ancient Greece, when philosophy and drama were meant to stimulate moral and emotional development. As philosopher Martha Nussbaum puts it, Hellenistic philosophy made itself "the doctor of human lives."[47]

Even popular talk shows can be therapeutic—at least those (such as Oprah Winfrey's) that are intelligent and sensitive about personal problems, as opposed to providing salacious material for an audience of voyeurs. Winfrey's show offers expert discussions of public affairs and promotes the reading of novels.

But most television programming is dreadful.[48] The standard of writing is poor; many plots are marred by gratuitous violence; and TV watching becomes an isolating, inactive leisure activity, in contrast to the kind of outgoing social experiences that generally make people happy and healthy. Even people who frequent bingo halls, playing the most tedious game ever invented, are measurably healthier than homebodies who go out less often.[49] Yet, as Robert Putnam has shown, face-to-face participation in voluntary groups has declined in the United States, partly because people spend time watching television.[50] They would get more out of television viewing if they discussed shows with others, say, on e-mail lists. And face-to-face conversations can be organized through existing organizations.

Dialogues about Andy Griffith

A new movement is sweeping through American churches: Adult religious groups are using inspirational television series for their study of ethics. Entertainment Ministry is an interdenominational Tennessee organization that prepares videotapes and manuals for such classes. I called Steve Skelton there, who told me that about ten thousand church groups, each with ten to fifteen members, have used his materials, and his organization is just one of many. His courses discuss the *Andy Griffith Show* of the 1960s. Each episode is a parable that comes with a biblical text and questions for reflection. After watching it, the church group discusses the moral theme—for example, commitment, mercy, or peace. I bought a set of his tapes and the manual.

Griffith played an amiable widower, the sheriff of Mayberry, who was bringing up his young son, Opie (Ron Howard), with the help of his aging aunt Bea. While Andy always displayed integrity and sound judgment, his jejune coworker, Barney Fife, did not always set a good example for young Opie, and Andy often had to intervene. However, there were no bad people in Mayberry; even the town drunk was accepted because, whenever he went on a toot, he would check into the jail overnight to sleep it off.

According to Skelton, "Andy Griffith insisted that each show contain a moral message." The writing was humorous, and the viewers never felt "preached at"—which probably accounts for its popularity. At every hour of the day, it is still being shown on television somewhere.

Critic Wayne Booth insists that, to enhance our experience of a drama or novel, we need to talk about it with others. Our fund of knowledge is essentially comparative in origin, and our friends' comments give us a basis for comparison. Judgment requires a community. Booth writes, "We do in fact 'appraise,' as an 'appraiser' arrives not at an absolute value but at a sale price implicitly comparative with that of similar houses on the market."[51]

However, I should warn you: Your relationships with fictive characters may be even more intensely emotional than those with the real people in your life. If, for example, you love a character but other members of your group criticize him harshly, you may feel hurt or even lose some friends. It's as upsetting as if you'd brought home your new boyfriend to meet your family and they took an intense dislike to him.

Ethical/Affective Criticism

Besides the comments of our friends, we also need reviews by critics who comment on a story's ethics and emotions. Critics sometimes *fear* criticizing repugnant cultural products and pull their punches. In my morning paper reviewer Kate Taylor writes about her own reaction toward a stage play whose characters she found morally repulsive: "As a critic this left me in a bit of a quandary: You can't just denounce a play because you dislike its characters and are disappointed that they aren't being punished for their crimes. Or can you?"[52] Yes, you can, Kate! Indeed, you owe it to us to do so. How did critical reviewers become so cautious, anyway, about expressing their moral and emotional reactions?

In the 1940s, American academics adopted an approach called "New Criticism."[53] Until then, critics generally appraised writing in terms of its plot, its characters, and their sensibilities. "New critics," on the other hand, emphasized the formal, technical aspects of the writing, such as the use of metaphor, imagery, themes, and meter. They introduced two new taboos: the "intentional fallacy" (the attempt to understand the author's intentions instead of analyzing the structure and style of the work) and the "affective fallacy" (the evaluation of a work in terms of its emotional effects on its audience). You may be astonished to hear such concerns called "fallacious," since they are the topics that you and your friends probably discuss after reading a novel.

New Criticism was most successful when applied to the analysis of poetry, but its strictures were applied to plays, films, novels, and television dramas as well, emphasizing the writing style, the acting, directing, photography, and other techniques of artistry, and ignoring the human relationships of the plot. The only way of gauging a character's personality and wisdom—by describing the critic's own emotional response—became unmentionable.[54]

After the 1960s, other theoretical frameworks, such as psychoanalysis, Marxism, feminism, postmodernism, and postcolonialism, replaced New Criticism. In some of these approaches a critic is allowed to refer to the external world outside the text itself (e.g., the class struggle, the status of women) and to express her personal values and emotions in judging the work. However, on the whole, critics remained chary about expressing distaste for a story on the basis of its moral aspects, lest they be deemed illiberal and censorious.

But the degraded status of "morality" cannot be blamed entirely on literary critics. Numerous other cultural changes during the twentieth century changed the connotations of the word. Anthropologists adopted cultural relativism. They stopped referring to any society as "primitive," for example, and learned to judge all forms of behavior in terms of the prevailing mores. Each society supposedly maintains a distinctive culture, and, according to relativists, there are no values that all cultures have in common. The search for universal ethical principles was deemed a hopeless cause. All cultures came to be regarded as equally valid, so that an action could be judged only by the rules of the local culture. (But, as psychoanalyst Erich Fromm pointed out, if relativism were embraced, one would have no basis for criticizing the Nazis, since most Germans fully endorsed Nazi culture. Cultural relativists could not acknowledge that whole cultures could be "sick," as Fromm[55] described Nazi Germany.)

Contemporary postmodernists in their turn also declare universal standards to be nonexistent. They claim that even empirical regularities, when discovered, should not be taken as general truths, for they occur in local contexts and are always historically specific. So much for science!

Meanwhile, in modern countries, the cultural dominance of traditional religion was gradually replaced by entertainment products that rarely stimulated self-scrutiny, let alone the philosophical reflections that Plato demanded. Relativism ruled unchallenged. To a considerable extent it still does. Nevertheless, we need outspoken reviewers who will sift through the cultural products competing for our attention. But ethical/emotional criticism takes courage.

I once ate dinner in the student pub before teaching an evening class at my college. There was an eight-foot screen for projected videos. As my burger was served, a scene from *Scarface* appeared. One man was applying a chainsaw to the face of another. I tried to cover my eyes and ears while hanging onto the burger. It was, after all, a student hangout, not meant for the likes of me, so I felt I had no right to complain. But in class I mentioned the event, musing over the fact that today the onus is on the viewer who complains, not on the person who selects off-putting films for a public eating establishment. Two students who had also eaten in the pub said they had seen me there and felt as I did, but they had waited for me to complain. After all, I was the authority, not they.

Emotions, Beauty, and Morality

Kate Taylor disliked a play whose evil characters were not punished for their crimes. She has every right to base her critique on her ethical/affective responses. But on the other hand, blame and punishment are not always the best solution. As other ethical critics have noted, mercy is sometimes a wiser option than punishment, for moral renewal sometimes occurs without retribution.

Literary critic Margaret Urban Walker makes this point in a provocative ethical analysis of Toni Morrison's novel *Jazz*. The book deals with the aftermath of the murder of a young black girl by her older married lover. The police barely bother to investigate the crime, and the murderer remains free, living with his bitter wife. For months they cry together, looking at a picture of the dead girl, and then they begin to put their lives back together. As Walker writes, "No one undertakes to exact a payment from [Dorcas's] killer. Instead, the lives of some of the living are repaired. They are, against the odds, replenished with abilities to value life, to trust once more, to give care and pleasure again. The story strikes me as a parable, but what is the parable about? Is it about another route to some resolution that ordinary justice also tries to achieve?"[56]

Walker's analysis is as appropriate to the Morrison novel as Taylor's analysis is to the play she reviewed. The two critics reach quite different conclusions about what should be done with a murderer, but that is as it should be. Situations differ. Both of these ethical critiques leave us wiser for having read them and perhaps more able to judge new situations. If I am ever a defendant confronting a jury, I hope the judge and jurors will have read many ethical analyses of fiction. (In fact, some law schools now offer courses in literature, taught by ethical/affective critics, intending to deepen the wisdom of the legal profession.) However, it would be a mistake to limit your own appraisal of literary and dramatic works to ethical considerations. There are other factors to take into account.

Consider the esthetic factor. Beauty is not the same thing as moral goodness, though some philosophers argue that the two qualities tend to go together. For example, philosopher Elaine Scarry maintains that perceiving beauty will improve our moral judgment.[57] Regrettably, I remain unconvinced. Some morally insensitive people are exquisitely perceptive when it comes to art or nature. Another wise moral philosopher, Martha Nussbaum, analyzes all kinds of cultural products, including music, from an ethical perspective.[58] Again I am unconvinced; music may move me without improving my character. Music is not necessarily mediated in the same cognitive way as ethical judgments. Sound vibrations have a direct impact on my nervous system whether I am consciously listening to them or not.[59] And psychologists studying infants say that when babies hear a wrong note played, they seem to recognize that there's a mistake. When a baby's mother sings to her, there is a decline in her level of cortisol, a chemical that indicates stress, which has nothing to do with an infant's "morality."[60] On the other hand, many great literary works of the modern era deal predominantly with the search for meaning. This *is* an ethical issue. Thus as I use the term, *ethical/emotional criticism* properly encompasses a wide range of soul work.

Managing Cultural Change

Ideally, this book will augment your mastery in using entertainment products, both in choosing stories for yourself and in influencing the array of cultural products on offer.

Sociologist Ann Swidler describes culture as a *tool kit.*[61] She suggests that culture is more a *resource* than a power that causally determines what we do. She critiques a common misconception that cultures are coherent and that people who share a culture have similar preferences and values. Instead, she insists that every culture contains a mish-mash of contradictory maxims and practices, which we draw upon in differing circumstances. We can always find a rationale for what we do, but our explanations do not add up to any consistent set of common principles. Our culture is, instead, a repertoire of actions, an array of varied possibilities, among which we select. (In chapter 9 I show how this metaphor describes our spiritual situation today; we each assemble our own personalized religion by selecting its component tools at a vast theological Home Depot.)

Swidler's "tool kit" metaphor does not predict what choices a person will make. It is a valuable corrective to deterministic theories of human behavior, but it may leave us open to two opposite errors—first, to overlooking the powerfully contagious influence of imitation and, second, to assuming that any cultural "tool kit" is as good as any other. I consider some cultures more useful and valid than others, and I suppose that you, too, want to distinguish between items that are better and worse.

Not all tool kits are equally useful for all kinds of jobs, and having a poor tool kit—an impoverished repertoire of cultural resources—can be a terrible handicap. Indeed, some tools, some ideas, can be worse than useless. That is why it matters that we choose fine novels and plays. The accessibility of great cultural products also matters.

As the joke goes, when all you have is a hammer, every problem looks like a nail. And if the hammer is at the top of your cultural tool kit, while other more effective tools are somewhere underneath, you may use the hammer because that's what you see. The solution is not to censor anything, not to throw away any tools, but to rearrange them, displaying the most useful ones more conspicuously and the others less so.

All cultures change. Change across *space* is "diffusion"—the spread of culture items ("tools") from one society to another. Diffusion results mainly from imitation. Foreign travelers or foreign mass media productions demonstrate practices that differ from local ways. The native people see, and copy, these odd foreigners.

Cultural change across *time* involves not only suggestion—the imitation factor—but also an additional notion: natural selection. Cultural change over time is largely a matter of evolution—the replacement of old "tools" by newer, more adaptive ones—as, for example, when cars supplant horse-drawn wagons and buggies. People imitate what they see, but then they may choose to keep only the practices that have worked well for them. At least I will assume—though perhaps I'm wrong—that usually the most adaptive items are the ones that survive.

Whenever you or I select one tool, then necessarily we ignore the other competing tools. Cars compete, in a sense, for our favor against buggies and stagecoaches. Computers compete for our favor against typewriters and adding machines. It's "survival of the fittest" in the tool kit, and the fittest tool takes over—the car and the computer.

This is probably how Swidler's tool kit culture evolves over time. But the defeated tools may not disappear without leaving a trace. We still have hieroglyphs in libraries, should you want to learn to read them. The hieroglyph still exists deep inside the kit, but it has lost its currency.

This evolution of culture occurs as people adopt or give up culture traits voluntarily. The disadvantage to this evolution is its slowness. To achieve an early breakthrough in the quality of global culture, we need to intervene, intentionally shaping policy through civil society organizations. Such groups will not eliminate the useless, antisocial, or obsolete tools in the cultural environment, but they may be able to encourage more prominent display of preferable alternatives.

Conclusion

"Entertainment" is often considered mere "diversion"—a frivolous respite from the serious challenges of reality. Such a definition falls short. As every bullfighter or gambler knows, entertainment can be real and fatefully serious. In the chapters ahead I'll mainly explore the type of entertainment—fiction—that delivers its impact with imaginary, rather than physical, encounters but is no less consequential for that. As we have seen, some novels and plays have changed the course of human history. Our challenge now is to develop new ones that also contribute to our highest human aspirations.

Stories contain implicit messages that may move the heart and mind, for good or for ill. Whether or not the authors intend it, stories may educate or mislead; inspire or exasperate; heal or inflame. We may learn as much wisdom from a beloved fictional character as from a brilliant therapist or spiritual adviser. The demonstration of a different way of living, when broadcast to a large audience, may stimulate enormous changes in the population. Serial stories especially have been shown to influence health and safety practices, birthrates, educational levels, crime rates, gender equity, energy conservation, habits of handling conflict, and spiritual values. Such stories, continuing in installments over time, have an astonishing power to address the most serious problems of humankind. We need to use that energy to stimulate a global culture of compassion, peace, and sustainable development. How can we maximize this potential, considering that today only a few hundred producers and writers are telling the main stories that are being heard around the world? How can we influence the people who influence *all other people*?

Unfortunately, few fiction writers are aware of their own impact on society. Often they prefer not to think about it, for the truth about their power poses many unsettling ethical, financial, artistic, and political problems. How can we foster the production and distribution of excellent, socially benign stories without infringing on freedom of speech for writers or freedom of choice for audiences?

Financing is obviously crucial. Money managers, not writers or artistic producers, determine what mass entertainment is produced and sold. The public constitutes an inarticulate market that expresses its demands only through box office receipts, magazine sales, Nielsen ratings, and cable subscriptions. A qualitative improvement in our cultural environment depends on the economics of the entertainment industry—an obstacle that I don't underestimate, but cannot address adequately in this book. At best, I can only stimulate debate and must leave residual problems for others to tackle.

Still, our vast array of options gives us a corresponding responsibility. In a capitalist society where entertainment is an industry, consumers can combine and influence the market demand for entertainment products. Merely by buying a socially deleterious story, we add to its profitability and thus contribute to its success in the cultural market, without intending either to sponsor its harmful effects on others or to be influenced by it ourselves. Thus we should keep our ethical wits alert when approaching the box office. And we should not be shy about judging quality bluntly.

We need more gutsy, insightful reviewers who will tell us what moods the story may evoke, what ethical messages, and what solutions to social problems it offers. Unfortunately, many reviewers have learned to eschew such criteria. Hence I'll devote a chapter to "ethical/emotional" criticism—the approach that Plato and Aristotle shared.

Chapter 3

Happy Bodies
Joy as Medicine

Are you happy? Given a yes-or-no choice, most people say yes. Of course, that does not prove just *how* happy they are.

Most people want happiness—but only to a limited degree. Aristotle maintained that moral education involves learning to feel the "right emotion to the right degree at the right time."[1] That sounds reasonable. At times you probably shouldn't be very happy. Suppose, for instance, it is moving day and the incoming tenants have arrived to take over your apartment, but your van has not come. Your dog is giving birth to a litter of puppies on the sofa. The heel of your shoe has broken off, and you don't know which cardboard box your other shoes are in. If you are humming a jaunty tune and snapping your fingers joyfully in this situation, something must be wrong with you. Facing such stress, you should be satisfied merely to cope and minimize your anxiety; positive happiness would be the wrong degree of the wrong emotion at the wrong time.

The absence of unhappiness may be attainable here, but that is not the same thing as happiness—delightful feelings such as joy, esthetic awe, laughter, or adoration. Happiness includes such moments as when your team has just won the trophy. Or when the robins and sunshine awaken you in your tent by the waterfall. Or when you watch Charlie Chaplin at the end of *City Lights* and smile and cry at the same time. We need such high moments of intense pleasure. The absence of unhappiness is not enough.

This chapter examines happy emotions—especially laughter and love—and their physiological effects. I explore the relationship between strong positive emotions and health. We'll examine the interaction between the mind-emotion-body system and the cultural system.[2] My big goal is to show the *connection between the biochemistry of our emotions and the quality of literary and dramatic products in our cultural environment.* However, I must defer further discussion of the cultural side until later chapters, when we'll connect the health-and-emotion system explored in this chapter to the moral, social, and spiritual insights of novels and plays.

This chapter is somewhat premature, for it needs evidence that is incomplete so far. Writing it is like assembling a jigsaw puzzle from which several pieces and the box cover photograph are missing. Although a picture emerges, a few features remain blank.

I can show three causal relationships. First, some feelings (emotions, moods, and temperaments)[3] have consistent biochemical effects within the human body. Second, emotional encounters and film clips that are chosen to elicit particular affects tend to produce biochemical effects in the body consistent with those findings. Third, such biochemical effects are consequential for health; they can make you sick or well. But more research is needed on these causal linkages.

We explore here the psychology of positive feelings. Later these insights will shed light on our relationships to fictional characters and to the real relationships in our lives, which are not so different from imaginary ones.

Being Happy

Some people feel that the very question "How happy do you want to be?" reflects a misguided belief that happiness is a proper goal, whereas it is actually a lucky side effect of attaining more admirable goals, such as treating others fairly, understanding what is true, valuing what is of lasting importance, and performing jobs for humankind. The avid pursuit of one's own personal happiness may seem self-indulgent compared to such virtuous objectives, for happiness should result from living well. It should not be an end in itself.

Fortunately, however, self-sacrifice is not usually necessary, for duty normally brings pleasure. When something unethical is going on, everyone involved is usually unhappy. Happiness may be both a cause and an effect of social well-being, just as an egg is both a cause and an effect of a chicken. Happy people more easily find a spouse and stay married. They are more likely to find and keep jobs, and to be productive.[4]

This same chicken-and-egg interplay of mutual causality also applies to the relationship between happiness and health. Good health fosters positive emotions and positive emotions foster good health, but I shall take emotions as the cause, with health or longevity as the effect. There is abundant evidence of that effect. For example, a study of old persons found satisfaction to predict survival time. For a seventy-year-old man in average health, a level of satisfaction one standard deviation above average promised to lengthen life by twenty months.[5]

That fact poses an intriguing puzzle: How, physiologically, does happiness affect health? Moreover, if your life situation is miserable, can you compensate and keep the benefits of happiness for your health and social relationships? If so, how? To address these questions, I'll review research on the physiology of human feelings and health.

If happiness enables one to be healthier and to live longer, why don't we all simply decide to be happy? Well, try it yourself and see. Close your eyes and change your mood from the one you were feeling just now.

Did it work? I think not. Most of us cannot instantly summon up any particular emotion. We do manage our moods to a degree but it is not like flipping on a switch. Most individuals are fairly consistent in their feelings, fluctuating around their own average level.

Set Points

An event may bring us joy or despair today, yet a year later it will no longer have an emotional impact. If you get a good grade on an exam, your mood will improve for a day or so, but not longer. If you argue with a coworker on Friday, your weekend will be spoiled, but you may be all right again by Monday or Tuesday. If you strike gold in your back yard or win an Emmy, you may be happier for several months, but eventually your mood will return to normal. There are hereditary differences between our temperaments, with some people usually jolly and others morose or cantankerous. Individuals have *set points*—the average level that may stay almost constant for a whole lifetime. Even prisoners in jail are about as happy as before, as soon as they get used to their new surroundings. Researchers have compared the average happiness levels of fraternal and identical twins who were reared either together or separately. They discovered that each person's set point is almost wholly genetic in origin.[6]

Having a set point seems to imply that you can't live more happily than at present, and even that your health is partly predestined by that set point. Nevertheless, David Lykken, the psychologist who established the existence of individual set points of happiness, maintains that it *is* possible to keep bumping one's mood upward above one's own set point level. It cannot be done once and for all, because we keep sliding back toward the temperamental level that nature gave us, but we can bump it up again and again by repeatedly having enjoyable experiences. Lykken advises us to cultivate "happy habits," giving ourselves little pleasures every day to keep us smiling.[7] He does so himself by walking his dog and baking lemon meringue pies.

Brain researcher Richard Davidson has gone beyond Lykken in showing the possibility of changing one's set point *in a lasting way.* Individuals differ in the symmetry of their brain activation, particularly of the frontal cortex. These tendencies already are obvious in ten-month-old infants.[8] Brain symmetry is related to temperament and health. The amygdala, a small, almond-shaped part of the brain, is active when people are anxious or depressed; the frontal lobes control moods by inhibiting activation of the amygdala. An especially active left frontal lobe signals a positive feeling (e.g., vigor, enthusiasm, and buoyancy), whereas an active right frontal lobe indicates unpleasant affect.

A person's set point also reflects the ratio between her good-to-bad moods— that is, between the activity of the two lobes. Davidson studied highly advanced Tibetan Buddhist yogis who had practiced meditation for many years. Meditation was already known to improve positive emotions at least momentarily. However, the researchers found enormous differences between the everyday brain functioning of advanced meditators and of ordinary persons. One monk, whom Davidson described as among "the most upbeat people I've known," had a pattern of brain activation toward the left by *three standard deviations* above the mean. Wow.

Davidson wanted to determine whether this practice might be effective with ordinary people, so he and a colleague, Jon Kabat-Zinn, gave meditation training to employees of a corporation and to a control group. Not only did the predicted leftward tilt in brain activity take place among the meditators, but their immune function was also improved. Even four months later, they had an increased left-sided activation, compared with their condition before they began.[9] Researchers now know that the brain's functioning changes its own *structure.* For example, trained musicians enlarge those parts of the brain that they use when playing. So do jugglers. London taxicab drivers, who memorize the street map of the city for use when navigating, strengthen the parts of the brain that they use within the first six months on the job.[10] The brains of people who undergo chronic stress actually decrease in size.[11]

These findings indicate that the way we habitually think and feel changes our brain in ways that reinforce those mental habits. I hope someone will soon give definitive answers to the question that interests me: By watching joyful movies and reading stories about compassion and altruism, can we make ourselves more joyful, compassionate, and altruistic in a lasting way? And, by watching horror films or war movies, do we impair our brains in a lasting way? Such a conclusion would be consistent with the research of Davidson and Kabat-Zinn. It would also parallel the brain changes that Steven Johnson has described as resulting from watching stimulating, complex TV and playing challenging video games.

Much of this book is an exploration of the management of moods. I hope to show ways of elevating your emotions above your own set point by choosing resources from your cultural environment to use or avoid.

Managed Emotions

Sociologist Arlie Hochschild maintains that in capitalist societies, the management of emotion is part of one's duty on the job—at least for occupations interacting with customers. This does not mean just hiding or repressing one's inappropriate moods, but also actively "working up" appropriate emotions for the role. Flight attendants must smile with enthusiasm, whereas bill collectors must look hard-boiled. It is not enough just to fake these feelings; one must actually feel them inwardly to portray them with conviction. Hochschild regards these demands for emotional management as a hardship that has arisen with commercialization.[12]

That may not be the experience of everyone, however. If happiness makes one healthy, then airline attendants, who are supposed to feel cheerful whenever they are on duty, may *benefit* from having to meet this requirement—at least insofar as they are able to carry off the performance well. Having to be up most of the time may be a blessing, not a burden.

But sometimes life offers only hardship, and we must simply try to meet it courageously. At such moments one is sustained by finding meaning in one's challenges. Such a capacity derives from doing one's spiritual homework beforehand, using the cultural resources of one's society.[13] For example, the Dalai Lama points out that Tibetans who were tortured while incarcerated by the Chinese invaders almost never showed any posttraumatic stress disorder after their release. Their emotional resilience can be attributed to their philosophy and religious practice.[14]

Devout persons of other faiths also tend to enjoy better health and to live longer than their nonreligious counterparts.[15] Where religion declines, spiritual movies, books, and television shows may provide healing insights that would otherwise be unavailable. But the spiritual notions that they teach may not work, just as not all religious teachings work equally well.

Findings such as these pose a challenge to medical science. Until recently there had been no accepted physiological explanations for the impact of emotions, spiritual development, or any other psychological condition on human health. Over the past thirty years, however, some breakthroughs have accounted for such phenomena by empirical science.

The Biology of Pleasure

It may seem far-fetched to discuss brain chemicals and hormones in a book dealing with the criticism of cultural products such as television dramas. However, scientific research supports this connection between human health and the cultural/moral environment. The mediating factor is our experience of emotions, which are biological yet influenced by cultural artifacts. A science called *psychoneuroimmunology* studies how our emotions and personalities influence our health. It explores the connections among the human immune system, the nervous system, and the endocrine (hormone) system. A generation ago, these were regarded as separate bodily functions, but recent discoveries show that they interact all the time.[16] The relationship between the immune system and the nervous system is bidirectional, with the brain influencing the immune system and vice versa. And the interactions also involve bidirectional influences by hormones.

One of the founders of psychoneuroimmunology was an intellectual with no medical training. Norman Cousins (1915–1990) was the editor of the *Saturday Review*; he also devoted enormous energy to halting the nuclear arms race.[17] Perhaps the challenges were too stressful. Upon returning from Leningrad in 1964, Cousins became critically ill at age forty with ankylosing spondylitis, a painful disease in which the connective tissue in the spine disintegrates. His doctor gave him a one in five hundred chance of recovering. But Cousins thought he might be experiencing adrenal exhaustion. He had read physiologist Hans Selye's famous book, *The Stress of Life*,[18] about the harmful effects of negative emotions on body chemistry.[19] As Cousins later wrote, "The inevitable question arose in my mind: what about the positive emotions? If negative emotions produce negative chemical changes in the body, wouldn't the positive emotions produce positive chemical changes? Is it possible that love, hope, faith, laughter, confidence, and the will to live have therapeutic value?"[20]

With the approval of his physician, Cousins found a nurse who was willing to administer massive vitamin C doses and run a movie projector. He obtained lots of his favorite Marx Brothers films and *Candid Camera* episodes, and his nurse read aloud from a trove of humor books. He checked out of the hospital and into a hotel, where his experiment wouldn't disturb other patients. The nurse took sedimentation rate readings before and after the laughter episodes. Each time, there was a drop of at least five points, which held up and was cumulative. Cousins's fever receded, and his pulse became normal. The gravel-like nodules on his neck and hands shrank. He went back to his job at the *Saturday Review* full-time. He became pain-free and resumed tennis, golf, and riding.[21] Cousins lived another twenty-six years, writing and lecturing on the relationship between positive emotions and health. Although his recovery is often attributed specifically to laughter, he made it clear that all positive emotions and states of mind were important.

Since 1964, when Cousins carried out his well-publicized experiment on himself, research has challenged the older models of physiology. Scientists discovered in 1985 that the central nervous system can directly affect the immune system by conditioning.[22] It may be possible to use the conditioning of the nervous system to heal the immune system.[23]

Conditioning is an automatic or subconscious type of reaction, but individuals can also control their immune systems deliberately by managing their thoughts and feelings. In 1990, researcher Howard Hall taught his human subjects various self-regulatory practices, such as relaxation, guided imagery, self-hypnosis, and biofeedback training. With these actions of the central nervous system, they were able to increase measurably the stickiness of their white blood cells—components of their immune systems.[24]

This experiment confirmed previous anecdotal accounts of healing the immune system through a direct psychological influence at the cellular level. Visualization, for example, has been reported to affect various white cells, as well as to improve the health of patients. How can such a practice work? Because of the similarity between the imagination and actual perceptions of reality. The central nervous system, when it perceives stimuli, sends messages directly to the immune system. But the brain does not necessarily distinguish between really perceiving something and simply imagining it vividly. Any visualized image—any perception in the "mind's eye"—can set off the same immune reaction as a real perception. That is why cultural artifacts such as fiction can have an impact on health: works of art are contrived to stimulate the imagination.

Emotional Chemicals

The older model of the nervous system, which had become established in the early 1920s, portrayed messages as electrical impulses traveling within each nerve cell (a *neuron*) by means of changes in the sodium and potassium ions. It further showed that a charge jumps from one neuron to the next by crossing the minuscule synaptic cleft between the two adjacent cells, where they almost meet. This transmission is possible because of the presence of certain chemicals—*neurotransmitters*—that are released, transmit the electrical impulse across the synapse, and are then reabsorbed by a cell (in the reuptake phase) to be destroyed or recycled. Messages run along these connecting nerves like telephone messages along a cable. This model is not incorrect, but since the 1980s, scientists have come to realize that it accounts for only 2 percent of the messages that are transmitted in the body. The rest of the communication system involves ligands and receptors.

On the surface membrane of a typical neuron, millions of *receptor* molecules may exist with roots reaching deep into the cell's interior. These receptors are made of proteins—chains of amino acids—that function as sensing scanners for the cells.[25] When the right *ligand* comes along that can fit a receptor exactly (just as a key exactly fits a keyhole), a "binding" process occurs. In binding, the ligand will bump onto the receptor, slip off, bump on again, and so on. While connecting in this way, the ligand transfers information to the receptor, which transmits it into the inner part of the cell, launching marked changes.

Ligands, which are smaller than their matching receptors, are chemicals that can be classified into three groups: *neurotransmitters*,[26] *steroids* (the sex hormones testosterone, progesterone, and estrogen), and *peptides,* which constitute perhaps 95 percent of all the ligands. (By the time all peptides are identified, there may be three hundred of them.)[27]

Receptors and ligands exist not only on neurons but also on other kinds of cells in the endocrine, gastrointestinal, and immune systems. Indeed, because of receptors and ligands, information is transmitted, not only across the tiny synapses but across long distances—sometimes from one end of the body to the other, and between cells that perform entirely different functions. A given type of ligand may be made in various organs of the body, often including the brain.[28]

A few receptors were identified in the 1960s, and Candace Pert identified a receptor for opiates in rats' brains in 1972. It was discovered that the brain manufactures its own opiates (enkephalins and endorphins) to fit that receptor, and that the release of endorphins creates happy emotional states. Pert assumed that peptides created anywhere in the body probably had specific receptors in the brain, and this line of investigation has paid off. Her study of peptides has convinced her that these little amino acids are the physical manifestations of emotions. She calls them "molecules of emotion."

This startling conclusion, which is shared by many other brain researchers, requires that certain previous assumptions be reconsidered—especially the assumption that particular parts of the brain are responsible for feeling particular emotions. Instead, what Pert has found is that the brain structures that had been thought to generate emotions[29] are especially densely covered with receptors for ligands, though some of the same receptors can also be found in other parts of the body. She believes that the binding of those ligands constitutes the experience of emotion. In some cases, though, viruses enter the cells via the same receptors, so that hypothetically a receptor that is already occupied by a ligand—a "molecule of emotion"—would therefore be inaccessible to the virus. If so, this would seem to be one of the several ways in which emotions are directly involved in the preservation of health.

Through such methods as positron emission tomography, or PET scans, as well as through more direct studies of animal brains, researchers have identified the emotional experiences that go with particular ligands. There are hundreds of such chemicals, but I'll mention only a few that are significant for health and emotional well-being alike. All of them are necessary for our survival under varying circumstances, so we need to keep them in a dynamic balance. If, as Aristotle said, moral education involves learning to feel the "right emotion to the right degree at the right time," then our bodies must be able to produce the right neurochemicals to the right degree at the right time. This is crucial, not only for our moral sensibilities but also for our health.

Such biochemicals are consequential. Thus the adrenal secretions epinephrine, norepinephrine, and cortisol, when imbalanced by stress, affect your heart rate, blood pressure, breathing rate, digestion, the mobilization of your protein and fat, the inhibition of your antibodies and inflammation, the rate at which your wounds heal, and your retention of sodium, to mention only the most conspicuous effects.[30] When you're stressed, you produce cortisol because you need it, but you don't want that to happen often, for its effects are largely harmful.

In the 1950s, medical pioneer Hans Selye discovered some effects of stress: enlarging the adrenal cortex, shrinking the thymus and lymph glands. It was Selye's observations that prompted Cousins to attribute his own illness to "adrenal exhaustion" and to use laughter as a drug to counter his own stress. Since then, researchers have shown that stress causes cardiovascular disease, arthritis, hypertension, elevated blood sugar levels in diabetics, and many immune-related deficiencies. Recent research more specifically suggests that minor, chronic stresses generally damage the immune system more than short-term emergencies or even tragedies, such as bereavement.[31] Also, we do not all experience stressors in the same way or produce the same biochemical responses. We differ in our ways of coping and even in perceiving our situations as stressful or otherwise. We should pay attention to the psychosocial factors that affect personal health and well-being.

Psychosocial Effects on Health

Life brings stress: the death of a family member, divorce, marriage, a new job, relocation, financial problems, and even such minor stresses as family holidays or such happy occasions as one's wedding. People with high numbers of such events tend to have more illness, to be ill longer, to have more severe symptoms, and to take longer to recover.[32]

Lonely, socially isolated persons are less healthy than those with warm, supportive social networks. This is true for both sexes, for all ages, for urban and rural persons, and for people living in different countries. The relationship between social engagement and health definitely is causal. In one Swedish study, those who had initially had the fewest social relationships proved to have a mortality rate 50 percent higher over the following six years than those with rich social lives.[33] Moreover, social support from other persons can counter the effects of negative circumstances.[34]

Researchers have studied the mechanisms by which loneliness and social isolation impair health. The immune system is crucial. For example, psycho-neuroimmunologists studied Ohio State University students; the loneliest students had lower levels of natural killer (NK) cells (which are responsible for destroying viruses and tumor cells), higher cortisol levels, less responsive T cells, and weaker immune responses when inoculated with a hepatitis B vaccine. Divorced or separated women had fewer NK cells than comparable married women.[35]

You cannot prevent the death of your spouse or children or ordinarily avoid moving house, changing jobs, or encountering financial hardships. Must you conclude, therefore, that your health and the length of your life are beyond your control?

Not necessarily. As we have seen, the way social support seems to help us is chiefly by stimulating us to produce certain chemicals within our own bodies. When you are sick in bed, your spouse may bring tea and aspirin—but these external aids are not why you may live longer. What counts more are the chemicals that your *own* body manufactures when you have friendly, supportive social relationships. As the Greek philosopher Epicurus noted, "It is not so much our friends' help that helps us as the confident knowledge that they *will* help us."[36] "Objective" circumstances in our lives have their effects primarily through stimulating responses that we generate internally.

Consider the effect of pets. People who own a pet tend to live longer than those without pets. Subjects' blood pressure is lower in response to a mild stressor if their pet is present.[37] In one study of heart patients, over six times as many people who did not own a dog died during the study as those who did own a dog.[38] Since a pet is usually around the house most of the time, the whole family may benefit without realizing it. Your cat or dog offers no practical help or advice that could explain its medicinal value. It is not Rover but *your affection toward* Rover that improves your health measurably.

Normally we do not realize that we make *ourselves* feel good when we see Rover or reminisce about happy outings with him. But it is possible to use biofeedback machines to observe our own processes, even while we are creating them.[39] Machines measure brain waves; PET machines scan and photograph our brains listening to music or visualizing Rover; and blood chemistry machines monitor the spikes and valleys in our production of, say, adrenaline or dopamine while we discuss different topics. Such biofeedback monitors can be useful. You can learn to meditate more quickly by watching your own brainwaves on a screen than by taking lessons from a skilled teacher. (Go for the alpha waves.[40] Their presence on the screen indicates moment by moment that you are successfully moving into a relaxing mental state, with proven health benefits for people under stress.)

I, for one, would not want to spend most of my day producing alpha waves. I like a wider variety of experiences. Like Norman Cousins, I need laughter but also some excitement and intense mental work. Each person may prefer a particular array of psychophysical states. Whereas stress is supposedly harmful, I have a friend who craves risk—who skydives for fun.

Here I'm discussing mostly positive feelings, leaving the darker emotions for a later chapter. And by "positive" I mean really *positive,* not just neutral. Many studies contrast three states: pleasurable, neutral, and unpleasant feelings. It is the pleasurable emotions that usually have beneficial health consequences. The same conclusion applies, whether we are comparing the effects of good *emotions* (e.g., love, laughter, and joy), good *moods* (e.g., euphoria and tenderness), good *attitudes* (e.g., optimism, tolerance, and compassion), or good *temperaments* (e.g., humorousness and warmth). Emotion comes and goes quickly, whereas temperament is long-term. All these happy experiences generally are favorable for health, and entertainment productions may increase or decrease them as much as real relationships do.

For space reasons I will limit my discussion to two emotions: laughter and love. Of the two, love will require more attention, since it must be distinguished from other, related emotional states.

Laughter: The Best Medicine

> And frame your mind to mirth and merriment, which bars a thousand
> harms and lengthens life.
>
> —Shakespeare, *The Taming of the Shrew*

To be rigorous, a researcher should distinguish between humor and laughter. We do not always laugh at humor, and often we laugh when nothing is funny at all. According to psychologist Robert Provine, about 80 percent of the time when people laugh, they are not amused but just being sociable.[41] Nevertheless, most researchers treat humor and laughter as equivalent, so they are not always sure whether the biochemical effects that they find are the consequences of laughing overtly or of simply *feeling* amused.

Another distinction also should be made, that between mirthful humor and ridicule or hostile humor. Fortunately, researchers typically try to amuse their subjects with funny film clips, so their laughter is usually mirthful, but that is not necessarily so. Some theories about humor portray laughter as an expression of hostility, which is, I think, mistaken, though indeed people sometimes do ridicule others cruelly. Probably such hostile, mocking laughter was more usual in centuries past than today. For example, it was formerly common to make fun of people with disabilities. According to Aristotle and Cicero, most laughter in their era was directed at ugly or deformed persons.[42] That is not the kind of laughter that this research deals with. Instead, we are describing true amusement—the pleasant surprise that happens suddenly when something unexpected occurs that nevertheless makes perfect sense if considered from a different perspective.

At UCLA's Norman Cousins Center for Psychoneuroimmunology, researchers are showing how laughter strengthens the immune systems of children with life-threatening diseases. They show films that make kids laugh, testing the physiological effects and the course of the children's disease.[43] Other researchers at Loma Linda University had already established that mirthful laughter strengthens the immune system. It increases the number of activated T lymphocytes, T cells, and NK cells.[44] Laughter is associated with the release of neuropeptides, endorphins, and enkephalins. It reduces cortisol and increases the production of immunoglobulin A, which is known to protect the body from various infections, notably the common cold.[45] Laughter is also an aerobic exercise that ventilates lungs, speeds up heart rate and blood pressure, quickens breathing, expands circulation, and increases the intake of oxygen.[46] In humorous situations, people with healthy hearts were found to be 40 percent more likely to laugh than those with heart disease.[47]

A team at the University of Maryland has experimented by showing twenty healthy volunteers a fifteen-minute segment of a 1996 Woody Harrelson comedy, *Kingpin,* and then, forty-eight hours later, the opening battle scene from *Saving Private Ryan,* a war movie starring Tom Hanks. After each film, the researchers measured changes in blood vessel reactivity with ultrasound. After the comedy, the beneficial blood flow increased by 22 percent—an amount comparable to that brought on by aerobic exercise. But it decreased 35 percent after seeing *Saving Private Ryan.* The author of the study, Michael Miller, explained that "anything that evokes an emotional response has an impact on the heart." Clearly that impact can be either negative or positive.[48] The research team recommends that people combine regular exercise with fifteen minutes of laughter a day for good cardiovascular health.

Various explanations for this significant health-related finding are possible, but it is clear that the inner lining of blood vessels, the endothelium, dilate with laughter or contract with stress. Miller adds, "Mental stress is associated with impairment of the endothelium, the protective barrier lining our blood vessels. This can cause a series of inflammatory reactions that lead to fat and cholesterol build-up in the coronary arteries and ultimately to a heart attack."[49] (In another paper presented on the same day to the 2005 conference of the American College of Cardiology in Orlando, Florida, researchers reported that depression raises the risk of dying from heart failure.) Other research has also shown that blood pressure is lower after people have laughed.[50]

Laughter also helps prevent and control diabetes. A Japanese study tested blood sugar levels after a meal when people were in audiences watching either a humorless lecture or a comedy show. Some of them were type 2 diabetics, others were healthy, but the results were the same: the blood sugar increased less after people had laughed from watching the comedy show.[51] Stressful entertainment, on the other hand, has harmful effects on these systems.

Another immediately useful finding is that laughter is a good painkiller. Its effectiveness goes beyond its ability merely to distract a person; interesting, neutral films and other activities such as working on mathematical problems do not have the same power to reduce pain as watching funny films. However, other films that are not funny (e.g., repulsive horror pictures) may also have an analgesic effect if they are highly arousing.[52] The explanation is still uncertain; this is one of those missing pieces from our jigsaw puzzle. Neutral dramas do not reduce pain in viewers, but some other arousing happy films, such as erotic scenes, often do. As communications researcher Dolf Zillmann has noted, "The prescription of amusing, captivating, cheerful, and satisfying [television] programming offers itself as a no-cost or low-cost pain-ameliorating strategy."[53]

Love Someone

Positive emotions arise mostly within friendly or (especially) loving relationships. The best treat you can give your soul and your body is to love someone. I want to explore now some of the complex experiences that often are referred to as if they were all the same: love, limerence (emotional excitement of being in love), and lust. Some of these distinctions will be obvious, others not. The most obvious one is the distinction between love and sex, though most people would claim that ideally they are connected, as when we call sex "lovemaking." But it is possible, though generally unpleasant, for people to have sex together even though they dislike one another.

Worldly and Transcendent Love

The distinctions among various notions of love require more elaboration. Love is one of the pinnacles of human experience, and everyone presumably wants as much of it as we can attain. I want to distinguish two ways of experiencing it, worldly love or transcendent love. As we'll see in a later chapter reviewing a television show, this distinction has important implications for meeting life well. To clarify the difference between worldly love and transcendent love, I need to digress and discuss the second dispute, to which I alluded in chapter 1, between our two favorite Greek philosophers.

Look at the painting by Raphael of Plato and Aristotle (fig. 3.1). Plato is pointing to the sky, while the younger man, Aristotle, is holding out his hand toward the earth. This image portrays the basic difference between them: Plato was preoccupied with eternal, universal truths that cannot be discovered with our senses. He was a mystic, like his teacher Socrates, pursuing higher truths. His pupil Aristotle, on the other hand, was mainly interested in this-worldly concerns of human relationships.

The dispute flares up even today when we are being offered entertainment with spiritual themes. Often these stories depict a character's attainment of psychological greatness as his rejection of wealth and social prominence in favor of contemplation, simple living, nonattachment, emotional neutrality, and an orientation beyond this material world. These are all aspects of *transcendence*. The term means "going beyond." It refers to levels of reality beyond physical perception.

To the mystic Plato, everything truly *real* is transcendent, lying beyond all the particularities that we may experience. Physical things only imperfectly represent timeless, invisible "Forms," which we should seek to know. He had little regard for Aristotle's pursuit of observable, empirical facts. He thought

Fig. 3.1. Plato and Aristotle are the central figures in a mural by Raphael. Plato points upward, indicating his orientation toward the transcendent, while his student Aristotle extends his hand toward the earth, indicating the priority he attaches to worldly matters.

that, as immortal souls inhabiting physical bodies only temporarily, we should pay attention to this invisible reality.

Plato's notion of reality as transcendent may sound spooky, but it's not—for not everything real occupies space and time. Take a melody, for example. It's real. It can be manifested in countless instances: played by a brass band; sung by a tenor in Italian; transposed into a higher key; read as sheet music; replaying endlessly in your mind; or hummed on a kazoo in your dream. In all these cases, it's still the same melody. Does it stop being real when nobody is playing it, listening to it, or even thinking about it? No. Without having any location in space-time, it's still the same tune. You could consider the tune itself—as opposed to particular instances of it—as transcendent.

Or take geometric forms. Every physical circle or triangle—whether drawn by your toe in the sand or by the world's most accurate instrument—only approximately represents a perfect, transcendent circle or triangle, which is an ideal Form, beyond space-time.

Consider the Pythagorean theorem, that old business about the squares of the sides of a right-angle triangle. It was proved by Pythagoras, the first person to call himself a philosopher. Plato insisted that logical reasoning, such as Pythagoras's proof, was the kind of thinking we should all cultivate. *Empirical* research, on the other hand, didn't count for much. Though you can discover certain facts by observing the physical world, your inferences will never be *necessarily* true, as are the proofs of mathematics or *logos*.

We can contemplate Forms, including such nonphysical ideals as love or justice, only in our mind's eye. To pursue truth, Plato insisted that you should philosophize—that is, contemplate Forms rather than the material world that is subject to circumstance.

Aristotle, on the other hand, regarded these Forms simply as abstractions derived from numerous empirical experiences. Unlike Plato and Socrates, he was not inclined to speculate about whether the soul survives death. Yet he had boundless empirical curiosity about the natural world and the social dealings of human beings. Aristotle might have been a poor *spiritual* adviser but a marvelous *moral* adviser, for morality reflects not eternal spiritual concerns beyond good and evil but worldly excellence in dealing with other people.

What does all this have to do with love? A lot, since much depends on whether you consider love a worldly experience or a transcendent one. I think it can be both—a biochemical physiological event and a timeless spiritual achievement. The trick is to figure out how the two aspects are related.

Enter Hanna Newcombe, a chemist and peace researcher. Like Plato,[54] she regards love as transcendent—as exempt from the first law of thermodynamics, the conservation of energy.[55] She writes:

Sometimes we mistakenly think that all entities are conserved, like matter and energy—which can neither be created nor destroyed (or at least the sum of matter and energy cannot). With conserved entities, we have to budget, economize, ration.... All finite resources obey the simple rule, "you cannot eat your cake and have it too."

[One] nonconserved entity is Love; we do not love our parents less because we also love our spouses and our children; we can love God and our country without feeling a contradiction .... We do not have in our hearts a definite quantity of love that we dispense to various persons or groups—we can have as much or as little of it as we please.... Love and friendship are the ideal renewable resources.... They can be created on demand. Why then do we get jealous? Well, partly because we begrudge the *time* (a conserved entity) which our friends spend with their other friends instead of with us. And in the case of sexual lovers, there is also the question of limited physical *energy* (a conserved entity), as well as parenthood of offspring. But partly jealousy stems from a misunderstanding about the nature of love as a nondiminishing entity.[56]

Transcendent love can be constant and ongoing whether one thinks about the beloved or not. It need not diminish with time, distance, or inattention. It is unconditional. When Shakespeare described love as "an ever-fixed mark/That looks on tempests and is never shaken," it was transcendent love that he had in mind. (Ordinary worldly love is shaken quite often, as we all know.)

If you consider love as transcendent—invisible, timeless, shapeless, and infinite—you can have all you want of it. But *expressing* it is a different matter. If, as Newcombe points out, you misunderstand the nature of love, you'll equate it to "worldly," observable, quantifiable relationships. Worldly love is what people do in their relationships as physical beings, and it's conserved. We never have enough time, energy, attention, or emotional capacity to do everything we'd like. We necessarily fall short. It is a mistake to measure love empirically in terms of worldly, quantifiable actions, for this leads us to question the love of others—or even our own. Of course, we want love, both visible and invisible, but we will always be disappointed if we believe that the visible manifestations are the only "real" love. Worldly love is conserved, hence finite. The assistance that we give others must be doled out with regard to probable reciprocity. I give to you, expecting you to give to me when I am in need. Worldly expressions of love must be budgeted according to some social principles, but to regard those expressions as "the real thing" makes human beings seem less loving than they really are.

The great sociologist Max Weber emphasized the distinction between these two ways of loving when referring to changes that the Axial Age religions introduced.[57] Before then, the worldly view of love prevailed. People were supposed to feel closer to their own family, neighbors, or tribe, say, than to outsiders, and their in-group solidarity involved mutual aid. But the new axial religions taught that everyone should love each other as if brothers. Indeed, we should love *everyone without distinction*: strangers, friends, foreigners, enemies—whoever comes along. That's transcendent love. It's unconditional; whether others deserve it or not, you're supposed to love them. And not just people: St. Francis loved animals and even the sun and moon in the same expansive way.

Such beautiful spiritual ideals are attainable, but only if love is considered transcendent—invisible and not material. Unfortunately, that distinction was not always recognized. The devout person was often expected not merely to love everyone spiritually but also to demonstrate love generously in material ways. Otherwise it didn't count as real.

Not surprisingly, this expectation interfered with economic and family relationships. Weber shows that the great world religions differed in how they taught people to manage the contradictions between family loyalty and "brotherly love" for every Tom, Dick, and Harry. In chapter 9, I'll analyze how one character in a television series tried to resolve the tensions that emerge for everyone when we try to love in both a transcendent and a worldly way. (Hint: worldly and transcendent loves are not mutually exclusive. There is no toggle switch. You can have both kinds if you're lucky, wise, and skillful.) But to experience love in a transcendent way is a spiritual accomplishment. How many people do you know who actually love their enemies, as Christ urged in the Sermon on the Mount? We'll come back to this topic later.

Love and Health

Love is the major theme of literature and drama, and its biochemical aspects have consequences for health and longevity. Stories and plays may stimulate such feelings in an audience, sometimes with profound effect. Referring to love and intimacy, cardiologist Dean Ornish has stated, "I am not aware of any other factor in medicine—not diet, not smoking, not exercise, not stress, not genetics, not drugs, not surgery—that has a greater impact on our quality of life, incidence of illness, and premature death from all causes."[58]

Ornish's books and the publications by cancer researcher Bernie Siegel summarize the scientific research on the health effects of love, so I need not recap them. This research is based on everyday worldly love relationships, but transcendent love also benefits health. For example, Mother Teresa's love for the dying street people of Calcutta was transcendent love, for it was given with no strings attached, not because those wretched people were beautiful or deserving. Nevertheless, that way of experiencing love is beneficial, both for the dying patients and for those who love them as she did.

Even observing such love affects people. Some years ago psychologist David McClelland asked Harvard students to watch a documentary film about Mother Teresa at work. A control group of students watched a more neutral film. Most of the students who watched the film about Mother Teresa then had a significant increase in antibodies, whereas the control group did not. However, not all those who watched Mother Teresa experienced an improvement in their immune response. To explain this result, the researchers showed them a photograph of a couple and asked them to write a story about the picture. Some students described the couple as sharing loving feelings. Such students had the largest increases in their antibodies and also reported fewer infectious diseases during the previous year. The students whose stories portrayed the couple in the photograph as unloving produced low levels of antibodies and reported having more illness during the previous year. Their perception of a photograph was a good projective test of their attitude toward life.[59] The capacity to recognize the goodness of a Mother Teresa is a subjective personal quality, a readiness to love and see love in the world.

Creating Love

The most common theme of songs, films, and popular psychological self-help books is the quest for love. It presupposes that the big problem is how to *get* love, how to make others feel warmly toward oneself. However, this concern is misplaced. What counts most is not *being loved* (although, of course, that can be wonderful) but rather *loving*. It is more blessed to give than to receive. Thus people who volunteer to help others not only can prolong the lives of the people whom they serve but usually *live longer themselves.*[60] Our quest is to open our own hearts, and that is not always easy. Every worldly love relationship—everything we do in space and time vis-à-vis another person—is conditional and susceptible to snags that can be cleared only by forgiveness, which comes from transcendence—often a daunting spiritual challenge.

Yet, loving rewards itself, both by creating grace in one's own social environment and by enhancing one's physical well-being. Loving feelings generate desirable biochemicals (e.g., immune antibodies, endorphins, dopamine, and the "cuddle hormone" oxytocin) during friendly encounters with acquaintances, such as sharing a meal[61] and especially when bonding with a cherished person.

As a physical sensation, love seems to me almost indistinguishable from joy. Both are wonderful. When I experience either of those emotions singly, it feels as if a balloon were being inflated inside my chest. But people differ; a friend of mine says she feels love inside her arms.

In itself love is the most positive of all emotions, but in real situations it combines with other feelings. A mother observing her beloved child in danger feels not a positive emotion but anguish. Two lovers who must unwillingly part feel, in their combined grief and love, "sweet sorrow." A grandmother may feel angry toward an adored granddaughter for tattooing her beautiful body. The anger doesn't cancel out the love but actually expresses it, for love doesn't necessarily "look like" love. In such cases, love may be present without being conspicuously in the foreground. But if negative emotions predominate for a long time, they may destroy love itself—at least the ordinary, normal experience of love with which we are most familiar. (Mother Teresa was able to sustain love transcendently, regardless of the circumstances.)

We usually enhance our images of loved ones, perceiving perfections in them that others may not notice. Is such a splendid image entirely the product of our own fanciful imagination? Or, conversely, are we truly able to see the beloved more accurately than other people do? This is a question that Plato formulated in the *Euthyphro,* asking whether we love something because it is lovable or instead call it lovable because we love it. Philosopher Ronald de Souza persuasively defends the former possibility—the *objectivist* answer. He claims that our emotions often recognize properties more accurately than our beliefs would otherwise allow.

Of course, our emotions are also capable of distorting reality and perceiving inaccurately, but that is equally true of anything else that we perceive. There is a principle that nobody needs to be taught: the importance of *veridicality,* the responsibility to perceive things as they really are. And when it comes to our emotions, there is a similar kind of rule: *We should love those who are lovable.* Distortions do occur, but we must nevertheless try to see the truth and emotionally to *feel* the truth.[62] To love that which is lovable is the rule governing worldly love, which is contingent on the circumstances of temporal existence. It's an economy of scarcity, where there can never be enough time, resources, or personal character to love everyone properly. Transcendent love follows an entirely different moral logic. It can love even that which is not lovable and which does not reciprocate.

Limerence

Another kind of love also fails the test of objectivity: *limerence*—the kind that one "falls into." It is involuntary, and when it strikes, one feels an attachment to another person that may not reflect how lovable he or she may be objectively. The word is not in most dictionaries. It was coined by psychologist Dorothy Tennov to prevent some common confusions between it and worldly love, transcendent love, and sex. For one thing, a different part of the brain is involved when feeling limerence than when experiencing sexual passion.[63] However, there are similarities among all four experiences.

One may love, in the sense of caring deeply about another person (worldly or transcendent love) without ever having fallen in love with anyone (limerence). And one may feel sexually attracted toward, or even have sex with, a person without being limerent toward him or her. However, limerence does include an element of sexual attraction. Having studied several hundred limerent persons, Tennov has listed the defining characteristics of the experience:

1. intrusive thinking about the object of your passionate desire (the Limerent Object) who is a possible sexual partner;
2. acute longing for reciprocation;
3. dependency of mood on Limerent Object's actions or, more accurately, your interpretation of Limerent Object's actions with respect to the probability of reciprocation;
4. inability to react *limerently* to more than one person at a time (exceptions occur only when limerence is at low ebb—early on or in the last fading);
5. some fleeting and transient relief from unrequited limerent passion through vivid imagination of action by Limerent Object that means reciprocation;
6. fear of rejection and sometimes incapacitating but always unsettling shyness in Limerent Object's presence, especially in the beginning and whenever uncertainty strikes;
7. intensification through adversity (at least up to a point);
8. acute sensitivity to any act or thought or condition that can be interpreted favorably, and an extraordinary ability to devise or invent "reasonable" explanations for why the neutrality that the disinterested observer might see is in fact a sign of hidden passion in the Limerent Object;
9. an aching of the "heart"—a region in the center front of the chest—when uncertainty is strong;
10. buoyancy (a feeling of walking on air) when reciprocation seems evident;
11. a general intensity of feeling that leaves other concerns in the background;

12. a remarkable ability to emphasize what is truly admirable in Limerent Object and to avoid dwelling on the negative, even to respond with a compassion for the negative and render it, emotionally if not perceptually, into another positive attribute.[64]

About 96 percent of Tennov's subjects called limerence a "beautiful experience," and 83 percent felt that "anyone who has never been in love is missing one of life's most pleasurable experiences."[65] Nevertheless, Tennov is keenly aware of the pains of limerence—especially when the limerent object fails to reciprocate the feeling. About half of her subjects said they had been deeply in love with someone who did not know of their feelings.[66] This experience can be excruciating; among a set of four hundred college students whom Tennov studied, 17 percent had often thought of committing suicide because of unrequited limerent love, and about 11 percent of them had seriously attempted it.[67] Forty percent never told members of their family when they were in love.[68] Evidently homosexuals typically experience even greater emotional turmoil about their relationships than heterosexuals.[69]

Tennov explains limerence in these terms:

> It endures as long as do the conditions that sustain both hope and uncertainty; it is unique in human experience for its control over our thought processes; and its power places the achievement of the limerent goal of reciprocation above responsibilities and above other relationships. Because the nature of the limerent experience depends on how one interprets the actions of another, it does not follow a standard or predetermined set of stages. And limerence is sexual because the limerent object is always desired as a sex partner; despite this, the limerent wish to obtain emotional commitment is greater than that of physical union. Limerence for someone other than one's spouse can cause major disruption of the family, and when frustrated, limerence may produce such severe distress as to be life threatening.[70]

She asked people what percentage of their waking day not by necessity consumed by other matters they spent in limerent fantasy. Many respondents said 85 or 90 percent, depending on the day. If they were busy attending a conference, say, it might be as low as 30 percent during that day, but it would return to a higher level when they were back at home.[71]

Tennov readily acknowledges that limerence is an irrational experience that can even be considered "crazy," yet she insists that it is not a form of mental illness but normal. It simply shows that normal people can have irrational experiences. Because her subjects were not a random sample, she cannot reach any conclusions about the frequency of limerence in the general population, except to say that it is common and, according to anthropological research, probably occurs in all the world's cultures.[72] The experience can strike, like a bolt from the blue, at any point in the life cycle, including old age. Recent research in Italy suggests that at least one-third of males fall in love again during their fifties—some of them with their own wives, others with younger women.[73]

Still, not every person experiences limerence. The most surprising fact that Tennov's research established is that many people have never fallen in love. Of those, some say they hope that it never will happen to them. Other nonlimerent persons said they supposed it would be nice but did not regard it as an intense need.[74] Though they didn't like to feel left out, they were completely befuddled by her descriptions of it.[75]

The lover cannot be satisfied with a response on the part of the limerent object short of full emotional reciprocity, and the deprivation feels especially grievous when the nonlimerent beloved has an easy-going, casual, nonobsessed attitude. According to one survey, more than 95 percent of us say we have been rejected at least twice by persons with whom we were in love.[76] Being the object of another person's limerence is unpleasant when one cannot reciprocate the feeling. The rejecters find the limerent partner's romantic persistence "upsetting because of the escalating danger to the friendship."[77]

Limerence tends to last about two years.[78] Then, if the sentiment is reciprocal and a pair bonding becomes secure, it usually declines—ideally to be replaced by love. However, unrequited love occasionally lasts a whole lifetime. (Think of Dante, who fell in love with Beatrice when she was nine and saw her only a few times before she died at twenty-four; his greatest work was about his adoration of her.) Instead of extinguishing ardor, adversity intensifies and prolongs it.[79]

Evolutionary psychologists explain the usefulness of limerence for the species by noting that the intense, obsessive, exclusive bond between lovers usually lasts long enough for the female to become pregnant and bear a child, thus establishing a new family.

Psychoanalysts also discuss limerence, generally calling it *romantic love,* and seeing as predominantly a benign psychological force that strikes us involuntarily, as if by lightning. It opens the personality up for change through an act of imagination that enlarges one's capacity to appreciate beauty and goodness. We desire reciprocity—that our lover be equally preoccupied with us. As Pascal noted, "We do not content ourselves with the life we have in ourselves and in our own being; we desire to live an imaginary life in the mind of others, and for this purpose we endeavor to shine."[80]

Still, limerence is not entirely exempt from the rule of veridicality, for we must fantasize in accordance with reality. Tennov distinguishes here between sexual fantasies and limerent ones:

> Limerent fantasy is rooted in reality—that is, in what the limerent person inter-prets as reality. Your limerent daydreams may be unlikely, even highly unlikely, but they retain fidelity to the *possible*.... As beautiful as a scene on a Caribbean island may be with you and Limerent Object dancing together in the moonlight, the scene brings the glow of bliss only when you are able to fill in the gaps, as it were, between present circumstances and the desired event.[81]

This observation is mostly correct, but we can evade the rule of veridicality by means of *vicarious limerence,* an experience that allows us a priceless opportunity to feel emotions that would otherwise not be available to us in realistic terms. One may call vicarious limerence an *exception* to the rule of veridicality, but it can alternatively be seen as a way of *conforming* to that rule. In any case, it is an especially common experience for the reader of novels or the spectator in a theater. The object of one's limerence may be a fictional character toward whom one gazes vicariously through the adoring eyes of another fictional character.

The Physiology of Love and Limerence

Is love good for your health? Certainly close, warm relationships and tender feelings are beneficial. What I have not shown are the physiological factors that explain those health benefits. Scientists are studying the love experience in the laboratory, and I shall review some of their research findings. They assume that both love and limerence are bodily, physiological experiences.

We can tell a good deal about the effects of emotions on our bodies if we simply pay close attention to our own sensations. However, when you are deeply limerent, you are thinking about your beloved, not checking your own blood pressure and counting your respirations or your salivary immunoglobulin levels. (However, some scientists actually do such experiments on themselves, even going so far as to make love while hooked up to machines that sample their blood and film their inner crevasses during orgasm.)

When I ask people where they feel love in their bodies, few of them can give full reports. I myself feel it in my chest, which is normal. Dorothy Ten-nov reports that almost invariably limerent persons describe the sensation of limerence as located in the midpoint of the chest. (So consistent is this answer that when someone replies "in my arms" or "all over," she infers that they are not really limerent but are describing affection or what I call worldly love. If they reply "in my genitals," she infers that they are not referring to limerence but to sexual feelings.[82])

Tennov cites researchers Beatrice and John Lacey, who found a two-way communication between the heart and the brain. Tennov speculates that the intrusive thoughts of limerence affect the heart rate, which in turn affects the thoughts. Heart rhythms vary throughout the day, depending on one's emotions. Stress and unloving feelings produce an erratic rhythm, as well as increase the body's cortisol levels, and thereby suppress beneficial immunoglobulin A (IgA). Even five minutes of feeling love will increase these IgA levels for several hours.[83]

What about limerence? The evidence for health effects here is more ambiguous. As we have seen, limerence is a period of excitement and stress. Often levels of cortisol increase. Moreover, limerence and obsession are closely related physiologically. One study proved the point at the University of Pisa in Italy.[84] Twenty subjects who had fallen in love during the past six months were compared with twenty patients suffering from obsessive-compulsive disorder and twenty normal controls. The results: Those subjects who had recently fallen in love were like the obsessive-compulsive patients; both groups had lower levels of serotonin than the control group. When retested a year later, the subjects' serotonin levels had returned to normal and their obsessions with their partners had diminished.

If this proves that limerence is "divine madness," the researchers do not think it should be cured; they consider it necessary for evolution that people be motivated to bond and form family units. Nor do the research findings discourage limerent people, who usually consider the experience a high point in their lives. And Candace Pert, the pioneer researcher into endorphins, agrees. She supposes that limerence produces "some of the classical neurotransmitters, like norepinephrine and dopamine, which are involved with excitement. If you are actually flooded with norepinephrine, viruses have a hard time getting in."[85]

Others studying the biochemistry of limerence believe that dopamine is the key. Dopamine produces euphoria, loss of appetite, sleeplessness, and intense motivation—symptoms generally present in limerence. If a limerent person's brain is examined under a magnetic resonance image (MRI) scanner and a photo of the limerent object is shown, four small areas of the brain light up—the same areas that respond to euphoria-inducing drugs. Looking at a picture of an old friend does not have the same effect.[86]

Dopamine acts in the reward pathway, notably the nucleus accumbens in the brain, which is involved whenever addiction takes place. When we fall in love, we undergo an intensely pleasurable experience and thereafter crave to repeat it by associating with the limerent object.[87] It may not be a metaphor, but a literal truth, to say that we have become addicted to a particular person.[88] According to Arthur Aron, a leading brain researcher who is studying limerence with MRI scans, "romantic love is probably best characterized as a motivation or goal-oriented state that leads to various specific emotions, such as euphoria or anxiety." Aron was reporting his group's findings, which provided the first physiological data to confirm a connection between romantic love and *motivation* networks in the brain.[89] As we'll recall in later chapters, limerence has extraordinary power to motivate our actions. Moreover, emotions in general are powerful engines that prompt us to change our lives.

However, more chemicals are involved in limerence than just dopamine. The sex hormones are important. So are the endorphins, oxytocin, and (in the male) vasopressin. (It accounts for males' social—if not necessarily sexual—monogamous commitment.) Phenylethylamine (PEA) also plays a part. It is released in the brain when one falls in love, creating elation.[90]

Scientists are at an early phase of research on these matters. It is already clear that a whole assortment of peptides are involved and that the combination probably varies with the emotion that is aroused, with the personality of the individual, and with the phase of the emotional relationship between the partners. It is not possible yet to distinguish sharply between the chemicals that accompany love and those involved in limerence—or, for that matter, lust.[91]

Lust

Psychologists who study emotion do not call sex an emotion but one of several drives, such as the appetites for water, air, and food. However, sex certainly can be a "feelingful" experience, and it also has favorable health effects.

Consider the effect of sexual feelings on pain. In a study at Johns Hopkins, college students were asked to put a hand in ice water and to keep it there as long as they could stand the pain. They were then divided into four groups. Group 1 was asked to think about a preferred sexual fantasy with their favorite partner. Group 2 was to think of a nonpreferred sexual fantasy. Group 3 was to think of a passive, neutral fantasy. Group 4 was given no particular instructions. The students placed their hands in the ice water again. The students with the preferred sexual fantasies were able to keep their hands in the water for three minutes, twice as long as those in the other groups.[92] Other research has shown that sexual stimulation and arousal can be as powerful an analgesic as morphine.[93]

This information is good news for people with chronic pain. Unfortunately, however, it is not well-known, and people rarely discover it independently. (Pass the word on! You can do a good deed every day or two by talking about this frankly with others.) The findings do hold up in real-life situations—especially when the sexual arousal goes beyond mere fantasy. Thus migraine sufferers can often obtain relief by engaging in sexual activities, either alone or with a partner.[94] One probable explanation is the marked increase of endorphins during sex.[95]

But the immune system is affected, too. A study of university students found that subjects who typically had sex once or twice a week had levels of salivary IgA about one-third higher than other students.[96]

There are other effects besides elevated IgA as well, though not all of them have been identified yet. The main question, though, is whether people who regularly have sex actually are healthier and live longer than other people—and the answer is yes. Several studies have established this point.[97] One study on aging at Duke University found that frequency of sexual intercourse was associated with lower death rates among men; for women it was not so much the frequency as the *enjoyment* of intercourse that was associated with a longer life.[98]

A more recent study was of nearly one thousand men aged forty-five to fifty-nine in Wales. Three groups were compared: those who had sex twice or more a week, an intermediate group, and those who had sex less than monthly. A decade later, the death rate from all causes was twice as high for the least sexually active group as for those who had sex twice or more a week. The death rate for the intermediate group was 1.6 times greater than for the active group. The frequency of orgasm was found related to death for coronary heart disease and all other causes. The overall death rate was reduced 36 percent for an increase of one hundred orgasms per year.

But, you may ask, which is cause and which is effect? Perhaps men with poor health and low energy are unlikely to have sex very often, and perhaps their preexisting poor health causes them to die younger. Or perhaps there are other factors, such as social class, age, alcohol use, depression, hypertension, smoking, or preexisting heart disease.

No. It was apparently the frequency of orgasm that counted. When the death rates were adjusted for these other variables after the initial interview, frequency of orgasm still made the greatest difference. The benefits continued to increase all the way up to levels of one orgasm per day and possibly beyond to even higher frequencies. As the researchers noted, "The association between frequency of orgasm and mortality in the present study is at least—if not more—convincing on epidemiological and biological grounds than many of the associations reported in other studies and deserves further investigation to the same extent."[99]

Solo sex is more taboo than sex between couples.[100] Nevertheless, it's probably more common than sex with a partner, and, so far as the research record shows, the biochemical effects and health benefits probably are equivalent. Unfortunately, however, this is another missing piece in our jigsaw puzzle: almost no scientific research has been done on this comparison. Very few surveys dealing with sexuality include questions about solo sex. I know of little evidence that autoeroticism or homosexual sex differs from heterosexual activity in its health effects. The only exception seems to be that some component(s) of the male ejaculate may improve the woman's emotional state. In one study, sexually active women who used condoms had more symptoms of depression than women who did not or who were not having sex at all. The antidepressant component of the semen has not been identified, though some researchers have speculated that it is prostaglandins.[101]

The Palette of Emotions

Love, limerence, and lust all are vital to human well-being. Eventually we may be able to explain our passion for particular lovers in terms of the combination of peptides we generate when we gaze upon them. But even so, we cannot produce those chemicals according to formula, and so our hearts may forever resist our commands. Love, limerence, and lust combine in baffling ways, merging or clashing with the other emotions.

For instance, both adrenaline and oxytocin may be produced during the sex act, yet they are somehow incompatible. The quality of each particular lovemaking event seems to vary according to the balance of those hormones. During sex, it is not uncommon for people to have shocking, obscene, or coercive fantasies. These exciting images stimulate exceptional levels of adrenaline and noradrenaline, thus enabling one to overcome inhibitions of one's enthusiasm for the activity. Nevertheless, according to some sex researchers, the excitement of such high-adrenaline coitus usually ends with disappointingly low levels of oxytocin, the "cuddle hormone."[102] The challenge is to get into exactly the right mood ahead of time—which is largely an act of imagination. This challenge is made more complex by the need to manage the combinations of other emotions that intrude: frustration from the job, worry about a sick child, envy of the handsome couple next door, even resentment (or worse) toward one's lover.

Anger or fear may be mixed with lust, creating strange hybrid feelings, such as violent sex. I know people who have had sex while being shelled in a war—not despite the fact, but *because* they expected to be dead within ten minutes. Soldiers and rapists have had orgasms at the moment of killing.[103] Moreover, contrary to Tennov's description of limerence, it is possible to be in love with, and to hate, the same person. This ambivalence is the opposite of lukewarmness toward a person. It also poses immensely difficult challenges for mood management.

Finally, the usual distinction between positive and negative emotions should not be considered absolute. For example, although we normally consider crying unpleasant, this is not always the case. There are also tears of joy and exultation. In the Middle Ages, religious writers commonly described crying as a sensual pleasure.[104] And several of my friends tell me that the most frequent occasion for their crying is to witness a breathtaking feat such as a perfect performance in an Olympic sports competition.[105] On the other hand, expressions that are normally pleasurable may occasionally be otherwise. Thus laughter may be bitter or even cruel—a way of tormenting another person by ridicule. People have actually been put to death by being tickled unceasingly.[106] Nevertheless, such qualifications are rare, so let's forge ahead, addressing positive and negative emotions separately. I'll discuss the negative ones in chapter 5.

Conclusion

I asked whether you were happy (*really* happy, not just moderately satisfied). I hope it is apparent by now that you frequently need to feel love, joy, laughter, spiritual awe, sexual pleasure, and limerence. Emotions are, in principle, available to everyone, but, of course, such intense emotions actually are *not* available all the time. Faced, then, with the inevitable deficit of happy emotions, what can you do to elevate your mood?

Many options exist—some more promising than others. Some conform to the common notion that one should always seek pleasure from "reality," not fiction, fantasy, or other solitary enjoyments. To many people this is sort of a moral principle. Indeed, most of us consider our fantasies as our most sensitive secrets because they are solitary sources of pleasure.

But for committed realists, the sources of emotional pleasure are limited. You can follow David Lykken's example: Walk your dog and bake for your friends to give yourself a "bounce" above your happiness set point. Or meditate; alpha waves are relaxing. Or phone a friend and chat. For laughter you might ask a friend to tickle you. (You cannot tickle yourself.) Or read some jokes every day.

Or join a "laughter club." (A yogi in India started a "laughter meditation" group in 1995 and the idea spread, so that thousands of such groups exist all over the world now. People meet in a park and deliberately laugh in unison, without even telling jokes.) If you crave romantic love, you could go hiking with a Sierra Club singles group or explore an online dating site.

If you can make real life fulfilling through such approaches, do so! However, every life has some temporary holes in it, and if the aforementioned "realistic" solutions do not patch yours, there are other means of mood management: the entertainment industry. Read a novel, go to a movie, or watch a TV show. Mood management research reveals that bored viewers tend to choose exciting or stimulating programs,[107] while frustrated, stressed, angry people, if allowed to choose between comedy and serious drama, usually pick comedy (which accounts for almost half of all television programming).[108]

Novels, film, and television dramas provide vicarious emotions. And afterward, you can reexperience the emotional scenes while walking the dog or baking pies. Whether you are living one of your own joyful adventures or vicariously sharing a beloved fictional character's fun, the biochemical effects in your body will be alike. In the latter case, your imagination mediates between your culture and your emotion. Therefore, in the next chapter I'll examine the experience of empathy, the imaginative process by which we appropriate another person's emotions.

Chapter 4

Empathy Plus

Tom Hanks played Chuck Nolan. A volleyball played a guy named Wilson. In the movie *Cast Away,* Chuck and Wilson, the only survivors of a plane crash, spend five years on a deserted Pacific island, becoming close friends. Chuck paints a face on the volleyball, talks to him, and even understands Wilson's replies. Eventually Chuck builds a raft and begins rowing, hoping to encounter a passing ship. When Wilson rolls off the raft and floats away, Chuck risks his life to swim out and save him, but fails. Distraught, he yells his apologies, then lies back on the raft, mourning and awaiting his own death. Theirs is one of the most touching human relationships I can recall in a movie.

In everyday life, a relationship with a volleyball would be evidence of pathology, but for Chuck it was a way of preserving sanity. People need to talk and express feelings. We need to imagine how others would react to our plans and actions. Besides, without considering it, we interact with characters every day who are just as imaginary as Wilson.

This chapter explores the psychology of inhabiting other worlds and personalities. We do so whenever we engage with fiction, the main kind of entertainment that this book discusses. To get into a story, the writer, performers, and audience must all "willingly suspend disbelief," as the poet Samuel T. Coleridge put it. Even more than that, we must actively *pretend.* Play-acting pretense is one of numerous psychological states in which we participate imaginatively in counterfactual experiences. (A few others are mental planning, daydreaming, imitating the behavior of a role model, vicarious living, and empathizing.) We'll explore such mental states here. They are the psychological underpinnings of entertainment, but they go beyond it, too, of course, for we experience them every day, in every conceivable context.

The first half of the chapter may appear familiar, as if about yourself. But later, as we turn to the complex consequences of empathy, we'll confront a quandary—the historic double-edged moral status of the storyteller's profession, arising from the human tendency to imitate (*mimesis*). Our capacity to live inside other minds poses a number of questions: Does preoccupation with fantasies impede our sense of realism? What limits, if any, do we impose on ourselves when we fantasize? Are animals and human infants biologically programmed to mimic others—and if so, does this help us understand other minds? When we observe art, are we engaging in vicarious experience? Is it more moral to be emotional about our personal lives than about fiction? What explains our emotional attachment to particular celebrities and fictional characters? Should we try to overcome such attachments? If empathy is a necessary aspect of moral growth, why do people so often imitate others and succumb to the ills of social contagion? And if empathy is morally desirable, why do we sometimes feel especially fond of flawed persons? Such questions will form our agenda here—but I won't promise satisfying answers for all of them.

Reality and Imagination

Let's distinguish reality from illusion, flimflam, and public relations spin. Yet we shouldn't diminish the imaginary by equating it to "fakery" or "fraudulence," for it is also the source of everything possible that has not yet been attained. Indeed, reality and the imagination each require the other.

The illusory can enliven us. As good sports, we gladly participate in shared fictions. We cheer our home team, pretending that the game is not just a made-up invention. Rather than undermine every celebration or pretension, we join in the collective spirit and support illusions. We season life with make-believe.

Some observers worry about this phenomenon. Neal Gabler's book, *Life the Movie: How Entertainment Conquered Reality*,[1] ridicules the manufacture of celebrity and the public's readiness to attribute prestige to those whose claims are sheer puffery. Gabler supposes the ersatz is replacing authentic art and public accomplishment. Though scorning this artificiality, he proposes no alternatives for those who allegedly cannot distinguish life from entertainment and who regard existence as an endless movie in which they themselves play bit parts.

Sociologists are less shocked than Gabler, without disputing his observations about the intertwining of reality and image. And some three hundred years before sociology began, another writer declared, "All the world's a stage, and all the men and women merely players."[2] Before Gabler, this comment was not regarded as a put-down but as an astute observation on the human condition. To enact our daydreams is simply human, for we are half-fictional creatures by nature.

Reality and the imagination each give rise to the other. Many daydreams are practical planning exercises, for actions are preceded by mental rehearsals—fantasized performances. If in a mental rehearsal we foresee an obstacle arising, we can revise our plans. The imagination spares us many real disasters.

Mental rehearsals can be as valuable as overt practice. For example, an opera singer on an airplane may sit quietly, rehearsing her entire role in silence. Nevertheless, her chest and throat muscles make tiny movements that electronic monitors could detect. Singers say that the ability to "think a note" is a necessary condition for being able actually to sing it. Athletes also develop their real skills by fantasizing perfect performances.

Reality and the imagination are usually considered as opposites, but this cannot be so; they converge in memory. True memories reflect previous *real* events. But a memory is so similar to an *imagined* event that occasionally we are unsure whether we're recalling what happened or what we only imagined or dreamed.

Images in our mind's eye, however fantastic, are built from recycled memories of real experiences. The real provides raw material from which the imaginary is constructed. And the imaginary yields a blueprint for constructing the next reality. We need imagination in order to function normally. And our imagination requires nutrients—a rich array of ideas from our cultural environment.

Consider how the brain works. You use the same brain structures for creating a mental image as for actually seeing or hearing. When you see a color, your eye sends specific signals to the brain. When you only *imagine* that color, the eye sends similar signals to the brain. Moreover (surprise, surprise!), if you imagine seeing red while looking at green, the signals that your eye sends to your brain correspond to what you were *imagining,* not what you were seeing.[3]

We visualize what may happen next, creating what brain researcher Antonio Damasio calls "memories of the future."[4] Such "memories" constitute a fantasy life inside our realism. We also have a commitment to realism inside our fantasies.

Imagining is a rule-governed activity. As writer Mason Cooley notes, "the imagination has rules, but we can only guess what they are." I'll try to guess at them in this chapter. The rules of daydreaming have much in common with the rules of accurate perception. Nobody has to teach us not to distort what we see or hear. We spontaneously obey a "reality principle" and even feel guilty if we discover that we have been fooling ourselves.

Similar principles regulate the content of our fantasies. We respect reality to some extent while we fantasize. For example, we may feel obliged to represent another person accurately in our imagination, just as in the physical world we try to see our environment as it "really is." Some informants have told me they don't permit themselves to visualize another person doing something he would never actually do. (For instance, one friend says she limits her erotic fantasies to men with whom she has had actual romantic encounters.)

Often we appropriate desired emotions vicariously from fictional characters. Suppose a novel or drama was emotionally significant but ultimately unsatisfying. You may become an editor, mentally revising the story while washing dishes. But the principle of realism imposes limitations. Despite the importance of the story to you emotionally, you may feel frustrated, unable to get the characters to follow your script instead of that written by their author. If you disliked the way *Casablanca* ends, say, you may not permit yourself to create a fantasy in which Ingrid Bergman and Humphrey Bogart stay together. To do so would be, one woman told me, like bringing tubes of paint into an art gallery and altering a Vermeer or Picasso. "Reality," having been produced by others, now has an objective existence that must be respected. I don't know whether this rule is universal or even very common, but I know it ruins the pleasure of many secondhand emotional experiences.

Intersubjectivity and Social Reality

Reality is stabilized by communication between persons. Suppose I do something and nobody sees me do it. I am not committed yet; I may change my mind and either undo the action or pretend I didn't do it. But suppose you saw me do it. If I don't realize that you saw it, I may still try to reverse my action or disclaim responsibility for it.

Suppose, however, I know that you saw what I did. I am probably stuck with my action. Still, if I am bold, I may pretend that I don't know that you know and forge ahead, disclaiming responsibility in the hope that you won't call my bluff.

But suppose *we both know that I know* that you saw me do it. Now I'll have to live with the reality I have created. (Unless, perhaps, you and I reach an agreement—say, by blackmail.)

The point is, when we know the contents of each other's minds, we almost have to agree on certain facts. We have to share a common version of reality that is stable. With that interpenetration of perspectives, our shared social reality seems "objectively true."

Your imagination has two aspects. You create some images independently, as, for example, when you daydream. But you borrow others vicariously. Empathizing is of the latter type. But I'll start with the first type: independent imagining.

Daydreams

About every ninety minutes, you are especially likely to daydream.[5] People in Western societies rarely talk about their fantasizing, perhaps because it violates an implicit rule[6] against wasting time. Freud believed that fantasies were unhealthy, but apparently he was wrong. Current research shows that it is not harmful to indulge your imagination. As Eric Klinger notes, "How much we daydream has no bearing on how happy or unhappy we are, or on how well or poorly adjusted we are, but *the particular style* of our daydreaming is related to these factors, because daydreams reflect our overall personality."[7] Klinger says that upbeat fantasies reflect a positive personality, while negative ones indicate personality problems.[8] But that may not always be true—notably in the case of sweet-but-shallow individuals who exclude their unpleasant thoughts from consciousness.

Comparing frequent to infrequent daydreamers, researchers find that the highly imaginative group can be hypnotized more easily than the low-fantasizing group. They are more affected by mental images. For example, they "might experience orgasms during purely imaginary sex, or they might become sick to their stomachs over televised violence or when they were afraid they had eaten spoiled food."[9] But this does not mean there is anything wrong with their minds. On the contrary, they are more creative than the low-fantasizers.

Empathy

Besides daydreaming, we imagine other people's experiences. This is *empathy,* a primary topic throughout this book. It means both knowing and feeling another person's thoughts and emotions. You empathize by creating in your mind's eye an accurate secondhand replica of your friend's experience. Of course, you can never feel her emotions directly because your nervous systems are not connected. Indeed, while empathizing, you don't always feel her emotion anyway. For example, suppose the hero of a movie is walking along, joking with a friend and not watching the pavement. You see that he is about to step into an open manhole. You feel anxious instead of sharing his humorous mood. We feel *for* the character, not necessarily *as* he feels. We don't give up our own identity when we empathize. Knowing what we know, we react to the manhole.

Sometimes we don't feel exactly as the other person does because we appraise the situation differently. As moral philosopher Adam Smith observed, we may "blush for the impudence and rudeness of another, though he himself appears to have no sense of the impropriety of his own behavior." Still, this is empathy.

Smith's 1759 book, *The Theory of Moral Sentiments,* is the best account of empathy ever written. Smith says that this "fellow-feeling" occurs "by changing places in fancy" with the other. He describes the sympathy we would feel for our brother if he were on the rack. "By the imagination we place ourselves in his situation, we conceive ourselves enduring all the same torments, we enter as it were into his body, and become in some measure the same person with him, and thence form some idea of his sensations, and even feel something which, though weaker in degree, is not altogether unlike them."[10]

Recognizing the necessity of empathy in ethical development, Smith urges people to expand their empathic capacity. Suppose, for example, we find ourselves as a spectator reacting in a very different way than our companion who is suffering. "The spectator must, first of all, endeavor, as much as he can, to put himself in the situation of the other, and to bring home to himself every little circumstance of distress which can possibly occur to the sufferer."

Smith has much in common with the sociological approach called *symbolic interactionism.* It, too, studies human interactions that involve adopting the perspective of another person, seeing imaginatively through his eyes—an experience that symbolic interactionists call *role taking.* Empathy and role taking are approximately the same, though empathy is a slightly broader concept, for it includes both thoughts and feelings, whereas role taking is primarily cognitive.

Empathy differs in degree. Watching a movie, we may empathize with all the characters, while nevertheless taking sides and "rooting" for only one of them. When we are emotionally committed to a character, we say that we "identify" with her. Identification is an especially intense level of empathy that, like empathy, is affected by our moral appraisal of the person.

Imitation, Mirror Neurons, and Social Learning

How do we come to understand the minds of others? Today most scientists, including physiologists and comparative biologists, favor a theory of empathy.[11] Normal human beings evidently are "hardwired" to empathize. Newborns watch the faces around them and mimic their expressions. Charles Darwin reported that his infant son showed a sad expression when his nanny pretended to cry.[12]

Babies also observe the gaze of others and look in the same direction as they are looking—a practice that cannot be explained as learned behavior. A simpler reason accounts for it: Every normal brain contains specific neurons that are designed to *mirror* the actions of others. These were identified first in monkeys' frontal lobes. Neurons fire when the monkey performs a particular action with its hand—say, pulling or lifting. The same "mirror neurons" will fire when that monkey observes another monkey, or even a person, performing the same action. Whenever you watch someone else doing something, a corresponding mirror neuron in your brain fires. This is the biological basis for your understanding another person's mind.

Brain researchers study human brains with positron emission tomography (PET) scans. One neuroimaging experiment compared different phases of imitating another person's action, separating the goal and the means of getting there. The imitation of goal and of means use different part of the brain.[13] The authors claim that, when observing someone's action, their underlying intention is even more important than their surface behavior itself. As kids develop, they must learn to read the goals or intentions of others from their actions instead of being just literal. To read another's intentions is to empathize or "role-take."

Fair enough, if you are a person. But suppose you are a guppy instead. Will you take the role of other guppies?

Yes, according to Lee Dugatkin, who explored the mate selection preferences of these tiny fish. Suppose we have two female guppies, Anna and Marian, each in her own tank. We introduce two virile males, George and Phil, to Marian's tank and wait until she shows that she prefers Phil. Then we transfer both males into Anna's tank, moving it close to Marian, who watches the three other fish getting acquainted next door. Eventually Anna chooses George. Now we put both males back into Marian's tank. Guess which male she prefers now. Correct: George. ("I want what she wants.")[14] The guppy brain may be minuscule, but it is capable of some primitive kind of imitation.

These findings are not unique; lots of animal groups develop customs that they learn by imitating each other. This observation has stirred up a controversy as to whether animals can have "cultures." Evidently local populations of animals do share traditions but arguably nothing that we'd call cultures. The question is important because imitation is a crucial means of transmitting culture—the issue that Plato posed and that will confront us again.[15]

Returning to human beings, How do we come to understand the minds and feelings of others? Now we need to know another fact: Paul Ekman has proved that people around the world reveal the same facial expressions when experiencing the same emotions. We needn't *learn* how to show anger, grief, fear, or other affects. Moreover, Ekman taught subjects to move their muscles in the particular way that normally *expresses* a given emotion; he found that assuming the facial expression actually *evoked* the corresponding emotion. If you pose to portray fear, say, or grief, you will feel fear or grief, to a lesser degree.

Combine this fact with the aforementioned tendency of infants and adults to mimic the facial expressions of others, and we can answer our question. How do we know what other people are feeling? By copying their facial expressions, we have an immediate physical sensation that *shows* us how they are feeling—not as an abstract notion, but as an emotion that we feel in our bodies. Empathy is the first experience by which we begin to know the human world. Behavioral mimicry is the channel that transfers emotion from one individual to another.[16] Imitation is, from the outset, involved in the empathic experience.

Vicarious Learning, Imitation, and Art

We learn by imitating. Indeed, *social cognitive theory* shows our dependence on observing and selectively copying others.[17] This fact may seem obvious to you (I hope so), but it was long ignored by psychologists. Until the latter half of the twentieth century, their main theory was behaviorism, explaining learning by the rewarding or punishing of particular behavior. But fortunately, we need not experience all rewards and punishments personally. We can learn vicariously by watching the outcome of others' actions, thereby sparing ourselves time-consuming, costly, and even fatal mistakes. Such vicarious learning results from empathizing with others—real or fictional. However, we choose our role models, emulating only those others whom we like and whom we seem to resemble.

Most entertainment involves vicarious emotions—but not always, especially if we count sports and the arts. Sport can be experienced either directly or vicariously. To the hockey player on the ice, it is physical (nonvicarious) activity that increases adrenaline, dopamine, and other biochemicals. However, as a spectator, supine on the sofa, you empathize and experience his excitement vicariously. For some men, this vicarious life is as fulfilling as the vicarious soap opera adventures of their wives. Their secondhand emotion supplements the real sources of positive affect in life.

Culture and biology work together in creating or appreciating art. Music has a direct (nonvicarious) impact on the listener's nervous system.[18] For example, therapists sometimes use particular rhythms that "entrain" with their patients' natural biological rhythms and lend physiological stability. Music's effect is not primarily a matter of role taking or imitation.

However, the emotional impact of music probably varies by culture or historical period—and therefore can be influenced by empathy or imitation. For example, at one time European audiences were not expected to applaud after a concert but rather to cry. Beethoven disapproved of the custom. Once when he finished conducting he turned around to face the audience and became angry when he found them weeping and waving their handkerchiefs at him. When he met Goethe, whose poems he had set to music, he played for him and Goethe cried. Beethoven scolded him for his "immature" response, and Goethe accepted the criticism.[19]

I think Goethe should have stood his ground. Tears were encouraged during the Romantic period, from the mid-eighteenth to the mid-nineteenth centuries. But I have occasionally been moved to tears by music, too—including Beethoven's own *Ode to Joy*—and I am not immature.

Composers can create emotional effects scientifically. For example, sudden changes in harmony often give shivers to listeners. Acceleration and syncopation tend to make the heart race. Grace notes tend to bring on tears. Sequences and harmonic movements that resolve tension by returning to the tonic also tend to cause tears.[20] We feel joy, fear, bouncy playfulness, anxiety, and numerous other moods as physical responses to music. We need not imagine being someone else to get these feelings.[21]

Paintings, unlike music, rarely have such a powerful emotional impact. I've never felt overwhelmed by a painting or any other work of plastic art. Millions of other people have—probably more often in previous periods than today. Emotional reactions to paintings used to be common in Russia, where the custom was to pray while gazing at an icon.[22]

Art historian James Elkins has written about weeping in response to pictures. One account was by one of his students. Tamara arrived in class directly from an exhibition of works by Caspar David Friedrich, a romantic landscape painter. One of the pictures had moved her to tears, and she said she had fallen in love with it. Her eyes were still red. "I was just standing there, and all of a sudden tears were streaming down my cheeks. I cried hard, for a while. It was wonderful."[23]

Elkins advertised an appeal for people to describe such experiences and received about four hundred letters. He also questioned art historians; in comparison with other groups, they were least likely to have cried or even to hold tolerant views of such a nonintellectual response to art.

The champion tear-jerking art collection today is a set of fourteen huge nearly black abstract paintings by Mark Rothko hanging in an octagonal chapel in Houston. Unlike the religious paintings that used to evoke tears, these portray the absence of God. Indeed, Rothko committed suicide before the chapel was completed.[24] Elkins says many other paintings also evoke tears by giving a sense of the absence of God.[25] Although he has never wept over a painting, Elkins offers suggestions from those who did so. He advises us to fantasize about the picture and not to think about what's proper.[26]

Not all crying spells are alike, and when two people are crying in front of two different paintings, their emotions may differ. (Similarly, weeping upon hearing of a friend's death feels entirely different from weeping while watching your sister receive a gold medal for figure skating.) Elkins supposes that everyone who sheds tears while looking at a picture has "fallen in love" with the painting,[27] but I question that conclusion. Comments from the guest book in the Rothko chapel express no love for the pictures but rather a sense of despair. Tamara's tears, by contrast, were manifestations of ecstasy and, as she said, love.

It is not clear which emotional responses to paintings are of vicarious origin and which from direct effects on the viewer's nervous system. Probably empathy was involved in the crying over Rothko and Friedrich. Presumably, the tears came from imaginatively looking through the eyes of the painter as he worked. However, I can't prove this and will generally omit the plastic arts, music, and sports from the forms of entertainment that I'll discuss. However, when drama moves an audience, that reaction is always vicarious experience.

If you cried at an art exhibit, a concert, or a play, maybe you needed it—not as way of *eliminating* unpleasant, bottled-up feelings, but as a pleasurable means of *stimulating* feelings that are scarce. Most people need more emotions, and they buy tickets just to get their feelings stirred up. Indeed, those whose lives run most smoothly may need especially strong stimuli to interrupt their routines. They are not overly emotional, but *under*emotional. They seek supplements.

Living Vicariously

When you run short of positive emotions, borrow one. There's nothing wrong with that. (My original title for this book was *Vicarious Emotions,* but some readers considered it insulting to call their emotions "vicarious." Why so? Many of my best memories are of vicarious experiences, and I keep looking for entertainment that will add to my collection.) When imagining what another person is doing, your brain goes through the same processes as his.[28] When you watch a James Bond movie, say, your brain gets much the same workout as if you were having the adventure yourself. Your blood pressure, heart rate, emotions, and peptides are stimulated.

Fiction is not the only source of vicarious experience. For instance, old men in nursing homes, with nothing to look forward to, may feel joyous about the achievements and prospects of their grandchildren. Their pleasure is wholly vicarious.

Today, we probably live vicariously more than any previous generation—through people on screens. As Marshall McLuhan wrote, the media are "extensions of the human body."[29] A camera lengthens the range of the eye, allowing us to see from Mount Everest or inside our own intestines. A microphone lengthens the range of the ear, allowing us to listen to the auction of a rhinoceros in Nairobi. Even more remarkable is the expansion of our hearts—our ability to feel along with people whom we have never met. We know what it was like to be a tough blonde nurse in a Korean War surgical tent. Or Napoleon's girlfriend. Or a pious New England woman accused of witchcraft in 1692. Media critic Charles McGrath has described his experiences with emergency room shows:

> Let's say you were to come speeding down the corridor on a gurney.... I know that the first thing to do is to get a "line"—an IV—into you and to order up a 1.25 milligram Solumedrol push. And let's have, what the heck, 5 of morphine. That should make you feel better right away. (The best way to install a line, by the way, is to use a No. 16 needle; pull the skin tight, so the veins don't roll, and go in slow.) All right let's type and crossmatch, let's get a blood gas, and I want chest film. Come on, let's move![30]

As we empathize, fictive experiences come alive. Who could sit through *Jurassic Park* or *Jaws* without feeling terrified? Who could see *Schindler's List* without feeling pity? Who could watch *Gandhi* without feeling inspired? Indeed, in a movie or TV audience we may actually feel more deeply than at any other time in our own "real" lives.

This fact troubles many people. They consider it a sad commentary on the unfulfilled lives of modern individuals. They believe we should feel more intensely about our real lives than about any film. I, on the other hand, am glad that my life is so dull that I never encounter dinosaurs, sharks, or Nazi guards except vicariously when watching a screen. Gandhi is an exception; I would love to know someone like him in real life, but since I don't, I thank Richard Attenborough and Ben Kingsley for filling that deficit.

No one empathizes equally with all characters; a play may simply fail to engage us as the actors intended. If you remain overly distant emotionally, you will get nothing from it, whereas if you are *under*distanced from a heavy drama, you may get upset instead of feeling well entertained.[31] Partly it will depend on the play and partly on your willingness, as an onlooker, to suspend disbelief and join actively in the pretense. Partly too, it depends on the rest of the audience. If they are deeply empathizing, it will be easier for you to do so, too.

Presumably, having a real experience yourself is usually more intense than just empathizing with another person who is having it. And, presumably, empathizing as an onlooker is in turn usually more intense than merely day-dreaming about such an experience yourself.

Researchers have confirmed my assumptions by comparing subjects' physiological reactions to real ice water, to vicarious ice water, and to fantasized ice water. The intensity of arousal declined in that order.[32] Also, when we watch television, an upsetting scene will usually arouse more distress in us if we know it really happened than if we know it is fictional.

Vicarious emotions tend to be exceptionally strong if you have bonded to the person with whom you empathize. Your emotional attachments make you care. The pain, joy, or death of a loved one will seem more vivid than that of an ordinary stranger.

Celebrities

On the other hand, not every stranger is "ordinary." Most of us can identify more than one thousand celebrities whom we have never even seen in the flesh—several times as many as the people we know in our own social world.[33] We may form surprisingly intense attachments toward these celebrity strangers, hating or loving them. A major conversation topic may be the latest doings of well-known persons whose activities we've been following. John Caughey reports that *all* members of one minor league baseball team invariably watch the soap opera *General Hospital,* so they can discuss it with each other or with women they meet in bars.[34] (See the appendix at the end of this chapter for a report of a European woman's prolonged attachment to a television character.)

Caughey studied seventy-two Americans who have been infatuated with actors or other media celebrities. He writes, "The intensity of those love relationships is often as strong as that of a 'real' love affair."[35] Although he acknowledges that these imaginary affairs may compensate for a lack of satisfying real relationships, Caughey does not think this explanation applies in most cases:

> It does not explain the suburban grandmother who had a lifelong "affair" with Frank Sinatra despite forty years of marriage. It does not explain why, in adolescence and in later years, artificial love relationships often persist after an actual lover is found.... [I]n some ways fantasy relations are often *better* than real love relationships.... He is there when you want him and gone when you do not. Real love relationships include all sorts of unfortunate realities.[36]

Caughey asks why fans become attached to one particular media figure, rather than another. He claims that the fan sees in the celebrity some qualities that they have in common, which the fan wants to cultivate further. The admired figure represents an ideal self-image.[37] In this way, such bonds channel a person's ethos and character development in a particular direction.

Attachments to Fictional Characters

My brief investigation of this topic supports Caughey's conclusions. Whereas his study dealt with media figures such as actors to whom fans became attached, my own queries dealt with fictional *characters* instead of the actors who played them. However, I found that the distinction does not hold up very well. People often do not know whether they are attached to the character or the actor. And sometimes the attachment begins with the character but turns to the actor.

One Valentine's Day, the *Globe and Mail* newspaper featured a long article in which local celebrities were asked to describe fictional individuals with whom they had fallen in love. Most of the characters described were from novels, but a few were from dramas.

This story prompted me to send e-mail to about forty of my friends asking whether they had ever fallen in love with a fictional character. I have asked this in other situations, too, such as at the hairdresser's. The majority acknowledge that they have experienced such a thing at least once, and a few have replied, "Of course. All the time." However, some reply smilingly to this question, "None that I would tell you about, dear!" One friend replied, "No, I'm a male," but several other males gave affirmative answers. Often acquaintances have replied fully, even eagerly. Here too their replies often did not distinguish between beloved characters and actors. My hairdresser says she has been in love with Mel Gibson for fifteen years. Her adult daughter is limerent toward Richard Gere.

One reply came from a woman sociologist who mentioned her crush on Lord Peter Wimsey, hero of the 1930s mysteries by Dorothy Sayers. I was startled to recall that I, too, had once entertained fantasies about Lord Peter, and my astonishment increased when my friend told me of her dinner party twenty-five years ago with three unmarried female anthropologists. The Sayers series came up in their conversation, and it seems that all the women had once been in love with Lord Peter. (That makes five of us.) No wonder: my friend described him as "attractive, witty, well mannered, sensitive, rich, respected, no ego or bombast, and he put women in the center of the world."

I placed a classified ad in the *New York Review of Books,* asking people whether they had ever obsessed about fictional characters. I received four replies.[38] Two were from women. One of them, Marta, had fantasized about Vladimir Putin, Jon Bon Jovi, and Russell Crowe (who are all celebrities but not fictional characters). She explained, "I would like to be better, so I simply imagine that

I am much better at everything and since I don't want to be left alone in my superiority, I must imagine that there is a man who would be able to handle me because he too is wonderful. If I am simply fabulous in my megalomania, then that person has got to match."

The other woman, Jillian, is a professor and novelist who at thirteen became obsessed with Alan Alda, who played Hawkeye Pierce, the leading character in *M*A*S*H*. She made tapes and kept a notebook, memorizing the lines. "To this day I can recite some comedy sequences from the script," she says. Her fantasies centered on meeting Alda and having him recognize her talent as a writer and wanting to perform some of her work. She also fantasized that Alda's wife, a children's book author, would read her work and write to her.

Jillian's obsession arose while her parents were having marital difficulties and she felt miserable. Her fascination began with an episode in which Hawkeye Pierce, the only doctor not struck down by flu, coped alone, heroically, with the crisis besetting the whole medical camp. "I may have grasped for the image of someone holding his own in adversity," she speculates. "Perhaps it kept me sane. I'm a happy person now. I learned to let go of obsessions by indulging them. If something fascinates me, I let it consume me for a while. Usually it runs out in a few months."

She had no romantic fantasies involving these celebrities, though she acknowledges having "come close." What she actually wanted, however, was "to *be* these people, live their lives, be like them, or have them in my life in some way." Marta's and Jillian's motives seem to be, as Caughey points out, to cultivate qualities that they have in common with the celebrity. The admired figure represents an ideal self-image.

Philip, my third respondent, was a fifty-year-old married professional obsessed with a Saturday morning cartoon/video game series. Philip writes "fan-fic" novels about its characters, who are animals that seem human. Occasionally a character refers to his "wing" or "claw" but usually to his "arm" or "hand." The most heroic characters are all aggressive females. I read some of Philip's novels. Always a small band of animals wage guerrilla war against the villain, who is human.

Philip's writing assumes that we, the readers, empathize with the "good guys" but never with the villain or his evil henchmen, who must be destroyed. Action films typically are of this polarized, blaming nature, which I will discuss in a later chapter. No conflict reconciliation is conceivable, for that would undermine the melodramatic premise of the action genre: a struggle between good and evil, where everyone is good or bad, never mixed.

In contrast to these "blaming" action stories, middle-aged people recall a delightful series of children's books featuring Freddy the Pig,[39] who could be a cowboy, magician, pilot, or detective. The villains were always pompous members of the Establishment, yet they could be funny. The lovable farm animals, although committed to social justice, had flaws. Characters were not black and white, but gray. One could empathize with them all, which is not the case with a true blaming story. Adults who have read the Freddy books get together every summer to talk about their old hero.[40]

I attribute these attachments, including Philip's bond with the female cartoon warriors, to two facts. First, the stories form a series. That format is necessary if the reader is to sustain an emotional relationship with characters. Second, as Caughey suggested, they represent the fan's ego ideal. An *ego ideal* is a conscious self-image to which a person aspires. We may have several ego ideals that are not much alike, for a normal personality contains a variety of subpersonalities besides one's own everyday self. They come from the experience of empathizing. I'll explore this from a combination of Buddhist psychology and object relations psychoanalysis. The Buddhist analysis relates to Plato's doctrine of transcendence.

Internalizing Others

Every normal person contains a whole array of personality systems. For example, every husband must maintain a stable notion of his wife's personality. He "internalizes" or "introjects" her self, and the wife internalizes his personality, too.[41] They do so by having repeatedly empathized, trying to experience what the other is feeling.

The self whom we have internalized may intrude in our thinking . Thus a husband ordering a hamburger and fries considers his vegetarian wife's disapproval, even if she is out of town. Internalization creates a conscience, or perhaps several consciences—one for each self that we have internalized. Not only does the husband's internal vegetarian wife monitor his consumption of meat, but she may argue with his internal cattle rancher mother. Luckily, the debates among his internalized selves aren't witnessed by the other customers in the fast food queue.[42]

Attachment

Both psychoanalysis and Buddhist psychology emphasize the centrality of attachment or clinging, though they disagree as to its value. *Attachment* is the forming of an intense, emotionally significant, usually prolonged relationship with another personality, normally in one's real life but sometimes fictional.

Limerence and the parent–child bonds are examples. We might include obsessive affection toward certain animals or even inanimate objects. (There's a musician in *Northern Exposure* who falls in love with a violin, but I'm not sure that such experiences actually happen to real people.) Object relations psychoanalysts claim that the personality is shaped by these intense, feelingful attachments to figures in our constellation of internalized selves. It is our passionate fascination with them that keeps us human, anchored in our community, on our planet.

To those aspiring to transcendence (e.g., Plato in his day, many seekers of enlightenment in ours) that is just the problem. Our emotional attachments confine us within our humanity, our bodily needfulness, our love for particularity instead of the eternal universals. To be free, they say, you have to extricate yourself from bonds, for nonattachment is the path of wisdom. Ultimately, you want to leave this illusory physical world behind and become totally transcendent. Plato and Buddhist psychology alike connect suffering to attachment. We *cling* to an object or, equally unfortunately, *resist* it, attempting to change or eliminate it. Resistance and clinging are sides of the same coin and, according to philosophies of transcendence, the source of misery. Suffering will end only when you become nonattached—which is hard to do. According to some Eastern teachings, that goal requires many lifetimes of renunciation. It is usual to begin by meditating, which involves *witnessing* oneself clinging or resisting without interfering.

Aristotle, unlike Plato, did not seek transcendence, for he regarded the physical world of space and time as the real home of humankind. Like him, I expect and often cherish human failings. I don't know many real people in hot pursuit of Nirvana—people fully committed to transcendence. However, we do see the tension between these contrasting values in specific cultures and individual personalities. We vary in our preference for aloofness, autonomy, and independent thinking, versus attachment to others.

Empathy and Imitation as Moral Processes

One test of another person's virtue is to empathize with her and see how the experience feels. If her act is reprehensible, you should feel uncomfortable and maybe even break empathy. (This is hardly an ultimate proof of right and wrong, but only a useful first approximation.)

When we empathize, we mainly feel what the other person feels. Because he, too, empathizes, what he may be feeling is the experience of yet a third person. I may imaginatively look through Eric's eyes while Eric is imaginatively looking through the eyes of Caitlin. In that case, to empathize accurately, I must also know Caitlin—or at least know Eric's impression of her. Our inner society is a "hall of mirrors" that includes selves based not just on our own experiences but also on the distorted accounts of others, including fictive characters.

What we internalize is not merely a self but reciprocal interactions. You probably began by internalizing your mom as a nurturant self[43] and a notion of yourself as reciprocally loving her. Thereafter you could comfort yourself by imaginatively loving yourself (or even patting or stroking yourself) from her perspective. The ability to do this gave you a convenient means of looking after yourself when necessary, even in adulthood.[44] Some psychoanalysts say that few mothers receive much nurturing themselves, and one way of filling their own needs is to nurture their dependent children while empathizing with them and thereby experiencing vicariously the pleasure of being cared for.

To be able to love yourself, you first imagine someone else loving you and empathize with that person. When I was about three, I internalized Jesus. In a biblical verse, Christ invites little children to come unto him, so I imagined him holding me and letting me touch his beard. Whenever my internalized mother skimped on affection, I could receive it from Jesus. A sophisticated woman friend of mine, now about seventy-five, continues such a relationship with Jesus. Not only does she pray throughout the day, but she says she constantly longs to be close to Jesus (though I don't suppose she wants him to pick her up and carry her around while she touches his beard).

From this crowd of internalized selves, some are peculiarly significant—especially ego ideals, who may be of the same or opposite sex. My ego ideals included unconventional women: Eleanor Roosevelt, Margaret Mead, and Ingrid Bergman. My politics are those of Roosevelt, and my career has been influenced by Mead and the psychoanalyst that Bergman plays in *Spellbound*.

It may be absurd to obsess over Hawkeye Pierce, Freddy the Pig, and the gallant Lord Peter Wimsey, but it is not abnormal. When I visited the Soviet Union in the early 1980s, children still internalized Vladimir Lenin. They encouraged themselves by approving of themselves from his perspective, just as I had nurtured myself from the perspective of Jesus. Even Soviet adults still depended emotionally on Lenin. The more I learn about him, the more I consider Jesus a better choice.

Attachment to a Self

You are not only the self you believe you are. Your repertoire includes many other selves as well. Everyday life is improvisational acting, and you may draw on them.[45] We lock ourselves in imaginary traps when we regard our own identity as given instead of self-created from our internalized selves.

There's a great story about this confusion involving actors Kirk Douglas and John Wayne. It seems that Wayne got angry when watching Douglas play Vincent Van Gogh in *Lust for Life*. He came over and criticized Douglas. "Kirk! How can you play a part like that? There's so goddamn few of us left. We got to play strong, tough characters. Not those weak queers."

"I tried to explain," recalls Douglas. "'Hey, John. I'm an actor. I like to play interesting roles. It's all make-believe, John. It isn't real. You're not really John Wayne, you know.'"[46]

He was right. John Wayne played John Wayne—and eventually he forgot that it was a role. He was attached to one self and resisted all the other selves that he had internalized.

Young American males made John Wayne into an ego ideal. They joined the army and went to fight in Vietnam. There many of them recovered some of their other internalized selves and turned against their John Wayne identity. Michael W. Rodriguez has described this moment of insight. It was the worst day in the war; soldiers were being blown apart by Claymore mines in the trees. Nobody in his platoon thought they would ever get out alive. But one man saw what their problem was. "John Wayne lied to us," he announced. "John Wayne is full of shit. We been thinking we're all John Wayne, and it ain't true."

Everyone concurred. One man added, "I get back to the World, man, I am looking that motherfucker up. 'John,' I'll say. 'You are a lying sumbitch.'"

A new lieutenant arrived on duty during this conversation. He said, "You guys are just now finding out that John Wayne lied to us? ... I learned that a long time ago."[47]

John Wayne's status as an ego ideal to American males is the exception that proves the rule. I suggested that one needs a *series* of stories to form an enduring attachment toward a character, but Wayne's movies were individual dramas. However, there were more than two hundred of them, and his character was always the same—his own personality. Thus the general rule is confirmed.[48]

The loss of an ego ideal is always painful, as any ex–John Wayne fan can tell you. Or any Russian. The Soviet people adored both Lenin and Stalin. As the evidence emerged about their crimes against humanity, the truth was almost unbearable; some people still refuse to discuss the topic. It would have been better never to have loved those dictators. Freddy the Pig would have been better. Everyone needs an ego ideal, yet much depends on choosing the right candidate. What matters is the ethos—the flaws and virtues—of our ego ideal.

Empathy toward the Imperfect

Everyone probably feels fond of certain persons who are weak, vulnerable, or far from accomplished. Think of Charlie Chaplin, for example. Robert Warshow describes him thus:

> Beneath all the social meanings of Chaplin's art there is one insistent personal message that he is conveying to us all the time. It is the message of most entertainers, maybe, but his especially because he is so great an entertainer. "Love me"—he has asked this from the beginning, buttering us up with his sweet ways and his calculated graceful misadventures, with those exquisite manners so perfectly beside the point, with that honeyed glance he casts at us so often, lips pursed in an outrageous simper, eyebrows and mustache moving in frantic invitation. Love me. And we have, apparently, loved him, though with such undercurrents of revulsion as might be expected in response to so naked a demand.[49]

We do love Charlie Chaplin, but not for qualities that we would look for in an ego ideal. We love some characters not despite but possibly *because* of their nonheroic personalities. To sustain empathy with them, we'll make allowances for their failings. Sometimes we almost prefer a person who tests our limits, so long as we can smile at him. If he seems good-humored and naive, we may be tolerant and appreciative, but not if his infractions reflect evil intent. But our empathy makes us vulnerable. We may suffer vicariously for a person or fictional character to whom fate is unfair.

In one e-mail list discussion of fictive characters, I found a woman with whom I generally agreed. Ellen and I shared a dislike for comedies about characters who are too shallow or crude to empathize with; we never laugh at them. *The Diary of Bridget Jones* and *Rushmore* were examples—and also slapstick shows and movies, such as those created by the Monty Python comedy troupe, which many people find hilarious. "Nobody could empathize with those characters," Ellen wrote. "When people laugh, they are ridiculing them. That's rude, like laughing at a handicapped person." I agreed. Some theorists claim that humor is basically hostile—that we laugh at people whom we dislike. That is not true of Ellen or me. We would rarely laugh at anyone we dislike. Only a character for whom we feel some fondness would we find funny. We especially laugh at foibles that we share.

I asked my e-mail discussion group whether they laugh at characters they dislike. Yossi, who lives in Israel, said that he does: "There are different laughs. When empathy is there, I would call it a benign laugh. When it is not present, I would call it a 'free' laugh (so I don't have to call it 'malignant'). The 'free laughs' are wilder and stronger. Maybe the best genre for that is cartoons. *Fawlty Towers* with John Cleese makes me laugh to tears, but I cannot empathize with a single one of the characters."

I rented *Fawlty Towers,* but I never laughed. I'll bet nobody ever became limerent toward John Cleese's character. Empathy is basic. If you feel empathy, you may intensify it, falling into limerence. But without empathy, there will be no limerence. If limerence occurs, it may be directed not toward an ego ideal but toward an imperfect character—an antihero—with endearing qualities.

Mimesis

Again we encounter the ancient Greek debate about the value—if any—of art, especially poetry and drama. Though it was best framed by Plato and Aristotle, the same controversy is still troubling modern people. In ancient times, it was part of the long-running, acrimonious dispute between poets and philosophers. People had to take sides: Did you endorse rational argumentation about abstract, universal ideas, or did you favor emotional enthrallment in stirring stories about mythic heroes, gods, and strange, half-animal creatures? Plato claimed that telling wild tales—especially to young people—ruined their education and led them to imitate the immoral behavior they saw onstage.

Defining Mimesis

Plato's criticism of Homer and the dramatists depended on his theory of *mimesis,* a term that is usually translated as "imitation." Mimesis covers a variety of concepts that are unrelated, if not mutually antithetical. Often the term refers to the *behavioral emulation* of another person—which is what I'll usually mean. Sometimes, however, it refers to the visual *resemblance* of two or more things (including figurative works of art). For example, if someone painted a portrait of a person or a picture of an animal, this representation would be mimetic. Or the evolving literary styles for representing stories may be described as mimetic trends.[50] Sometimes the word refers to the *impersonation* of another person or even an animal, including by an actor onstage. Sometimes it refers to the *production of music* by singing or playing an instrument. Sometimes it refers to some kind of *metaphysical similarity,* as, for example, the Pythagorean belief that the physical world is a mimesis of the immaterial realm of numbers. Sometimes it is applied to a *work of art* itself, sometimes to the *artist or performer,* and sometimes to the psychological effect that the artwork has on its *audience.* What confusion!

Logically, we should give different names to these different concepts instead of trying to see them as related phenomena. Unfortunately, I am in no position to redefine such an ancient word. I think the best general translation might be *simulation,* but I don't want to add to an already ridiculous list.[51] Normally, as I use the word, *mimesis* will refer to the behavioral emulation of another person, for that is the only aspect I consider a problem today.

But the larger problem did haunt Plato. It related to the primacy he assigned to transcendence and unemotional, eternal matters, as opposed to worldly concerns. He explained his theory best in Book X of *The Republic,* a Socratic dialogue about the nature of justice. There, Socrates and his young philosophers imagine a utopian city-state and decide how it should be run. They are concerned with rearing the elite guardian youths who will effectively rule there, and they decide that art, poetry, and drama should be banned to keep the youths from being swayed by untruth and emotions. Poetry would lead to all manner of social ills, since it is inherently mimetic.

Plato reasoned along these lines. God created the world and all its creatures, including ourselves, to mimetically represent particular divine "Forms." Physical entities that the senses can perceive are only representations (copies, or simulations) of these true, perfect Forms.

So what about a carpenter who is constructing a bed? True, he is following the ideal model or Form of a bed, but his mimetic carpentry is second-rate in comparison to God's mimesis. And what about an artist who is painting a *picture of the carpenter* building that second-rate imitation bed? At best, the artist's mimesis will be three degrees away from the Forms that constitute reality and truth. That is, the painting is a *mimesis of a mimesis.* The painting is a mere appearance of a bed, not a true bed. "Beds," says Plato, "are of three kinds, and there are three artists who superintend them: God, the maker of the bed, and the painter."[52] So as not to be distracted from God's realm of Ideas, he would exclude painters and poets from the utopian city.

I've never met anyone who took Plato's metaphysics seriously as a reason to shun music, dance, poetry, or drama. Many people, however, *are* concerned about the effects of popular culture on young people—and for excellent reasons. It is true, as he worried, that audiences—especially in crowds—sometimes are swept up in contagious responses, lose their critical judgment, and copy what they see others do. (Why else, for example, would tattoos and eyebrow rings ever become popular?)

Unlike Plato, we suppose that imitation can be harmful, benign, or a combination of the two. It certainly cannot be abolished, for it is the means of transmitting culture itself. But sometimes culture is harmed by the imitations of what has been witnessed. What determines whether the consequences will be benign or deleterious? Primarily, as Plato argued, it is the use of rational criticism, even against the stirring emotionality of public events.[53]

Empathy and mimesis are so interdependent that they are considered almost synonymous. The connection between them creates a dilemma. On the one hand, empathy is the basis for morality; on the other hand, to imitate others is morally dubious. To be sure, we learn vicariously from role models, but this is presumably rational. What is more troubling is *uncritical mimesis* in which one stops thinking and simply apes another person's ways. Such influence appalled Plato—properly so. It seems contradictory to encourage empathy while discouraging mimesis, yet I will propose that as the solution to Plato's concerns.

Plato wanted to prevent imitation, partly to prevent social conflict. He did not quite explain how imitation causes conflict, but a recent writer has done so with a theory of "mimetic rivalry." This was a French literary professor, René Girard, whose psychological account describes a familiar experience—*mimetic desire.* As a source of contagious competition, it plausibly explains much human discord.

René Girard's Theory of Mimetic Desire

Girard's unusual theory arises from his rejection of the assumption that we are the source of our own desires. He claims that people often don't know what to desire. We learn through mimesis, the nonrational identification with others, in the following way.

While we are feeling uncertain or insufficient, we encounter someone (usually a real person, but sometimes a fictional one) who apparently has everything we lack. Enthralled and eager to become like such a person, we imitate him as closely as possible. In fact, we imitate his motives by *desiring whatever he desires* or whatever seems to satisfy him. And in adopting his desires, we may become his rival for satisfying them. (Remember our guppies? Girard might call Marian's imitative preference for George an instance of "mimetic rivalry.")

Girard sees mimesis as the main, if not the sole, source of all our own desires and, therefore, as the source of many of our problems. However, he says that we don't acknowledge the mimetic origin of our desires but instead hide our fascination for the other person—the "model" or "mediator" whom we emulate.

Nevertheless, our imitative experience often opens a destructive conflict with the mediator over the objects that we now both desire—at least those that are in scarce supply. If we simply empathically shared the model's wishes inwardly without pursuing them overtly, there would be no problem. And if unlimited persons could pursue the same desires without competing, there still might be no problem. (Probably it would be all right for the whole world, through mimesis, to acquire the current enthusiasm for yoga, for there's plenty of yoga for everyone—unless one does it competitively.) Unfortunately, however, in many cases, if we try to fulfill our new wishes, we find ourselves in rivalry with our model/mediator over some finite, "conserved" object of our common desire, such as money, prestige, or a particular guppy named George. Plato had failed to explain *why* our imitating creates conflict. Girard explains it this way: We try to *appropriate* the model's desired object, which without mimesis we would never have wanted at all.

Immanuel Kant claimed that all vainglorious desires arise from comparing ourselves to others instead of paying attention to our own real needs. We display "a reluctance to see our own wellbeing overshadowed by another's because the standard we use to see how well off we are is not the intrinsic worth of our own wellbeing but how it compares with that of others."[54]

Our model may become involved in the dynamic, too—possibly by actively trying to *instigate* our desire for whatever he has. By desiring it and envying him, we confirm his good taste and amplify his satisfaction and prestige. For example, a husband may enjoy realizing that other men desire his beautiful wife. He may show her off precisely to make other men envious, for their desiring her may be an aphrodisiac to him, validating his own marital choice.

Much depends on whether the model is what Girard calls an "external" or an "internal" mediator. By *external*, he means that the model is socially so remote from his imitator that there can be no realistic rivalry between them. This distance may be geographic, or it may arise from the fact that the model is a fictitious character in a novel. Or it may be a matter of status. You can't compete against a celebrity (who is by definition an external mediator), whereas if you desire the "top salesman award," say, or the same corner office that a colleague desires, you will resent her every achievement. The colleague is an internal mediator, in Girard's terminology, and the closer the similarity between yourself and the internal mediator (model), the more likely you are to start a mimetic rivalry.

There is no limit to the number of persons who may become involved in imitating each other. When we see others around us avidly desiring a thing, we also may get caught up in these contagious wishes, as in the case of fashions and fads that come and go. Market fluctuations result from this mass imitation of desire—and loss of desire when the market crashes.[55] Collective pathologies such as racism and nationalism occur because people selectively imitate particular populations, thereby creating artificial boundaries that exclude people who are "different." History is replete with instances of panics and stampedes, booms and busts that show how mimetic rivalry threatens social order and precipitates violent conflict. Even if rules and prohibitions say how people are supposed to behave, runaway mimesis may break down social hierarchies and smash prohibitions.

In a tribal, preindustrial society (one that lacks an effective state), such rivalries are hard to manage. There are no formal institutions of law and order. Suppose two mimetic rivals try to grab the same desired object, and a struggle ensues. As Thomas Hobbes made clear, "Considering that many men's appetites carry them to one and the same end; which end sometimes can neither be enjoyed in common, nor divided, it followeth that the stronger must enjoy it alone, and that it be decided by battle who is the stronger."[56] So mimesis can lead to rivalry, which can lead to violence. And one violent act evokes retaliation, which in turn will be avenged by another act of violence, endlessly perpetuating the cycle until no one is left standing.

Even today, the remaining Stone Age–like societies have far higher homicide rates than the inner cities of democratically governed states. Girard shows that typically, Paleolithic and agrarian societies arrive at this solution to a rivalry crisis: they sacrifice a scapegoat. This person may be marginal to the society and in no way responsible for the conflict, but a unanimous consensus is established, pinning the blame on him, and he is killed or expelled. Immediately after his murder, the scapegoat may be regarded as a powerful figure, possibly even sacred, for not only was he deemed responsible for all the troubles, but his sacrifice has brought peace.[57] The community's attitude toward him becomes a blend of hatred and gratitude. Thereafter, to prevent the outbreak of new mimetic rivalries, prohibitions are reinstituted and rituals are enacted that allude to the terrible, violent preceding period and the sacrificial murder.

In modern society, such performances are no longer necessary, says Girard. Instead, we have institutions of justice that identify and punish blameworthy individuals. As soon as the legal penalty is imposed, that's the end of the matter. Relatives don't carry on the cycles of retaliation further. Sacrificial victims are still punished by the state, but the violence is limited.[58]

As civilization advances, there's a tendency to give up sacrifice in favor of less violent ways of managing mimetic rivalry, Girard says. Here we see some of the differences between high and popular culture. In popular fiction, for example, the characters are sharply defined as good or bad, and we usually know that the bad ones will, in the end, become victims of a sacrificial punishment not unlike the older scapegoating system. (I'll discuss this "blaming" theme in later chapters.) In high culture, on the other hand, the distinction between good and bad is less clear, and the denouement may not be sacrificial. (Here we may find a potential basis for a culture of compassion, but its moral ambiguities will have troubling aspects of their own.)

Girard applies his model to humankind everywhere and in every age. He cites cases from literature and ethnography depicting mimetic desire as regrettable, though understandable. As for mimetic *rivalry,* it is hard to dispute his conclusion that it is an immensely dangerous and widespread source of conflict. However, he offers no solutions for overcoming it. The more I accepted his observations, the more haunted I felt by their pessimistic implications. His theory calls for a reply—as follows.

Mimesis is not always pathological. We all do it, usually without serious consequences except when it leads us into rivalry with our mediator. Besides, is it true, as Girard suggests, that all our desires come from imitating others? Surely not. If you're caught in a blizzard without a hat or boots, you'll spontaneously generate desires without emulating a model. Surely our bodies must be the main source of our desires. And, apart from mimesis, we also must have desires that arise instrumentally to carry out the projects that we have set for ourselves as meaningful goals. But it is true that many of our conflicts do derive from mimetic rivalry. The challenge then is to find ways of forestalling them. How?

Avoiding Mimetic Rivalry

My first clues came from reading Girard more closely.[59] Nowhere in his writings, so far as I can find, does he explain mimesis as resulting from empathy or role taking. Apparently I had unwittingly imported the idea of empathy into his theory, presuming that he considered the two processes inextricably linked.

But can we have mimesis without empathy? Or empathy without mimesis? Yes and yes.

As for mimesis without empathy, it happens whenever we yawn contagiously after seeing someone else yawn. Also, when we buy a brand name because we have seen a billboard, we are experiencing mimesis without empathy. All direct instances of suggestion taking place outside relationships are mimesis without empathy. (Remember, people behave more aggressively if a toy gun is visible in the room than if a badminton racket is present. There is no empathy involved in this mimesis.)

What about empathy without mimesis? Obviously, such a thing is possible, for it is vastly more common than empathy that *is* followed by mimesis. For example, when you are excited by the football game on television, you do not (I hope) tackle the coffee table or leap into the air to intercept the forward pass. If you watch a movie about World War II, you may feel the patriotic fervor, but you won't enlist in the army the next day. Almost always, when we follow others' experiences vicariously, we can enjoy their feelings and desires while retaining our own identity. (I empathized with John Belushi in *Animal House* without throwing food at anyone afterward.) Good parenting requires you to empathize with your child without engaging in mimesis—without imitating her immature behavior or desires.

On the other hand, many of the fictional or mythic characters whom Girard describes seem to experience mimesis without empathy. They imitate and take on the motivations of the other without evidently feeling with her, without experiencing her feelings vicariously.

Yes, mimetic rivalry causes trouble, but I now believe that it often comes from the *absence* of empathy. At least, that is true of me. If I try to take what another person wants or possesses, it is usually because I do not fully imagine how the loss will make him feel. I appropriate his desired objects only if I am thinking about my wants, not his. If I empathize, I will feel his sorrow, his pleasure, his desire—and this vicarious perception will influence me morally.

I conclude, therefore, that mimesis is distinct from empathy. We don't have to imitate the other person's desires and activities to have an empathic experience. Indeed, it seems that empathy often is an antidote to mimetic rivalry, rather than being its source. In Buddhist psychology, one of the four highest virtues that a person should cultivate is *mudita,* a capacity to feel the joy of others along with them. *Mudita* is empathic experience and exactly opposite to mimetic rivalry. There is no word in the English language for *mudita,* though we have plenty of words for its opposite—such as envy. *Mudita* may be more common than mimetic rivalry. For example, when a young ballerina stars in *Cinderella,* her grandmother feels no envy but may feel as proud as if she herself had danced. Such secondhand emotions are richly rewarding in our mortal existences.[60]

With empathy, I subjectively put myself into your shoes. If then I imitate you overtly, I am experiencing *empathy plus something else.* Empathy per se is not dangerous, but mimesis sometimes is. To imitate a movie star's haircut merely adds variety, but to imitate *The Basketball Diaries* (as the shooters did at Columbine High School) brings disaster.

Girard suggests that it is less dangerous to imitate an *external* than an *internal mediator,* for that will preclude real competition with the model. Since fictional characters are always external mediators, Girard would seem to be advising you to imitate them instead of your cousin or a coworker. But some external mediators are monstrous—Rambo, for instance.

Girard implies that mimetic desires arise because one feels insufficient, lacking in purpose.[61] If our lives are meaningful, presumably we won't imitate the desires of others but will think rationally for ourselves. Thus the problem is an existential, moral, or spiritual issue: How do we discover meaning on our own, without emulating others?

Girard evidently does not address this question directly, but we can draw ethical inferences from his theory, as follows: Mimesis becomes the source of motivation when one's own life is empty. In that meaningless state we try to "keep up with the Joneses," measuring our well-being by comparison to other people rather than our own real needs. Mimetic desire and, even worse, mimetic rivalry are the consequences of existential emptiness. Later we'll explore meaninglessness further.

Conclusion

I've tried to reconcile the ancients. We can, I think, agree with *both* Plato and Aristotle. Drama can give us false lives, as Plato argued, or heal us, as Aristotle contended. What it does depends largely on whether we respond with mimetic desire or with empathy.

Certainly social contagion and imitation are empirical realities. Therefore, Plato's criticism of the theater is well founded. Even though mimesis is not the inevitable outcome of empathizing, copycat behavior does happen. For example, I recently read news of a murder perpetrated as imitation of *The Sopranos*. Such events pose ethical problems for authors, an issue to which I'll devote a whole chapter.

I have celebrated empathy. I think we should increase it and especially *diversify* it. We lose out by limiting our empathy to familiar, accepted groups. It is a worthy spiritual project to empathize, quite deliberately, with people who seem unfamiliar or even unappealing. Adam Smith was right: Expansive pluralism, rather than a constriction of empathy, offers the prospect of overcoming narrow loyalties and parochial worldviews. Our challenge is to empathize while avoiding the dangerous effects of mimesis.

We can acknowledge Plato's rightful concern about the value of the theater—without concluding, however, that its dangers are unavoidable. I admit to being mostly on Aristotle's side of the debate; and, like Aristotle, I'm in no rush to leave the social and material life of this planet. (Still, we have not finished with the question of transcendence.)

We don't have to choose between rational philosophizing and the social learning that comes from empathizing with drama. However, Plato was right on this point: We need to discuss emotion-laden stories rationally and critically.

In most cases of modern entertainment, that philosophizing part simply never happens.

Appendix to Chapter 4

Gwen's Vicarious Love Affair

I want to present here a remarkable illustration of a psychological experience mentioned in this chapter that most people probably don't disclose, even to their best friends. I met a woman on a chat group whom I'll call Gwen. We began a private e-mail correspondence, and eventually she consented to a personal interview by transatlantic phone call. I present it here in an emended form. I've never met Gwen in person, but her comments provided evidence for several theoretical generalizations, as presented in this chapter. Readers differ in their opinion of her. Some pity her; others think she sounds perfectly normal and say they have been through similar periods themselves. How common is this experience?

Gwen demanded absolute anonymity. I may say that she is an English-speaking woman living somewhere in Europe with "senior citizen privileges." I won't identify her beloved television series or its actors. Her husband, formerly a prominent businessman, has suffered dementia for several years and lives in a medical facility, where she and their married daughter visit him every day. Gwen had worked in his firm until his health forced them to sell it. Now she socializes, attends cultural events (especially operas), works on NGO committees, and reads novels, but she rarely watches television—except tapes of her favorite show.

Several years ago she began to watch a syndicated English-language drama series every day and became obsessed by it. Before she had even learned the main characters' names, she was thinking about them eight or ten hours a day. She wondered what it all meant. Her husband still lived at home but was quiet and forgetful. They had a cook, a cleaning woman, and a secretary, so he wasn't a burden. They still were having sex as often as before. She felt okay, except for pains diagnosed as fibromyalgia.

Gwen fell in love with the show's lead character, Randall,[62] who was younger than her stepson. She explained to me:

> I had forgotten how much love increases sexual desire. I started slipping away about twice a day alone for sex while imagining being Randall and Vivienne—his

girlfriend in the story. But it was a "family" show, so I had to fill in lots of missing parts to make the story work out right.

I had the best sex of my life while thinking about those two people. Both sides of the relationship were essential. While I was fantasizing, I never once imagined being *myself* with Randall. That would be impossible. I am twice his age. Instead, I imagined being Vivienne loving Randall. Then in a few seconds, my perspective would automatically shift. I would imagine being Randall loving Vivienne. From one perspective to the other, alternating many times. Sometimes it didn't matter which of them I was at any given moment—I think in a sense I was both of them simultaneously. It was bizarre but wonderful.

From my own point of view, I can't say I find Vivienne interesting. However, I usually looked at her through Randall's eyes, and he was crazy about her, so when I empathized with him, I was crazy about her too. And then, a minute later, I would "become" Vivienne and I'd be watching him and adoring him.

The odd thing is how it affected my fibromyalgia. Every time I had one of these passionate sex experiences, my pain vanished for hours at a time. You say it's endorphins that cause that? Well, I don't know about endorphins, but whatever it was, was wonderful! It still is, when it happens, which is less often lately. Of course, my husband is no longer able to function in that department, though we both still feel affectionate.

The two lovers sometimes said things that displeased me. For example, Randall once told Vivienne that he didn't want children. She accepted that, but I did not. For one thing, when I imagined them having sex but not wanting a baby, the sex was just blah for me. It went nowhere. I had to imagine that they both wanted pregnancy—and preferably right away. So there I was, stuck. I couldn't change the story, because, after all, I had seen them say it on television, so that particular script definitely had been written and couldn't be changed. But I couldn't have sex anymore. It stopped me cold for days. The whole time, I was developing arguments to convince Randall to change his mind. I invented a lot of dialogues. Sometimes I even spoke them aloud when I was alone. I don't know why it was so important to me—especially at my age! I have my daughter and my step-son. Why should I care whether other people have babies or not? Fortunately, another episode soon showed Vivienne talking to a neighbor about babies in ways that allowed a happy resolution to the issue. I got past the problem and resumed my great romance....

I joined the _____ e-mail discussion group [about the show] and found that I wasn't the only obsessed person. Both sexes were preoccupied with the show, but none of us alluded to our secret fantasy lives. You know how they are. Mostly we discussed the plots. Some people talked about the actors. Initially I hadn't even known the names of the actors but gradually I learned a bit about their personal lives.

This began to blur the distinction in my mind between the character Randall and the actor, Andrew. I learned that Andrew was married, and I saw a picture of him with his wife. I began to create a few fantasies of him with her instead of his being Randall with Vivienne. Still, I kept watching the episodes over and over and loving them. The stories stayed fresh a very long time....

After about three years my husband went into the facility where he lives now. I expected to become terribly depressed about him, but it's not so bad. It's like getting old; it creeps up so gradually that it's not a shock. If he were in pain or miserable, I would be too, but he has come to terms with it. Not only does that make it easier for me to accept it, but, to tell the truth—and I wouldn't want anyone else to hear this—I have actually been incredibly happy until recently. I was having a vicarious love affair that was perfectly legal, that didn't interfere with my being a good wife. I love my family as much as ever....

But it is coming to an end, alas. During the past eight months, there have been some changes. First, some of the romantic scenes that I had reused so many times began to lose power as erotic fantasies. But Randall was still "it" for me—I couldn't switch to some other love object, except Andrew, of course. Gradually I invented more adventures for Andrew and his wife, and these were wonderful too—though no longer twice a day. Again I would oscillate, being now the wife loving Andrew, then Andrew loving the wife, and so on. I suppose I lost interest in Randall and Vivienne along the way. I still think about Randall or Andrew every day, but mostly it is the Andrew side of him, not Randall anymore. I have seen some other movies that Andrew made, so I have other images of him that don't look at all like Randall.

But then I read on the Internet that Andrew was seen appearing too attentive toward another woman. Oh, my, that was awful. I couldn't push it out of my mind, but it stopped my erotic life cold. Strange. I hadn't felt particularly sad about my husband, but I felt depressed about an actor I had never met. I wanted him to have a happy marriage for otherwise I couldn't be happy vicariously, to use your expression.

Fortunately, some other stories came out that contradicted the rumor about the other woman. Everything I have seen lately indicates that Andrew adores his wife. That's only hearsay, but it was enough give to my emotional life another lift.

Still, I was gradually falling out of love with him. Not that I wanted to. I didn't have any guilt about enjoying this perfectly proper fling. In fact, it was priceless just for reducing my fibromyalgia pain. I would keep feeling erotic indefinitely twice a day if I could. But I can't.

Something odd happened a couple of months ago. I am one of the sponsors of a company that helps young actors and playwrights stage their original productions. We decided to put on a festival and award a prize, so we wanted some big names as judges. I had heard that Andrew would be near here for several months, so I wrote his agent and asked him to serve as a judge. The answer came back right away: no. He turned me down flat. I was so disappointed!

Now that, I am afraid, is really the end. When he turned me down, that was reality. I can't argue with it. I can't fantasize it away. He turned me down. That has shut down my erotic connection to Andrew—I don't have any basis for it anymore. Reality has spoken. It's the end of the affair. Don't laugh. Now I'm back to the state of mind I was in before I ever saw that television series. It's not a bad state of mind—but it sure falls short of what I had come to enjoy!

I wanted to reassure Gwen or comfort her, but I didn't know what to say. Finally, I asked, "But why should that matter? You said you didn't play *yourself* in your fantasies with him; you played his wife. He didn't reject his wife, so why can't you go on fantasizing about him and her together, just as you did before?" She answered:

Because there are limits on how I can think. He didn't reject his wife, but he rejected *me*. That cancels any permission I could give myself to imagine being him and her together. I'm not saying this is logical. These things don't run on the basis of logic. The heart has its own reasons. But I'm all right. Besides, I still have those videotapes to watch when I need an emotional lift.

Chapter 5

Bad Vibes

If you often jump out of airplanes for fun, or if you love suspense, action, horror, tragic, and war movies, this chapter is for you. After emphasizing that happy emotions are good for both your body and soul, I must now face some awkward facts. People often choose entertainment that evokes terrible emotions, such as terror and grief. Why? Don't they know that these feelings are deleterious? Don't they find them unpleasant? If so, why do they pay good money to experience them? How can anyone enjoy tragedy? Or is "enjoyment" beside the point? Are there other attractions to painful stories that offset the unpleasantness involved? Or do people differ so much that what is painful for one may be enjoyable to another? Are there certain times when all of us enjoy experiences that seem disagreeable at other times? We'll deal with these questions in this chapter.

It seems impossible to explain all entertainment preferences in terms of the goal of mood management. In fact, no one single motivation will account for all these preferences. However, mood management may explain most choices, including complex affects that may be unpleasant. We must examine several possible explanations.

Let me reject one theory right away: that what you experience when watching a film or reading a story is not *real* fear or grief, but something different.[1] Quite a few writers take this position, though it is hard to imagine why. According to this argument, since you know that the story is fictitious, you must surely realize that no one is in actual danger, and therefore, logically, you *must* not feel as you would when watching, say, real cowboys and Indians shooting each other.

Related to the "it's not real" theory is another notion: that the emotions you experience in the movies are simply memories of your own previous feelings, now restimulated by the events on the screen.[2] This theory considers the emotions to be real, but as your *own* revived ones rather than new responses to the new situation.

There is no way to disprove either theory, but I know of no reason to accept them. True, you don't usually feel as intensely about fiction as about a real massacre, but your feelings seem to be milder versions of the same emotions.[3] Indeed, your physiological reactions (e.g., blood pressure, respiration, adrenaline content, brain activity) suggest that your emotional arousal is real and sometimes quite intense. People generally know *when* they are aroused, even if they aren't sure *what* combination of emotions they are feeling or what triggered it all. As we shall see later, this uncertainty can explain a great deal.

Why We Watch What We Watch

Besides using entertainment for mood management, sometimes you may just want to feel *interested*. Plots are likely to hold your interest if they include surprises or mysteries to figure out. (Hence the popularity of crime shows.) Interest is independent of pleasure/displeasure, but it is related to arousal of both the limbic cortex and the autonomic nervous system. People can be interested in sad, fearful, delightful, and amusing situations. Another factor making a story interesting is that it provides you with information that you regard as relevant to your own life. If it does so, you may watch, even if it upsets you.

As Steven Johnson has shown, the trend in television dramas has not been toward "dumbing down" stories and writing. Quite the contrary. TV writers today keep you on your toes, moment by moment. Characters are of ambiguous morality, and viewers can't be sure whom to trust. These writers know how to keep us interested. And, according to Johnson, to watch such challenging stories makes us smarter.[4]

I think that only a minority of the audience actually work hard at following such complex stories. Nevertheless many others also enjoy the surprises. My son, for example, hates any show if he can guess what will happen before the end of the episode. Unpredictability, in itself, seems to be his main criterion for appraising a drama.

But if TV writers are making us more intelligent, they are not necessarily making us more thoughtful, sensitive, caring, or moral. These interesting, complex, fast-cut, unpredictable stories are not necessarily profound.

It should not be necessary to choose between *interesting* and *deep* programs. The two qualities aren't incompatible.[5] I think *The West Wing* does a good job of maximizing both values. It always has one story thread that deals with a genuine political issue, and all of the characters speak quickly and wittily; you have to work to keep up, yet the values and intellectual challenges are excellent.

Occasionally, even a light comedy or love story provides wise insights. That makes it doubly difficult to explain the popularity of entertainment displaying gruesome malevolence. "Action" or horror shows that evoke horrific reactions may nevertheless attract people in droves. I think it's simply because such stories are *interesting* for a brief time, though often forgettable within an hour or so.

Do high box office receipts prove that modern people have lost their moral bearings and prefer violence and ugliness? Maybe so, but we moderns are not the most insensitive society in history. Recall the Roman circuses. For five hundred years, slaves and prisoners were killed for the entertainment of cheering crowds.[6] Ancient Rome was truly a culture of violence. Its brutality was reflected in its conquests to expand the empire and in the way newborns and slaves were treated. Nor were these habits often challenged. Philosophers such as Marcus Aurelius and Epictetus said nothing critical of the practices. Seneca was an exception; he thought it uncivilized that anyone should take pleasure in "seeing a man made a corpse."[7]

By late in the second century, the Christian Bishop Tertullian scolded his flock for attending gladiatorial shows. But his reasoning was strange: He promised Christians that if they would stay away from them, they could watch an even better spectacle after the Day of Judgment, when nonbelievers would be tortured with worse sufferings than any inflicted at earthly circuses—and (whoopee!) those tortures would be everlasting![8]

In comparison to Rome's spectacles, Hollywood productions are mild and gentle. And mayhem, violence, and horror are not the most popular forms of entertainment. Most viewers choose comedies and sitcoms instead.[9] (The same goes for children; violent cartoons are not particularly popular, with the parents or the children.)[10]

Then why do studios continue to produce mayhem/violence/horror films? According to communications expert George Gerbner, many shows of that kind are profitable only because of foreign distribution.[11] Violent stories hold attention around the world and can be comprehended more easily than, say, a conversation with dubbed dialogue or subtitles. Violence and mayhem can be produced cheaply and is easily exportable. If the studios' only source of revenue were from the domestic market, they might even stop producing gruesome shows. Nevertheless, some people love mayhem/violence/horror shows. This challenges my theory that people select programs for mood enhancement. This puzzle should trouble us for the same reasons that the popularity of gladiatorial contests troubled Seneca.

Painful shows don't leave viewers in a better mood. Studies show that children and college students alike continue experiencing fear after viewing scary programs. Often they say they regret having seen the show. Almost half of them report having trouble sleeping or being afraid to go into certain rooms of their own house.[12]

There are major gender differences in entertainment preferences. Females tend to choose romantic tearjerkers, whereas "thrill-seeking" males tend to choose action, sports, violence, pornography,[13] and horror.[14] These differences reflect traditional roles, since males are supposed to be protectors of females. Watching horrific entertainment gives young people a chance to demonstrate gender-appropriate behavior. A young man who was my research assistant once told me that he enjoys taking girls to horror movies because they get nervous, need comforting afterward, and are likely to spend the night with him! And actually, there is empirical evidence that he's right.

In one experiment, paired male and female subjects were required to watch the movie *Friday the 13th, Part III* together. Later they rated their enjoyment of the film, the extent to which they felt intimidated by their viewing partner, and the extent to which they were romantically attracted to that partner. Actually, the female was a confederate who was supposed to display fear, mastery of fear, or emotional neutrality while watching the film. Males enjoyed the film more with a woman who displayed fear. Females enjoyed it more when paired with a male who showed mastery. The female confederates were ordinary in physical attractiveness, but they were rated as being much more attractive when they displayed fear. Obviously, the opportunity to show mastery of fear is an important factor explaining the males' enjoyment of mayhem/violence/horror shows.[15] Apparently they misconstrue their own pleasure in achieving the appropriate displays, wrongly believing it to be enjoyment of the frightening film itself.[16]

Moreover, women subjects in whom fear had been induced became more aroused sexually than females in an emotionally neutral, nondistressed state.[17] Anxiety distress has also been shown to facilitate subsequent genital arousal in both sexes.[18]

Personality influences the selection of genre. You can test your own personality on the Internet. Various tests are available, such as the Myers-Briggs Type Indicator. Most research of this kind uses Hans Eysenck's scales, which rate people according to a threefold typology: extraversion (vs. introversion), neuroticism (vs. stability), and psychoticism (vs. socialization). *Extraverts* are characterized by sociability, affiliation, and positive self-esteem. *Neurotics* have high levels of anxiety, emotionality, shyness, social isolation, and a negative self-image. *Psychotics* (as measured by Eysenck's test) tend toward egocentricity, sensation seeking, and autonomy; they typically are impulsive, dogmatic, and socially deviant.[19] People scoring high on neuroticism tend to avoid light comedy and adventure stories, preferring informative television programs and "downbeat" music. Those scoring high on psychoticism have little interest in comedy and a strong preference for graphically violent horror movies and "hard" or "rebellious" rock music.[20] Extraverts typically cannot bear to watch horror films. This is evidently because they empathize and hence suffer more with fictional victims than do introverts (people who score very low on the extraversion scale).[21]

When TV viewers are asked why they choose particular types of shows, they give two different motives. The first is "mood management" (preference for relaxation, entertainment, and arousal). The other is "social compensation"—defined as a way to make up for a lack of companionship, to escape from the world, or simply to pass time. Extraverts almost always name mood management as their primary aim, while the shyness and loneliness of neurotics explains their social compensation viewing motive. Extraverts emphatically deny that television programs can substitute for interpersonal relationships.[22] For them, the emotional content only *supplements* real companionship.

There is evidence that this account is true. Researchers have found lonely people *less* likely than others to develop emotional—"parasocial"—relationships with television characters or celebrities.[23] And instead of compensating for a lack of romance, love stories usually are chosen by viewers (especially women) whose own romantic lives are highly fulfilling. Moreover, they often insist that their emotional involvement with fictional erotic affairs improves their own real love life.[24] The use of fiction for substitution shows an emptiness that makes one vulnerable to mimesis—the tendency to imitate characters and be swayed by their example.

Emotion as Arousal

Pleasant emotions make you healthy and unpleasant emotions can make you sick.[25] Emotions involve the endocrine system, the immune system, and the nervous system—the brain and, most conspicuously, the autonomic nervous system, with its two aspects, the sympathetic and parasympathetic systems, which function to counter each other. Some negative emotions (not grief, but preparation for flight or fight) involve the arousal of the sympathetic system, which can dilate pupils, activate sweat glands, increase heart rate and respiration, release adrenaline and glucose, and inhibit bowel activity. Other emotions (e.g., contentment) accompany the activation of the parasympathetic system, which tend to slow an aroused organism down by constricting pupils, decreasing the heart rate and respiration, and stimulating tears, salivation, and digestion.

One problem for researchers is that none of these peripheral effects of the auto-nomic nervous system necessarily operates in sync with the others. There is no unique way of measuring the arousal of the sympathetic system, and research seems to yield different findings, depending on the indicators used to measure it.[26] Hence the conclusions that I'll record here are likely to be revised as further investigations are completed.

While it is impossible to determine which *particular* emotion a person is experiencing by measuring her visceral activity (blood pressure, heart rate, etc.) and/or PET scan, researchers can often guess from such evidence whether she is feeling a positive or a negative emotion. In general, negative emotions arouse the sympathetic nervous system. Also, a PET comparison of the brain hemispheres shows whether her inclination is to approach (e.g., that she feels happiness or anger) or instead to withdraw (e.g., that she feels sadness or fear).[27]

Positive emotions "undo" effects on the autonomic nervous system that were activated by negative emotions. Happy feelings speed the restoration of the organism to its prearousal state. One study stimulated fear in subjects with a film, then showed them another film known to induce contentment. Indeed, their fear did dissipate more quickly than when the second film was sad or neu-tral.[28] Negative emotions can have bad health effects, unless they are "undone" by some offsetting positive feelings.

Negative emotions are autonomic responses to an appraisal that the organism or some of its goals are in danger. In such situations, endocrine responses occur automatically. However, by an act of will, it may be possible to suppress overt muscular reactions.[29] Psychologist Robert Levenson has explored the physical effects of intentionally inhibiting expressive behavior—especially the effect of suppression on the autonomic nervous system. He studied the suppression of disgust by showing subjects a filmed amputation of a limb, instructing them not to reveal their feelings. They managed to reduce emotional expressions but not eliminate them totally. Some subjects reduced their body movements, slowed their heart rates, and reduced their autonomic arousal. However, in other parts of the body (e.g., sweat glands), their arousal was *heightened*. This reflects the dual nature of the autonomic nervous system, whose two sides (sympathetic and parasympathetic) function in contrary ways. The slowing of the heart rate is mediated by the parasympathetic system.

Levenson sees the same thing happen in his clinical work. For example, in marital counseling sessions, one spouse may "stonewall"—suppress any emotional expression by inhibiting facial and bodily movements. But his or her sweat glands may become increasingly active. Why, in a parasympathetic slowdown, does the *sympathetic system* become activated? Levenson believes this is because the inhibiting of visible emotion requires real work—"bracing" and "braking" actions throughout the body. But Levenson believes that such autonomic activity probably harms health only when it is sustained and chronic and when the autonomic arousal exceeds metabolic demand.[30]

Not all stress is equally harmful. When you're running or playing tennis, you're stressed, but the metabolic demand is appropriate for the activity. But, "if this same level of cardiovascular arousal were produced when the person was relaxed and sitting still, then the arousal would be in excess of the metabolic demand."[31]

Hence, when you're feeling negative emotions, it is a good idea to use up the heightened energy or reduce the emotions quickly. You might go for a walk or play tennis to "metabolize" the emotional arousal. Or scratch your dog.[32] Or play a CD (music directly affects the central nervous system, reduces stress, and increases levels of immunoglobulin A).[33] Read a novel or watch a pleasant, comforting movie. Happy emotions may hasten the restoration of your sympathetic arousal back down to a healthy normal state.

Catharsis

But don't jump to unwarranted conclusions. There's a common belief that we store up bad emotions in our bodies, carry them around with us, locked up in tense muscles, until something happens that rekindles our old pain; to pour out this emotion leaves us feeling cleansed and relieved.

Basically, scientists now reject this theory. Not emotions, but memories, are stored in the body. To be sure, there can be emotional "markers" attached to a given memory. When we recall it, we also recall the feelings that went with it and may (or may not) create a new emotion to match the old one. This theory, proposed by leading brain researcher Antonio Damasio,[34] denies that emotions remain locked up in the body until finally liberated.

Damasio's "marker" hypothesis argues against one of the oldest psychological theories ever proposed, Aristotle's concept of *catharsis*.[35] Again we encounter the 2,500-year-old debate between Plato, who worried that theatergoers might imitate the antisocial behavior shown onstage, and Aristotle, who believed that audiences could actually benefit from seeing terrible stories portrayed. Catharsis was what made it beneficial.

How can empathizing with a suffering protagonist do our souls good? Until recently, the only plausible defense of tragedy was Aristotle's explanation—catharsis—which now is basically discredited. Aristotle assumed that we are all haunted by painful memories that we try to ignore in our daily lives. The author of a tragedy gives us an opportunity to revisit our past and feel pity or fear for the wretched protagonist who reminds us of our own old anguish. The revival and discharge of that feeling supposedly "purges" us, so that we leave the theater with our spirits restored and our soul calmed.[36] Aristotle's notion of catharsis still informs much contemporary drama and psychotherapy—not surprisingly, for the theory had a distinguished history; it was promoted by both Aristotle and Sigmund Freud.

Early in his career, Freud became convinced by an older psychiatrist, Josef Breuer, that hysterical patients could be relieved of their symptoms by reliving the original trauma that had caused their neurosis. Freud used this cathartic approach without success, then replaced it with a more cognitive theory. He claimed now that what brought relief was his new "talking cure." The excavation of a painful memory was now thought to help a patient only if the previously repressed event was discussed and remained accessible to her conscious mind thereafter. It was the transfer from the unconscious to the conscious mind that healed.

Freud abandoned the quest for catharsis, although many subsequent therapists still pursue it.[37] Some empirical researchers have concluded that there is no evidence that catharsis ever happens.[38] Nevertheless, tragic dramatists still seek to create moments of catharsis for their audiences. So do many contemporary psychotherapists, who attribute much human suffering to past traumas that must be faced before the personality can be whole again. They do not expect pent-up feelings to be released all at once. Usually several sessions are required before the patient can recall the old pain without being overwhelmed. In both the theater and therapy, it is widely assumed that when you feel sympathy for a character, your pain is *projected* from your own past misery, rather than being freshly generated by empathy.

You may have had cathartic experiences—as if a hidden tap were turned on and amazing feelings poured out of yourself. However, this phenomenon is rare. Sociologist Thomas J. Scheff has examined instances of catharsis. He says that in therapy it hardly ever ends the patient's symptoms.[39] He believes that acting out anger is virtually never cathartic. Still, he believes that catharsis sometimes does happen in the theater.

Scheff's theory of catharsis relates it to identification and empathy. This notion is compatible with Aristotle's. He suggests that there's an optimum psychological distance from the drama, such that the audience is brought into contact with their repressed emotions without being overwhelmed. Only then may catharsis occur. When we're emotionally remote from the action, we don't get much out of the play, but when we are too caught up in it, the feelings simply compound our distress rather than releasing it. For example, *The Exorcist* frightened audiences so much that their restimulated fears were overwhelming and no catharsis took place.

Scheff advises playwrights to create a "controlled identification" in the viewer by making the character morally exemplary yet similar to the spectators. When handled skillfully, the outcome is a profound esthetic and psychological experience, yet it is such a difficult accomplishment that few dramatists are able to bring about catharsis. Instead, they often overwhelm adult audiences. Some early films for children, such as *Bambi,* caused distress by underdistancing the audiences from the pain.[40]

Scheff's advice seems sound, but even if playwrights follow it, they cannot attain their intended results with every audience. Psychological distance from the drama depends only partly on the writing or production; it also depends on audiences' personalities and values. Introverts are more distanced from the play than extraverts and can watch more distress without reacting emotionally to what they see. And even if catharsis sometimes occurs, there is no evidence that it changes the personality, for either better or worse.

Another reason for skepticism about catharsis comes from the way that Method actors use their own experiences as a resource for generating required emotions. Suppose an actor wants to be able to cry on cue and to continue doing so six times a week for the whole run of the play—possibly several years. In preparing for this, he finds a sad memory from his own life and learns to relive it for the sake of the tears that it provokes. If crying discharged the grief connected with the memory, the actor would be in trouble within a week or two, for his daily spell of crying on stage would be a disastrous catharsis. He'd be unable to cry again unless he found another past memory to draw upon. This does not seem to happen. Leonard Bernstein once said that he had seen his own musical play, *West Side Story,* performed a thousand times, and he had always cried at the end. Many actors have cried more than that onstage.

Cognitive Therapy

Thus most psychologists have discarded the notion of catharsis in favor of cognitive therapy. Improvement sometimes occurs after a patient recalls a painful experience, but, according to cognitive therapists, this happens only if the patient reinterprets the experience and reconstructs its meaning.

An example of this effect can be seen in experiments by James Pennebaker, which initially seem to support the notion of catharsis. The researchers assigned healthy undergraduates the task of writing about a stressful life experience of theirs a few hours at a time for four successive days. The control group wrote about a superficial topic instead. The immune systems of all subjects were studied; also noted was the frequency of their visits to the university health service over the next term. In comparison with the control group, the subjects who wrote about emotionally intense experiences not only showed improvement in their immune responses but also less frequently sought medical care thereafter. One might attribute this outcome to catharsis, but the researchers attribute it to changed cognition. It was students whose writing showed increasing insight whose health improved.[41]

Even though most psychologists have abandoned the theory of catharsis, many people continue to believe that it's healthy to "vent" one's rage and to cry. In fact, research shows that to display anger increases the likelihood that one will behave aggressively. In one study, most women believed that crying benefits their health and psychological well-being. However, they must have been mistaken, for crying was associated with worse, not better, health, and it did not reduce stress.[42]

When Negative Emotions Are Positive

I've examined the catharsis theory in connection with this question: Why do people choose books and dramas that distress them? If we eliminate catharsis as an explanation, I can think of only two other logically possible accounts: first, that the distressing stories may be accompanied by other insights or feelings valuable enough to outweigh the displeasure or, second, that the supposedly "negative" emotions are actually pleasurable—at least sometimes. I think both are true. Preference for tragedy is mainly explained by the former, whereas the choices of horror, war, and suspense shows are mainly explained by the latter theory. Indeed, I think audiences do choose frightening or horrifying shows for the purpose of mood management—but the moods they seek are opposite to the happy ones we've discussed so far.

Some negative emotions are morally desirable and worth experiencing. This is especially true of pity, one of the feelings that Aristotle considered central to the value of watching a tragedy. Pity is a finer emotion than resentment, hatred, or blame. If you see a terrible act being perpetrated, your normal response is to blame the wrongdoer. If a drama makes you empathize with her instead, your hatred will be converted to pity, and you may become a more forgiving person with fewer inner resistances than before. The point is not to "purge" yourself of pity but rather to increase it. I consider this the chief benefit of tragedy, though my opinion is not widely shared. Nevertheless, I don't propose that we watch mainly tragedy, for the direct joys such as laughter, love, and sexual pleasure are generally more valuable.

Tension or conflict is essential to any engaging narrative. A story has to involve at least one character with an unmet desire that may perhaps never be met. You, in the audience, experience that desire vicariously by empathizing. You care about the obstacles and the attempts to surmount them. No desires and no obstacles, no story! The obstacles may be terrible, even life-threatening. The negative emotions are essential to drama. So what needs to be explained?

Perhaps that question arises only if we assume that mood management is a fiction consumer's major concern. (For some people, interest is more important than emotion.) Anyway, there must be some tension. If we want to experience euphoria, then we must be prepared first to encounter certain obstacles, for then, having surmounted them vicariously, we may rejoice empathically with the fortunate character whose plight had worried us. Had the hero attained his great victory effortlessly, in the end there would be no celebration and no elation. Again, what needs to be explained?

A lot—even if we concede that mood management is not a primary objective for all readers and theatergoers. But if not for mood, why do people want to see distressing scenes? What do they get from them?

Here's a comparison. Ancient Greek tragedies contained a great deal of violence and suffering. Yet physical violence never was depicted onstage.[43] Instead, a runner might rush in, announcing that a terrible battle was being waged in the streets below. Someone might even stand at a window peering out and reacting with shock. However, the bloodshed would not be shown, since to witness it was considered too excruciating for the audience to endure.

Compare that delicate Greek sensibility to the following newspaper article about the opening of a new film in February 2001, which was attended by numerous celebrities: "A theaterful of grossed-out celebs groaned their way through the gory *Silence of the Lambs* sequel *Hannibal* at the Ziegfeld Monday night. Regis Philbin covered wife Joy's eyes during a scene in which Anthony Hopkins slices out pieces of a brain. *Everybody Loves Raymond* co-star Peter Boyle shuddered and shook his head during a disemboweling scene. Everyone tittered."

The difference between aesthetic standards needs to be explained, including the disparity between the Greek sensibility and that of the Romans, who thirsted for *real* (not play-acted) gore and agony. True, a drama must include some tension, but audiences do not need to witness disembowelings in order to experience pity.

Some people claim to enjoy such anxiety-provoking scenes, but research indicates that they are bad for the heart—even for people who *want* sympathetic nervous system arousal. Whereas laughing at a comedy improves beneficial blood flow, watching such stress-inducing films as *Saving Private Ryan* has harmful effects, diminishing blood vessel reactivity by about 35 percent.[44] Maybe you should keep this information in mind when deciding whether to watch violent films or whether to let your friends display them in your presence.

But let me offer a theory about why people sometimes want unpleasant stories. This theory comes out of Buddhist psychology.

Metaemotions and the Tragic Sense

Previously, I mentioned the Buddhist project of ceasing to cling to or resist experiences. Such clinging or resisting is a "metaresponse"—a response *about* another response. A metaresponse does not destroy the original response. Both sentiments persist, though often with an uncomfortable tension between the conflicting tendencies.

Indeed, we often experience emotions in combination with a metaemotion. A normally timid man may feel *proud* of himself for, this time, being justifiably *angry*. A devout woman may feel *angry* with herself for feeling *proud* instead of humble. A young woman may feel more *confident* of her sexual attractiveness for being *frightened* watching a Dracula movie and a young man may feel more *confident* for successfully *hiding his fear*. You may feel *guilty* for falling in *love* with your best friend's lover. I may feel *sad* because I *no longer feel love*. A widow may feel *a longing* for an old familiar *sadness* that is diminishing over the years since the loss of her husband. A Scoutmaster may feel *ashamed* for having *laughed* at a Cub Scout who was confiding an important secret that seemed trivial. We may feel *humiliated* for having failed to *laugh* at the punch line of the bartender's joke. A medical student may feel *afraid* that her *disgust* is about to overwhelm her as she dissects a cadaver. A tango dancer may be *embarrassed* about becoming sexually *aroused* by his partner.

These dual emotions can be overlaid with yet additional metaemotions—conceivably five or six more emotions *about* other emotions. (The concepts "resistance" and "clinging" are inadequate to portray such complex layers of metaemotions.) For example, a young male may feel *proud* of his *mastery* of the *fear* that he experiences in a horror show. Here the fear itself still arises and is still unpleasant, but the moviegoer contains his reactions to it. This accomplishment enhances his dignity, self-respect, and manliness—agreeable metaemotions that motivate him to attend a terrifying movie.

The joint arousal of two or more distinct emotions is probably the best explanation for the enjoyment of tragedy or suspense. Aristotle thought that the point of going to the theater was to feel fear or pity for the protagonist's terrible fate. Fear or pity is unpleasant, but one may enjoy the metaemotions that accompany it. For example, philosopher Susan Feagin has described the "metaresponse of satisfaction":

> We find ourselves to be the kind of people who respond negatively to villainy, treachery, and injustice. This discovery, or reminder, is something which, quite justly, yields satisfaction. In a way it shows what we care for, and in showing we care for the welfare of human beings and that we deplore the immoral forces that defeat them, it reminds us of our common humanity. It reduces one's sense of aloneness in the world, and soothes, psychologically, the pain of solipsism.[45]

Pleasant metaemotions compensate for the vicarious suffering we endure while engrossed in a tragedy. Pity, in particular, is a feeling that generally transforms inner turmoil into a calmer, transcendent acceptance that may endure after we leave the theater.

Philosopher Robert J. Yanal accepts the theory of metaemotions, but he considers another condition necessary, too: what Coleridge called the "willing suspension of disbelief." However, Yanal observes that this suspension of disbelief is always partial, for otherwise we might lose our grip on reality and become overwhelmed.[46] He asks us to compare our feelings when watching *King Lear* to the emotions we'd feel when watching a nonactor *really* undergoing the terrible events that befell Lear. Or suppose we were to witness a man's *real* eyes being gouged out, instead of the fictional Gloucester's. We would feel intense anguish.[47]

Indeed, tragedies sometimes go wrong and leave audiences distraught instead of satisfied. For example, countless viewers have experienced depressions lasting weeks or months after watching some distressing episodes of *Northern Exposure*. Yanal, however, seems to assume that we can instantly withdraw our "willing suspension of disbelief" and deny the characters any further attention. Not so. A viewer may form intense attachments to a fictional character—a bond that is, like limerence, involuntary and irreversible. As every lover knows, once we have given our heart, we can't readily reclaim it, even when the beloved leads us through unbearably painful situations.

Not all tragedies are successful. A great playwright needs a "tragic sense," which is very different from a sense of religion. Although Greek tragedy emerged from religious rites, the two orientations have different psychological effects.[48] Religion confronts unhappy predicaments, but it restores our trust that the universe is a good and meaningful place, even when the situation appears distressing. Tragedy is different. As philosopher Richard B. Sewall describes the tragic vision, it is not for those who cannot live with unsolved questions or unresolved doubts, whose bent of mind would reduce the fact of evil into something else or resolve it into some larger whole.... [T]he vision of life peculiar to the mystic, the pious, the propagandist, the confirmed optimist or pessimist—or the confirmed anything—is not tragic.... The tragic vision impels the man of action to fight against his destiny, kick against the pricks, and state his case before God or his fellows.[49]

Tragedy and Transcendence in the Book of Job

We see the contrast between religion and tragedy in the devout biblical character Job.[50] Satan challenged God by saying that he could make any man lose faith, and as a test, God allowed Satan to do anything whatever to Job's family, reputation, and property, so long as Job himself was not killed. Satan set about killing Job's children and destroying his property. But Job only said, "Naked I came from my mother's womb, and naked shall I return; the Lord gave, and the Lord has taken away; blessed be the name of the Lord." He did not charge God with wrongdoing.

Next Satan obtained God's consent to afflict the wretched man with boils, from head to foot. Job's friends came to visit, stayed seven days, but spoke not at all, watching him sit in agony in the ashes, his skin covered with worms and dirt.

At last Job cursed the day he was born. Now he was a tragic figure. His religious friends tried to convince him that he must have been wicked to deserve this punishment, since Jehovah was just, but he challenged them and God alike: "Teach me, and I will be silent; make me understand how I have erred.... I will say to God, Do not condemn me; let me know why thou dost contend against me. Does it seem good to thee to oppress, to despise the work of thy hands and favor the designs of the wicked?"

Because Job knew he was blameless, he dared to hold God to account. Then the Lord answered him as a voice from a whirlwind, describing in poetry the majestic expanse of the universe, and challenging Job: "Who is this that darkens counsel by words without knowledge? Gird up your loins like a man. I will question you, and you shall declare to me. Where were you when I laid the foundation of the earth? Tell me, if you have understanding.... Will you condemn me that you may be justified? Have you an arm like God, and can you thunder with a voice like his?"

Despite God's extraordinary self-defense, He never explained his actions to Job. However, He was more pleased with this audacious, tragic man than with the pious ones who had tried to placate Job with religious platitudes. Job did gain some glimmer of the infinite scope of God's creation, which made his own troubles seem less central to the ultimate plan, and he stopped complaining. For His part, God restored Job's health and gave him a new family and twice as comfortable a life as he had enjoyed originally.

Maybe we should be satisfied by this upbeat, triumphant ending, but we aren't. Job's lamentations remind us that life is impermanent and full of suffering, and we do not forget it just because a new family and new wealth are provided. These can make up neither for Job's original losses nor for his physical pain. The only answer to the innocent sufferer is God's mysterious message from the whirlwind: that Job cannot understand His ways, for His universe is simply too vast for human comprehension.

Our metaresponse to this story is the same sense of transcendence that Job himself finally experienced when he admitted to God, "I have uttered what I did not understand, things too wonderful for me, which I did not know."

In the end, Job's tragic sense evidently lost out, and he regained his religious faith—but, if so, it was no simplistic religiosity. The pleasure we readers gain from this story is a metaresponse to Job's suffering. It is not joy, but a consoling vision that reconciles us to a God who would otherwise appear cruel. Job receives no answer to his question, but he transcends it. Either our vicarious living of Job's tragedy will be satisfied by this metaemotion, or it probably cannot be satisfied at all.

Positive and Negative Arousal

"Bad vibes" include a variety of negative emotions including suspense, horror, mayhem, cliffhanging adventures, and creepy creatures such as vampires, ghosts, and giant man-eating insects. We'll turn now from the tragic feelings involving our parasympathetic to the (mainly unpleasant) arousal of our sympathetic nervous systems.

Early in the chapter, I hinted at the points I am going to make here. I noted that people usually know *that* they are aroused, but they may not know *why*—exactly what event or thought set off this heart-thumping adrenaline rush. Now I need to go back about forty years to an astonishing experiment by psychologists Stanley Schachter and Jerome Singer,[51] the authors of cognitive labeling theory, which is still accepted today.

Imagine you're the subject of their experiment; I'll tell you how you would probably react. Suppose you are given either an injection of adrenaline or a plain saline injection. If you get the saline, you will not feel anything in particular, but if you get the adrenaline, your sympathetic nervous system will be aroused by it. Now suppose I tell you truthfully that you received adrenaline; again you will not feel emotional because you will realize that any "keyed-up" sensations just arise from the injection.

But suppose instead I lie and say that the adrenaline was a vitamin injection or some other innocuous substance. Then I put you (actually pumped up with the adrenaline) either in a room where a lively party is going on or in a room with someone obnoxious who is trying to annoy you. Now what do you feel? In both situations you will realize that you are somehow aroused, and you will try to figure out the cause of this experience. If you are in the room with the party, you will probably conclude that you're excited and having fun; you will describe your emotion as euphoric. If you are in the room with the annoying person, you will label your own state as anger, and you may even display your anger.

On the basis of such experiments, Schachter and Singer proposed a two-factor theory of emotion: that in order to experience an emotion, you need both *physiological arousal* and a *cognition* explaining that arousal. The cognition need not be the correct interpretation; you may be persuaded by external circumstances or by another person what to believe, and in any case the effect will be the same—you will actually experience whatever emotion you have cognitively labeled.

This experiment shows that sympathetic arousal is not proof that you're feeling a negative emotion. (When the subjects believed their situation was pleasant, the adrenaline gave them euphoria.) Whether arousal is negative or positive depends on whether you welcome it. For example, coition involves heavy breathing, strenuous heart action, a rise in blood pressure, and other sympathetic reactions, but usually it is considered positive.[52] If sympathetic arousal can be either pleasant or unpleasant, we need to consider further what explains the variability. First, however, we need to add another set of observations.

Excitation Transfer

Dolf Zillmann has proposed what he calls *excitation transfer theory*. He points out that it takes a while for the body to return to its normal baseline state after having been aroused. Suppose you are frightened enough to become highly aroused—it doesn't matter by what. Say, for example, you find a cobra swaying right in front of you. Then, almost immediately, you discover that you are not in danger after all, for the cobra is a realistic toy that your best friend is operating by a remote control device. What are your reactions? At first you may yell and jump away, but when you recognize the truth a moment later, you may howl with laughter and jump up and down with exuberance. It may be the most fun you have had all month.

Now, a question. Suppose you had not been frightened or surprised by the cobra. Suppose your friend had described the toy before unwrapping it, and you both had played with it casually together from the beginning. Would you have screamed with laughter or jumped up and down in euphoria? Probably not. Your two strong emotions are causally connected.

The explanation has to do with excitation transfer. In most negative emotions the sympathetic nervous system is aroused, but the same arousal can also feel positive, as when an injection of adrenaline may make you feel either euphoric or angry. While you are in a state of arousal and haven't returned to your normal condition, if another situation arises with a *different, arousing emotion,* you are going to add that second arousal onto the arousal that you already are experiencing, which will increase the total. You will be far more aroused during the second emotion than if you had entered it from your regular baseline condition. Sympathetic nervous system effects are cumulative, and while you are in the second emotion, you'll attribute the whole arousal to it and therefore will experience that emotion as being far more intense than it might have seemed without the "priming" of the initial arousal.

Zillmann and others have experimented with this effect and say it explains much about the intensity of emotions. For example, he applies it to the common situation in which a couple become gradually less enthusiastic about sex over their years together. There is now less arousal than the first few times when they made love. Zillmann mentions some of the stimulants that the couple may adopt, such as sexy garments and the infliction of pain as a stimulus. He reports that in societies where promiscuity is widespread, sexual excitement is rare because people have already seen and done practically everything. Precisely in those societies, it is common for people to engage in a certain amount of violence in connection with intercourse—biting, scratching, and the like. Zillmann sees this as a last resort, a way of reviving flagging excitement after everything else has failed. Sex, begun after violence has already created considerable sympathetic arousal, is intensified.[53] Presumably, any other way of arousing the sympathetic system would also intensify the second emotion—be it sex or something else. And as we have seen, fear aroused by a horror film may increase a woman's sexual responsiveness immediately thereafter.

Similarly, other researchers have studied the excitement produced by skydiving. Beginners in this sport feel intense anxiety before and during their fall. When they finally find themselves safe on the ground, their sympathetic nervous system cannot immediately return to its normal baseline state, though now there is no longer anything to fear. As a result, the jumpers convert their arousal from anxiety into extraordinary euphoria. As skydivers gain more experience, they become less anxious about each jump, with the result that the surplus arousal left over at the end is also diminished. The high that had been so glorious during the first few skydives diminishes correspondingly, and the jumper may even begin to look for a more dangerous sport that yields the elation that had formerly followed skydiving.[54]

Zillmann explains the pleasures of violent or suspenseful fiction in terms of excitation transfer theory. Cliffhanger films, for example, evoke mostly negative emotions while the audience is watching the protagonist struggle to survive. However, as soon as he has triumphed over all the impending disasters, the empathic viewers feel immense relief—a pleasurable emotion that is intensified by their residual arousal. Only those viewers who have suffered along with the hero during the dangerous phase are able to reap the reward—the euphoria that accompanies his successful return to safety.

Excitation transfer theory also goes far toward explaining the glee that audiences often display at seeing the "bad guy" being shot down in a hail of bullets. This pleasure (and it *is* pleasure to some viewers, even if not perhaps to you and me) is only possible because the antagonist has been seen brutally and unjustly harming others. When he finally gets his comeuppance, the audience feels justified in rejoicing. As Zillmann points out, "*displays of monstrous gratuitous slaughter and the distress they evoke are a necessary prelude to the portrayal of righteous maiming and killing that is to spark euphoric reactions. Without such prelude, violence cannot be righteous and, hence, is rendered unenjoyable—at least for nonsadists.*"[55] Thus our emotional reaction to a character's suffering will depend on our appraisal of his morality. Retribution may seem sweet to us when it represents justice—when it has been earned by a character whose evil deeds we have witnessed. In later chapters we'll explore the conditions under which painful outcomes may appear just or unjust.

Next question: Why do *some* individuals experience arousal as pleasurable while *other* individuals intensely dislike it?

Thrill Seeking

It may seem bizarre to suggest that some people were "born" to prefer horror and action films rather than romantic comedies and family films, but that may be the case. Psychologist Marvin Zuckerman has identified a personality trait that he calls "sensation seeking." (Some call it "thrill seeking.") His research does not deal primarily with taste in films and fiction but with the enjoyment in real-life situations of emotions that others find aversive. Sensation seeking, as a type of personality, is physiologically determined[56] and hereditary. Identical twins have quite similar scores, even if they have always lived apart. People who share a particular variant of the gene named DRD4 crave sensations and thrills.[57] This tendency of theirs will concern us repeatedly, for it influences their choices of entertainment, how they live their lives, and even the content of Hollywood shows.

Sensation seekers like change. They easily become bored and, to avoid that, they want more stimulation than other people. At first, they react strongly to a new stimulus, but soon they lose interest, become restless, and want another new or more intense sensation. For example, when sensation seekers have control of the television remote control, they keep switching the channels, trying to follow two different dramas at the same time. They may be, on the average, slightly more intelligent than low sensation seekers, but they do no better in school, probably because school does not offer enough stimulation to keep them aroused.

There is a strong connection between sensation seeking and Eysenck's psychoticism. Indeed, the two traits are virtually synonymous. Those high on the psychoticism scale are nonconformists who like sensational, novel, even risky, forms of entertainment.

But Frank Farley, a psychologist who studies what he calls "Type T" personalities—the *T* standing for "thrill seeking"—maintains that these people tend to be creative leaders at the forefront of human progress. (I prefer his word or the term *sensation seeking,* since *psychoticism* seems unduly insulting.) Farley believes that North Americans have more genes for Type T behavior than Chinese in the mainland, for example. North Americans or their ancestors migrated here—a risky venture that calls for a thrill-seeking gene. Farley thinks the famous Kennedy family must have inherited the gene, for they are born leaders, but their adventures have often produced tragic outcomes.[58]

As for beliefs, Type Ts are open-minded. When it comes to art, they especially like complex pictures that are asymmetrical and ambiguous, and that suggest movement.[59] When it comes to humor, they usually enjoy incongruous jokes that remain unresolved or nonsense humor. Low sensation seekers, on the other hand, want the punch line to resolve the incongruity.[60] (Notice: Both of these traits remind us of the complex TV and video games that, according to Steven Johnson, are making people smarter by giving their brains speedy, demanding workouts. Are writers catering to Type T viewers?)

Sensation seekers are likely to smoke and to use drugs. They tend to be gourmets who enjoy spicy ethnic foods and will readily try new foods, even ones that low sensation seekers would regard as disgusting.[61] Sensation seekers tend to choose risky jobs such as journalism and to supplement these thrills in their spare time with other exciting adventures, such as travel to dangerous areas.[62] (I think here of my friend, a female war correspondent who covered some of the bloodiest battles on the planet during the 1990s. After returning home to safety, she became depressed by the lack of excitement. Her solution was to take up skydiving.)

Sensation seekers keep less of their money in cash or accounts available for unexpected contingencies than do low sensation seekers.[63] Sensation seekers are sexually more permissive and active than the general population.[64] They tend to enjoy gambling, and, when their gambling is pathological, they only enjoy it if they are risking larger sums than they can afford.[65] Some antisocial criminals seem motivated by a desire for excitement, and they must take unnecessary risks in order to feel that thrill.[66]

Sensation seekers don't intend to do anything dangerous; they simply believe that what they are doing is safe, whereas other observers are not so sure. For example, they will drive fast but use seat belts; they will climb the rocky face of a cliff but double-check their safety harness before going up, feeling utterly confident because of it. They do more dangerous things, but feel *less* anxious than other people.[67]

Who do you suppose likes horror and action films? Thrill seekers, of course. They say they enjoy being frightened, and in fact they go more often to scary pictures than do low thrill seekers. They have a strong sense of curiosity about gruesome and morbid events.[68]

Genetics explains most of the individual differences in sensation seeking. However, we all vary from one time to another in our enjoyment of change and intense experience. Sometimes we want stability, peace, and quiet; at other times we want novelty. To explain such intrapersonal variations, we turn to psychologist Michael J. Apter's research, which may actually seem clearer if portrayed in terms of symbolic interactionism.

Instrumental and Expressive States of Mind

George Herbert Mead introduced the distinction between instrumental and expressive acts. An *instrumental* act is one phase of a larger act, intended to help reach the goal of that larger act. An *expressive* act, however, is performed for its own sake—not as a rational, goal-oriented activity but for the sheer pleasure of doing it. We all do some instrumental and some expressive acts, though perhaps in differing ratios.

Apter refers to instrumental and expressive states of mind—or sometimes to "serious" versus "playful" states, by which he apparently means instrumental and expressive. He suggests that everyone alternates as if by a toggle switch between instrumental versus expressive orientations,[69] for no intermediate position is possible. Spontaneously and suddenly, we switch back and forth several times a day between seriousness and play.

The instrumental state is the more common state of mind for most people. It's a rational, goal-oriented attitude in which we are organizing thoughts and behavior toward desired ends. The expressive state, on the other hand, is not rational, for we are motivated only by the pleasure of doing it. Consider the distinction between being serious and playing or joking. We sometimes say we are "half-joking," but ultimately that's impossible. If someone demands to know whether you are serious or not, you had better be prepared to say whether you really mean what you said or were only kidding. To be serious is a way of being instrumental, and to joke is a way of being expressive, though there are many other such ways as well, such as art, music, games, sports, and gambling.

Apter's objective is to explain the attraction of danger, which involves our ambivalent attitudes toward arousal. When we are in the serious, instrumental state of mind, we like to be calm and purposeful, and we don't welcome arousal. If arousal happens despite our wishes, we experience it as anxiety. The more intense it is, the more unpleasant. However, when we are in the expressive, playful state, arousal can be pleasant; we experience it as excitement or even euphoria or ecstasy.

But danger often accompanies arousal. To those seeking excitement, the risk is the attraction. Apter describes an event in his hometown in Wales when the city council announced that a promenade along the seafront was in dangerous condition. Crowds flocked to walk along it, crossing over the rope that was put up to protect them from getting dangerously close: "The young ducked under it, the old stepped over it, and those in wheelchairs—and even mothers pushing babies in prams—had it lifted for them."[70] In an expressive state of mind, one wants excitement, and the closer one gets to the dangerous edge, the more exciting it is—assuming that the cliff does not actually collapse, which the danger-seekers do not want.

Still, some people take more risks than others, and Apter must explain why. He says that some people believe there is a "protective frame" around them that keeps them safe. This is an imaginary zone that is somehow portable, in that they carry it with them into new situations. It may involve, for example, certain skills they have acquired that make them confident of their ability to survive. When no protective frame is experienced, people will not try to get close to the dangerous edge. The pleasure of excitement requires both the danger and the protective frame, just as the fun of seeing a tiger in the zoo requires both the tiger and the protective cage he is in. No tiger, no fun! No cage, no fun!

On the other hand, suppose you are in an instrumental (serious, rational, goal-directed) state. You will not seek arousal, and if it comes anyhow, you will experience it as anxiety. So long as you are in your preferred state of low arousal, you will describe your condition as "relaxed." If, however, you switch into an expressive state, you will experience that same low-arousal condition as "boredom." Boredom is a state of low arousal with a negative valence, and relaxation is a state of low arousal with a positive valence.

What determines whether you prefer low or high arousal? That depends on whether you are in an instrumental or an expressive state. Here's a scenario that may seem familiar. When you come home tired after work, you want some peace and quiet, so you can relax and read your mail. If something does arouse you while you are in this serious state, you will feel anxious until it's resolved. and you can again indulge in a period of low arousal. After an hour or two, though, having relaxed enough, you may switch into an expressive, playful, excitement-seeking mode and go to the yard to pitch horseshoes. If you were to continue resting on the sofa, you would feel bored. Indeed, horseshoe pitching may not be stimulating enough to satisfy your desire for excitement; if that sport bores you, perhaps you should go dancing or play squash. If you are truly a thrill seeker, you may even go bungee jumping when the excitement-seeking impulse strikes you. If not, you may simply settle for a video—say, a Bruce Willis movie or *Night of the Living Dead*—and get your adrenaline rush vicariously.

Is Thrill Seeking a Social Problem?

Both relaxation and excitement are normal, enjoyable emotional states that everyone experiences often. Their opposites—boredom and anxiety—are also "normal" but not enjoyable and, when experienced intensely, they can be pathological.

Compared with anxiety, boredom receives little attention, except from a few writers such as Erich Fromm, who called it "one of the worst forms of mental suffering." Sensation seekers (or, in Apter's terminology, those whose expressive state of mind is dominant in everyday life) are especially susceptible to boredom, and in their effort to avoid it, they sometimes put themselves and society at risk.

Some sensation seekers are creative people who contribute greatly to society—at least if they find constructive ways of satisfying their cravings for danger. It is apparently not possible to eliminate the excitement-seeking tendency, since it has a neurochemical basis and is as much genetically determined as the color of one's eyes or the shape of one's ears.[71] Therapy is not effective in reversing sensation seeking. What is required instead is to identify the trait and find benign ways of satisfying it. But because risky, intense stimulation is precisely what sensation seekers want, they may not settle for anything less.

Historically, humankind has needed daring people—especially men who willingly stood at the entrance of the family's cave and fought off saber-toothed tigers and marauders from the next valley. Courage and hardiness are required to launch bold new projects and address physical and social challenges, such as settling frontiers and fighting wars.

Such aptitudes are characteristic of the risky, sensation-seeking personality. Enthusiasm for battle may even be part of both our genetic and our cultural heritage, but there are enormous variations between individuals in this respect. Most soldiers hate war, but some love it. Here is one Vietnam veteran explaining how sensation seeking led him to war:

> I had no illusions, but I volunteered for a line company anyway. There were a number of reasons, of which the paramount was boredom.... I cannot deny that the front still held a fascination for me. The rights or wrongs of the war aside, there was a magnetism about combat. You seemed to live more intensely under fire. Every sense was sharper, the mind worked clearer and faster.... You found yourself on a precarious emotional edge, experiencing a headiness that no drink or drug could match.[72]

Apter reports that males and females do not differ appreciably in the balance between instrumental and expressive states of mind. They do differ, however, in their ways of increasing or lowering their arousal.[73] Men are more likely to choose such stimulants as hang gliding and joining the army. Since there is no way of reducing the genetic risk-taking tendency, the best answer is to identify socially useful ways of pursuing arousal.

Substitutes for Risk Taking

About a century ago, psychologist William James delivered a famous speech at Stanford University on "The Moral Equivalent of War." James was a fervent pacifist, but he foresaw World War I and believed it could not be averted unless arrangements were made to divert the enthusiasm of young men away from military arousal into more socially useful activities. He proposed a conscription of all men (not considering young women in this context) to perform hard, challenging, dangerous work comparable to the bracing demands of a soldier's life. In 1906, the task ahead seemed to involve "taming" nature, and so James called this challenge a "war against nature." That title would not attract support today, but a "war to *protect* nature" might appeal to many, especially if it involved dangerous but useful work to eliminate pollutants from wetlands or protect endangered rhinos from poachers.

An even more promising program might be based on the UN peacekeeping forces and disaster relief organizations: a corps of trained persons ready to fly anywhere in the world to rescue people from floods, forest fires, invasions, and earthquakes.[74] Probably conscription would be unnecessary, for the opportunity would appeal to youthful volunteers seeking meaningful ways of experiencing danger in the service of society.

There's a serious shortage of danger in today's world, and it is becoming more scarce every day because of a "civilizing process."[75] A few generations ago, one might aspire to become a saint or a hero, but that is not likely today. Saints and heroes have to perform excellent deeds of service in a context of risk, and the risk is diminishing as fast as democracy and affluence are growing. As a society develops and guarantees citizens their human rights and a decent standard of living, there are fewer wars and fewer necessary reforms for which to sacrifice oneself heroically. One can take a secure job in a good firm and have a pleasant life, but there are few opportunities to perform dangerous altruistic deeds. Such an organization as the "International Rescue Corps" proposed here, or even William James's conscription scheme, may help make up for the shortage of worthwhile risks for youths.

In the meantime, we may consider some possible stopgap measures, including vicarious thrills through entertainment. I personally loathe horror and war films, crime and action TV shows, but I score near the bottom of the thrill-seeking scale. Such shows cannot be defended by arguing that they are "cathartic"—that they reduce the tendency of audiences to behave in antisocial or violent ways. They do not. In fact, they tend to increase such behavior somewhat; the causality is small in magnitude but too serious to consider negligible at any level.

Moreover, people become habituated to the shows that excite and horrify them. Producers must keep introducing more shocking actions, in a never-ending escalation of advertisements for behavior that we hope the audience never emulates, though in fact, they do.

On the other hand, millions of people evidently enjoy mayhem/horror/violence in entertainment products. The appeal is not (as catharsis theory would suggest) because the viewers want a way of *ridding* themselves of stored-up unpleasant emotions, but rather because they specifically want to *arouse* those emotions, which they experience as enjoyable—either because of certain associated metaemotions or because they find them pleasurable, where other people would not.

They may be choosing films about risky activities as a substitute for real, live dangers that are too scarce in their lives to give them the arousal they crave innately. Unfortunately, for some individuals with extreme needs for thrills, it seems that the vicarious excitement derived from films is not enough to satisfy; they prefer real, active dangers such as bungee jumping. Unpublished research by Jo Groebel in the Netherlands suggests that the relationship between sensation seeking and the consumption of violent entertainment is not linear.[76] People are increasingly attracted to violent shows in proportion to their need for thrills—up to a certain limit. Those with still higher needs for thrills require more than action films or other vicarious arousals; they are satisfied only by experiencing *real* danger for themselves.

Such extreme thrill-seeking individuals are rare, however. Violent entertainment does attract many people who have relatively high levels of aggression and a high need for physical arousal or excitement. If you are one of those thrill seekers, bear in mind that your needs are not typical. Conceivably, you may use cultural products to substitute for more dangerous real challenges, such as driving recklessly or gambling. Whether or not you actually *need* such forms of entertainment and benefit from them, you have a right to choose them anyway, just as I have a right, as a predominantly serious-minded, instrumental personality, to avoid them. In the final chapter we'll consider ways of giving people more choice.

Conclusion

To some extent our tastes differ for inborn reasons. We may be extraverts who abhor horror films, for example, or sensation seekers who love them. We know that watching stressful movies (e.g., *Saving Private Ryan*) harms people physiologically. However, there are individual differences. It remains to be discovered whether thrill seekers are harmed as much as other people by entertainment that arouses the sympathetic nervous system. In any case, it seems wise to metabolize the arousal quickly after such exposure, or offset it by watching a comedy, say, or a love story.

But sometimes we can all benefit from tragic dramas or fiction—not by means of catharsis, as Aristotle supposed, but rather by feeling pity for the characters. Pity is a more humane emotion than the anger that blaming stories induce. It may make us more sensitive to life's moral complexities and hence more compassionate.

Another benign effect of distressing stories is that we may have metaemotions that offset the harm done by the primary emotion. For example, we may feel rather proud of ourselves for observing such terrible events as those in *Schindler's List*. Our enhanced self-respect may outweigh the anguish we must undergo to win it.

Whether a particular emotion is negative or positive may depend on the interpretation we place on it. When pumped up with adrenaline, say, we may suppose either that we're feeling hyper because of an annoyance or that we're feeling excited by a lively party. According to excitation transfer theory, we often convert the surplus arousal left over from one emotion (such as fear of falling) to quite a different one (such as euphoria).

When we are in an instrumental mood, we usually don't want much arousal; if it comes, we experience it as anxiety. If we're in an expressive mood, we probably want arousal; if it comes, we experience it as excitement; if it's absent, we feel bored.

Modern society offers few outlets for thrill seekers who want to make a social contribution by their courageous actions. Possibly new occupations should be invented just for such people. We differ in our emotional needs and should have maximum freedom to choose our entertainment—including freedom to avoid the kinds that we find unpleasant.

Chapter 6

Artistry and Ethics

Imagine you're a serious creator of fiction. You've learned that your work may be more consequential than you had known. For example, your novel or soap opera may keep thousands in your audience from catching the flu or may relieve their fibromyalgia. Your sitcom may reduce the birthrate in Uzbekistan. Your movie may prompt dissidents in a dictatorship to march in the streets demanding democracy. Or may stimulate a new Nazi movement. Or may increase the popularity of smoking. Or may start a civil war. (When introduced to Harriet Beecher Stowe, Abraham Lincoln said, "So you are the little lady who started this big war!") How will you carry on your creative work in light of these responsibilities?

This chapter addresses the ethics of producing cultural works that affect audiences' emotions, health, or social values. But don't expect a simple list of rules. Indeed, we'll discover that several ethical principles are mutually contradictory. Instead of simplifying your moral problems, I'm about to complicate them. Sorry.

What do ethics have to do with a writer's decisions about what, and how, to write? Even to ask that question makes people nervous. Already there are too many fanatical ideologues spoiling fun in this world. I feel as queasy as you probably do about bringing it up—as, nevertheless, I shall do. The only moral aspect of culture that is discussable in polite liberal society has to do with limiting the exposure of *children* to video games, television violence, sex, and other "adult topics." But we'll deal with grown-ups here.

This thorny issue of moralistic criticism arises during every cultural revolution—including Iran's 1979 Islamic Revolution against the shah. In her book *Reading Lolita in Tehran,* Azar Nafisi described her dramatic confrontations with revolutionary students in English literature classes at the University of Tehran. The dispute centered on the appropriateness of the reading she had assigned them—F. Scott Fitzgerald's *The Great Gatsby,* the morality of which suddenly became controversial. In a mischievous spirit, Nafisi set up a mock trial in her classroom, assigning the fiercest Islamic critic the role of prosecuting the book for teaching immorality. A liberal female student was the lawyer for the defense, while Nafisi represented the novel itself.

The young prosecutor ranted in the predictable way, attributing the "cultural rape" of Islam to the novel for supposedly preaching illicit sex. He called the adulterer Gatsby a charlatan who earned his money illegally and who represented the American dream. The whole of American society deserves to die as Gatsby did, he concluded.

The defense attorney Zarrin was a stylish young woman who pointed out that novels are not moral in the usual sense of the word; they can be called moral if they challenge the absolutes that we have unthinkingly accepted. *Gatsby,* she said, was not about the love of money, but about the vulgarity of materialism. Instead of approving of the rich, Fitzgerald shows their dishonesty and their carelessness. The rich characters Tom and Daisy let other people clean up their messes.

Then Zarrin put Professor Nafisi on the stand to represent the book. Nafisi gave Fitzgerald's own explanation of the novel: that it is not about adultery but about the loss of dreams. You read it to learn how complicated marriage and fidelity are. A great novel, she said, "prevents you from the self-righteousness that sees morality in fixed formulas about good and evil."[1]

Her students understood her point, but few of them spoke out in favor of the book. Already their peers' revolutionary zeal was too powerful for most of them to confront, and self-censorship was becoming the order of the day. However, Nafisi's argument should inform our own use of ethical/emotional criticism. She does not exclude ethics as a basis for criticism, but she does show that bigoted, unintelligent critics will be bigoted and unintelligent, whatever critical methods they adopt. It is not that morality is irrelevant but rather that a brilliant writer's moral insights question the narrow, moralistic *formulas* of ideologies. By excluding stories about adulterers, charlatans, and liars, the revolutionary Muslims would exclude an ethical exploration of carelessness, loss of dreams, and lack of empathy—moral lapses that are not on any official list of sins but that make *Gatsby* a great literary work. Nafisi's insights remind us here that ethical criticism can be as stupidly applied as anything else; intelligently applied, however, it's the most illuminating way to analyze fiction. Let's work from that standpoint.

Some Uncontroversial Ethical Issues

I'll clear the ground by mentioning a couple of arguments that I am *not* going to make.

Sex-and-Violence?

Complaints about the harmful effects of entertainment mostly refer to an unpleasant hybrid thing called "sex-and-violence"—though, fortunately, in real life the two experiences rarely go together. I prefer to distinguish between them.

The more sex people experience, the better off they generally are, and fictional products can help make up for certain real-life deficits. I know an eighty-six-year-old widow in a retirement home who complains that it is hard to find love stories either on television or in video stores. She loves sex, so long as it is sweet and romantic. She's right. Check out your own TV and you'll find it's scarce—except for dangerous or impersonal, exploitive encounters. The deleterious social effects of pornography probably come less from imitating sexual scenes than from being *put off sex* by the sleazy or shallow imagery.[2] I know two people who claim that watching virtually any episode of *The Sopranos* will deactivate their libido for several days—and it is not a remarkably pornographic show. Not all erotic movies are pornographic, but only those showing demeaning or abusive sex. I'll be more concerned here with the effects of antisocial exemplification than with sex.

Only Upbeat Stories?

Next: I won't propose that writers should create only happy, bland stories. Yes, I did indicate that positive emotions have important health benefits for audiences. Vicarious joy, laughter, and love tend to make you healthy, while autonomic arousal may have either positive or negative health effects. Theoretically, then, one might insist that every writer should produce only life-affirming, pleasant stories full of joy, laughter, and love. On ethical grounds we might consider abolishing antisocial, painful plots—but I won't.

Censorious proposals won't fly. First, audiences are too diverse for those restrictions. We differ widely in our emotional needs. Besides, any given story may convey multiple messages, some of which contradict the others. Different personalities will see different meanings in the same story and prefer different genres. Yes, *most* people do benefit most from humor, love, and joy. However, neurotic introverts tend to prefer sad stories about human misery, and risk takers or sensation seekers prefer thrillers, horror shows, and war movies. Sometimes a tragedy will be good for *your* soul, too. In selecting entertainment, therefore, adults (though not children) are entitled to freedom of choice. (But free choice also means freedom from exposure—the right to avoid unwanted material. This principle, if taken seriously, creates programming challenges.)

The Steep Price of Freedom

Let's acknowledge that freedom of choice is not risk-free. Modern societies place few restrictions on the public display of disturbing stories. As a result, all of us have witnessed thousands of dramatized murders and sadistic acts. Even a saint would become desensitized by such habituation. Whenever we watch pornography or violence over an extended period, the shock diminishes. The violence in films must constantly escalate just to provide audiences with a constant level of arousal, since normal persons gradually become less sensitive to the pain of others. Unfortunately, professional critics are overexposed to such stories, so they tend to stop noticing or mentioning violence in their reviews. The problem becomes normalized, invisible, uncontroversial.

Nevertheless, mimesis continues occurring around us; it actually influences your life expectancy to a small but nontrivial degree. A few people are especially susceptible to the suggestive effects of antisocial plots, and anyone may become their victim. For example, Marc Lepine, the Montreal loner who killed fourteen female engineering students, habitually watched violent, pornographic videos. Yet in liberal democracies, Lepine's freedom of choice generally trumps security for women. So far, I don't know any way of preventing such tragic instances of mimesis. But we should acknowledge it as a price we're paying.

To revisit the Dalai Lama's question: In a world where only two of every five persons practices a religion, how are we learning compassion? Not from Hollywood, apparently. A movie producer named Peter Livingston made a documentary about the twenty-five most popular films of all time. Only two of them showed natural death, and only one had a birth in which the baby survived. However, Livingston calculated that *nine billion people were killed,* though not all these killings were shown on the screen. In *Star Wars,* a blue planet called "home" is vaporized, accounting for six billion. In *Terminator 2,* three billion are killed. In *Independence Day,* there are 427 million more, and so on. Only two films (*Mrs. Doubtfire* and *Home Alone*) had no killings at all.[3] Our fiction is not teaching compassion or loving-kindness.

These murders do influence audiences. Since the 1950s, more than 3,500 studies have examined the relationship between media exposure and violent behavior. All except eighteen have found a positive correlation.[4]

136 ◆ *Chapter 6*

Ratio of Audience Empathy

What would reduce the impact of this violent entertainment? An improved ratio of positive to negative suggestions. The main determinant of antisocial imitation may not be the *total amount* of cruelty shown but rather the *ratio of audience empathy for the perpetrators relative to that for their victims.* For example, my all-time favorite film, *Gandhi,* has several scenes of mass violence, including a massacre. Conceivably, some viewers might imitate those actions, but that is highly unlikely, since the movie promotes *non*violence. We do witness fighting, but we empathize with, and interpret it through the eyes of, Gandhi and his followers. We are, therefore, appalled by it.

This explains another puzzle. Japanese and American films show the same amount of violence, but far less real violence occurs in Japan than in the United States. Why? Part of the reason is that in Japanese films, the violence is only perpetrated by villains against "good guys." The films also show the pain that it causes and the harm it does to the characters they care about. In the United States, by contrast, the agony and other terrible consequences of violence are rarely shown. This makes it more acceptable or even fun to watch.[5]

The question is, In a liberal democracy where entertainment is an industry, how can citizens influence the content of the stories in their cultural environment? Without proposing any new rule book, I'd like to see a shift in the "center of gravity" by, say, 30 percent toward civility and compassion. That's not a revolution but a realistic goal that would make a perceptible difference in our culture. In the final chapter I'll consider some possible strategies, but in this chapter I want to move past the mainly self-evident points that I've discussed so far and turn to the ethical ambiguities that creative writers face.

Harder Issues

Since the advent of Romanticism two centuries ago, it has been widely assumed that ethics is irrelevant to writing fiction. Supposedly, authors merely "express themselves" and are not held accountable for any consequences of their work.

But no human activity is beyond ethics if it influences other people. At a minimum, the writers should adopt the principles that guide physicians: "Do no harm." But even that is easier said than done. It's often unclear just what harm a story may do.

All vicarious experiences have effects—physiological, psychological, and moral. The Greek dramatists wisely allowed no violence to be shown onstage, while audiences today get to observe disembowelings. So where should a writer draw the line to protect the public?

What are the emotional effects of empathizing with a character who is morally skidding? Should the audience be led to break empathy during a character's downfall and begin hating him? And are audiences demoralized when fate treats characters unfairly, bestowing good luck on the vicious and bad luck on the decent? Writers need to address such issues.

Every story contains an implicit worldview. For example, a novel may imply that only fools are altruistic or truthful, and that life punishes their folly. Or that the world is dangerous and no one can be trusted. The prevalence of such messages, along with the body count in our living rooms, are indicators of our culture's quality. Are there any basic principles to reduce the harm writers do?

Aristotle's Advice

Unlike Plato, Aristotle believed that plays could be psychologically and morally therapeutic. In *The Poetics* he offered advice on how to write tragedies that worked. (A second, lost book was supposedly about writing comedies.) No other guide has ever been so influential among dramatists as *The Poetics*. It's largely a technical handbook, but the aspect that interests us is its ethical admonitions on protecting the emotional well-being and morale of audiences. Whereas one might consider it wise to prevent spectators from empathizing with such miserable, immoral characters as Medea, Creon, or Electra, Aristotle intended for us to suffer along with them, since the psychological benefits would only come to those who empathized unreservedly, fearing for the characters and pitying them along the whole route to their terrible destiny.

We should feel fear and pity, yes, but not bitter disillusionment. The emotional and moral benefits for spectators supposedly depended on a second factor: the *fairness* of the denouement. Insofar as fate meted out an unjustly harsh penalty, Aristotle supposed that the audience would be distraught, demoralized, and spiritually wounded. Thus he believed that the ethics of good storytelling required that the universe be shown to pay people back fairly. This emphasis on *equitable retribution* still informs most playwriting today.

Aristotle insisted that a plot should not violate our basic sense of fairness, for audiences cannot derive pleasure from witnessing the miscarriage of justice. A play should not shock us morally by suggesting that ethical commitment is pointless. He advised poets who wrote tragedies:

> The change of fortune presented must not be the spectacle of a virtuous man brought from prosperity to adversity: for this moves neither pity nor fear; it merely

shocks us. Nor, again, that of a bad man passing from adversity to prosperity: for nothing can be more alien to the spirit of tragedy; it possesses no single tragic quality; it neither satisfies the moral sense nor calls forth pity or fear. Nor, again, should the downfall of the utter villain be exhibited. A plot of this kind would, doubtless, satisfy the moral sense, but it would inspire neither pity nor fear; for pity is aroused by unmerited misfortune, fear by the misfortune of a man like ourselves. Such an event, therefore, will be neither pitiful nor terrible.

There remains, then, the character between these two extremes—that of a man who is not eminently good and just, yet whose misfortune is brought about not by vice or depravity, but by some error or frailty.[6]

Thus the only type of protagonist who may properly come to a sad end in the tragedy is a middling character who committed an error. If a truly bad person were punished, we would enjoy witnessing the inflicted retribution instead of feeling pity, as we are supposed to feel when watching a tragedy.[7]

Many playwrights still follow Aristotle's advice by ensuring that, in the end, characters get their just deserts. When they do not, we leave the theater feeling dissatisfied. Such dissatisfaction may be countertherapeutic, and the witnessing of injustice may discourage ethical behavior on the part of the viewer. Since mass media entertainment is consumed today by millions, the potentially grave aggregate effects should be considered.

Aristotle's recommendations cannot have influenced all playwrights, even the Greek tragedians or Shakespeare. He wrote this advice after Aeschylus, Sophocles, and Euripides were already dead. Moreover, *The Poetics* was not translated into English until the eighteenth century, and no Latin translation appeared in England until 1623, seven years after the death of Shakespeare, whose tragic heroes sometimes suffer more from their outstanding virtue than from errors.[8] That is, they have excellent qualities that are not ordinarily flaws. Only in the unlucky circumstances of a specific plot do their virtuous traits predispose them to failure or catastrophe.[9] Nevertheless, even without Aristotle's excellent advice, the greatest tragic playwrights independently conformed to his main recommendations by retaining our empathy for the doomed protagonists until the end.

Tragedies that fulfill Aristotle's advice create in us a mixture of pain and peaceful resignation because of our sympathy for the protagonist, who at the end seems pitiable, though he may be more a villain than a hero. Though we have seen unforgivable wrongs done, the loathing that we might feel toward a perpetrator in real life becomes here an acceptance of the irresistibility of destiny. We sustain our empathy despite everything—which is not necessarily the case when it comes to new dramas that are produced today.

Just Deserts and Dispositional Theory

Dolf Zillmann has also addressed the question Aristotle had posed: What does it take to satisfy an audience? His main answer is called *dispositional theory,* and it has been tested empirically. Zillmann shows that we must form intense wishes for the characters, and these wishes are determined by our *empathy* and our *affective disposition*—the extent to which we like or love a character. He suggests, not surprisingly, that our affective dispositions virtually control our empathy toward characters.[10] The more we like a character, the more we identify with him and want fate to be kind to him. But what determines whether we like a character? Zillmann agrees with Aristotle that this depends on the relative excellence of his morality.

Dispositional theory has been tested on child and adult subjects alike. Most people over ten to thirteen years old do like or dislike characters depending on their moral-ity. For example, Zillmann and Jennings Bryant made a children's film about two princes: one good, the other bad. The bad prince got the upper hand and banished the good one to an unpleasant region of the kingdom. However, the good prince eventually returned to power and was able to punish his tormentor. As options, he had three possible punishments: *equitable* (giving the bad prince the same punish-ment that the bad prince had planned for him), *too mild* (being too forgiving), or *too severe* (being more brutal than the bad prince would have been).

Normal young people enjoyed having punishment dealt to the bad prince, who had fully earned it.[11] However, they were disturbed if too much or too little punishment was imposed. If the bad prince was underpunished, the children disliked him intensely, and to some extent they even disliked the good prince for failing to impose adequate punishment. If the bad prince was punished in an unnecessarily brutal way, however, the children pitied him and stopped disliking him. They liked the good prince only when he imposed "fair" punishment—nei-ther too much nor too little. (Zillmann did not present another option, wherein the bad prince would see his error and apologize for his wrongdoing. In such a case, I think the children might have partly forgiven him and wanted him to receive little or no punishment. We need much more research on the emotional responses to moral redemption.)

Most adults react as the children did. "Tit-for-tat" is basic to the principles of justice. We exult when the hero gets the girl and the bank robbers go to jail or at least lose their loot bag. Indeed, as noted in the preceding chapter, some audi-ences become gleeful when the bad guys are blown to bits, but this is only true if their sympathetic nervous system had been aroused previously by watching the horrible deeds of these villains, who came to deserve their terrible fate.

Zillmann says that "*respondents must be made to care about characters, either in a positive or in a negative way.*"[12] Playwrights must make us regard protagonists as our friends, and antagonists as our enemies. They must be seen doing good or evil and thereafter we will wish appropriately good or bad fortune for them. If the writer does not make this happen, we will neither enjoy the drama nor consider ourselves well entertained.

But notice: The fair retribution that Zillmann is proposing does not have the moral impact on audiences that Aristotle had in mind. This "fair payback" outcome, as exemplified in the story about the two princes, resembles a violent action film more than a Greek tragedy. Aristotle wanted the payoff to be fair so the audience would be able to accept the sad fate of a character whom they pitied. The ordinary action plot, on the other hand, leaves us gloating when the bad guy gets his just deserts in the end. Our exuberant satisfaction is not the spiritually beneficial experience that Aristotle wanted audiences to undergo—quite the opposite!

On the other hand, the principle of equitable retribution makes for a good comedy. Probably Aristotle's recommendations for comedy (admittedly, without the second book of *The Poetics,* we have to guess about this) would fit Zillmann's recommendations perfectly. Develop a good and a bad character, make us care about the good one, and end the play by having him encounter good fortune, whereas the bad character fails to reach his goal. Then we'll be satisfied.

But Aristotle was mostly concerned with tragedy, and he wanted us to feel fear and/or pity. To make this happen, the protagonist had to be a "gray" character—neither all good nor all bad; the audience had to come to care about him or her; and he or she had to encounter a terrible fate. The protagonist's bad end must be fully deserved, yet the audience should continue to empathize with him the whole time. This is a "fair" denouement but not an upbeat comedy.

This desire for equitable retribution—tit-for-tat—is normal but not by itself the highest level of morality. It's not insightful unless accompanied by the pity of a tragedy following Aristotle's guidelines, which gives us a new acceptance of human frailty. Tit-for-tat neither elevates the soul nor points us toward any solution of conflict. As Gandhi said, "An eye for an eye and a tooth for a tooth leaves the whole world toothless and blind."

Still, the principle of equitable retribution is deeply rooted in the human psyche and cannot be disregarded. There is nothing transcendent about it, but it provides a basis for organizing society in a workable way. Aristotle was a practical man; he admired politicians for skillfully managing the contingencies of social life in the physical realm of space and time. His worldliness, as contrasted with Plato's transcendence, acknowledged the pivotal importance of judgment, of choosing between limited options. Fair retribution—justice—is the best we can expect for living morally in a world not of our own making. The pity that Aristotle wanted us to feel was his way of reminding us that even just deserts are never completely just. We must, indeed, devote our worldly love to those who deserve it. But we can feel fleeting transcendent love even for those who do not deserve it—and such moments of uncontingent, pitying love are the spiritual insights that Aristotle wanted dramatists to convey.

Blaming Plots

> It is the act of an ill-instructed man to blame others for his own bad condition; it is the act of one who has begun to be instructed to lay the blame on himself; and of one whose instruction is completed, neither to blame another nor himself.
>
> —Epictetus

Stories that involve just retribution may differ enormously, depending on whether we do or don't empathize with the protagonist during his immorality. I'll call the latter type of drama the *blaming plot*. It is far more common now than the kind of plot Aristotle favored, which depends on unreserved empathy and pity. To blame is to exclude from empathy; the more we empathize, the less we blame. The blaming story falls short as a therapeutic spiritual exercise. Still, both types of story have advantages and disadvantages.

Empathy can hurt. To accompany a troubled person as she makes bad decisions can be a painful experience from which ultimately one may or may not learn something of value. Since this pain may even compromise your immune system, you may prefer not to take on such challenges as a habitual regimen of moral self-discipline. My advice: Don't overdose on tragedy—and far less so on action films, which, with their attitude of blame, withhold empathy and contribute nothing valuable to the soul.

Yet blaming stories have huge audiences because they offer something that many enjoy. The *excitement* is apparent; thrill seekers need autonomic stimulation, from whatever source. I'll argue later that blaming also confers *meaning* on lives that are otherwise vapid. Hence I'll approach criticism with a certain diffidence, rather than seeking bossily to deprive others of their preferred forms of entertainment. Still, my greatest hope would be to replace the culture of blame with problem solving as a habit of mind.

Blame is the opposite of empathy. However painful empathy may be (and nobody can sustain it all the time), it recognizes a common humanity that sees beyond punishment, reconciling us to the inevitability of personal failure. My concern about blaming is based on my sense that the habit of *finding fault with others* is a precondition for overtly violent behavior. It's probably easier to reduce the resentment portrayed in fiction than to reduce the violence. If blaming is a psychological prerequisite for physical aggression, then much suffering may be prevented by redirecting attention at early stages toward more promising ways of solving problems. That's my theory, anyway. Rather than complaining about the undesirable content of popular culture, I prefer to propose favorable alternatives, such as fostering audience empathy, even toward blameworthy characters.

One objective of the culture of blame is to single out characters with whom audiences should never empathize. Whereas I understand the basis for this concern—that empathy sometimes leads to direct mimesis and the contagious imitation of despicable behavior—it's generally counterproductive. Better: expand and diversify, rather than constrict, the range of the persons with whom we empathize.

The problem is not that our stories lack moral messages. On the contrary, wrongdoers usually are punished for bad deeds. Theoretically this should support ethical standards, but in fact it promotes punitiveness. One impediment to compassion is the rigorous judgmentalism that finds and pays back evildoers. The social value of retribution is assumed.

One cannot eliminate this orientation completely, for it is the basis of justice and social order. People must be held accountable for their actions within the rule of law. Fortunately, however, in real life legal demands are often moderated by other values, such as mercy, tolerance, and good humor. Only in entertainment do we see an extreme imbalance between punitiveness and tolerance. The overemphasis on law and order makes for exciting drama but warps our souls.

This prevailing bias is a *culture of blame.* Even a slight correction for it could significantly improve the average quality of the stories that we tell each other.[13] Audiences are harmed by the incessant assigning of blame and heartless imposing of retribution. Such values are so widespread today as to seem incontestably valid. However, whole societies have flourished that did not believe in blame—including that of Greece during Aristotle's day. It's worth asking, How did the transition take place from a culture that did not blame to the one with which we are familiar today? The progressive change is visible in a trilogy of plays by Aeschylus.

Transition to Blaming

During most of the classical period when the great tragedies were written, terrible actions were described fully, but the wrongdoer was not blamed. Playwrights wrote about characters whose monstrous deeds were ordained by fate. For example, it was predicted that Oedipus would kill his own father and marry his own mother. Everyone who knew about the prophecy took extraordinary measures to ensure that it could never happen.

Nevertheless, it did happen. Upon learning the truth, Oedipus blinded himself and left his homeland, not because he deserved blame for his actions, but because he was somehow "polluted" and would contaminate his city by his presence. Instead of attributing guilt, the Greeks of that day viewed wrongdoers much as we consider someone who, through no fault of his own, carries a virus that makes him dangerous to others. He is not blamed, but he has to suffer the consequences anyhow.[14] A "polluted" tragic character might feel humiliated for his flaws but would not feel guilty as you or I might feel, for his culpability would be considered something that happened to him, rather than something for which he was responsible. Usually the gods were the source of his shortcomings, for they were not constrained by human rules of justice or decency. The Greeks managed to worship gods who we today would consider capricious, unfair, petty, and malevolent.[15]

Greek ways of handling conflict changed historically. Prior to the sixth century B.C.E., Athenians and members of other societies dealt with their personal conflicts by cycles of retaliation such as blood feuds. Then Solon paved the way for democracy by establishing a legal code and changing the tradition of private vengeance into a system of justice. Conflicts were to be resolved before presiding judges in public councils, which were juries of peers.

We see evidence of that shift toward justice in the great trilogy by Aeschylus, *The Oresteia,*[16] which depicts the aftermath of the Trojan War. Throughout the first two of these plays, the leading characters follow the custom of retaliation. Agamemnon returns home after the Trojan War, bringing along his mistress, Cassandra, daughter of his slain enemy, Priam. His wife Clytemnestra awaits him, still enraged by his sacrifice of their daughter Iphigenia, which he had performed a decade earlier to propitiate a god and secure favorable winds to carry the fleet to Troy. The vengeful Clytemnestra slays Agamemnon, whom their other daughter, Electra, adored.

Still mourning years later, Electra awaits the return from abroad of her brother Orestes, who must avenge the death of their father by slaying their mother, Clytemnestra. When Orestes finally shows up, he feels understandably conflicted about his obligations but eventually carries out the murder. Then he is pursued by the avenging Furies, who consider his murder of his mother worse than her vengeful murder of her husband. The retaliatory cycle goes on.

But eventually, in the third play, Orestes seeks a sensible solution. He appeals to a jury of citizens to decide the matter, and they exonerate him in a contentious courtroom trial that hinges on deciding whether he is legally sane.[17] For the first time, the notion of personal responsibility and a rational system of justice are displayed as crucial to the denouement of a Greek tragedy.[18] Nevertheless, even here Orestes's fate is actually determined by the gods, and there is no implication that he is to be blamed or exonerated on the basis of his own free actions. His actions were partly decreed by destiny and partly the result of his natural impulse to avenge his father's death. At that point, Greek justice still did not involve blame.

The gods on Olympus seem to us petty and self-centered. However, these traits need to be seen within a cultural context in which shame was a powerful emotion and guilt was hardly noticed. Homeric Greeks were extremely concerned with their honor and reputation for heroism. Their stories do not suggest that their inner lives, their "souls," were well developed at all. Their gods had many of the same qualities, resenting any slight to their status, whether by another god or a man. They might punish a person for attaining too much success, which might represent an arrogant challenge (*hubris*) toward the gods' superiority.

Greek individuals had little insight into their own personalities. Whenever they behaved in some impulsive or irrational way, they explained it away in terms of *Ate*—an intervention by the gods. ("I was not myself at the time, for Dionysus had muddled my thinking.") Modern psychologists would identify such reasoning as projection. Whereas this kind of explanation did allow people to avoid personal blame, it also had disadvantages. It implied that the gods had no sense of true justice and did nothing to assist people who morally had earned their support. These gods were not fair and could not be expected to perform miracles to make human affairs work out right.

Perhaps it was asking too much of shame-oriented gods to be ethically fair, but in any case, during the Archaic Age,[19] there were times when the gods (especially Zeus) were addressed as agents of justice[20]—however underdeveloped their divine notions of justice might be. But everyone could see that bad people often succeeded when fine people suffered. How could a just god allow such undeserved results to occur? (This is, of course, the question we call "the problem of evil.")

The answer, to be satisfying, required one to think of results as emerging over a longer period than a single lifetime. And, with that prolonged time span in mind, two different answers became possible. The first theory suggests that perhaps the fair payoff for good or evil will come, not to the *individual* who deserves it but to his son's family, or even to his grandchildren. Perhaps suffering or prosperity is inherited in the family from the good or bad deeds of the ancestors. Or, according to the second theory, perhaps equitable retribution will come to *oneself,* but in a subsequent lifetime.[21] This is the theory of reincarnation, which often goes with at least a rudimentary concept of karma as well.

The Greeks adopted both explanations, though not necessarily at the same time or by the same theorists. Early in history, the patriarchal family was extremely strong. Fathers were treated as kings. During that period, the notion of inherited familial suffering prevailed.[22] Later, however, the notion of reincarnation gained wider (though certainly not general) acceptance. I am not convinced that the Greeks had a fully developed theory of karma, which would be an important element in making the notion of reincarnation satisfying. (*Karma* is a mechanism by which fate might actually be postponing fair rewards and punishment even while appearing unfair in terms of the payoffs meted out in a single lifetime.)[23]

The problem of evil is both a problem of spiritual morale and also one of theodicy—of justifying God's ways to humankind. Plato's opposition to drama reflected his notion, as an idealist, that goodness was real, whereas to us it is only an abstraction. He wanted people to be oriented toward ideals that were neither visible nor properly representable. And he recognized the disparity between his own optimistic idealism and the tragic vision that accepted the possibility of insoluble problems of evil and suffering.[24]

For his part, Aristotle, in his *Poetics,* omits any discussion of the gods as an explanation for the outcome of a plot. This omission, in fact, changed the assumptions on which drama was based. Theater had emerged from religious rituals and always had remained, to some extent, an expression of devotion. Now Aristotle was counseling playwrights to make their plots work out fairly, so that the audiences would not be shocked or demoralized by the endings—but to what purpose? Evidently he was not trying to preserve their faith in the fairness of the gods, for the gods were no longer even mentioned. If the gods were no longer the cause of the characters' failings, how were these mortals to remain psychologically blameless?

Aristotle's answer turned on the characters' tragic mistakes, which must be punished, but he does not explain how human beings happen to make such errors. Possibly the new absence of such an explanation accounts, in part, for the emergence of a culture of guilt in Greek society, replacing the culture of shame and of blamelessness. By the early Hellenistic period, the Greeks had begun *internalizing* blame,[25] even as they came increasingly into contact with other Eastern societies, including Judaism.

Jews, from the earliest times, had borne a heavy consciousness of guilt. Theirs was never a culture of shame, as that of Greece had been. Eve's mistake with the apple was not just embarrassing. It was *sin.* Upon discovering what His creatures had been doing, God launched an accusation against them. Soon all four characters—God, Adam, Eve, and the serpent—were blaming each other. For their guilt, God expelled the couple from paradise. After that, matters went downhill: Cain and Abel, Sodom and Gomorrah, and Lot's wife—guilty sinners all. Nor has it ever stopped.

This was the consciousness that Christianity inherited. A pious Christian is supposed to examine her own soul, anticipating Judgment Day, for Christianity elaborated the Jewish notion of an afterlife in heaven or hell. Many stories reflect this anticipation of damnation. Although most serious narratives today are secular, offering no theological vision whatever, our main characters remain marked by guilt and will pay heavily for their deeds in the denouement, and the readers will not pity them.

The historical Western preoccupation with blaming can be attributed, I think, to the strength of our guilt culture. However, in urging that we cultivate a more generous spirit to replace our culture of blame, I am not proposing that we revert to a culture of shame. Nor is there any other single alternative theory that opposes the culture of blame. Instead, countless possible alternatives can be contrasted to our inherited, guilt-driven habits of mind. I'll illustrate a few.

Without Blame

A more advanced sensibility is often one that does not attribute blame. To show what it is like to approach problems without identifying culpability, I'll tell four stories and then compare them.

Blameless in El Salvador

Here I'll quote an article by Canadian peace worker Karen Ridd, who worked during the 1980s as a volunteer with the Committee of Mothers of the Disappeared of El Salvador. Ridd writes:

> They are a group of women who formed in the height of Salvador's repression, women who came together as a result of running into each other, time and again, in that horrific search for the bodies of their disappeared loved ones—husbands, children, sisters. Again and again they saw each other, at the morgues, the police stations, the jails, the body dumps where they turned over body after body, hoping/not hoping to find their lost one. And in running into each other time after time, their commonality began to draw them together. They saw that their strength would lie in union. So they formed the Committee of Mothers of the Disappeared,

one of the groups in the vanguard of the protest against the repression, violence, and injustice suffered by the people of El Salvador.

The story that I will recount took place in 1989. In the middle of the night, a bomb placed in front of their office blew open the front of the building. The office is used also as living quarters. It is a place where women who are too threatened to stay in their own homes can come for some measure of safety. Women from the countryside bring their families and stay there while they search in the city for their disappeared relatives. So it is a place filled with people, mostly children and women. Bombs such as the one detonated that night are not an entirely uncommon occurrence. They are a terrifying and dangerous one.

After the blast, soldiers gathered outside the building, preparing to storm through the gap created by the explosion and raid the office. Inside the office women moved quickly and quietly, soothing the cries of the children. Then they began to make coffee. The foreigners inside the building were aghast. It is 3:30 in the morning, a bomb has just gone off, the soldiers are about to drag everyone away—and the mothers are making coffee. Have they lost their minds?

When the coffee is ready, the women pour it into cups and take it, steaming, out to the soldiers in the street. They are young, the soldiers in El Salvador. Some of them are scarcely sixteen years old. It is the middle of the night, they are tired, cold, and miserable. Probably they are a little nervous too. They take the coffee, not hesitating, and drink it.

In that moment, something changes. For having drunk the coffee someone has offered you, having shared that symbolic meal, having partaken of someone's hospitality, it becomes impossible to turn around and raid their office, dragging them away. The soldiers finished their coffee, handed back the mugs, and slipped quietly away. The women began to reconstruct their wall.[26]

Blameless in Japan

This one is a Zen detective story about a sword-carrying brigand who was robbing houses in a village. When he entered the Zen master's house, he found the owner in deep meditation. Brandishing his sword, he asked him where he kept his money. The master pointed to a jar, which the thief seized and carried away.[27]

But the local policeman was able. He captured the brigand, recognized the jar, and hastened to ask the Zen master whether it belonged to him.

"No," replied the master calmly. "A man came in here a while ago and asked me where my money was. I gave it to him. So it's his."

Blameless in a Church Group

David had spent time in an institution for the criminally insane. His deprived childhood had left him with many problems. Lately he had been volunteering in a church-related service organization, but suddenly a large sum of money disappeared there, and, for several reasons, the staff concluded that he had taken it. If charged and convicted, he would get a long prison sentence. Trying to talk with David did not work, for he angrily denied the theft. The group appealed to a local conflict resolution center for help. A meeting was set up and a panel agreed to mediate.

It was a moving evening. Tanya, a volunteer who had spent some of her wedding gift money replacing some of the missing funds, spoke warmly of her relationship with David. Then David spoke of the support he had received from the other volunteers.

Finally, David asked the director, "If I tell the truth, am I going to go to prison?"

The director raised his arms in relief and exclaimed, "Hallelujah, no!"

This admission was followed by expressions of respect for David's honesty—and lots of ideas about how to help him. David was promised a retroactive birthday cake. A follow-up session helped him find a way to carry out some conditions of his agreement, and afterward he made restitution. He took correspondence courses, trained as a mediator himself, and found his first paying job, where he is doing well.[28]

Blameless in Germany

In his book *Explaining Hitler,* Ron Rosenbaum explores the range of accounts that have been offered to explain what made Hitler into *Hitler.* None of them can be confirmed, but neither can they be disproved absolutely. For instance, there's the theory that Hitler's father was the illegitimate child of a peasant woman impregnated by a nineteen-year-old Jew. Or that when he was a hospital patient as a soldier in World War I, a psychiatrist hypnotized him and gave a grandiose posthypnotic suggestion that he should become Germany's savior. There are several theories about his genitals (that he had only one testicle; that he contracted syphilis from a Jewish prostitute and passed it on to his niece, who committed suicide; and that a billy goat bit his penis when he was urinating into its mouth). Or that Hitler watched his mother die in agony because of the malpractice of a well-meaning but misguided Jewish physician. There are dozens of other explanations. Rosenbaum reports that every person who related a theory explaining Hitler's horrible character believed that his preferred explanation was sufficient to exonerate him of guilt in court.[29]

Explaining Blamelessness

The preceding four stories illustrate a few rationales that can be offered for lenience toward wrongdoing. There is no one single culture that is the contrasting counterpart to the culture of blame; instead, there are infinite possibilities, some of which reveal themselves surprisingly, or even as jokes.

Whenever a joke is being told, a tension is created that makes us apprehensive. Then, suddenly, we given a perfectly logical but unexpected interpretation, which instantly eliminates our tension. Our laughter releases it physiologically. For laughter to occur, the situation, as newly reinterpreted, must be shown as unexpectedly so absurd that it can't be taken seriously. And having laughed at a character's ridiculous problem, we can no longer blame him for making the wrong choice. Our laughter has exonerated him. Comedy is therefore hardly an appropriate milieu in which to debate an ethical question.

Or so it would seem. On the other hand, when we discuss our moral problems with sensible friends, we often choose them for their sense of proportion. And we can benefit from empathizing with someone who knows how to laugh off a problem at the right moment and put it into a more tolerant perspective. Thus humor is often an eminently sane response to a human dilemma.

Still, we cannot laugh off everything. When an action is truly immoral or cruel, we cannot smile or let the malevolence pass without comment. Humor offends in such cases, especially when it ridicules a character toward whom we feel strong empathy or attachment.

Let's consider again the four stories shared in the previous section. How might we explain the blamelessness illustrated in each one?

Explaining Blamelessness in El Salvador

Despite Ridd's astonishment when the mothers served coffee to the soldiers, it is not hard to comprehend the women's reasoning. No one present was to blame. The soldiers had carried out the bombing, not by free choice but because they had been ordered to do so. Disobedience would have invited punishment. The story illustrates the principle that blame is mitigated by lack of free choice.[30]

Explaining Blamelessness in Japan

The thief might well have been prosecuted. Certainly he had not earned exoneration. We have to guess at the Zen master's motive for showing compassion.[31] Probably it was based on Buddhist psychology, especially the theory of karma. According to this view of causation, both the master and the thief were brought to this situation by their own actions (possibly in previous lives) and will create their own future circumstances by the way they handle this event. Showing loving-kindness adds merit to one's karmic ledger and demonstrates one's transcendent insight about what is important and what is not. A Buddhist culture does not foster attachment to money or short-term vindication.

The Zen master presumably does not oppose the institutions of justice. He simply transcended law enforcement, at least on this occasion, possibly thinking that to impose retribution would be spiritually short-sighted. Buddhism holds that when people do wrong, it is not because of evil intent but because they do not realize that we are all one and that they are actually harming themselves. Malefactors therefore should be more pitied for their ignorance than blamed.

This reasoning is unfamiliar to Western minds. We might, however, benefit from it as an alternative to the law-and-order motif in our culture of blame. More often in the West, mercy is granted culprits at the stage when the judges sentence them, rather than during the phase of apprehending and charging them.

Explaining Blamelessness in a Church Group

The story of David is exactly opposite to the typical whodunit. It illustrates what is called "an ethic of care," in contrast to the ethic of justice.[32] Instead of tit-for-tat retribution, the caring community seeks to solve problems with restorative justice and to reintegrate the offender as an accepted member of society. The objective is to resolve the harm resulting from his wrongdoing.

The church group did not allow the theft to go unnoticed, as did the Zen master. There is no theory of karma here, no sense of transcendence, but rather a concern for problem solving and reconciliation. Presumably the group is motivated by Christian forgiveness. However, some non-Christian groups (notably aboriginal U.S. and Canadian tribes) are also committed to restorative justice instead of punishment and blame. The principle illustrated here is that caring often succeeds where fair retribution fails.

Explaining Blamelessness in Germany

In collecting the various explanations of Hitler's behavior, Rosenbaum also inadvertently collected evidence as to how people explain it *away*—how they think about the mitigation of guilt. None of his stories (if confirmed) would provide adequate grounds for acquitting Hitler of war crimes. In the new International Criminal Court, he would be convicted and sentenced to lifelong imprisonment but not executed.[33] To be sure, we can see now that he had some kind of horrible mental disorder, but to millions of German voters, *Der Führer* seemed not only normal but virtually superhuman. It would be impossible to declare him blameless on grounds of mental incompetence.

The story illustrates the ambiguity arising from an important legal principle—that mentally incompetent persons cannot be blamed for their actions.[34] If Hitler had suffered massive damage to his prefrontal cortex, for example, he would indeed have had grounds for acquittal of war crimes. But even if found blameless, he could never be forgiven and accepted back into society, as David was in the preceding story.

The Gold Standard of Blameworthiness

Ron Rosenbaum maintains that more people want to explain Hitler's behavior than to blame him and that to them, to explain means to exculpate or excuse. That is not my perception. I see almost nothing adduced to mitigate his guilt for genocide. Indeed, I see Hitler as uniquely important wherever the culture of blame prevails.

One illustration of this can be seen in a controversy that arose in 2002 over the planned production of a CBS miniseries on the young Adolf Hitler. This announcement evoked protests. People worried that the series might rekindle admiration for Hitler and his despicable politics.

As an example of blameworthiness, Hitler's life is in a class by itself. Yet the production of his biography presents the same challenges that arise every day when other morally depraved protagonists are portrayed on stage or screen. There is always a chance that the villain will be depicted in a sympathetic light, so that viewers will imitate him. Yet that possibility never seems to worry producers, whereas the Hitler miniseries was regarded as uniquely dangerous.

We might ask, Why a biography of Hitler? Why not of Roosevelt or Churchill instead? Or Raoul Wallenberg, Simone Weil, or Eleanor Roosevelt? We have much more to learn and apply in our own lives by studying great human beings than those who brought the world to catastrophe. I wouldn't ban the Hitler biography, but I doubt that anything ennobling will come of watching it. Why, then, are people fascinated by his pathological life story and afraid of its power?

My answer: He is blameworthy, and we can renew our commitment to blaming him by reviewing his life once again in every postwar generation. We need Hitler as a symbol—the gold standard against which to measure other wrongdoers, for much of our energy is devoted to allocating blame for evil.

A powerful argument in favor of the culture of blame can be seen in the writings of Hannah Arendt, who witnessed the war crimes trial of Adolf Eichmann, the bureaucrat who ran Hitler's death camps.[35] Eichmann's intentions were, in Arendt's opinion, utterly banal. He never hated Jews, had no personal desire to kill them, and got sick on the only occasion when he watched them being murdered. In fact, he wanted only to do his job well. Her inference about his lack of intention to do evil would ordinarily argue for a defendant's acquittal. However, contrary to the arguments of both the prosecution and defense, Arendt insisted that this should *not* mitigate his responsibility. Admitting that her opinion was unusual, she noted:

> [It is assumed] in all modern legal systems that intent to do wrong is necessary for the commission of a crime. On nothing, perhaps, has civilized jurisprudence prided itself more than on this taking into account of the subjective factor. Where this intent is absent, where, for whatever reasons, even reasons of moral insanity, the ability to distinguish between right and wrong is impaired, we feel no crime has been committed.[36]

But in judging Eichmann guilty, Arendt considers it irrelevant that the man actually seemed unable to distinguish right from wrong. Her own verdict is based instead on the much older principle: "that the very earth cries out for vengeance; that evil violates a natural harmony which only retribution can restore."[37] Possibly Aristotle would have agreed, for he, too, insisted that only after witnessing just retribution could playgoers feel satisfied—though he would expect them nevertheless to pity Eichmann.

Whether or not we accept Arendt's opinion that vengeance should be legally legitimate, we still need to distinguish between pity and forgiveness. Forgiveness can only be given freely. It is not obligatory.[38] And, although a Greek tragedy fills us with pity for both the evildoers and their victims, it does not release anyone from a painful end. The suffering must be completed, since forgiveness is generally impossible. Thus we pity Medea, a monstrous woman who killed her own innocent children to punish her faithless husband. Yet, whether or not we blame her, we see that her future must inevitably be terrible. And, whether by vengeance or some other mechanism, the lives of Eichmann and Hitler must end badly. Both were beyond the credible possibility of redemption.

Yet even in the case of Hitler, empathy can be a positive ethical influence. Insofar as empathy causes problems, it is more because of those whom we exclude than because of those whom we include. The world needs to understand Hitler—*plus* the Germans who brought him to power democratically, *plus* the great historical figures of his day who saved civilization, and especially *plus* the people whose lives he destroyed. We need to widen our view. Hitler refused to empathize with Jews, Gypsies, gays, and numerous other categories of people. In this mind-set lay the origin of his immorality. If, in empathizing with him, we come to pity him, this will not diminish our horror for the suffering he caused. Hitler was the author of one of humankind's worst tragedies. The value of a tragic drama comes from the pity it evokes in us. This is altogether different from exculpation or forgiveness.

Blame Is a Force That Gives Us Meaning

Blame provides an antidote to meaninglessness. People can mask their emptiness by stimulating adrenaline and dopamine with entertainment full of vicarious personal risk. Typically, they pick a violent movie or at least an agonistic battle of wits between FBI agents and terrorists, vampires and their slayers, emergency physicians and prevaricating patients, or homicide cops and murderers. A blaming plot must identify the bad guy and incarcerate, slay, or dematerialize him. As René Girard suggests, those who find life meaningless are especially likely to imitate the characters they watch. Thus the quest for meaning has social implications beyond private existential emptiness.

The less meaning we see in our daily problems, the more vicarious stimulation we may require.[39] Indeed, the distinctive pathology of modern civilization has been identified as the pervasive "lack of meaning"—an alienation most apparent in postmodern cultural relativism, which denies all meaning, except very locally and for a short term.

Therapists call meaninglessness a hidden epidemic. About one-quarter of the populations studied in Europe and North America express a sense that their lives are meaningless.[40] Carl Jung wrote that about one-third of his patients were not clinically neurotic but were suffering from the aimlessness of their existence.[41] Symptoms include boredom, drug dependency, alcoholism, and depression. According to personality inventories, those suffering from meaninglessness are disproportionately likely to be neurotic, introverted, hedonistic, and interested in excitement and personal comfort rather than idealistic or involved in community service or organized groups.[42]

However, no psychiatric symptoms may manifest at all. Some one-fourth of a sample of one hundred successful Harvard alumni also said that their own lives feel meaningless. Indeed, the tragic vision of our era is expressed in such bleak works as Beckett's *Waiting for Godot,* T. S. Eliot's *The Wasteland,* and Arthur Miller's *The Death of a Salesman.* These unheroic literary portraits do not resemble earlier tragedies, when protagonists had plenty of meaning in their lives, even if they failed to meet the challenges.

Boredom is easily masked by exposure to blaming plots. I think there's a causal connection between two cultural patterns: a sense of meaninglessness (which is often hidden) and a preference for violent entertainment apportioning blame. If I'm right, then to decrease violent blaming stories would only exacerbate the boredom—unless the decrease is compensated by prosocial, but equally intense, programming. Today writers tend to draw upon two institutions for their blaming plots: the criminal justice system and warfare.

Justice, Moral Blame, and Violence

Justice institutions count among humankind's greatest inventions. We benefit from objective judging by citizens who are not parties to the dispute, adherence to accepted laws, and standardization of punishment. Previously, the only redress available to victims of wrongdoing had been through private tit-for-tat vengeance. Without jurisprudence, no society could function as a modern democracy or economy.

The identification and punishment of wrongdoers makes for exciting plots. Detective stories bring the villain to justice, and solving the mystery somehow seems to restore harmony to the universe. But such stories reinforce the adversarial logic of blaming. Indignant blaming confers purpose and meaning. Some people even come to depend on it for their motivation and sense of orientation.

The same can be said of war, the most aversive activity known to human beings—apart from those who find it the ultimate entertainment. Chris Hedges has described this excitement honestly. After thirteen years as a full-time war correspondent throughout Central America, the Persian Gulf War, and the Balkans, Hedges wrote a memoir of his career, acknowledging that, like many other people, he had been addicted to war, unable to give it up: "The enduring attraction of war is this: Even with its destruction and carnage it can give us what we long for in life. It can give us purpose, meaning, a reason for living.... It gives us resolve, a cause. It allows us to be noble.... There is a part of me—maybe it is a part of many of us—that decided at certain moments that I would rather die like this than go back to the routine of life."[43]

Hedges acknowledges that war involves taking sides and blaming the enemy. He also admits that every warrior's attribution of blame for the horrors of battle requires indifference to the sufferings of those he kills, yet the mourning and veneration of his own dead.[44]

This dividing of human beings into those who do and do not deserve blame irresistibly seizes everyone involved in a war, including the journalists who cover it. Hedges admits remorsefully that reporters come to see their mission as the maintenance of "their" side's morale. Therefore, they rarely disclose the wrongdoings of their army when reporting from the field.[45]

Here blaming—the exclusion of the other side's experience from our empathy—yields untruth. Hedges does not say how to stop polarizing humankind into "blameworthy" and "innocent." Indeed, he believes it cannot be prevented during armed hostilities.

But polarization during war is an extreme version of everyday blaming—which can be *countered* as a cultural habit. Doing so may sometimes keep blaming from intensifying to levels at which war becomes thinkable. It is for the sake of a culture of peace that I criticize the culture of blame and violence. We can't eliminate all violence from society, but maybe we can reduce it. The starting point is to recast some past-oriented, blame-apportioning plots into future-oriented, problem-solving ones.

Amending Aristotle

While *The Poetics* has favorably influenced countless playwrights, preserving the immune systems and morale of vast audiences from emotional devastation, the time has come for a reappraisal of certain of its recommendations. I'll propose four amendments to Aristotle's advice: (1) a change in his guidelines concerning "equitable retribution," (2) a broadening of his notion of morality to include emotional appropriateness, (3) the addition of a brand-new rule advising writers to protect the attachments of their audience, and (4) the general maintenance of "ethical pluralism" in stories that portray immoral actions on the part of likeable characters.

Equitable Retribution as Moral Validation

Aristotle urged that characters receive a fair payoff for their morality. For a comedy, you invent good and bad people, and you ensure that they receive correspondingly good or bad luck.[46]

But tragedy is another matter, for despite being fair, you want the audience to empathize, especially with the protagonist, who must be morally "gray." Our sympathy for him will purify us, for pity is a finer emotion than hatred. Yet fairness will be sustained, and with it the morale of the audience, who see that ethical commitment is rewarded.

Zillmann's recommendation resembles Aristotle's except that he doesn't expect to produce pity, but only a simpler—even a shallow—satisfaction for the audience. Yet both Aristotle and Zillmann consider it demoralizing for a truly good character to incur undeserved misfortune. I want to amend this notion.

Probably as many tragedies violate the principles of fair retribution as conform to them. Indeed, we see increasingly often in films that criminals and rogues triumph in the end, as, for example, in *The Good Thief, The Italian Job,* and *Ocean's 11.* The audience is supposed to feel elated, having identified with the likeable robbers and killers instead of the cops. I can't justify such a denouement. Even a regular blame-apportioning potboiler would be better than such "crime does pay" romps, which induce mimesis among suggestible young theatergoers. Here Aristotle is exactly right.

On the other hand, there are countless stories about morally exemplary characters who encounter terrible destinies. Among them are such films about the Holocaust as *Life Is Beautiful,* in which the hero, a very good man indeed, perishes. In my perception, most viewers can tolerate such endings without lasting demoralization, which suggests that a reappraisal is required of Aristotle's theory.

We can tolerate seeing our beloved characters encounter hard circumstances, losses, or even death. If they get sick, lose their money, or are eaten by alligators, we don't feel that the author cheated us. What we cannot bear is that they end up with their moral accomplishments or failings unrecognized, deprived of the respect or love they had earned. Whether luck punishes or rewards them materially, in any fair conclusion their moral status must be confirmed for all to see. We demand that virtue be validated.

Suppose, for instance, a good character is mistakenly believed by the others to be evil. Suppose, further, that he dies, much to the satisfaction of the other characters, who never learn about his goodness even after his death. The audience will feel demoralized by this ending. Thus the issue of fairness remains important. Morality need not be paid off in material rewards or punishments, but eventually goodness or evil should be recognized.

A fair denouement sometimes includes redemption. The wrongdoers repent and seek forgiveness. Whether or not they receive a harsh fate in material terms, their remorse usually wins our forgiveness. Blaming plots, today's staple of the crime-and-punishment genre, rarely end with redemption, which is regrettable. The restoration of faith in wrongdoers inspires audiences, revives our hope, and even boosts our immunoglobulin A—at the price of rendering characters' blameworthiness ambiguous. But not all characters are credibly redeemable.

Emotional Appropriateness as a Moral Dimension

In advising writers to mete out fair retribution, both Aristotle and Zillmann assume that the morality of the characters determines whether we like them and wish them well. Contrary to their theory, we may like someone who is not good if she has high "emotional intelligence," to use psychologist Daniel Goleman's felicitous expression.

Our affective dispositions and empathy toward characters can't be explained entirely in terms of their rectitude. Hearts are not attracted exclusively to highly moral individuals. If you review your own relationships, you'll discover endearing foibles that have appealed to you. I myself tend to feel fond of people whose flaws I share and can therefore easily forgive. I am less attracted toward paragons whose ethical excellence makes me feel puny in comparison.

My preferences are not unique. As Joseph Campbell once commented, "The perfect human being is uninteresting—the Buddha who leaves the world, you know. It is the imperfections of life that are lovable."[47] Nevertheless, the perverse proclivities that I share with Campbell fit neither Zillmann's nor Aristotle's model, for they both assume that our affection for characters will be proportional to their virtues.

How, then, can we reconcile the incongruity of liking people for traits irrelevant to ethics? Consider, for instance, the public's liking of John F. Kennedy and Bill Clinton, even after their morally questionable sexual adventures had become well-known. Clinton could probably have been reelected after his impeachment, had the Constitution not limited him to two terms. Why were these men more beloved than admired?

Because of the broad nature of morality, which includes our appraisal of the other person's emotional intelligence. Before a character makes any fateful ethical decisions, we see his emotional reactions and we already begin judging him. Both Kennedy and Clinton empathized when they listened to Americans talking about their problems. Not every politician is so warmly and appropriately responsive.

Is it fair to blame a person for his emotions?[48] Perhaps not, for feelings arise spontaneously and cannot be controlled precisely, even when one wishes to do so—which anyway is not always a good thing to attempt. There are no laws against any emotions. Our only legal obligations are to perform certain actions overtly. Nevertheless, our feelings show how we are oriented. If a person's emotional reactions are inappropriate, we expect her to run into trouble. In many plays, the protagonist's flaws first becomes apparent when she shows a questionable emotional orientation.

We hold each other accountable for our feelings. When we describe a person's character, we mention traits involving both feelings and habits of mind. Consider a few such adjectives: Silly. Stubborn. Truculent. Generous. Petulant. Resilient. Energetic. Demanding. Idealistic. All of these attitudes involve composites of feeling, thinking, and behaving tendencies. And all of them can be considered "moral" dispositions. We judge people morally without evidence as to whether they habitually violate ethical or legal rules. If someone giggles a lot and speaks primarily about frivolous matters, he will be considered an unpromising candidate for positions of authority. Such a verdict is a *moral* judgment.

We can keep both Aristotle's and Zillmann's theories of audience empathy if we widen the meaning of moral perception to include appraisals of emotional appropriateness. Within that wider definition, we do usually want writers to allocate happiness or unhappiness to their characters on the basis of their moral performances.

Protect the Audience's Attachments

Generally I have avoided proposing rules of ethical writing, but I do want to elevate one principle to that status: Always protect the attachments of readers toward your characters.

We can watch our beloved characters face hardship, deprivation, and suffering. We can even accept the tragic loss of those whom we love. *What we cannot accept is the loss of love itself.*

A talented fiction writer may make us love a character as deeply as we have ever loved any real person. Intense empathy, attachment, and limerence are among life's greatest experiences. Deep love does not happen every day, and for a few unfortunate individuals it may never happen. Love is transformative; it restores your emotional well-being and preserves your health. It opens the personality to change and, yes, makes you vulnerable. Yet its greatest danger is the possibility of its loss. The loss of love undermines resilience, saps courage from the soul, and renders life meaningless.

In many tragedies, good persons are brought to ruin or death. If we loved them before, we love them in their desolation and after their demise. The other characters who loved them beforehand also still love them afterward.

Hardly ever does a writer depict a good character whom we have come to love deeply as failing morally in the end and depriving us of any basis for forgiving him. To make us love, and then hate, a character who remains unredeemed at the end of the drama is possibly the most harmful plot a writer can create. We can bear losing a loved one, but it is far worse to lose our love for that person.

The best stories involve flawed but beautiful persons whose lives zigzag unpredictably. We must live with their imperfections, hoping for redemption. We intend to stick with the hero until the end. But occasionally we cannot do so. The protagonist can go so far wrong that we must give up on him and *break empathy*. Our friend has now become an enemy, and, in distress, we wish for his downfall.

I e-mailed about forty of my friends, asking them, "Can you think of a novel, film, play, or movie in which the lead character is initially the hero or heroine—someone whom you like or love—but who later behaves so badly (or has such inappropriate emotional reactions) that by the end of the story you actively dislike him or her? Did you break empathy with the character? How did you feel at the end?"

Of the replies, only ten stories were named that contain reversals from strong positive affect to strong negative affect. One friend named a suspense film, *Jagged Edge*, which he now wishes he had not seen. Another mentioned a David Mamet film starring Steve Martin, *The Spanish Prisoner*, which surprised and disappointed him because a presumed hero turned out to be a villain. Someone mentioned both *The Music Man* and *Breaking the Waves* as glorifying the worst kind of patriarchal abuse. He said many people had walked out of the theater during the latter film, which he had hated. Two people mentioned the same film, *The Talented Mr. Ripley*, and reported disliking it intensely. One person named both *Othello* and *Macbeth*, but it is not clear whether at the beginning he had strongly liked both protagonists, or only mildly so. (Mild liking would disqualify the play from this category.) Another friend mentioned the film *Talk to Her*, in which a formerly likeable man rapes and impregnates a comatose woman. One man mentioned the protagonist of a novel, *The Count of Monte Cristo*. Finally, one friend mentioned Vikram Seth's novel, *An Equal Music*, whose protagonist she came to dislike. She said she would never read another novel by Seth.

The impressive thing is that, all told, forty of my friends could think of only ten such plots. That indicates that the hero-turns-villain phenomenon must be extremely rare—and for one clear reason: people hate stories of this kind. Not one person said he or she had ever enjoyed a story in which it had been necessary to break empathy with a previously beloved character, if empathy had remained broken at the end.[49] Such a plot is almost a certain formula for failure. (*Othello* and *Macbeth* may be exceptions, but I myself never loved either protagonist at the beginning, nor did I break empathy with them at the end. I pitied them both.)

Beyond these ten, a few informants mentioned stories in which the reversal of affect was considerable but the empathy remained unbroken. One friend mentioned several novels in which we mildly dislike characters at the beginning and really hate them by the end (e.g., Tom Wolfe's *Bonfire of the Vanities* and Russell Banks's *Continental Drift*). Another person mentioned several novels by Margaret Atwood in which we feel distant from the protagonist all along. In *Alias Grace* we do not know at the end whether or not Grace was a murderer.

Then there is Joy Kogawa's novel *The Rain Ascends,* in which the protagonist Millicent only slowly acknowledges that her beloved father is a pedophile who has abused three hundred boys, including her own son. This story does not count as one of the plots I was looking for because, although it is *about* the experience we are interested in, it is the protagonist who experiences the disillusionment, not the readers. We retain strong sympathy for Millicent until the end, and indeed, she manages to retain her love for her father, despite her terrible disappointment in him.

Finally, we return to *The Sopranos.* I don't classify it among the empathy-breaking plots because we know from the beginning that Tony Soprano is both a ruthless murderer and a lovable guy with a soul. The writers have not tricked us into loving someone who will later shock us (we are shocked from the outset), so I would not count this writing as unethical. If we are willing to empathize even slightly with Tony, we know we are entering a difficult relationship.

Still, the difficulty is greater than we may have considered. We are supposed to stay with him emotionally, no matter what he does. I found that painful. For example, Tony was once arrested. I found myself wanting him to outwit the FBI, though I knew he was guilty. Yet I also had a metaresponse of guilt—of hating myself for wanting evil to win out over morality and justice. (This is the reverse of my metaresponse of feeling pleased with myself for suffering with the protagonist of a tragedy.) Indeed, after watching every episode of *The Sopranos,* I felt physically unwell, depressed, and disgusted throughout the next day or two, as if I had personally participated in those reprehensible acts. Both empathy and the breaking of empathy can hurt. Eventually, I chose the latter course and stopped watching. I had never really loved the guy, which is fortunate because if I had, the empathic rupture would have hurt too much. All writers should pay attention to this possibility and protect their audiences from unnecessary suffering.

Ethical Pluralism in Stories about Likeable but Immoral Characters

So far, I have not questioned Aristotle's recommendation that we learn to empathize with and even pity morally imperfect characters. In general, he was right. However, every writer must consider the harm that may come from the audience's identification with gray characters. Different answers are possible. According to Zillmann's theory, we must be made to care about the characters—and that requires that they display good morals. But some shows today are extremely popular, though the characters are mainly villainous.

True, we can learn *something* by empathizing with almost anyone, so we may willingly explore life through the eyes of appalling people. Our affection for them may overcome the blaming habit that I've criticized, teaching us that human beings can be evil in some ways while also possessing redeeming qualities. This is an important lesson.

On the other hand, according to research on learning, if we like an immoral character and see ourselves as resembling him, we're more likely to imitate him than if we hadn't empathized at all. This evidently does happen. James Gandolfini, the actor who plays Tony Soprano, considered quitting the show after a couple of seasons because his character became a cult hero, and it worried him. Adolescents wrote, expressing a hope to be like him when they grow up. Gandolfini was particularly bothered that Tony killed his best friend. "People ask me to come and talk to their kindergarten class about Tony Soprano," he said. "It boggles my mind, and I say, 'Are you watching the show?'"[50] Gandolfini denied, however, that the show was saying that crime pays. "Tony Soprano is miserable, and so is everyone he works with. We never glorify the violence."

Another actor, Joe Pantoliano, played Ralph Cifaretto, a member of Tony's mob family who was vastly nastier than his boss. The exasperated Tony finally murdered him. Later, in a *New York Times* interview, Pantoliano said, "I've always felt as an actor that the antagonist was a more interesting way to go. I think Iago is a more interesting character than Othello." But the violence and the apparent lust for it from fans troubled him. "As an actor, it was my duty to the character to justify his behavior, at least to myself. Now that I'm not Ralph anymore ... I hate him."[51]

The question is, How can a playwright depict morally spotty characters without suggesting that the audience should internalize their deplorable values?

One solution, in a single play, is to make sure the evildoers suffer in the end. However, in an episodic series, this will not work. The wicked protagonist would be finished during the first show, whereas he must keep going for years.

A better approach is to maintain ethical pluralism throughout the series by including characters who comment negatively on the others' bad deeds. In a Greek tragedy, this is the responsibility of the chorus, usually several players who remain onstage observing the drama. They represent the values of normal society, so that when anticipating a murder, they express shock, articulating the values of society.

In today's dramas, no Greek chorus is on the set commenting as Tony Soprano whacks his enemies. However, Tony's psychiatrist, Dr. Melfi, performs that function. He doesn't tell her everything about his illegal activities, but she understands the general idea and indicates that his misery comes from the ethics that he is repressing. Her presence allows for the expression of a value system that the other characters couldn't plausibly hold. A different television series, of course, might use the heroine's hairdresser or the hero's bartender as the show's Greek chorus.

The plurality of moral perspectives needs to be *explicitly articulated* to make the audience think about what they have seen. This advice goes against certain artistic notions. A great writer may just hint at a character's underlying intentions, letting readers reach their own contradictory conclusions. However, if Dr. Melfi, for example, is to supply a wiser perspective than Tony's own, she must express it plainly, not just show subtle dismay on her face. Learning is cognitive. Even if life itself keeps disproving our theories and prejudices, we usually keep them until someone challenges them explicitly. That is what therapy does, and that also is how stories can have therapeutic effects.

Sensation and Meaning

The twenty-five most successful movies (the ones mentioned earlier that killed nine billion people) were popular. People paid to see them. Blaming is exciting. It gives us meaning, just as hatred and wars give us meaning. Something important is at stake. We feel alive, committed, engaged, justified.

If a primary motive for blaming is to mask the everyday lack of meaning, then writers face an ethical dilemma. If they diminish the culture of blame, they must provide some compensation. This is possible. The entertainment industry can stimulate the autonomic nervous system—including adrenaline, cortisol, dopamine, and the nucleus accumbens area of the brain, which is responsible for the uptake of dopamine[52]—by portraying the novel adventures of people who are living bravely and meaningfully in the service of humankind. But this approach will require new thinking.

Researcher Mary-Wynne Ashford distinguishes between two problems, both of which may manifest as boredom: unsatisfied sensation seeking, on the one hand, and meaninglessness, on the other. (Some people experience both.) Sensation seekers often are dependent on aggressive or hostile entertainment.[53] The thinness of their sense of meaning may give rise to a fascination with blame, which masks the emptiness while also creating the psychological conditions for mimetic rivalry and violence.

To address meaninglessness as a source of boredom, a more cognitive approach is needed. This is compatible with the production of more arousing, pro-social entertainment. Writers can address meaninglessness as a core existential problem, ideally by pointing toward answers instead of merely illustrating the despair that it causes. Stories can assist meaning seekers by showing potential sources of genuine purpose.

Viktor E. Frankl was a psychiatrist who created "logotherapy" as a treatment for meaninglessness. He offered no generic answers to it but helped individuals locate meaning, moment by moment. Frankl wrote that "mass neurosis of the present time can be described as a private and personal form of nihilism; for nihilism can be defined as the contention that being has no meaning."[54]

Frankl spent much of World War II as a Jewish prisoner in Nazi death camps. His book recounts not only horrors but also inspiring insights. Even while suffering physically, he remained free inwardly and sometimes felt joy. He thought often about his wife and spoke to her in his mind. She was already dead, though he had no way of knowing it. The meaning of his life, at such a moment, was just to keep on loving her. He wrote, "In a position of utter desolation, when man cannot express himself in positive action, when his only achievement may consist in enduring his sufferings in the right way—an honorable way—in such a position man can, through loving contemplation of the image he carries of his beloved, achieve fulfillment."[55]

Frankl shared with the other prisoners his awareness that, moment by moment, life presents us with *assignments directed uniquely to oneself.* Life "calls" on us, he said, and we must actively discover its full message as we go through our day. That is its meaning. Happiness is a by-product of our search, our willingness to make the most of each possibility. Frankl's own call, his vocation, his assignment, usually was to ease the mental suffering of the other prisoners, and even of the guards, whenever that was possible. Many prisoners chose to die with their integrity intact rather than submit to degradation. Sometimes, Frankl wrote, all that life presents us is suffering. Even then, we can discover meaning in our assignment. But more often, we have options, and the meaningfulness of life consists of our willingness to seek and fulfill the unique tasks to which life summons us.

When prisoners lost purpose in their lives, Frankl tried to recall them to the projects they had taken seriously before or the people they had loved. When he failed to rekindle their meaning, he said, they always died within a few days. They gave up, got sick, or even threw themselves onto an electric fence.

Other therapists agree that the neurosis of our time is meaninglessness and nihilism. (John Lennon's murderer, for instance, claimed that his motive for killing had been to make his life significant.)[56] If contemporary life feels meaningless, it is partly for lack of daunting challenges to satisfy those who want thrills. In fact, as we bring democracy, health, and human security to the planet, fewer dangerous challenges remain open for risk takers. They may become even more dependent on vicarious thrills from entertainment or go out for real dangers, such as extreme sports, that lack social value.

I am not a sensation seeker at all (quite the opposite), but one defining moment of my life occurred when I was seven. My grandmother was the Sunday school teacher that day, and she was explaining heaven to us kids. She said that it was a wonderful place with no problems whatever. Anything you desired, you could have instantly, effortlessly. There would be no pain or deprivation or difficulty. Instantly I made up my mind. I will refuse to go there! Heaven would be unbearably boring. I intend to go someplace that has plenty of problems.

Instead of too many problems, this world has a shortage of them. We complain about all our problems, but the excellent ones actually are so scarce that we settle for trivial ones, such as acquiring more stuff than we need, killing time with crossword puzzles, or traveling to resorts where there is still nothing to do.

People need more real problems—life-and-death catastrophes that must be handled. Or scientific problems for which a brilliant discovery will make a big difference. People need to contribute to the world. Probably there are endless excellent problems that we can't recognize when we see them. There's nothing wrong with crosswords, but if you were Albert Einstein, you'd find better puzzles. He discovered relativity by imagining what he would see if he were riding a photon through the depths of space. As my professor Karl Popper once said in a lecture, a creative person is someone with a good nose for a worthwhile problem.

This little homily may seem to contradict Frankl's advice to accept what life hands us, for we can find moments of joy even in the worst places on Earth. But Frankl said more than that, too. He said that we have to search actively for the assignments that life hands us. They aren't apparent. We need a good nose. We always miss some of our assignments, and some people miss most of theirs—which gave Frankl the opportunity to serve by helping prisoners and patients find meaning. He had a great nose.

The absence of personal meaning in one's life leaves a void that may be filled with mimetic desires, keep-up-with-the-Joneses values, and shallow distractions, including entertainment oriented toward the search for blameworthy characters.

Unfortunately, most writers today seem to lack good noses. They could be telling stories that prompt audiences to address a whole range of new, complex, and important issues.[57] They could create plots about significant controversies and bold, wise characters who take risks for humanitarian causes. Instead, we get to study the life of Hitler. And we get movies in which one baby is born and survives, two people die naturally, and nine billion are killed.

Conclusion

The ethical responsibilities of fiction writers are complex, requiring that contradictory concerns somehow be balanced. Vicarious experiences with fictional lives may have genuine health consequences for audiences; but even so, some people may conceivably benefit from stimulation that harms others, and there is no way to predict the outcome reliably now. Moreover, both empathy and the experience of breaking that empathy may cause suffering. A related contradiction is that empathy for an imperfect character may induce our imitation of him or, alternatively, may deepen our compassion for human frailty. There is no way of codifying these considerations as rules for writers.

However, in his day Aristotle did try to advise tragedians about how to take ethical care of their audiences, and his admonitions are a good starting point for us today. He expected that their empathy would endure until the protagonist met her terrible fate. Pity was essential for the spiritual growth of the theatergoers, yet the characters must also receive equitable retribution, according to the morality of their lives. Only a protagonist of "middling" character could properly be allocated such suffering in the end. This did not involve blame, for the Greek culture was oriented toward shame, not guilt, and one's faults could be attributed to the gods. Then and now, empathy is necessary for rich human relationships and for normal moral development. Yet, it can be so painful that we cannot always sustain it. Some amendments to Aristotle's advice should be considered.

For one thing, I have suggested that a character's overt morality is not the only determinant of our love for her. Her emotional appropriateness is a moral dimension that attracts or repels us, too, whether or not she violates laws or standards of decency.

Today immoral characters (including emotionally inappropriate ones) generally are objects not of our pity but rather of blame. This cultural habit means that modern audiences often lack the spiritual benefits that come from empathizing with challenging "gray" characters.

Moreover, the casting of blame instead of pity is a major obstacle to a culture of peace. Polarization cannot be prevented in wartime, but the everyday habit of finding fault can be reduced, and it is the first step toward extreme polarization. Writers can redress the cultural imbalance in modern society by providing more endings that involve redemption and restorative justice. However, sensation seekers may view such a shift away from blaming themes as a deprivation if they have depended on blaming plots as a source of meaning. Writers therefore must compensate for this deprivation by pointing toward constructive, yet arousing, ways of living.

Indeed, every author has some responsibility for us, who have trusted him by following his character where he has led us. Every empathic rupture is hard on our souls. Writers should never induce love in us for a character and then turn him into villain on whom we must give up, losing our love.

The duties of writers are not simple matters that can easily be codified. Instead, they must balance contradictory considerations to protect the well-being of the public. But this is a high calling that, when performed well, is among the greatest contributions to humankind.

Part II

To choose stories, we depend on critics who watch or read on our behalf ahead of time, informing us about their own ethical and emotional reactions. We need critics whose sensibilities are trustworthy, and they need to know what to look for. Here I illustrate by reviewing two television series in terms of how they fulfill some of the uses for entertainment.

Individuals will always differ in our needs for cultural products. We require better ways of obtaining the kinds of products that meet those individual needs. Yet entertainment is not just a private consumer activity; it is also the way to re-create the world collectively. It is our pleasure, our responsibility, and our greatest resource as a society.

Chapter 7

Justice and the Thrill Gene

Drama can provoke us to question taken-for-granted theories and everyday social institutions. But actually this is rare. As we'll see in this chapter, cliffhangers and cop shows are never combined with social analysis. You're not supposed to think much while you're watching—which (I hate to admit) proves that Plato was right: stirring dramas give you more emotion than wisdom. For smart ideas, you need logical discourse—the kind of reasoning that a philosopher employs. Or a *Northern Exposure* writer. Or a theologian, sociologist, legislator, or criminologist.

Arousing stories may have valid, urgent social implications that writers don't make explicit. "Show, don't tell," they say, and what is shown must be fast-paced. The characters' motivations and what they learn from their experience shouldn't be discussed.

That's a big mistake. Plato and Aristotle aren't actually incompatible. We learn from both our feelings and our reflective discussions. Tolstoy ended *War and Peace* with an essay on history and militarism—without spoiling his novel one whit.

We'll explore in this chapter exactly the kind of show that, according to Steven Johnson, makes us smarter for watching it. It has multiple storylines; the editors cut scenes fast; and lots of facts are left unexplained, so that we must guess at the writers' intentions. You have to work hard to figure out what is going on—and the effort may indeed strengthen your intellectual muscles. It may not, however, deepen your insights or make you mull over the implications.

Street Time is an agonistic television series about criminals and law enforcement officers. It was better than average for its genre, and it made a powerful point that we in Western societies need to learn. But because that message was conveyed without discursive analysis, no viewer would be led toward reforming the criminal justice system. Only afterward, as I considered what the show *should* have said, did I explore alternatives that it might have presented to all of us. Here's how it all began.

I had not been able to observe the production of *Northern Exposure,* as I felt I needed to do. Fortunately, its star, Rob Morrow, was shooting a new series, *Street Time,*[1] only four miles from my home. I was permitted to observe production during the summers of 2002 and 2003. Though *Street Time* was a violent thriller—poles apart from *Northern Exposure*—it was atypical, for it rarely apportioned blame to the characters, and it treated most criminals sympathetically. It was mainly about the relationship between a parole officer, James Liberti, played by Scott Cohen, and a hashish smuggler parolee, Kevin Hunter, played by Morrow. The two men were remarkably alike, except that one of them was in charge of the other.

I sat on the set knitting, getting to know the people and the story they were creating. I said I was doing anthropological fieldwork and that they were my "tribe." If an actor wanted to chat, she knew she would not be bothering a knitter, whereas she would not have spoken if I had been reading. Without knitting I might also have watched too intently, making my tribe consider me some kind of vulture.

Richard Stratton, the show's creator and producer, generously allowed me to be present on the set for about three hundred hours and gave me tapes to show in my living room every week to six friends, who discussed each episode afterward. Thus I was able to compare the production and the consumption ends of the show to see which creative intentions were fulfilled and to theorize about how. But my larger objective was to see how a gritty crime show might offer reformist criticism of social institutions—in this case, the criminal justice system. Later I'll analyze the plot with that in mind, but first I'll describe the people on the set.

An Ethnography of Television Production

A comparative ethnographer can do no better than compare *Street Time* to a 1979 book by Ben Stein. *The View from Sunset Boulevard*[2] describes the worldview of the writers and producers of American television shows. There were then only about three hundred active television writers and producers. Stein liked them all, though initially his values differed from theirs. He considered the Hollywood television world liberal. He compared them to other people with whom he was more familiar—probably a conservative lot, since he had previously worked for Richard Nixon.

Many of these people came from New York. Few of them had academically prestigious educations. They were not deeply informed about current affairs. Extremely optimistic and cheerful, they displayed enormous social skills, such as tact and friendliness. Instead of living wildly, they worked hard and then went home faithfully to their wives and children.

Stein's writers and producers infused their scripts with their own values. They regarded businesspeople as evil—and the bigger the business, the worse the businessperson. They accepted conspiracy theories, such as the notion that the world is run by multinational executives with links to the Mafia.

Mostly city born, the producers and writers viewed small towns as dangerous, reactionary places, contrary to the traditional portrait of the small town as the repository of all that is good about America. Shows are almost always set in Los Angeles or New York. The producers prefer New York because it is more stimulating.

Television producers invert traditional values, wrote Stein. For example, they do not emphasize religion or education. They portray mainstream religion as irrelevant, while education is downright suspect.

> Generally a highly educated man is a fool or a knave. Study or introspection is worthless. Deep thought is the villain's tool. Humility and modesty are ruses and tricks. On television, if you've got it, flaunt it.... Speed, action, squealing tires, and screeching brakes on Topanga Canyon Boulevard are what count. On television everyone with money has a swimming pool and only villains have a library.[3]

Television crimes are mostly violent, says Stein, and committed by well-to-do people, not members of a minority group. Why? The writers blame violent street crime not on the criminal but on a larger social failure.[4] If we see a petty thug, he is supposedly controlled by business or the underworld.

Stein claims that television dramas portray rich people as bad, and poor people as good. These beliefs were a residue of Marxism; many of the writers had been leftists and were proud of it, though their attitudes also included an element of capitalism. The producers liked the entrepreneurial system, while disliking big corporations. Stein did not suggest that the views of TV writers and producers resembled those of their viewers. He accused prime-time television of attacking the old American culture.

Do these dramas influence public opinion? Stein did not pose the question, but clearly the answer is yes. However, television genres rise and fall, depending on what the ratings suggest that the public wants. Presumably televised values also shift, though researchers have rarely analyzed their political impact.[5]

When I compare Ben Stein's portrait of Hollywood television culture to the *Street Time* producers, I find remarkable resemblances. The show is set in New York, and, yes, one of the coproducers and both of the male stars are New Yorkers, born and bred. (Stratton himself grew up in Massachusetts.)

Yes, the *Street Time* producers and writers have "enormous social skills"—reportedly better, in fact, than the average Hollywood producer. The cast and crew really seem to like each other.

Yes, they work hard and go home faithfully to their families. In fact, Stratton even brought his family to work with him. His two young sons were on the set almost every day, and his wife told me they are home-schooling the kids.

Yes, their social values are liberal. I'll bet they are not Republicans.

Yes, religion is rarely mentioned in a script. The parolee Kevin Hunter is a WASP and his wife Rachel Goldstein is Jewish, but when their son Sean asked what *he* is, they just said, "Whatever you want to be."

Yes, education never comes up. I can only recall seeing one book in the apartments or offices of any of the characters. Kevin has a degree in business administration, but nobody has intellectual inclinations.

Yes, there is a lot of violent crime, and, yes, it is rarely performed by minorities. When shown, blacks or Latinos are good people in difficult situations. We rarely feel wholly unsympathetic to characters.

Yes, rich people are bad—at least to judge by the only superrich woman in the story. And yes, despite this, there is a tendency to favor capitalism. Kevin is in the marijuana business—definitely for profit. He also runs a nightclub and sells art in a pricey gallery. There is no implied criticism of commercial activity. In short, Stein was spot-on correct in his predictive description of the *Street Time* producers.

In another sense, too, the *Street Time* creative workers share a cultural value with other television artists: *realism.* Theirs may be the most realistic show of its genre. It aims to surprise, but only with events that might occur in real life. Everyone involved with this show values spontaneity and immediacy. The actors seem natural, and the cinematography and lighting make them look authentic rather than handsome. To assure the verisimilitude of the parole office, a real U.S. parole officer watches, flagging any inaccuracies.

Life as a Source

The show's creator, Stratton, is an unmatched expert on marijuana smuggling and the life of prisoners and parolees, for this has been his own life. Morrow's character is based on that life.

Fig. 7.1. Richard Stratton, about a year after his release from prison. Photo by Wayne Maser.

Stratton is an extremely likable man. Yet he was a thrill seeker who tested every rule as a boy and was even sent to reform school. He began importing marijuana from Mexico while he was in college, then dropped out of university entirely to smuggle tons of hashish at a time, making $12 million or $15 million per year. Besides numerous houses, he owned ranches, an airplane, and a horse farm—and went through cash like water. He knew that he was collecting material for stories and that eventually he would be a writer. He was caught, but after his first arrest, he skipped the country to go to Lebanon, where he lived the high life leading a hippie mafia group for a year, still plying the hashish trade.

Yet, he told me, "Even then, I felt the spiritual emptiness of what I was doing. It wasn't satisfying my creative urges. I felt that making money was a gamble. Win or lose, it's really not about that. It's about this crazy adrenaline high we become addicted to. So before I went to prison, I knew I was neglecting what I really wanted to do. And then when I went to prison, I resolved to change that. I would find something more lasting."

In 1982, he slipped secretly into Los Angeles to collect a $6 million debt, but he was arrested instead. This time, he would serve time. He was thirty-six years old. The federal agents offered him leniency in exchange for testimony against his friend Norman Mailer, whom they believed to be a drug kingpin. He was not. Stratton refused, so the judge imposed a twenty-five-year prison sentence. It was a turning point in his life, he told me one day during lunch: "Being in prison is kind of like being in a monastery. A place to reflect on who you were and how you got there. That's what it became for me. I had meditated before, but in prison I got into it seriously. I started reading books about the growth of the soul and the inner journey." He also started reading law in the prison library and writing seriously. He wrote a novel about risk takers in the drug trade.

After eight years, Stratton successfully appealed his case. Out on parole (a phase that is called "street time"), Stratton married and, with his wife Kim Wozencraft, published a magazine for ex-convicts. When he met the producer Marc Levin, they began working as a team, making documentaries about prison life—an experience that kept them more comfortable with spontaneity and improvisation than the average filmmaker.

The idea for *Street Time* occurred to Stratton when he was sitting in the parole office waiting room with other parolees, many of whom knew each other. Whenever a parole officer opened the door to summon someone, everyone hushed up, for they were not supposed to speak to other parolees. This and the curious relationships between the officers and parolees struck Stratton as a wonderful topic for a television series.

Improvisation

The *Street Time* show is remarkable for its realism and its extensive use of improvisation. In mainstream productions, actors can rarely even negotiate a change in the script. But with astonishing frequency, *Street Time* actors ad-libbed or conferred with the director and Stratton, who often incorporated their views into the script on the spot. During the second season, whole scenes were occasionally improvised. The script was then written, after the fact. The actors truly loved this extraordinary opportunity, and everyone agreed that it improved the quality of the show.

Dealing with Showtime

The creative makers of television and films normally clash with the producers in Hollywood who handle the financial end and whose opinions tend to be formulaic. Producers typically watch what is popular on other channels and try to copy that—generally meeting the resistance and barely disguised contempt of the creative workers.

These usual conflicts—and eventually some unusually serious ones—emerged in *Street Time*. After every episode was edited by the director in Toronto, it would be sent to Hollywood to the cable executives, who could reedit it to suit their tastes. And even before the filming began, they had a say about the plots. For example, early in the show Stratton's writers planned for the parolee Kevin Hunter to commit a murder. The executives turned this idea down—not because they didn't want to show violence (they actually wanted more of it) but because they believed it would make Kevin irredeemable. I think they were right, but Stratton doesn't believe that anyone is irredeemable. And as far as realism goes, his experience carries weight. For example, I saw an astonishing memo to his writers in which he explained:

> I agree that Kevin has to take steps to kill Goldie. This actually happened to me. I went to pick up my brother-in-law at the time (though the marriage was common law) and had a nine millimeter under the seat and I was going to kill him. I was convinced he was going to send us all to prison. He started telling me a sob story about how ineffectual he felt around his wife, and so on, until I totally lost the nerve and drove him to a bar where we spent the rest of the evening drinking. He died in a plane crash (doing a deal behind my back with my airplane) a couple of years later. But putting the gun to his head? Maybe.

Values in Showbiz

Being on the set gave me time to talk—or even argue—with the producers and actors. I'll mention two such debates: (1) moral ambiguity and retribution, and (2) the relative merits of explicitness and subtlety in writing.

Moral Ambiguity and Retribution

Since Aristotle wrote *The Poetics,* drama has reaffirmed the rightness of a universe that gives each of us, ultimately, our just deserts. But no longer. Today, most dramatists prefer realistic plays, and realism recognizes that life is not just. Innocent people are wrongfully executed, with no one ever discovering the truth. Guilty people get away with murder. These things happen. To say so is realism.

If the villain goes unpunished and the hero unacknowledged, the audience will be upset. But *how bad* can a protagonist become without losing the empathy of viewers—or without causing them to switch off the TV in disgust? The answers to this question differ from one genre to another. In melodramas, we used to see unmitigated villainy, but it was always punished, and we cheered when the evildoer got his comeuppance. There was no empathizing with the likes of him.

Today's morally ambiguous plots are the antithesis of melodrama. We empathize with the whole ethically gray cast, and some of us wind up imitating an attractive but unprincipled character, who often fares quite well in the end. Therein lies the seductive depravity for which television, not unfairly, is accused.

The two male stars of *Street Time,* Scott Cohen and Rob Morrow, both told me that they would never play a monstrous character with whom the audience must break empathy. Yet both of them have played villains. Cohen said, "If I play a villain, the audience has to like me. The way I approach any character is that there is something in him that creates empathy." (But I broke empathy with him at the end of season 1.)

There are real problems in this business of "humanizing" villains. Empathy does increase the probability of mimesis. Morrow insists that it is irresponsible to "humanize" Hitler unless the terrible consequences of his actions are also made apparent within each episode of the show.

In *Street Time,* both protagonists make huge moral mistakes, but the ugly outcomes of their bad decisions don't occur until later in the series. A viewer of any one episode may have the impression that "crime pays." How can writers neutralize this message before the denouement, when (usually) crime stops paying so handsomely?[6] A plurality of moral perspectives can be offered. One way is to write comments into the script that criticize the questionable actions of the lovable protagonist. Yet dramatists dislike such commentaries, which they consider "spoon-feeding" the audience.

Spoon-feeding

Greek drama began with the chorus. Later one actor stepped out from it and performed—and then more and more actors. But the chorus remained, witnessing and articulating the opinions of mainstream society about what was going on.

When I suggested to Morrow that *Street Time* needed a "Greek chorus," he immediately understood my rationale. If a character justifies his criminal behavior, another voice is needed to express noncriminal opinions. Such alternative perspectives can be presented by anyone—even an anonymous passerby who can be overheard discussing a moral issue like the one in the plot. Morrow expressed misgivings. "Comments should only be used as a last resort," he said. Normally the dramatic situation should carry the viewer along.

Fair enough. Writing is richer for being subtle and ambiguous. Declarations may spoon-feed certain readers at the price of spoiling a delicate insight for others. Hence a creative storyteller sometimes must choose between clarity and subtlety. Stratton particularly likes to leave matters ambiguous. While admiring his artistry, I am not convinced that the moral impact on the audience is negligible.

I had lunch with Michelle Nolden, the actress who plays Rachel Goldstein, the spouse of the marijuana dealer parolee, Kevin Hunter. Again I mentioned having a Greek chorus make comments representing the values of normal society. Nolden pointed out that Kevin's parole officer does so, though morally he is as ambiguous as Kevin. She said:

> What often keeps us in check is not pure. We've got this great character, Liberti, who plays the opposite side of Kevin: "You'll go back to prison if you continue to do this. Think about your family." But we know that he is harming his own family, too. That's why I think it works so well, because the "Greek Chorus" is also flawed. Everybody is flawed in real society. The church is flawed because it's made up of people with power. The government, the institutions that keep us straight, are flawed as well.

Only later did I recognize the basis of our dispute. Nolden is a realist, and I'm an idealist. Even if all the characters are flawed, I want someone to point toward a deeper truth, a more valid resolution. Nolden's position is postmodern, I think. There is no truth, say postmodernists. There is only this perspective or that perspective. The best you can do is change from one flawed perspective to another, for you can never transcend such limitations. I would not be satisfied with such a relativistic view, for it treats both faith and rationality as delusory.

But Nolden is thoughtful. She said, "I want to be involved in dramas that get people talking. I don't want to sway people one way or the other. I'm in favor of putting it out there and letting people make their own decisions. There is still a lesson to be learned—that people can be disillusioned with society."

Another reason why Nolden would rarely use comments is that she does not believe that audiences should be thinking. "If there is too much commentary," she said, "they end up in their heads. You need to get them in their gut, so that they are feeling it before they are actually thinking it. They should simply be lost in their feelings. Then afterward, they can think about it. Some people need to be banged over the head. Other people need more subtlety."

That's the issue, of course—how to balance subtlety and spoon-feeding. I prefer shows that have a message, but, all too often, I miss the intended message. Unlike Nolden, I don't believe that people usually do think about a drama's implications afterward. I myself rarely do so. If we don't grasp the meaning at the time, we never will.

To change our way of living, someone has to influence our minds, our way of thinking. Experience alone doesn't do that, for learning is not primarily inductive. What we see depends on what we look for, which in turn depends on our theory.[7] We don't notice what our theory does not consider real. So I need, as Nolden put it, to be "banged over the head" to see that a belief of mine is wrong, and I want screenwriters who will do so—but with a fine, artistic touch, please.

The Sensation-Seeking *Street Time* Characters and Their Story

Both Kevin Hunter and James Liberti had the variant gene. Every cell in their bodies contained a copy of it. Probably all the other parole officers, including James's partner Dee, also had it, as did Kevin's hash-smuggling partners. Otherwise, they would have led more sedate lives. The DRD4 gene shapes a person's desire for excitement, and these folks wanted lots of it.

These two guys with the same problematic DRD4 gene dealt with it in very different ways—neither of which we can fully endorse. Kevin had been importing millions of dollars worth of hashish before he was caught, and James was (secretly, so far) a gambling addict. But how should we wish for them to live? How can they satisfy their need for thrills without harm?

They were both in their late thirties. James, the parole officer, had a beautiful blonde wife and three young kids. Kevin, the pot smuggler/parolee, had a beautiful brunette common-law wife and one son. But James was an armed officer of the law, authorized for the next five years to veto almost anything Kevin might want to do. I'll tell a little of Kevin's story here, paying attention to justice, blame, and his inborn craving for adrenaline. (This is only a minor fraction of *Street Time*'s numerous plots, for each episode also involved other stories in which James or his partner Dee dealt with their parolees.)

Most crime plots, of course, revolve around catching blameworthy characters—regrettably so, since blame does not foster virtue. However, without much blaming, *Street Time* teaches a different message: every action has consequences. And, when it comes to crime, those consequences often compound problems and lead inexorably toward more dangerous actions.

Recidivism: Karma or Just Bad Luck?

During Kevin's first interview with his parole officer, James predicted that he would be back in the marijuana business within a month. He was overly opti-

Fig. 7.2. Scott Cohen, played by James Liberti, with Kevin Hunter, played by Rob Morrow, who is in handcuffs. Street Time *still courtesy of Sony Pictures Television.*

mistic. It was actually less than a week, though it would take much longer for the long arm of the law to seize him.

James's prediction was not based on any particular intuition about Kevin personally but on statistical probability. Around 75 percent of released American prisoners are rearrested later.[8] The odds aren't good.

One of Stratton's purposes was to reveal the pressures toward recidivism, which affect even such likable guys as Kevin. The explanation of a reversion to crime always involves both character traits and circumstance. Kevin's character traits were, to some extent, inborn. He had the thrill gene. As he explained his smuggling career to his father, "Tell you the truth, it started with a love of pot. Then it was the excitement of doing the deals, the rush—and then it was the money—and then when the money got so huge it didn't matter anymore, it was all about the rush again."

But Kevin did not understand until too late just how dangerous it was for him to be outside the law—how a mistake early in life would come back against him, time after time, with cycles of increasing harm. This is mainly because being an "offender" meant that often he couldn't afford to tell the truth, lest he be sent back to prison or penalized in some other way.

And the consequences are long-lasting. For example, his parents had written him off as a disgrace. During his five years in prison as a kingpin hashish dealer, Kevin had left his money with his brother Peter for safekeeping, but Peter and Kevin's brother-in-law Goldie had spent it, buying a nightclub and the down payment on a new load of hash.

Now Peter and Goldie needed Kevin's expertise with the new load. They would withhold the money they owed him so that, to regain what was his, he would have to help them, however reluctantly. Because that money came from his life of crime, Kevin could not use the law to recover it or to prosecute his brother, even if he had wanted to do so. Indeed, because Kevin, now a felon, could not get a decent job, he was vulnerable to Peter's pressures to help with the new smuggle.

But subsequent consequences would continue unfolding. For one thing, Peter and Goldie were under surveillance by the federal Drug Enforcement Administration (DEA). In order to facilitate the surveillance, the DEA agents forced James to let Kevin run the nightclub—exactly the kind of business that would subject him to additional criminal temptations and pressures. James thought this amounted to entrapment, but he had to go along with the DEA, who secretly planted bugs in Kevin's office. None of this would have happened if Kevin had not been a drug kingpin.

When Kevin made a success of the nightclub, he was able to sell it for $175,000—but James took $150,000 of it in payment of the $500,000 fine. Kevin was back into financial vulnerability and had to take charge of the new smuggle to keep the inexperienced Peter and Goldie from bungling it. Again, his past experience was constraining him in the present.

Next Kevin was photographed with a known hash dealer. Then the Mafia found out that he was about to clear millions of dollars from the new smuggle, so they shook him down for a portion of it. Since he could do nothing legal to protect himself, he cut a deal with the Mafioso: they should "take care of" another enemy who had stolen most of the proceeds of the new smuggle, and he'd share whatever money they could recover for him. This led to mob murder.

And so it goes. One bad deed leads inevitably to something even worse. Had Kevin never sold marijuana—or had the marijuana trade not been illegal—he could have taken a good job and ignored his rotten brother and brother-in-law. I won't rehearse for you the whole sequence of events, but I've diagrammed the chain of causality, with bad deeds making it necessary to resort to even worse deeds, and on and on. Kevin refers once to his belief in karma—and that is exactly what the plot of this series depicts. I call the diagram "Kevin's Karma" (fig. 7.3). This chart shows the most powerful argument I can imagine for the

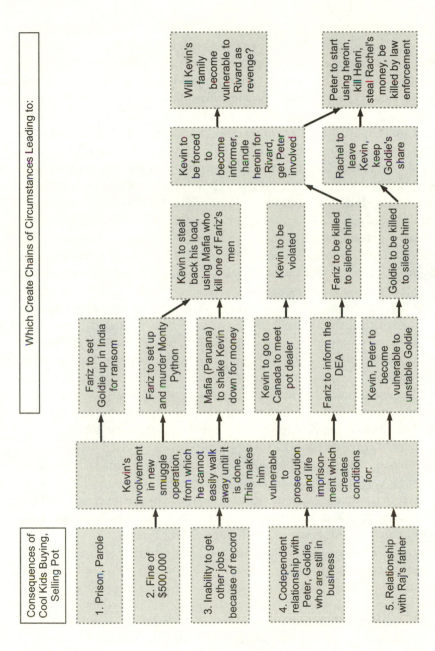

Consequences of Cool Kids Buying, Selling Pot

Which Create Chains of Circumstances Leading to:

1. Prison, Parole

2. Fine of $500,000

3. Inability to get other jobs because of record

4. Codependent relationship with Peter, Goldie, who are still in business

5. Relationship with Raj's father

Kevin's involvement in new smuggle operation, from which he cannot easily walk away until it is done. This makes him vulnerable to prosecution and life imprisonment which creates conditions for:

Fariz to set Goldie up in India for ransom

Fariz to set up and murder Monty Python

Mafia (Paruana) to shake Kevin down for money

Kevin to go to Canada to meet pot dealer

Fariz to inform the DEA

Kevin, Peter to become vulnerable to unstable Goldie

Kevin to steal back his load, using Mafia who kill one of Fariz's men

Kevin to be violated

Fariz to be killed to silence him

Goldie to be killed to silence him

Kevin to be forced to become informer, handle heroin for Rivard, get Peter involved

Rachel to leave Kevin, keep Goldie's share

Will Kevin's family become vulnerable to Rivard as revenge?

Peter to start using heroin, kill Henri, steal Rachel's money, be killed by law enforcement

Fig. 7.3. Kevin's Karma. The plot of Street Time illustrated the fatal consequences that unfold endlessly as a result of living outside the law.

181

legalization of marijuana and numerous other activities that are now treated as crimes.

Someone else might just call this sequence of events bad luck, and that's a fair theory: moral luck.[9] The quality of one's behavior is always contingent on circumstances that are not (at least not immediately) within one's control. To believe in karma, as Kevin does, is to assume that luck is not random—that his own past actions have brought his currently disastrous moral circumstances on himself, and that now he has few opportunities to avoid further catastrophes. I won't speculate here as to whether crimes should be attributed more to the offender's character traits or to his circumstances—either from karma or random moral luck. In any case, Stratton portrays most cases of recidivism sympathetically, knowing that it is always at least partly of situational origin.

Was Kevin's luck karma or random? You can see it either way. It began with Kevin's initial foray into selling illegal pot. That put him outside the law, and all the other events followed naturally, almost inevitably (Kevin's karma explanation). But if selling pot had been legal, none of the rest would have followed. You and I have the power to make it legal, but we haven't, so everyone is paying the price (Kevin's bad luck explanation).

The important message of *Street Time* is that one particular circumstance is enormously fateful: the status of being, either at present or in the past, outside the law. The status of criminality, as a condition, sets up endless other unfavorable circumstances from which you and I, as noncriminals, are exempt. Having to keep secrets or lie (which every criminal must do) spoils one's relationships and makes one vulnerable to others' unwelcome demands, from which there is no legal recourse. (You can't sue; you can't ask for police protection; you have to resort to "self-help" measures, which are usually illegal in themselves.) If you're smart and lucky, you'll figure out how to use the Mafia for your own purposes, as Kevin did—with a ghastly result: murder. Thus serious consequences for society—gangland killings—result almost inexorably from the criminal justice system that is supposed to protect us. Criminalizing the marijuana trade requires a huge, expensive enforcement staff and makes sellers into felons, vulnerable to pressures that keep them locked in a cycle of recidivism. The costs to society clearly outweigh the benefits.

Stratton *shows* us all that but doesn't *tell* it to us, so we never get it. My six intellectual friends sat in my living room watching Kevin's karma unfold (which went on much longer than I have described—thirty-six hour-long episodes). Never once did our conversation turn to the obvious inference: that marijuana should be legalized. Had Stratton introduced a few comments pointing out what I have just said, we would have seen his point. Along with Plato, I believe that philosophizing is a good thing.

But Stratton is an artist, and my friends did enjoy having to think fast to keep up with his unexpected twists of plot. Complex stories are more *interesting* than easier ones. The plots contain puzzles, and if you work hard to figure them out, you'll hone a particular skill. However, my high-IQ friends actually didn't work hard to make sense of the blur of fast-moving events, and, when they did try, they often failed.[10] Stories just zipped past us—surprising us, but leaving us confused. I taped the conversations that followed two seasons of both shows, and, looking back on those conversations, what strikes me is that the discussions rarely were oriented toward figuring out the complex plots. Instead, we talked about the human side of the characters—their emotions, their relationships, their attitudes—which is not what the writers evidently expected us to notice. It seems to me that ethical/emotional criticism is exactly the kind of analysis that people normally do, unless they have been trained to think like literary critics or philosophers. Now I want to explore a couple of other ways in which Stratton's subtle writing stimulated our emotions more than our understanding.

Stratton's Subtle Writing

James and Kevin are equally the protagonists of *Street Time*. We like both of them, and James likes Kevin. (As the resentful object of James's close supervision, and because parole officers don't disclose much about themselves to their parolees, Kevin had no reason to reciprocate James's liking.) My living room audience, on the other hand, was supposed to like James for helping Kevin, though in fact they did not understand that he was being helpful.

Who Gets to Arrest Kevin?

My friends did know that James and the DEA were meeting and cooperating, but mainly *competing*, for the chance to arrest Kevin. We also were cued to prefer James over the unscrupulous and merciless DEA. Then we were shown that the DEA had a photo of Kevin inside Canada, meeting with a convicted marijuana dealer. Kevin could have his parole revoked on both counts: for leaving the United States and for associating with a known criminal. James wanted to "violate" him—return him to prison for a year. But the DEA won out; Kevin would remain free, so as to be caught in his big new operation.

My viewing friends did not see why they should prefer James's plan over the DEA's, since they liked Kevin and wanted him to remain free. I had to explain twice to them that there are two very different ways in which Kevin could be sent back to prison. First, if he violates the conditions of his parole even slightly (by associating with another offender, say, or smoking marijuana, or going out of town without permission), James can instantly send him back to prison to serve more of the term for which he was on parole—usually a year. However, if Kevin is caught in a *new* smuggle, he will have a new trial; and as a kingpin drug dealer, if convicted, he'll return to prison for the rest of his life. James feels sure that Kevin is indeed conducting a new smuggle, but there's insufficient evidence to convict him. Therefore, James can do Kevin a favor by "violating" him for a short time rather than leaving him free to get caught in the new crime by the DEA. My friends did not understand that James might actually show kindness by violating him. Nowhere does the script spell out these facts, though they are crucial for making sense of the story. It took me several months to figure it out. My friends said they would never have understood without my explanation.

Stratton also loves to explore moral ambiguity, though again without forcing us to draw any inferences from it that challenge our ethical assumptions. The next section describes one such instance.

Murder as an Act of Charity

Every parole officer has a partner to accompany him where he should not go alone. James's partner was Dee Mulhern (played by Erika Alexander)—the most interesting woman in the series. Dee is tough, funny, sexy, and black. We never get to know her inner emotional dynamics, but she is a good friend to James.

One of Dee's parolees is a Hispanic woman, Carmen, who is being forced to keep working in the drug business. Dee cannot protect her. An old man, Sam Cahan (played by Red Buttons), is one of James's parolees. He spent twenty years in prison as a mob boss. Now frail (he uses two canes to walk), Sam lives with his dying wife. In the parole office waiting room one day he encounters the badly bruised Carmen and gently asks who has done this to her. Shortly afterward, Carmen's attacker is murdered by a hit man. This is Sam's generous gift to her.

Next Sam's beloved wife wants his help in dying. Tenderly, he gives her the pills she has put aside for this moment.

Suspecting Sam of ordering the hit on Carmen's attacker but unable to prove it, James "violates" Cahan just after his wife's death. The embittered old man resolves to get revenge.

Gene, James's bookie, was working for Sam, who had instructed him to toy with James's gambling addiction by increasing his credit limit. By the time Sam was released from prison, James owed $25,000 to Gene but could not pay even a fraction of it. His wife Karen had found out about his gambling and had thrown him out of their home. Now Sam comes to James's hotel room to complete his revenge. He taunts James for his hypocrisy, then tears up the $25,000 marker and throws it in his face, saying, "Enjoy the rest of your pathetic life."

Here Stratton questions the grounds of blameworthiness. Murder is wrong—isn't it? But the law enforcers could not protect Carmen, so Sam did so—at considerable cost to himself. He helped his wife die, as she requested. Even his revenge on James was ambiguous—less cruel than one might expect. Another mobster might have broken James's legs for failure to pay a gambling debt, but Sam makes a gift to him of $25,000 by tearing up the marker. Is this vengeance or generosity?

Is Sam an evil man? Nowhere in the script are such questions uttered, and I doubt that many viewers reflected on the moral ambiguity they were shown. It did not come up in the postviewing discussions in my living room, though my friends did like Sam. If Stratton wanted to make us rethink our morals, he needed to "spoon-feed" the question to us by having two characters discuss Sam's moral ambiguity aloud. The affection we felt for the old man definitely had opened us up for sympathetic reflection on this issue.

Stratton had his own moral objective: to deepen James's sensibilities. (He told me that James began as a Roman Catholic and gradually became a "Zen Catholic.") James was a hypocrite at that point, and Stratton would have him change, but we would never be privy to his thoughts as he became less judgmental, less ready to allocate blame. Thus his growth would not become a basis for our own growth.

Emotional Appropriateness and Empathy

Zillmann, among others, claims that we like and empathize with characters primarily for their moral excellence. I agree—if we include in our definition of morality a person's emotional appropriateness, which is probably even more decisive for his reputation than adherence to legal or social norms. We can explore that question in watching *Street Time*.

My friends inevitably compared James to Kevin, and also their families to each other. Although no one liked Rachel at first, this was not just because they disapproved of her hedonistic values, for they disliked Karen Liberti even more, though Karen behaves conventionally. The difference must be attributed to the two women's differing feelings for their families. Rachel loves her family and understands their failings. The Hunters have fun and are affectionate. We enjoyed their

Fig. 7.4. Kevin Hunter, played by Rob Morrow, with his common-law wife, Rachel Goldstein, played by Michelle Nolden. Street Time *still courtesy of Sony Pictures Television.*

joint bubble bath and their playfulness when helping Sean with his homework on gorillas' teeth. Rachel loves sex. In one scene when she is very pregnant, she and Kevin "spoon." The set was closed, but I listened to the soundtrack, which gave me a lovely oxytocin trip—the only one in the whole series. (Regrettably, this sweet, erotic scene was edited out by the Hollywood producers, who had retained lots of pornography. Stratton was outraged, and this time he was right.)

Contrary to Zillmann's theory, my viewer group's greater empathy toward the Hunters could not be attributed to their moral superiority but only to their higher emotional intelligence. They are more capable of mutual pleasure, which we shared vicariously.

Empathy was, indeed, affected by our moral appraisal of characters—which again was mostly a matter of emotional appropriateness. At the end of the first season, James Liberti wins his competition against the DEA and is able to violate Kevin—put him away for a while, since the evidence is too weak to convict him on the new smuggle.

The scene begins just after Rachel has gone into labor. The couple have decided on a home birth with a midwife. Now they happily await the next contraction.

Just then, James arrives with two U.S. marshals. When Kevin opens the door, James arrests him and has the marshals handcuff him. Kevin protests that his wife is in labor. Terrified, Rachel has a powerful contraction. Her water breaks, and Kevin tries to go to her, but the marshals throw him down and hold him there. James runs to phone the midwife, yelling the whole time. When he tries to help Rachel to the sofa, she howls that she wants her husband's help, not his. Kevin, still pinned down in the entry hall, can do nothing but yell, too: "Breathe! Breathe!"

James delays the arrest until the midwife's arrival. Rachel is in hard labor now, and each man seems to be competing to outshout the other. "Breathe, Rachel!" yells Kevin, while James shouts his own instructions and keeps telling Kevin to shut up. Eventually, he lets the marshals uncuff Kevin, who runs to kneel beside his wife, caressing her as she weeps and moans. Then two midwives arrive. Kevin is handcuffed again and led away. Two hours later, Rachel gives birth to a baby girl.

I was so upset by this episode that, despite being present only as an observer, I actually spoke up to protest against it. James Liberti treated a woman and baby in a way that I, and probably most other women, could never forgive. He burst into the apartment with two U.S. marshals, stomping around like a storm trooper, bellowing to prove that he was the dominant male in charge of this woman. Kevin's response was not much better; he kept competing to outshout James.

I was watching the monitor outside the set with some other women. Two were mothers; the rest were not. I was horrified at the abuse we were witnessing. Surely every baby has a right to a decent birth! Childbirth is excruciating at best and becomes far worse if the woman is being traumatized. The women who had given birth agreed with me. The others looked blank or simply said, "That's what would actually happen in such a situation. The police are brutal to the guys they arrest." This wasn't about Kevin but about Rachel and the baby.

"Do you know how men actually treat women who are in labor?" I asked. "They get very quiet and solicitous. The woman takes priority over all other concerns. Everything else can wait. They whisper and make her as comfortable as possible."

Rob Morrow came out between takes, and I stopped him. "That's a despicable scene," I said. He looked startled, then said to Stratton, "She may be right." Richard was not fazed. He and Marc Levin said they were glad I had registered emotion, because it meant that the episode was exciting. "We humanized James," Stratton said. "We eventually let him uncuff Kevin until the midwife came."

Morrow then focused as only Morrow can focus, discussing the scene with Stratton and Levin, and never looking toward me again. That was okay—it was Scott Cohen who most needed to rethink the way he was playing this scene.

Cohen came out. I said, "Scott, women are going to hate you after this scene." He swore at me and walked away. On the next takes, his yelling was even louder.

Eventually I left, saying that if I had been viewing at home, I would have turned it off, never to watch the show again.

The next week, I went to observe the editing. When we got to that point, Levin said to the editor, "All that yelling! Let's cut out as much as we can." About half of the scene was deleted, but the final cut was still so cruel that I permanently broke empathy with James Liberti. He had become irredeemable to me—a change that would influence my responses to him throughout the following season.

Throughout the next season, the characters undergo strange changes—especially Kevin, who was playful and warm before but becomes cold and hard now. He's back in jail for a year, thanks to James. Rachel visits him often, bringing their baby along. We see some tough action scenes, and several of Kevin smoking pot, but nothing as interesting as Stratton's description of his own soul-searching mysticism in prison. He had told me, "Before I got released from prison, I often felt as though I could spend the rest of my life there. It would not have been difficult. I had reached the level where it didn't matter to me anymore where I was located. I felt I could continue to do it because I was so involved in the journey I was on. It wasn't until I knew I was getting out that it began to get to me a little."

Stratton added that prisoners usually become depressed when they get out. "They go through periods when they think, 'I was actually better off when I was in prison.' Just about everyone I've talked to who has spent a significant amount of time in prison has gone through such changes when they got out."

But Kevin just closes up emotionally and stops expressing his disappointments or telling Rachel the truth. Even when emotional guardedness seems unnecessary, the script instructs the actor to "feel it but cover the feeling"—but that was, I think, a mistake on Stratton's part. Why should Kevin pretend not to be hurt? By now, because of his inappropriately stony affect, my friends disliked him and even stopped empathizing with him.

This personality change is happening while James is showing his feelings *more,* so that my friends were increasingly liking him. I did not share their opinion, for I still held the dreadful childbirth abuse against James and would never empathize with him again.

There was some basis for Kevin's change. He expected to be charged with new crimes and put away for good. When this possibility looked imminent, Rachel came to visit him in prison. He told her to get on with her life. Then he whirled and walked away. She screamed at him in rage.

James came to her apartment. She was alone, but let him in, then angrily went back to washing dishes. When he gave her the news of Kevin's probable new indictment, she screamed at him, then hysterically started smashing dishes.

He put his arms around her to settle her down, but, between her sobs, she began kissing him wildly. In a moment they were ripping off their clothes. The last thing James had ever expected was to have an affair with Kevin's wife—but it happened.

What did Stratton intend by these developments? My theory (and Stratton has not verified my guess) is that he wanted to promote James's growth by having him go through several instructive experiences. As a strict Catholic, James had been brought up to distinguish sharply between right and wrong. He had applied rules strictly to offenders too. But early on, he was humbled by his own gambling addiction and by Sam Cahan's criticism of him for hypocrisy. Later, even harder lessons were in store. Besides having James learn through his parole work, Stratton wanted him to learn at a deeper level by discovering the ubiquitous consequences of limerence and the cravings of the body. What could humble him more than having an affair with the wife of an offender?

But why would *Rachel* turn to James for comfort and sex, considering the passionate, affectionate quality of her marriage? Answer: She would never do such a thing unless Kevin had abandoned her. Hence, working backward from his end objective, Stratton reasons that he must make Kevin reject her coldly and withhold the truth from her, so as to motivate her affair with James. This is just my theory, but it fits what Stratton told me: that actors (notably Rob Morrow) had started seeing the drama strictly through their own characters' perspectives, whereas he, as the author, had the bigger picture in mind. Morrow had protested against these personality changes.

Who is right? One cannot glibly reject Stratton's panoramic view. Indeed, my friends viewed James and Rachel's affair compassionately. Compared to all the meaningless couplings with hookers and exotic dancers, their affair was truthful and touching, though of course also troubling.

But Kevin was weakened to make room for this storyline. To motivate Rachel as Stratton wants, Kevin must behave coldly, withhold the truth she needs to hear, and even tell her to "get on with her life," though his inappropriate affect can only diminish our empathy for him. Indeed, this was the biggest disappointment of the second season to the viewers in my living room. However heavily his poor moral choices weighed against him in our minds, his emotional inadequacy seemed far more deplorable.

Appraising *Street Time*

Street Time's artistry is outstanding. The writing, acting, and technical work are excellent. How shall we rate it in ethical/emotional terns? Ambiguously, with one thumb up, one down. I empathized with many characters, without loving any of them, and would never have spent time with them in real life. Great fiction asks, "How should human beings live?" But the *Street Time* characters do little soul work, nor do they learn from their own mistakes. A few other characters were unmitigated villains all along, and some of my friends rejoiced in their demise as, one after another, they are killed. As a cautionary tale, the message is "Don't live like this." Unfortunately, some viewers *will* imitate the worst characters anyway. The world is not a better place because of *Street Time*.

But the show implicitly challenges the culture of blame. Just for this, it almost deserves our approval. The episodic stories involving James's and Dee's parolees show that it is false to divide human beings into good and bad people. The line between good and evil runs down through every human heart. Law enforcers are neither better nor worse than most others. For example, during the last few episodes, the head of the parole office follows orders from the Justice Department by insisting that Kevin Hunter (who had never handled heroin before) become a dealer to entrap a bigger criminal.

My main regret was that Kevin does not grow. Within one minute after I first met Rob Morrow, he told me that his morals had come largely from movies and television. Then he said he had been deeply disappointed because his character in *Northern Exposure* had not been allowed to grow but added that this show would be different. It wasn't. Kevin's growth was sacrificed during the second season to allow James to develop. The only thing that Kevin learns is the grave consequences of letting the DRD4 gene run him.

Street Time has multiple, probably contradictory, influences. Its most obvious moral impact is deleterious: By showing antisocial acts without offsetting commentary, it will lead certain susceptible viewers to imitate them. It is really wrong to overlook or deny this harm.

On the other side, it reveals the unmistakable flaws in our institutions for managing crime. Prison does not reduce crime rates but rather increases them. Our system of justice is based on distinguishing sharply between blameworthy criminals and righteous enforcers. Stratton's insight is that such a division is false and hypocritical, so he should illustrate a better alternative, one that doesn't categorize offenders as blameworthy moral outcasts. He does know of such better approaches; I discussed restorative justice with him. He might have demonstrated it in action, had he chosen to do so. Though he proposed no alternatives to the present flawed system, he did prompt me to explore "community justice" on my own. I wish other viewers had pursued the same question, for it convinced me that our criminal justice system needs a radical change.

Up to 80 percent of all offenders who are sent to prison go on to commit more crimes. It costs the state $90 to $200 per day to keep a person in prison.

According to Stratton, only about 10 percent of the people in U.S. prisons really need to be there—the predatory criminals who cannot be controlled and who would continue to victimize others.

It is great for a dramatist to prove to us that an important social institution needs to be reformed. Stratton didn't achieve that, but he started the process. A little discursive commentary might have let the notion penetrate into our consciousness—that our present criminal justice system only traps people such as Kevin Hunter into recidivism and personal tragedy. Having established that point, Stratton could make even greater contributions, not by dramatizing yet more thrilling crimes but by showing us a better alternative system: community (or restorative) justice. (See the appendix to this chapter.) He might have launched a prison reform movement story along innovative lines.

For a start, judges might send to prison only perpetrators of violent crimes rather than property crimes. This would reduce the prison population by about half. Another distinction sometimes is made between crimes with and without victims. Prostitution, drug use, and gambling can be considered crimes without victims, since all the participants engage in these activities willingly. Arguably it is wrong to charge people for crimes without a complaint from a victim. However, as we have seen with Kevin and James, "victimless" activities may harm one's family or other people indirectly.

Risk-seeking behavior poses interesting examples of this. Risks should be confined to oneself, but everyone has a right, and some people conceivably even have a need, to take risks. The question is, Can persons with the DRD4 gene put their risk taking to good use in the service of society? James Liberti's career was dangerous and, as he became more empathetic to parolees, also mainly constructive.

But what could Kevin Hunter do to substitute for the rush of smuggling? We know exactly what he would do. As Richard Stratton, he would become the creator and producer of a television series. That job has the perfect amount of adrenaline and dopamine to substitute for hashish smuggling. May he have another show that is just as good as *Street Time*— or, even better, one that points toward solutions..

And I have another recommendation for Stratton: Don't just show. Tell, too!

Conclusion

Street Time portrays most characters as ethically gray so that the audience continues to empathize with them, despite their obvious flaws. Relatively little blaming takes place in the story, contrary to the situation with the typical crime show. This moral ambiguity has both advantages and disadvantages. It is always ethically questionable to make wrongdoers attractive to audiences, for people do imitate the characters they like, and in a TV series, the harmful effects of a character's wrongdoing may not show up for years after it is done. No doubt some people were influenced by the show in negative ways. Others, however, may have learned from it how to recognize hypocrisy and judgmentalism.

Most professional actors and producers appreciate subtle writing and dislike spoon-feeding. When my living room audience watched the show and discussed it, they enjoyed the complexity and ambiguity of each episode, which was invariably challenging to follow. Nevertheless, they often missed crucial facts that were required to make sense of the plot. Artistry has its price: it is less intelligible to viewers than spoon-fed stories. (If Steven Johnson is right, my friends gained a few IQ points just from trying—often unsuccessfully—to figure out the plots. I can't attest to that. Besides, I think the moral and emotional impacts of the stories are more important than the mental calisthenics involved in following them.)

But a creator's socially important message may not influence the audience as intended because it is not made apparent. *Street Time*'s main message is that being outside the law—however one gets there—leaves one vulnerable and usually draws one back into further illegal activities. The consequences of criminalizing marginally antisocial behavior are overwhelmingly deleterious for society and for anyone identified as criminal or ex-criminal. The show makes that point very convincingly, but because it is never articulated, probably very few viewers ever learn it.

One important use of entertainment is to cause audiences to reflect on social problems and solve them politically. Episodic television dramas, especially, can play an enormous role by informing the public on vital issues and influencing opinion. We need to use it far more effectively in addressing the world's problems. I'll return to this point in my concluding chapter.

Appendix: A Brief History of Community Justice

In world history, modern criminal justice institutions are unusual.[11] For more than five hundred years, medieval Europe used community justice, in contrast to the state justice that we see in *Street Time*. Then, and in many other premodern societies, no written laws identified "crimes." Occasionally, of course, some people harmed others. The response might involve negotiation, restitution, compensation, or (as a last resort) vengeance or recourse to an official court, which was used mainly to pressure people to acknowledge responsibility for the harm they had done.[12]

Community justice was not necessarily more cruel than state justice, which had begun in the Roman Empire. State justice had involved rational, formal, codified laws, created and administered by the state. However, Roman laws were forgotten by the sixth century, as the empire disintegrated. For the next five hundred years, Europe reverted to community justice by mediation, without written laws. An offence was defined not as law breaking but rather as the wrongful harming of another. The needs of the victims and offenders were addressed, not the claims of the state.

During the eleventh and twelfth centuries, the pendulum swung back. Roman law was recovered and became the basis for church canon law, which involved applying rules, establishing guilt, and fixing penalties. Crime was now sin against God. No longer did Christianity emphasize forgiveness or redemption, but rather the infliction of pain for punishment. The "inquisitorial" system developed. A person might be charged by the church court, whether or not there was any complaint by a victim. Torture became a way of finding out the "truth."

England was never influenced as much by canon law as was the Continent, but even there a uniform system of criminal law developed, with the state taking initiative for administering justice. Fines might be imposed, but the money would not go to the victim but rather into the state's coffers. A crime was now considered an offense against the state and abstract rules, not against a victim. Indeed, the victim's needs and wishes became irrelevant in the prosecution of the case. Punishment became the standard practice. A defendant was either guilty or not guilty, for there were no degrees of guilt. This led people to think categorically about blame (as James Liberti did initially). It led offenders not to repent and apologize, but to deny responsibility for their actions, since lawyers usually advise clients to plead not guilty, no matter what they have done.

As a reform against the harshness of punishment, Quakers proposed an innovation: the penitentiary, where an offender might spend time in solitude, doing spiritual penance. Immediately, however, this penal institution became yet another way of inflicting pain on offenders. Rather than reform, a penitentiary typically stimulates resentment and additional crime.[13]

However, certain categories of offense are treated more flexibly; these are in civil law, where one citizen may still sue another for harm done. Civil law mostly involves liability and obligation—concepts in which there can be degrees of responsibility rather than simple "guilt" or "innocence."

Fortunately, most acts that could be criminalized are not handled as such. Probably both you and I could have been incarcerated a few times for foolish acts that fortunately escaped the attention of law enforcement authorities. Countries vary in their use of incarceration. In the early 1990s, the United States had the highest incarceration rates in the world. Then in 1994, laws proclaiming "Three strikes and you're out" drove rates of imprisonment even higher.

In recent years, a movement has begun to replace the harsh, hierarchical forms of state justice with new versions of community justice. In many of these cases, the victim and the offender meet with community members, discuss the problem, and agree on ways of righting the wrongs, insofar as possible. The offender must be held accountable for what happened, but, instead of dwelling on his blameworthiness, everyone looks to the future and addresses the needs that were created by the wrongdoing. (See the case of David in the preceding chapter.)

This new form of community justice—usually called *restorative justice*—is vastly less expensive than conventional courts and systems of punishment and supervision. It usually reduces rates of recidivism, in comparison with the conventional practices of state justice.[14] However, its main advantage is that, unlike state justice, it pays particular attention to reducing the distress and harm experienced by the victim.

Chapter 8

The Right Emotion

Don't just show. Tell, too!

Unlike *Street Time, Northern Exposure* fulfilled this principle beautifully, letting its characters express their inner conflicts, often by quoting literary classics. The two shows differ in other ways as well, addressing entirely different concerns of their audiences—and maybe even different parts of their brains. If Simon Baron-Cohen's "systemizing" brains prefer the mental workout involved in following *Street Time*, "empathizing" brains must prefer the interpersonal subtleties and soul-searching conversations of *Northern Exposure*.[1]

If *Northern Exposure* were a painting, it would be by Hundertwasser. If it were an opera, it would be *The Magic Flute*. If it were a cathedral, it would be by Gaudí. In contrast to *Street Time*'s dark, realistic feeling tone, it is light, colorful, insightful, and playful. I've watched certain episodes thirty times, for the same reason I've gone to *La Traviata* a dozen times: they're gorgeous works of art. But here instead of discussing either show aesthetically, I'll address their emotional and ethical messages.

Street Time seems tailor-made for pointing out institutional flaws and stimulating a reevaluation of the modern criminal justice system, though in fact it does not do so. *Northern Exposure*'s characters, however, lead their viewers through two different explorations: (1) our moods and interpersonal sentiments and (2) our spiritual orientations. I treat these topics in separate chapters. In this chapter I focus on the former matter—interpersonal ties—and reserve discussion of contemporary soul work for the next chapter. If the present chapter belongs to Aristotle, the following one belongs to Plato.

Appropriate Emotions

> Anyone can become angry—that is easy. But to be angry with the right
> person, to the right degree, at the right time, for the right purpose, and
> in the right way—this is not easy.
>
> —*Aristotle*

In contrast to this quotation, perhaps you believe, as Plato did, that anger is *never* really right—that we should become wise enough to overcome it and all the other strong emotions too. People who do believe that tend to avoid certain topics—such as partisan politics—to keep from riling anyone up. Unfortunately, avoidance of important human issues limits the significance of one's life. Plato usually sidestepped that problem by addressing profound topics at an abstract, philosophical level instead of taking positions on concrete political issues.[2]

Plato's transcendent idealism survived him by many centuries. The Stoic philosophers, especially the Roman Seneca (1–65 C.E.), sought to eliminate all passions, especially anger, though on more secular grounds than Plato's. Even today, millions of spiritual seekers, and even lots of polite nonreligious people, try to dampen their desires and strong feelings, cultivating instead a "view from eternity" that is dispassionate and wise. *Northern Exposure* also avoided serious controversies, usually keeping its tone light—but occasionally, as we shall see, avoiding anger when anger was appropriate.

In other respects, its writers (until nearly the end) were, like Aristotle, fully oriented toward human flourishing in the flesh, not encouraging their characters to become unemotional or self-sufficient, but rather to feel the right emotion to the right degree, at the right time, for the right purpose, and in the right way. Aristotle considered it right to *grieve,* for example, when a friend dies, since that shows the importance of the relationship. He considered it right to feel *angry* when something important is attacked.[3] He explained that "those who do not get angry at the people at whom they should get angry seem dense.... For they seem to be without perception or pain. And a person who is not angry will not defend himself. But to allow oneself and one's loved ones to be trampled underfoot and to overlook it is slavish."[4]

Still, our emotions need to be educated, because they are shaped by our beliefs and our values. For instance, if we overvalue material possessions or social status, we will respond with the wrong emotions at the wrong time. We can cultivate insights about what is worth valuing by watching other people, including *Northern Exposure* characters, as they display appropriate feelings. Few of the scenes will stimulate your adrenaline or cortisol (the writers never wanted to stress us), but many will give you happy moments of dopamine, serotonin, and (occasionally) oxytocin. Plus useful tips on how to increase such moments in your real life.

A person's emotional appropriateness is a moral quality that influences how much we like her. Yet we often cannot agree as to whether a response is appropriate. Viewers of *Northern Exposure*—like the readers of any other story—react to it differently. Try it and see. Assemble your friends in various small groups and show them all the same movie. Even if you know them well, you won't be able to predict how they will react.

If you laugh when someone else is crying, which one of you is being emotionally appropriate? How can you tell? It's hard to say. Appropriateness means responding to at least three kinds of cues: to oneself, to one's companions, and to "reality." That gives us at least three different standards of appropriateness—which may not all be compatible. I'll explain.

Expressiveness—Appropriate to One's Internal Condition

Appropriateness may involve the *expression* of one's own temperament. ("To thine own self be true.") Some of us are pretty forthright about disclosing our attitudes, whereas others try to not to display their feelings unless the circumstances are exactly right. Most people like expressiveness in others, though we don't all like it to the same degree. I mostly admire the integrity and honesty of an open personality. It's a matter of being appropriate to one's own inner nature. An expressive person is taking responsibility for being exactly who he is, and everybody can see what they're dealing with.

In the last chapter, I said that my living room viewing group came to dislike Kevin Hunter because he stopped being expressive. But a few members of the same group would later dislike Joel Fleischman, the protagonist of *Northern Exposure,* for being *too* expressive, especially in his grouchiness. Personally, I loved him for it—mostly, I think, because he doesn't curry favor with anyone. All the characters in *Northern Exposure* are highly expressive, which makes them appealing, though few of them are as open as Joel or, especially, an outlandish wild man named Adam.

Perceptiveness: Appropriate to External Circumstances

The second kind of appropriateness is the ability to size up external social situations with insight. Call it *perceptiveness.* This is usually the strong suit of empathic individuals, who are good at taking the role of others and imagining their intentions and inner conditions. Of course, some situations are truly complex and ambiguous, so that different observers will reach contradictory interpretations, even if they are all empathic. That's why it's valuable to bring friends together to discuss books or plays; you'll always gain a variety of perspectives from them. An insightful reviewer will reconstruct the story especially appropriately, taking account of factors and motives that the rest of us may not have noticed. There's a gift to "reading" other people and their stories sensitively and accurately.

Agreeableness: Appropriate Accommodation to Others

The third kind of emotional appropriateness I've called *mimesis*. That occurs when we imitate the feelings expressed by others around us. There's nothing inherently wrong with doing this; in fact, it's often the sociable thing to do when friends get together for entertainment. The rule (and it's a good one) is this: Do your best to enjoy the occasion, and show it! That will give others more opportunity to get into the experience too. At a Red Sox game I once attended, a woman near me had accompanied her husband, but, instead of watching, she read a book the whole time. The people around her got angry and let her know it. She was being a wet blanket. An entertainment is an expressive occasion—an occasion to feel intensely and cut loose in expressing it. Save your instrumental rationality for critical discussions of, say, politics, philosophy, or medicine. Be kind. If you know your companion has a crush on Brad Pitt, maybe you shouldn't criticize his acting as you leave the theater. Good entertainment leaves pleasant emotional associations. It's appropriate to avoid contaminating good ones.

As Arlie Hochschild has pointed out, we often manage our emotions as a gift to others. Sometimes we *repress* feelings (e.g., at a former lover's wedding we may rigorously suppress any sadness), and sometimes we *work feelings up,* either as a way of being sociable with our companions or as a duty to our employer to make the customers feel welcome.[5]

Audiences have collective personalities. We imitate each other unconsciously when we're watching together. Every stage actor can sense the difference from one performance to the next. "Claques" of people used to be hired to sit in the audience and express specific feelings loudly at the right time, to stimulate the others. Thus the third way of being emotionally appropriate is to work up whatever feelings will allow the other members of the audience to enjoy the occasion as they want to do. I have sometimes been upset by sharing a movie or TV episode that I particularly loved with friends who cut it to pieces with their criticism. If this goes on long enough, it spoils my empathy with my beloved characters and leaves me sad or angry.

This third kind of appropriateness may appear to pose an ethical problem. At its worst, it is fakery. At its best, it may feel incompatible with the first type of appropriateness—the open expression of one's true inner state. Still, it is not inevitably fraudulent to "work up" an emotion, any more than it is fraudulent of an actor to work up the feelings that he creates for a performance. Not everyone can do it readily, but when the emotion has been worked up, it's real. The actor's body reacts physiologically in ways that are identical to natural emotions in real life. It's not immoral to be a good sport and create an emotion to fit the occasion—unless you habitually become a chameleon, which is a character flaw in itself.

The management of incompatible kinds of emotional appropriateness is an existential problem, but not usually a difficult one. You just choose whether to be loyal this time to your own inner nature or to your companions. In your discussion group, you can criticize bluntly or preserve your friends' love for a character. If this appears to be an unpleasant dilemma, there's one way out: don't go. If you don't think you can get into the spirit of your friends' outing to the ball game or opera, stay home and read a book.

Tuning Your Mind-Set

Every viewer must contribute some kind of mental readiness to "read a story intelligently." This is especially apparent when it comes to humor, for our minds have to be set in a particular way to receive the intended amusement. Of the thousands of books that analyze humor, almost all try to explain what is funny about the joke or the situation—not what there is in our *own minds* that enables us to "get it." The paucity of writings on this subject is surprising, since performers know how much depends on the mood of their audience. We have to tune our mind-sets to receive the story that is being sent. I want to explore that process here, particularly with respect to humor.

There are two main ways in which our inner "receiver" must be tuned. First, we must switch from the instrumental to the expressive mode. In chapter 5, I described Michael Apter's theory about thrill seeking as an expressive kind of experience—the state of mind when you carry out activities for their own sake, not for any practical purpose. Playing with your pet, joking, hugging friends, rock climbing, and enjoying friendly games of backgammon all fall into this expressive category, while working and communicating factual information are instrumental activities. To get the proper meaning of another person's activity, you must recognize her intentions as "serious" (instrumental) or "nonserious" (expressive). Here the knob on your mental receiver is a toggle switch, not a dial. There is no third position besides instrumental and expressive.

You must also tune for "lightness-darkness," and that knob is a gradient dial. Lightness usually goes with expressiveness. But not always: At work, some of your colleagues approach their instrumental tasks lightly, with grace and ease. Conversely, among the expressive entertainments are such intense experiences as bullfights, which are anything but light. In *Northern Exposure,* the grumpy protagonist, Dr. Joel Fleischman, is expressive but sometimes dark; it is *we* who supply the lightness by smiling at him—as most (but not all) viewers do.

Audiences must adjust their mind-sets appropriately to receive the kind of message that is being sent, though the senders are not always successful in signaling that a light or dark, expressive or instrumental, message is on the way. You have probably found yourself chatting with someone who evidently expected you to say something funny when your message was simply factual; both of you must have felt slightly awkward when the anticipated punch line failed to arrive. The opposite situation is even more embarrassing—when your interlocutor fails to get the humor that you intended.

One such instance occurred many years ago when I was working at Harvard. There was a famous psychologist on the faculty named David McClelland, a Quaker who had published an article analyzing the typical personality traits of people in India. I belonged to a lunch group that met weekly to discuss research on India, and on one occasion, my Indian friend Amar Kumar Singh presented his ongoing project, complete with tables on the blackboard. I knew instantly that it was a retaliatory send-up of McClelland, for it was about the supposedly typical personality traits of Quakers. Unfortunately, I was the only person present who recognized it as a joke. I wanted to rescue my friend but could think of no way to do so. After Amar had gone on for twenty minutes, I actually crept away, ashamed of myself for abandoning him but unable to bear what was bound to happen. When I saw him an hour later, he was still humiliated. When he had confessed that it was a hoax, several people had become angry. Evidently Amar was as ineffective as I often am at sending cues so others can react with emotional intelligence.

Northern Exposure was a comedy, but you might watch it a long time without laughing out loud. You'd smile a lot, though, even at characters who display conspicuously low emotional intelligence. The *Northern Exposure* characters take each other lightly—a generosity of spirit that, after a while, some viewers begin to emulate in their own lives. As complex people, the characters are morally gray (or perhaps I should say "speckled," for they are far from drab) but not evil, and their failings usually amuse us. Probably the best moral lesson of the show is on how to respond intelligently to emotional stupidity.

When Joshua Brand and John Falsey, the creators of *Northern Exposure,* were asked what they intended their series to illustrate, they replied, "A nonjudgmental society." And indeed, they invented a town whose inhabitants displayed uncommon tolerance, rarely blaming anyone. Instead of watching the central person in a scene, it will pay you to watch the *other* characters who are observing or interacting with him. For example, if a character is having an irrational "hissy fit," the others around her will generally either show civil inattention[6] by hardly noticing the outburst or seem mildly entertained by it. Even when witnessing a transgression, they may regard it as just an expression of feelings, not as a threat to society. Emotional confrontations may be treated merely as interpersonal blips, not as truly menacing announcements of intent. The inhabitants of Cicely, Alaska, have a talent for finding the appropriate emotion, and it is rarely heavy. To "tune our minds" to match theirs, we need to understand how to take an "antihero" lightly and how to regard humor in post-Freudian terms.

The Antihero

Though movies and plays often require us to empathize with warped characters, they seldom offer us finely developed personalities for our empathic exploration. *Northern Exposure,* however, assigns us the challenge of empathizing with its protagonist, an above-average antihero, a smart, caring physician with great spiritual potential but underdeveloped social skills—a natural-born complainer.

An antihero is not a villain but merely a protagonist who lacks the qualities we expect of a hero, such as courage or idealism. (Think of most Dustin Hoffman roles. Or Mr. Bean.) He cannot become our ego ideal. Still, our emotional training assignment may consist of learning to feel affection precisely for such a character's flaws by taking them lightly and empathizing with him. This is not impossible. Polls showed that most *Northern Exposure* fans liked the irascible Dr. Joel Fleischman best of all the characters.

Joel can be compared to another antihero, the perennial pessimist Jaques in Shakespeare's *As You Like It.* That play is full of characters having fun—all except Jaques, who expresses his moroseness to everyone in sight. He is both one of the least popular and one of the *most* popular Shakespearean characters. Nobody exactly laughs at him, but the people who like him do enjoy his crankiness and smile wryly at him as they would when unexpectedly glimpsing themselves in a mirror on a bad day. It is Jaques who utters that famous "seven ages of man" speech that begins, "All the world's a stage/And all the men and women merely players." It ends with a gloomy commentary on old age: "Last scene of all/That ends this strange eventful history/Is second childishness and mere oblivion/Sans teeth, sans eyes, sans taste, sans everything." Old age is hard to laugh at, but we smile at Jaques's sourness, since he is describing facts that we accept cheerfully—except occasionally when we are deeply in the dumps.

Freudian and Post-Freudian Humor

If we are to "tune our mind-set" to enjoy Jaques or Joel, we need a theory explaining how anyone can find them amusing. I think the best account begins with Freud's theory of humor, as amended by British philosopher Simon Critchley. In 1905, Freud wrote *Jokes and Their Relation to the Unconscious,* a theory that laughter reveals one's pleasurable sense of unconscious superiority to the butt of the joke.[7]

To see his point, watch any late-night talk show. The host's opening monologue will be a cruel attack on prominent figures of the day. One cannot admire these jibes morally, and indeed Freud did not like jokes as much as what he would later call "humor," referring less to laughter than to smiling.

Freud wrote about humor in 1927, long after proposing his famous distinction among the ego, superego, and id. The superego originates when the ego splits in two, with one side becoming a disciplinarian toward the other side. To laugh at a *joke* is to treat another person as a child and oneself as a superior adult, as the critical superego. But as Critchley explains, "Now in adopting a *humorous* attitude towards myself it is precisely the other way around: I treat *myself* as a child from an adult perspective; I look at my childlike, diminutive ego from the standpoint of the big, grown-up superego.... Humor ... is an anti-depressant that works by the ego finding itself ridiculous.... I would argue that humor recalls us to the modesty and limitedness of the human condition."[8]

Here we see ourselves as antiheroes and find ourselves amusing. How are we able to do this? Critchley explains that after 1905, Freud's notion of the superego evolved in a gentler direction. By 1927, when he wrote about humor, it deserved a new name, which Critchley now proposes: "Superego II." "If 'superego I' is the prohibiting parent, scolding the child, then 'superego II' is the comforting parent."[9]

This gentler superego allows us to relinquish the glorified, superheroic aspirations that come from identifying with one's ego ideal. Thus one comes, as Freud wrote, "to resign oneself also to being a human being. To be a superman is to refuse all that en bloc, that is, to refuse the human condition."[10]

When Critchley claims that humor comes from viewing oneself as ridiculous, he seems to mean literally *oneself*. Yet one might regard another person as oneself and gently smile at his ridiculous qualities, as if at one's own failings. That is surely possible when we *identify* with another, such as Jaques or Joel. From the tolerant perspective of our Superego II, we smile at his grouchiness and accept the limited human condition.

This identification is deeper than ordinary empathy. After all, Joel and Jaques do not laugh at themselves or find their own crankiness amusing. If we merely empathized with them, we would see nothing humorous in their situation, either. It is *our own* Superego II that smiles at *their* imperfect egos, as if acknowledging our own childishness. Moreover, one beautiful effect of identifying with antiheroes is that we surmount our tendency to blame.

Superego II's generous affection is transcendent love. One doesn't deserve it, but it's given anyway. Such tolerance undermines the culture of blame. If Supergo II multiplies in a society, its benign outlook will enlighten not only the criminal justice system (as I suggested in the preceding chapter) but perhaps even public attitudes toward international affairs, diminishing blaming as a legitimation of warfare. Thus a show such as *Northern Exposure,* though ostensibly dealing only with personal relationships, is a visionary exercise, disciplining our hearts in larger ways. Much can come of learning to love characters who mirror our shortcomings and of comforting them with the smiles of our own Superego II.

But even Superego II has moral limits, and sometimes a hero or an antihero turns into a genuine villain or emotional moron. Whenever a character whom we love transgresses so gravely that we must break empathy with him, our superego is responsible for making that judgment. Whether it is the verdict of a tough Superego I or a loving Superego II, such an empathic rupture is excruciating, for it means that the character with whom we have identified must now be considered morally depraved. We bear some sense of guilt. Such distress should never be inflicted on trusting audiences. It's the opposite of the pitying resignation we derive from a great tragedy. Still, the antihero must come close to the edge sometimes, to impart new and beneficial ranges of tolerance to audiences as they explore moral predicaments. Now I want to apply the principles that we've explored so far to analyzing my favorite TV series.

Northern Exposure and Its Creative Sources

Executive producers Joshua Brand and John Falsey created *Northern Exposure* as an eight-episode summer filler in 1990. Critics and audiences loved it, so six months later the team reassembled, produced another eight episodes, and kept going for a total of 110 episodes.

The MTM Tradition

Brand and Falsey had learned their craft in TV's finest seedbed, an independent production company called MTM Enterprises. Named after its first series, *The Mary Tyler Moore Show,* MTM introduced "character comedy" to sitcom writing. Previous television comedies (e.g., *I Love Lucy*) had involved a funny, confusing situation but little human development or exploration of ideas. The denouement reduced the confusion without making viewers reassess their values. With MTM, however, the problems were emotional, and the solutions involved relationships.

Some producers argued that a comedy series cannot allow characters to develop, but MTM sitcoms did so. In fact, what was reduced in the MTM comedy was the *plot.* A similar situation might recur in several episodes. Each new version differed not in the plot but rather in the personal qualities of the characters, who had changed over time. All MTM comedies were character driven, involving an ensemble of complex personalities—usually colleagues in a workplace. The quasi-family structure permitted individuals to grow within the group rather than by leaving home.[11] (In this respect *Northern Exposure* departed from the MTM model, for no one grew much while Brand and Falsey ran the show.)[12]

MTM shows used intertextuality and self-reflexivity—styles in which the script refers to other texts or to itself. Modernist writing often displays such allusions. In *Northern Exposure,* hundreds of books, films, and authors are quoted, and their ideas are debated.

The plots of *Northern Exposure* involve three emotional motifs. First, Cicely exemplifies a *nonjudgmental community*; people are emotionally intelligent, with vast tolerance for ambiguity. They take each other lightly. Second, *Northern Exposure* employs the oldest narrative device, the *hero's journey,* wherein a protagonist is sent on a quest into a strange, magical land to confront difficult challenges. (In this case, it might more aptly be called the "antihero's journey.") Third, the series contains a romantic relationship characteristic of the classic Hollywood genre of the 1930s and 1940s known as the *screwball comedy.*

The Hero's Journey

We arrive in Cicely (population 844) along with its new physician, Dr. Joel Fleischman. Alaska has paid for this 28-year-old doctor's medical education at Columbia University, on condition that he practice four years in that state. His sojourn in Alaska represents the archetypal journey depicted by mythologist Joseph Campbell.[13] If his quest was for wisdom, he did not undertake it voluntarily. As a Jewish New Yorker of working-class origins, success has never come to him from adventurousness but from well-honed habits of reasoning and of complaining volubly. Still, great stories require the hero to venture into a faraway land where bizarre things happen, and so fate has brought Joel to a place where modern medicine is considered no more credible than the shamanic lore of the Tlingit Indians.

Ancient heroes did not begin as individuals. They had to earn their distinctiveness by their quest, but they would return home strengthened in the end. To Carl Jung also, individuation was supposedly the proper outcome of psychological maturation.

However, as Campbell pointed out, beginning perhaps with King Arthur's knights, Western heroism has come to involve a different kind of personal development. Each knight entered the forest alone, not in a group but already formed as an individual.[14] Indeed, Campbell believed that modern people need a new myth that replaces the hero's quest for individuation with a quest for a much older sensibility: a feeling of community. Such is the motif of *Northern Exposure*—at least until season 6.

Unlike the Cicelians, Joel lacks any spirit of thrill seeking. He is no knight, whether of the Camelot or the Don Quixote type, but a fully modern Western individual who sets off already knowing his own mind. Fortunately, he has psychological strengths. He is empathic enough to understand his patients' emotional troubles. He is capable of introspection and prayer, and of acknowledging his own abundant shortcomings. He is faithful to his fiancée, Elaine, who remains in New York studying law until she throws him over, early in the series. He is committed to medicine, even calling up faraway specialists and searching obscure journals for answers to clinical puzzles.

But Joel has far to go in his emotional development. He is materialistic and petulant, grumbling about trivial obstacles. He is oblivious to Alaska's mountainous beauty and afraid of its wildlife. Yet, as Campbell pointed out, we love people for their flaws more than their perfections, and most viewers adored Joel, even as they laughed at him. He won my heart in the pilot episode by throwing a public temper tantrum worthy of a two-year-old. I knew at a glance that I would receive a vicarious emotional education by following this man's excursions into strange places where I can never go.

Screwball Comedy

Whereas most Cicelians are light and nonjudgmental toward each other, that is not true of two people, Joel and his landlord, Maggie O'Connell (played by

Fig. 8.1. Rob Morrow played Dr. Joel Fleischman and Janine Turner played bush pilot Maggie O'Connell. Northern Exposure *still courtesy of Universal Studios Licensing LLLP.*

Janine Turner), who take each other all too seriously. Joel forms an ambivalent attachment to this stunning but difficult feminist bush pilot. They crave, yet dislike, each other.

Maggie comes from a rich family and is well educated but often flagrantly irrational. The boyfriend whom she accompanied to Alaska froze to death on a glacier. She has remained in Cicely, flying and servicing her own plane and ferrying mail. She wears boots and short hair and is hostile to men—especially Joel. (My Superego II finds it harder to indulge her personality than Joel's.) In Cicely she is considered "cursed" because four boyfriends have died accidentally. Her current boyfriend, Rick, will be felled by a plummeting satellite shortly after Joel's own fiancée Elaine sends him a Dear John letter.

Maggie is impulsive and devoid of introspection. She criticizes Joel for his rationality, scientific skepticism, and avoidance of risk. Her defensiveness is tolerated gently by the Cicelians—except Joel, who openly laughs at her. Their spectacular public fights will be interrupted occasionally by tender scenes. No plausible motivation is ever given for the mutual ambivalence of their relationship. After showing touching affection and intimacy, Maggie will again display shock and revulsion at herself for wanting Joel as a lifelong partner.

Brand and Falsey did not concoct this unlikely romance out of thin air but used the well-worn template of the screwball comedy, which had been popular in Hollywood films fifty years earlier. Screwball lovers engage in egalitarian, anarchic, and combative relationships that sometimes remain unconsummated. They are intelligent, verbal, and assertive. Both partners are ambivalent and fight constantly, despite their mutual sexual attraction. Clark Gable and Claudette Colbert in the 1934 film *It Happened One Night* provide a classic example.[15] Other famous films of the genre are *Bringing Up Baby, The Philadelphia Story, His Girl Friday, Adam's Rib,* and *The Awful Truth.*

For decades Stanley Cavell taught a philosophy course at Harvard that analyzed screwball comedies. He was almost unique among serious critics in regarding this type of film as important.[16] He liked how it showed characters addressing humorously the ethical complications of establishing or reestablishing a marital relationship. Often the couple had divorced but would finally renew their union. Cavell explains that "the concept of marriage, understood as remarriage, as a search for reaffirmation, is not merely an analogy of the social bond, or a comment upon it, but it is a further instance of experimentation in consent and reciprocity."[17] In these comedies, the marriage is saved not by promising each other a quiet conventional life but by rejecting that aspiration. Thus Walter and Hildy Burns, the journalistic team of ex-spouses in *His Girl Friday,* revive their life together by rushing off to cover a news story instead of having a honeymoon. In discussing this film, Cavell speculates about how they will find happiness. The Burnses' answer, he says, consists in their capacity for adventure, improvisation, and risk taking.[18]

For Joel and Maggie, too, the main conflict concerns their readiness to take risks together, but in their screwball comedy, it is the man, not the woman, who avoids physical danger. Maggie enjoys frightening Joel by hitting every air pocket when flying him around in her Cessna. Yet she has her own fears, which she will never fully surmount. As a wise old hermit tells her in the third episode, the risk that Maggie cannot bear to take is to pick a stable, family-oriented man such as Joel who lacks any dangerous hobbies and is likely to *live.*

Joel and Maggie differ from previous screwball comedy characters by parting in the end instead of continuing their spirited, mutually autonomous romance within marriage. If we take their relationship as seriously as Cavell proposed, we will feel exploited, for the couple will not commit to each other, and we will feel duped by the previous appearance of intensity in their ambivalent love.

Feminist critic Christine Scodari attributes their inexplicably nonchalant final parting to the influence of the MTM culture, where lively screwball antics were not thought to preclude friendship but to rule out a committed love relationship. Female viewers typically would like to see such free, adventurous interactions continue within a marriage, says Scodari, but most male viewers evidently do not consider that outcome possible or appealing.[19] As a woman, I, too, wanted Joel and Maggie to spend the rest of their lives zig-zagging between tenderness and combat. None of the men agreed; in fact, one male friend dropped out of my viewing group because he hated the couple's "bickering."

In *Cheers* and *Northern Exposure* (both produced by MTM alumni), the erotic consummation is immediately preceded by mutual threats of, or actual, violence. We are invited to suppose that this physical fight is sexually arousing. Afterward, however, the writers face the problem of reviving the sexual tension, lest the show's ratings drop. Typically, says Scodari, male viewers do lose interest, but women do not. The fate of Joel and Maggie was determined by this depressing MTM maxim. Whether or not Brand and Falsey shared this aesthetic, they left *Northern Exposure* in the hands of a cynical storyteller, David Chase, who ended the screwball romance. He also transformed Brand's nonjudgmental utopia into a dystopic precursor of the Mafia families that would inhabit his own show, *The Sopranos.*

Northern Exposure, having begun brilliantly as a comedy, ended as a tragedy, marked by reversals in all three of its guiding motifs. First, the nonjudgmental society turned judgmental; those who had previously displayed emotional intelligence began to act without insight. Second, the antihero turned heroic, now seeking self-realization and abandoning the lessons he had been sent to learn and the patients for whom he had previously cared. Third, the screwball romance came to an implausible end just after Joel had overcome the failings for which Maggie had previously rejected him.

It is not obvious why writers so often prefer sad endings today. I cannot accept Erich Segal's argument that comedy has died because happiness is impossible in this brutal modern world.[20] Perhaps it is merely a matter of fashion. For whatever reason, sad endings to dramas are considered more artistic—or perhaps only more realistic, in a period when realism is valued highly. In any case, they are not required by the logic of the plot. Therefore it is hard to justify these insults to the human immune system. As Campbell suggested, less medically, "sober, modern Occidental judgment is founded on a total misunderstanding of the realities depicted in the fairy tale, the myth, and the divine comedies of redemption. These, in the ancient world, were regarded as of a higher rank than tragedy, of a deeper truth, of a more difficult realization, of a sounder structure, and of a revelation more complete."[21]

The Cicelians

Several regular members of the ensemble appear in most episodes. Maurice Minnifield (played by Barry Corbin) is the town's big man, yet sometimes a buffoon. He was a pilot in the Korean War and then an astronaut. Upon retiring to Alaska he bought fifteen thousand acres of land and set up a logging business, a radio station, and a newspaper. A burly Oklahoman who wears a NASA cap instead of a cowboy hat, Maurice combines sophistication with bigotry. He lives alone in a superbly furnished log house on Cicely's outskirts, raising orchids and collecting wine, antiques, and art. In middle age, he has fallen in love with an innocent, uneducated teenage beauty queen from a Saskatoon trailer park, Shelly Tambo (played by Cynthia Geary), whom he has brought to Cicely, planning to marry her.

But Shelly soon realizes that Maurice is not right for her. An attraction blossoms between her and Maurice's best friend, tavern keeper Holling Vincoeur (played by John Cullum). He is old enough to be her grandfather yet virile enough to satisfy her exceptional libido. Holling is a French Canadian who spent years as a trapper. After being mauled by a grizzly bear named Jesse, he quit shooting animals (except on film) and bought a tavern, the Brick. Shelly moves into his apartment above the bar, working as a waitress alongside her new "squeeze."

Ed Chigliak (played by Darren E. Burrows) is a sweet, earnest 18-year-old. The offspring of a single white woman and an Indian father, he was a foundling. The tribe raised him collectively, but he yearns to find his parents. Now he works part-time for Maurice Minnifield and lives in a rented room with his videotapes. Ed will soon decide on a career as a filmmaker. Whenever any issue comes up, he will reflect on the countless films he has watched, searching for a similar moral situation from which to learn how to respond. (We can learn ethical/emotional criticism from him.) He supplements his job with Maurice by working for Ruth-Anne Miller (played by Peg Phillips) in her general store. Finding himself "called" to become a shaman, he also enters training with a native healer. Despite his youthful naiveté, Ed is Joel's archetypal guide and helper in this strange wilderness.

Marilyn Whirlwind (played by Elaine Miles) is Joel's receptionist. A thirtyish round Indian woman of few words or facial expressions, she lives with her parents and spends her time in the office knitting or just sitting. Yet she does have interests. She dances in native rituals and Cajun two-step competitions; she keeps ostriches; she once took a vacation trip by herself to Seattle; and upon occasion she attracts male admirers.

Ruth-Anne Miller is a brisk, outspoken widow of seventy-three who runs the general store and keeps mail for townspeople to pick up. Like Holling, she is a bird-watcher, and they sometimes go together into the bush with cameras. Ruth-Anne can be supportive, especially toward Ed, whose self-esteem is never secure. Like many other Cicelians, Ruth-Anne combines ordinariness with sophistication: Her sweatshirt proclaims "Born to Bingo!" and her loose dentures click when she talks, yet she starts studying Italian so she can read Dante's *The Divine Comedy.*

Chris Stevens (played by John Corbett) comes from a dysfunctional West Virginia family. His mother was an alcoholic, his father a thief who rarely was at home. As a teenager Chris had gone to prison, where he read voraciously. Eventually he wound up in Cicely as a disk jockey/philosopher/artist/intellectual/minister who constructs large metal sculptures. He conducts the weddings, funerals, and other ceremonies. Everyone turns to him for counseling, and on Cicely's radio station, KBHR, he reads wonderful books aloud.[22]

Chris is a dead ringer for Jesus. In fact, he appears as Christ in a few scenes, and in person he, too, is infinitely forgiving and supportive. He wears tattered clothing, lives in a metal trailer in a yard piled high with old junk, and rides a Harley-Davidson. Like other Cicelians, Chris is a risk taker. Women are attracted by his extraordinary pheromones, and he occasionally falls in love, but only briefly. No new girlfriend reappears in subsequent episodes. Probably Chris is too lost in his thoughts to be preoccupied long with a lover.

His closest relationship is with Bernard (played by Richard Cummings Jr.), a black motorcyclist who sits down beside him one morning in the Brick. An accountant living in Portland, Bernard has been overcome by an impulse to buy a Harley and ride north. Chris is working on a huge metal sculpture, and Bernard offers to stay and help him. They soon discover that they are half-brothers, born on the same day, sons of a white traveling man who divided his time between two families, black and white. Neither "twin" had heard of the other before, but they are attuned telepathically from then on.

Adam and Eve (played by Adam Arkin and Valerie Mahaffy) are a wild couple who live in the woods. Initially Adam was thought to be a myth—a legendary, dangerous, local "Bigfoot" creature—but he turned out to be a Vietnam veteran, avoiding human society, who threatens everyone who comes near. He is also a superb professional chef who seems to know everything—possibly because of obscure connections to the CIA. His wife is a consummate hypochondriac who studies medical books and diagnoses grave diseases in everyone she meets. This hilarious pair is the most popular—yet the most emotionally unintelligent—couple on the show, which proves that we don't hold inappropriateness against characters so long as they are funny or, like Joel, lovable antiheroes.

A Polis on the Frontier

Brand and Falsey set *Northern Exposure* in Alaska because that was the "final frontier" in American society. Apart from Ed and Marilyn, whose tribe has inhabited Alaska for thousands of years, the townspeople came as bold migrants. Maurice was a rapacious entrepreneur, Chris was a wandering ex-criminal, Ruth-Anne followed "the open road," and Maggie came in rebellion against her conventional family. Only Joel has come against his will, and he alone misses the high culture of the East. This frontier town is free of class conflict. Cicelians neither defer to nor resent the only local plutocrat, Maurice.

The frontier especially attracts thrill seekers, and Chris worries about the loss of challenges for explorers and danger seekers—in Alaska especially, but everywhere else, too. In a wistful soliloquy on the radio, he calls the space program a substitute for human adventure. Our rockets are our surrogate risk takers.

But if you have to settle for a place on earth, Cicely is a good choice. The seedy old mining town resembles a Greek polis in its acceptance of diverse public opinions. Although all small communities can be oppressive, almost totalitarian, the one safeguard of Greek freedom was this: Citizens could always voice their opinions openly in public meetings. Cicely's town meetings are frequent, and debates are lively. Thus, during a Russian flu epidemic, the town meeting blames it on Joel. In other meetings the townspeople express their preferences for radio programming, collectively refuse to ship a dead stranger off to Anchorage for an autopsy, and decide to peek inside a mysterious unclaimed package covered with foreign postage stamps.

In ancient communities, members exchanged services as gifts, rather than by cash payment. The same pattern holds true in Cicely, where anyone sick or with car trouble can count on her neighbors. Cicelians rarely use the phone but drop in on each other unannounced—a practice that is unacceptable in cities. Many people use the same keys and can come in even when a house is empty. Ed, in particular, habitually walks in and makes himself at home. As he explains to Joel, Indians don't knock—it's rude.

It is Chris, KBHR radio's "Greek chorus," who best understands the meaning of community, as when, for example, he reads aloud Einstein's thoughts on the human bond: "Strange is our situation here on Earth. Each of us comes for a short visit, not knowing why, yet sometimes seeming to divine a purpose. From the standpoint of daily life, however, there is one thing we do know: that man is here for the sake of other men—above all for those upon whose smiles and well-being our own happiness depends, and also for the countless unknown souls with whose fate we are connected by a bond of sympathy."[23]

Joel's assignment in Cicely, we soon decide, is to acquire this warm sense of community by learning that he exists for the sake of others. He must learn to be appropriate with others. Already he's open in expressing his own feelings—sometimes overly so. Now he needs to empathize more and feel as others do, at the right time and for the right reason. As he learns perceptiveness and agreeableness, so will we viewers.

We recognize the appropriateness of Cicelians in three ways. First, we appreciate their light responses to those whose emotional intelligence seems to be, at least temporarily, subnormal. Second, we observe their generous use of "restorative justice" for infractions that the official criminal justice system would treat more sternly. And third, we watch their kindness toward one another. I'll give examples of all three.

Responding to Low Emotional Intelligence

Tactlessness is the negative aspect of Ed's guileless personality. The ever-resilient Ruth-Anne turns seventy-five without mentioning it to anyone. When Ed finds out how old she is, he starts worrying aloud about her dwindling life expectancy. She has broken a toe, and he annoys her by hovering oversolicitously. The locals have not given her a party or a gift, so he secretly begins organizing a belated celebration at the Brick. He asks Chris what to buy her for a present and ponders earnestly Chris's offhand suggestion: "a gift that keeps on giving."

That evening, after she closes up the store, Chris helps her hobble over to the Brick, where they find the whole community assembled for a surprise birthday party. Ruth-Anne beckons Ed over for a hug, and he hands her a peculiar gift: a glass fruit jar full of dirt. He explains mysteriously that he could only put a small part of the gift into the jar but will take her to see the rest of it. On the next day, they walk along a spectacular panoramic cliff overlooking a river. Here he points out the rest of his present: a small plot of land for her grave.

Anyone else might be astonished by the insensitive mind that has imagined such a gift, but Ruth-Anne is not fazed. She smiles involuntarily, but then recovers and looks around appreciatively. It is, she announces, a beautiful place to spend eternity. And now she wants to dance—right here, on her grave.

The camera slowly moves back a great distance, and we hear a cello. For a long time, Ed and Ruth-Anne joyously dance. It is an inspired, magnificently appropriate, emotional scene.

Justice in a Nonjudgmental Society

Unlike *Street Time,* which illustrates, as a cautionary tale, the flawed workings of the criminal justice system, *Northern Exposure* illustrates instead an alternative approach to handling crime. In Cicely the culture of blame does not prevail. Whenever possible, the Cicelians use informal restorative justice without punishment. This approach is especially easy to do when the "criminal" is their most beloved citizen—their pastor, Chris Stevens.

Suddenly Chris is arrested for crimes committed years before. A white-haired female judge arrives in town to hear his case, and it seems certain that he will be extradited to West Virginia. Chris considers it pointless to defend himself since he has indeed violated parole by leaving Wheeling. Resigned, he attributes this turn of events to his accumulated karma. The other Cicelians also accept the inevitable verdict with fatalism—except Maurice, who hires the only lawyer in town, Mike Monroe.

The prospects are dim, Mike knows, but he gets an idea: to challenge the warrant on grounds of identity. When court begins, he tells the judge that the man standing before her is not the same Chris Stevens named in the warrant. He argues that Chris has undergone such an extreme personality change as to constitute a new identity. This is a preposterous argument, he knows, but it is the only angle he can think of, so he asks Maggie to fly to Anchorage and look up legal precedents involving identity. There aren't any.

During the recess, Chris returns to KBHR, where Bernard is substituting for him as DJ. A caller phones in, asking about the metaphysics of changing identity. Was this like what had happened to Saul of Tarsus on the road to Damascus? A blinding light and suddenly he's Saint Paul? Chris himself is uncertain about the nature of his redemption. Has it made him over or just returned him to his true inner nature? Most theologians, he realizes, take the latter view, but he has no fixed opinion.

That night, the Cicelians throw a farewell party for him at the Brick. Joel commiserates with his ill-fated friend, but Chris is resigned, comparing his case to that of Herman Melville's character Billy Budd. He recounts the plot to Joel. The sailor Billy Budd, beloved by the rest of his crew, unintentionally kills an officer on board. The captain sorrowfully concludes that, to maintain order for the good of the state, he has to punish the guilty. Billy is hanged.[24]Joel seems more depressed by this story than Chris himself, who as usual can admire both of the contradictory arguments.

The next day, Mike calls a series of character witnesses. Shelly describes how Chris heard her confession once when she had become addicted to television. The judge is astonished to learn that Chris is the town minister, having answered an ad in *Rolling Stone* for ordination. Holling tells of having neglected to pay his income taxes for thirty-three years; Chris bailed him out with a loan of $9,000. Maggie tells about the time when her mother visited and accidentally burned down her house. Chris had been looking in the ashes for something to fling with the giant medieval siege weapon he was building. He chose her charred piano. The fling was so moving that Maggie forgot all about her problems.

Now the judge adjourns to review the evidence. When she returns, she says that the fingerprints give her no choice but to turn Chris over to the state of West Virginia. However, she notes that sometimes the removal of an offender imposes a burden on the community worse than his offense itself. It is acceptable to postpone the sentence on such an occasion—which this one seems to be. Therefore, she orders freedom for Chris for up to three years, until the town hires another disk jockey. If they fail to do so by then, Chris must be turned over to West Virginia—*if they show up asking for him.*

State justice has just bent to fit Cicely's version of community justice. In this case, no punishment is imposed at all, for everyone can see that the culprit has already redeemed himself. Chris escapes the doom that Melville portrayed as an inevitable outcome of formal legalism. Could such an appropriate outcome occur in a real U.S. courtroom? One member of our e-mail discussion list is a high-ranking federal judge. When we asked him whether such a verdict might actually hold water, he genially advised us not to expect it. But from the standpoint of ethical/emotional criticism, the beauty of this work of fiction is its illustration of how we should live—how society can be changed for the better.

Emotionally Appropriate Friendship

Only since the early 1990s has the concept of emotional intelligence become popular. It was introduced by the psychologist Daniel Goleman, who says it is often even more important in life than ordinary intelligence, which is an entirely different quality. For example, he points out that a "pure-type" high-IQ male is usually critical, inhibited, unexpressive and detached, and emotionally either bland or cold. A man who is high in emotional intelligence, by contrast, is outgoing and cheerful, not prone to fearfulness or worry, responsible, with a rich but appropriate emotional life, and fully capable of friendship and caring relationships.[25] Numerous Cicelians are brilliant in the intellectual sense and also gifted with emotional intelligence, but in these respects, no one surpasses Chris Stevens. His emotional appropriateness is visible in almost every episode, as I'll illustrate here by depicting a situation in which he becomes involved unwittingly in Ed's love life.

Working part-time in Ruth-Anne's store, Ed is suddenly overwhelmed by the beauty of an auburn-haired customer named Lightfeather, who seems to viewers conspicuously plain and lacking in personality. However, Ed is a virgin and his time has come. He hastens to Chris's broadcasting booth and, while the next record is spinning, consults him about how to pursue Lightfeather.He wants Chris to write a letter for him, for no one else in town can match Chris's gift with words. Chris has some misgivings about providing this assistance but does not resist long. He writes an erotic poem for Ed, portraying Lightfeather as his Harley-Davidson motorcycle. "I want to ride, ride, ride you!" declares one steamy verse.

The poem is amazingly successful. By the time Ed pays his first visit, the girl's heart already belongs to him. Lightfeather is milking the cows amid hay, which provides a perfect locale for a glorious first tryst. Soon Ed is seeing his beloved regularly and reporting back to Chris, requiring ever more help.

For Lightfeather the chief attraction is the poems. She demands more and more of them, and Chris keeps writing them for the younger man. Ed is invited to dinner at Lightfeather's house and has to give an account of his career aspirations, for he is getting serious. When he tells Chris he wants to marry her, Chris points out that eventually Ed will have to start speaking for himself without help.

Predictably, Lightfeather hears Chris on the radio describing how he had fallen in love with a Harley Hog. Recognizing him as the author of the verses that have touched her soul, she flees to his radio booth and discloses her craving for such phrases as "hot roaring machinery" and "swelling fuel tank." Chris gives her a reading list and agrees to compose one last poetic letter ("Shall I compare thee to a summer's day? ...") if she will then leave.

Poor Ed. He gets dumped for his deception and sits in his room grieving. Chris comes to see him, full of remorse and apologies. Ed admits that he begged Chris to write those letters. He says he always wondered what sex would be like, but it was much better than he had ever imagined. Now he is disconsolate.

"I know you're not going to believe this," replies Chris, "and I know you're hurting, but this experience is going to transmute itself. It is. You do something like this, and it tears you apart. But eventually it becomes one of your fondest memories."

A day or two later, Chris sees Ed in the Brick and asks how he is doing.

"Oh, I feel bad," says Ed. "But I guess it feels kinda good. I think I'm starting to transmute the experience already."

"Yeah," replies Chris. "You were apple juice, and now you're apple cider."

These scenes are moving for aesthetic reasons. The actors are superb, evoking feelings a viewer may not have recalled since his own youth. And if we ask ourselves how we should live, we might point to this scene, admiring Chris's emotional appropriateness and the perfect insights he shares with Ed. We want to live life just that way.

To call Chris "moral" in this situation is to lose something in the translation, but that idea is worth considering anyway. We worry at first that Ed may get so deeply involved in a relationship with an unpromising young woman that he will be unable to retreat without grave complications. We want him to have this relationship, and we want it to be sweet but temporary. Instead of mourning with him, we are glad that Chris's ethical lapse worked out as it did and that Chris acknowledged his mistake in writing the letters for Ed. Had he refused to apologize or sympathize, we would have seen this as a moral flaw.

To appreciate the excellence of Chris's responses, we can compare the incident to a far better-known case. Cyrano de Bergerac, famous for his immense nose, loves Roxane, who from a distance loves Christian, a handsome but unremarkable young soldier whom she does not yet know.[26] Believing himself too ugly for Roxane, Cyrano writes love letters on behalf of Christian that win Roxane's heart. Before Roxane has a chance to discover the truth, as Lightfeather does, Christian is killed in battle. Roxane enters a convent and spends the rest of her life there, mourning and receiving regular visits from her dear old friend Cyrano, who never sets the record straight. After fifteen years, Cyrano appears one day, dying. Only then does Roxane learn that the man she has always loved is Cyrano. If she had realized earlier who had authored those old letters, she would have married him, but now it is too late. "I have only ever loved one man," she says, "and I have lost him twice."

As a teenager, I loved the self-sacrificing Cyrano. Years later, I realized that what he had done was not noble but unspeakably cruel. Had Roxane married the tongue-tied, callow Christian under the false impression that he was the author of the love letters, her life might have been ruined. And her life was ruined anyway, for she and Cyrano might have had a wonderful marriage, but he cheated them of that possibility by his deception. And during that whole time, he was proud of himself for keeping the old secret honorably.

Any admiration of Cyrano was misplaced. Today I would admire him more if he had apologized to Roxane for the deprivation his lie had caused her, just as Chris apologized to Ed. He would have had to tell her the truth—that her affection for Christian had been manipulated. Such a revelation, coming after Christian's death, might have seemed disrespectful. The only way I can imagine Cyrano helping her cope with this sad truth would be to state, as Chris did, that her pain would eventually transmute itself into a fond memory of her first great love. That's a message we all need to hear sometimes. And we can all learn by observing and empathizing with an emotional genius such as Chris.

Myth and Logos

Even in Alaska, we've not left behind the ancient quarrel between philosophy and poetry—or at least *Plato's* ancient quarrel, since Aristotle (who was every bit as much a philosopher) took the side of the poets, insisting that much is learned from plays and Homeric myths. It's just that what you learn from poetry may be lost if you translate it into systematic exposition. This issue remains important to us because *Northern Exposure*'s characters tell myths to each other all the time, and the series itself is a modern myth.

Some have called the show a modern fairy tale, but I think that's mistaken. A fairy tale is an optimistic wish fulfillment escape from real life—always with a happy ending. A myth, however, reminds us of the finitude of human existence and tells us something serious, perhaps even mystical, about how to live.[27] As Bruno Bettelheim notes, "The myth presents its theme in a majestic way; it carries spiritual force; and the divine is present and experienced in the form of superhuman heroes who make constant demands on mere mortals."[28] That's what I get from *Northern Exposure* for, even when it seems light and playful, I can see it symbolizes moral struggles between human desire and larger powers. It speaks to the soul. Fairy tales don't.

Yet Plato's philosophy, in its own way, also speaks to the soul, though its language is rational (actually, Plato made up myths of his own, even while criticizing the practice).[29] The Greek philosophers who developed rationality or systematic exposition called it *logos,* in distinction to an earlier way of thinking, *muthos*—which we call "myth." Logos (the source of our word *logic*) was critical enquiry that might involve questioning, considering proofs, and arguing, as opposed to accepting the speaker's personal charisma or the poetic beauty of his expressiveness. Logos arose with the emergence of democracy in Greece, for it offered compelling ways of persuading an audience.[30] Myth, on the other hand, was a pre-urban way of thinking that characterized Homer's *Iliad* and *Odyssey,* which dated to the Bronze Age—and of course myths are told in all other preliterate societies as well.

The Cicelians do not consider it necessary to choose between myth and logos. They accept without question all kinds of rationally inexplicable magical experiences—yet they also weave logos into each discussion. The townspeople are natural-born intellectuals in an enchanted world. If a myth were a finger, it always point toward the moon—the larger meaning—which they debate with passion and intelligence. At first, Joel is frustrated talking with them because he is a logos man, par excellence, and he can't understand how any sane person could imagine, for example, that trees can talk or that there is value in thinking like a fish. Over time, however, he, too, learns to communicate in metaphors—a skill that actually proves clinically useful.

Joshua Brand's writers accepted Carl Jung's explanation of myth as reflecting humankind's inherited "collective unconscious." People in all societies supposedly have a similar cast of symbolic figures inhabiting our dreams and myths—archetypes such as dragons, witches, and Merlin-like old wise men.[31] Jungian folklorists find similarities among dramas and dreams around the world. However, most other psychologists doubt that archetypes can be listed or that human beings have a common "collective unconscious" hard-wired into our nervous systems. Joseph Campbell did believe in Jung's collective unconscious, and *Northern Exposure* draws on Jung's mythic themes.[32] Some of the most interesting applications of the mythic imagination in the show are those proposed by a Tlingit shaman.

Healing Myths

Healing stories are metaphors that insightful people or healers use to illumine others' existential predicaments and ailments. For example, in Hindu medicine, carefully selected tales are told to psychologically disturbed individuals, who are supposed to meditate on them, visualizing both their personal problem and a solution to it.[33] In Alaska, too, Native shamans often tell healing stories to their patients.

Ed is preparing to be a shaman, which will combine his storytelling in two careers: as a filmmaker and as a healer. He is training with a wise native healer, Leonard Quinhagak (played by Graham Greene) but, because of low self-confidence, actually is neither working on a movie script nor studying for his career as a medicine man. He doesn't know what path to take and is getting stomach aches from thinking about his shortcomings.

Leonard begins feeling low himself. He has acquired a tape recorder with which to collect healing stories from whites. However, whenever people tell him a legend, it always turns out to be a creepy urban myth rather than anything inspiring or healing. "White people don't seem at all concerned with using mythology to heal themselves," he tells Chris sadly. "In fact, they seem intent on making each other feel worse. So I'm abandoning the project."

But he goes to see Ed, who is watching Orson Welles's film classic *Citizen Kane* for about the twentieth time. Ed says that his stomach never hurts while he watches it. However, he adds, when it ends he'll still have to figure out what to do with his life.

This conversation makes Leonard think: Perhaps white people's healing stories are *movies*. The scene that touches Ed most is about Kane launching a newspaper—*getting going* with his project. Leonard says, "The path to our destination is not always a straight one, Ed. We go down the wrong road, we get lost, we turn back. Maybe it doesn't matter which road we embark on. Maybe what matters is that *we embark.*"

That message sinks in, for later we see Ed settling down with new determination, beginning to write a script. Yet what strikes me is that the film alone didn't convey the wisdom. It was Leonard's philosophizing *about the film* that worked. Myth combines with philosophy in a fruitful synergy, illustrating Plato's basic point: that the meanings of deeply significant stories do not necessarily register until a wise comment is added to explain them.

Joel's emotional intelligence increases in Cicely and he begins inventing healing stories, too. For example, he creates a sexual fantasy to help Shelly. Halfway through the series, Holling and Shelly get married and she becomes pregnant. This condition delights her but also brings about a disappointing change. Whereas she and Holling have previously enjoyed a remarkable sex life (an average of four times a day), she now has lost the inclination altogether. She consults Joel, who reassures her that her libido will eventually return. But then, surmising what is inhibiting her, he tells her to close her eyes and imagine a fern that is growing. He says, "Now in order for that fern to keep thriving, it needs to be tended. It needs food. And it needs … water. Without it, that fern shrivels up. So that's what you have to do. You have to water the plant."

A light goes on as Shelly realizes what he is driving at, and she smiles. "Oh, yes!" she nods happily. "Water the plant!" End of healing myth. Life presumably returns to normal that night, up in the Vincoeur "love grotto" above the tavern.

Joel was learning. Aristotle would have laughed.

Toward Joel's Community Spirit

Joel's quest was assigned to him by life—which is usual for a hero on a journey. From the beginning we consider his main developmental task to be not individuation (which he already possessed) but rather to acquire a sense of community.

Community Spirit in Cicely's Thanksgiving

Every viewer can see the solution to Joel's misery in Cicely: He should stop resenting his exile and embrace his role. Yet he resists learning that lesson. Whenever he finds himself turning into a Cicelian, he reacts with dismay. Still, his low emotional intelligence appeals to every Superego II.

A gorgeous street scene opens the "Thanksgiving" episode, as the Cicelians decorate with pumpkins and skull faces for their autumn celebrations—American Thanksgiving, combined with the Day of the Dead,[34] which originated with native people. While the whites prepare a potluck feast in Holling's bar, the natives organize a parade of ghosts and vultures and assemble stashes of overripe tomatoes, which they throw at white passersby, who laugh whenever they are smacked. Joel is unaware of this native custom until Ed, calling out in a friendly way, lands a red, juicy one on him.

Shocked, Joel makes his way to the office to wash up. Marilyn explains to him that the Indian tradition is both a celebration and an occasion for expressiveness. This is an annual opportunity for oppressed people to vent their antagonism toward whites in a playful way. Joel insists that he is not white but Jewish—and *his* ancestors had been oppressed, too.

But matters are about to get worse for Joel. He receives a letter from the state of Alaska informing him that an extra year has been added to his term in Cicely. His original contract was in 1986 dollars, but with inflation he owes five instead of four years in payment for his medical education. Learning that he had no legal case against the state, he falls into depression, lying on the floor under his desk, immobilized. Whenever he sees patients, he is downright hostile. He dreams he is the replacement for Sisyphus. Now he is the guy rolling the boulder uphill.

Meanwhile, Chris is feeling depressed, too. Only upon seeing some large cans of green beans in Ruth-Anne's store does he realize why: he is homesick for prison. "These were the beans!" he tells Ruth-Anne. "Every Tuesday and Thursday for three years, these babies had a regular spot in the corner triangle of my dinner tray! I'm going to buy all these beans."

On the radio later, he recalls fondly the best Thanksgiving of his life—in prison. In fact, he is so homesick that he calls and arranges a sentimental visit with his old buddies, live on KBHR. They chat excitedly about who is in solitary, who stabbed whom, who is on parole, and who has gone states' evidence. Chris is elated to hear their voices.

Joel, for his part, is still miserable. The Indians invite him to march with them in their parade, but he does so gloomily. Then the whole crowd heads to the Brick for the feast. It is a gorgeous scene—the quaint old Victorian bar, the music, the exuberant Indians in wacky costumes, platters of food circulating. Ed sits down at the table beside Joel, who complains that his sentence in Cicely is longer than that of many convicted felons.

In his mind, he is "doing hard time." In the most beautiful setting imaginable, Joel feels wretched and believes himself incarcerated. Yet Chris, who has experienced real incarceration, knows that it, too, can be enjoyed. We all construct our own social reality, and we can find sweetness or misery anywhere.

This episode provides one of the loveliest lessons of *Northern Exposure,* and I thank Josh Brand and David Assael for writing it and showing us how to live. It perfectly illustrates Joseph Campbell's observation that we love people not for their perfections but for their imperfections. I laughed at Joel throughout the episode, though I also loved him. It was easy to empathize with him because I have been exactly the same kind of jerk a thousand times myself, making myself miserable in the midst of joy and abundance. (Haven't you?)

I interviewed Michael Fresco, the director of "Thanksgiving," who had another insight about the episode. He pointed out how much fun the Indians and whites had with the tomatoes as a way of handling the anger native people still feel, for valid reasons. Marilyn explains to Joel what the whites have done to Indian society, as Fresco recalled:

> The whites had brought chain saws and Ben and Jerry's ice cream and hundreds of TV channels to them—but they also brought smallpox, pollution, and other horrible things. Indians were ambivalent and celebrated with a totally fictive tradition—throwing tomatoes at white people.
>
> Concurrent with that Thanksgiving show, I did another show that also took place in a small town. And in that show the natives were also very angry at the whites. But they seized City Hall. There was a big standoff and guns were drawn. The whites were outside shooting. It was so hard-hitting! We tried to address the same thing—that the natives were angry and ambivalent. But wow! The way *Northern* addressed it was very, very clever.

The Community versus the Doctor

The exact opposite of the "Thanksgiving" plot can be seen in an episode called "Northern Lights." Produced during the fourth season (before the show was turned over to Chase) and written by the gifted team of Diane Frolov and Andrew Schneider, it should have been a winner, but to my mind (and I am far from alone on this opinion), it is the worst mistake of the entire series. Whereas in "Thanksgiving" the Cicelians display their typically generous forbearance, yet the emotionally immature Joel resists their heart-warming community spirit, in "Northern Lights" it is the opposite. Cicely withholds from Joel what is due him and abuses him with gratuitous cruelty, yet eventually he swallows his pride and abjectly crawls back to join the community. Whereas "Thanksgiving" filled me with joy, "Northern Lights" filled me with bitterness and even hatred.

There are three storylines, two of which actually are beautiful. The story takes place during the darkest, coldest weeks of Alaska's winter. Chris is constructing another huge metal sculpture but feels dissatisfied with it, so he abandons his first try and begins borrowing as many lamps and lighting fixtures as he can find.

Now a derelict man arrives in town, camping in a tent and scrounging through trash cans. At first Maurice is contemptuous, but then he discovers that the man is a veteran like himself. He takes him into his home, gives him some odd jobs, and urges him to reestablish himself in respectable society. The guy refuses. It seems that he had once seen lights at night that could only have been a UFO. By speaking publicly about what he saw, he had become an outsider, yet in his pride, he has refused to keep quiet about his experience. Maurice pleads with him. He, too, had seen strange, inexplicable lights as a pilot and astronaut, but he learned to keep them to himself. But the hobo will make no such concession for the sake of being socially accepted.

The third story in the episode involves Joel, who is eagerly preparing for his trip to the Caribbean—a vacation to which he is legally entitled in his contract with Alaska. At the last moment, however, word comes that the state has cancelled his vacation for lack of a qualified substitute. Incensed, Joel asks the other Cicelians to support his demand. They respond with total indifference. Now feeling like a victim of the class struggle, Joel summons up the courage to defend his rights against the power structure as a heroic working man. He will strike! He arranges for the doctor in the next town to be on call, then declines to treat any patients until justice is done. (Luckily, nobody is sick anyhow.)

Led by Maurice, the townspeople strike back. They seize Joel's personal belongings and lock him out of his cabin. When, in shock, he asks how they could treat him this way, everyone shrugs. Shelly says she is just showing team spirit. Nobody seems angry—just callous. Even Ed lines up with the community.

Joel has to move into the tent in the snow that the hobo has vacated. For days he huddles there in the frozen dark, eating from tin cans and sticking to his principles. Eventually, however, he caves in. With hardly a word, he returns to his office and smoothly resumes his work, as if the town has not crushed and humiliated him decisively. He says something to Marilyn about going with the flow. The Cicelians are equally nonchalant. They are assembling outdoors to see Chris's new sculpture, and when Joel shows up, no one reacts. Ruth-Anne offers to give him her latest oil painting. Then Chris switches on his gigantic light sculpture—thousands of old lamps from people's basements strung together in the street. The town glows. Everyone is happy.

Well, not everyone. Along with millions of other viewers, I was devastated. The writers had made me love a dozen characters and then turned them into cruel monsters with whom I had to break empathy. I loathed all of them now. I felt as if I had found out that all my dearest companions in real life were actually vicious, heartless criminals who had only been masquerading as kind, nonjudgmental, moral friends. This was the experience that made me realize the importance of preventing empathic ruptures and preserving the audience's loves. It also made me realize that fiction and everyday life are equally real and can be equally close to one's heart. That week, I lost a friend to cancer—someone who had been dear to me for thirty years—but I did not grieve. Instead, I was glad that she was finally released from her long suffering. Nevertheless, it was the worst week I experienced for years because I lost my love for my Cicelian friends. I doubted I'd ever be able to forgive them. I was sleepless from the stress. My cortisol levels must have reached record highs.

A few people on the e-mail list tried to justify what had happened. After all, Joel had gone on strike. I agree that physicians' strikes are ethically questionable, but they do happen—sometimes on a large scale. And Joel's marginal moral decision about the strike could not be compared to the extraordinary evil of Cicelians seizing his belongings and forcing him to live in a tent in Alaska's cold. He could have frozen to death. He had looked after them, but now they treated him worse than a hobo stranger. Ethically, Joel should simply have gone, as planned, to the Caribbean and used his contract to defy the state of Alaska. (My grandfather was the only doctor in an Oklahoma town smaller than Cicely. Every summer he went to California to visit his daughters, but no one considered that trip unethical. If he had said he was on strike, however, his patients might have taken offense.)

Besides my empathic rupture with the Cicelians, I was disappointed in Joel. Even the hobo was more honorable: he accepted permanent exclusion from normal society rather than conform to pressure. Joel, however, capitulated. Though my Superego II easily smiled at his emotional inappropriateness in other episodes, including "Thanksgiving," his failings on such occasions reflected immaturity, but not serious moral inadequacy. In "Northern Lights," however, he did not get angry when he should have. There is a time when one must be angry—when failure to be outraged is a serious character flaw. As Aristotle said, a person who is not angry will not defend himself, and it is slavish to let oneself be trampled underfoot. In "Thanksgiving," Joel has every basis for learning to appreciate a sense of community, but he does not learn it. In "Northern Lights," he has no basis at all for feeling part of the community, yet the writers ask us to believe that he *does* so. This is bad writing. It teaches the viewers nothing valid about either emotional appropriateness or moral integrity.

I am not suggesting that Joel should be violent—only that he is cowardly. (To Mohandas K. Gandhi, cowardice was the worst flaw. Even courageous *violence* was morally superior to cowardly nonviolence. Of course, courageous nonviolent action was best of all. He said, "Noncooperation with evil is as much a duty as cooperation with good.") In "Northern Lights," the Cicelians' cruelty is evil and should not be accepted. Instead, the writers should have invented an effective way for Joel to take a stand without harming anyone.

Conclusion

I'm still leaning toward Aristotle. We can, as he said, learn from good drama. A play, by simulating a situation, lets us figure out in advance how to handle real life. Thinking it through ahead of time allows us to prepare. Joel Fleischman is a crash test dummy, going through wrecks in our stead and showing what might happen to any of us. That's why his story can seem so important to us. We'd miss our learning opportunity if we stopped empathizing with him whenever the situation becomes painful.

I hope the world never betrays me as viciously as Cicely betrays Joel in "Northern Lights." But if that happens, what should I do? Even to consider this possibility is emotionally and physiologically so stressful that it can be justified as a plot only if it demonstrates how we should live. The writers of "Northern Lights" teach the wrong message. Luckily, by applying logos, I finally recognized some of their errors—and also some of my own.

I've promoted transcendence repeatedly in this book. I've advised empathizing instead of blaming. Use restorative justice instead of legalistic punishment. Smile tolerantly at antiheroes. Take other people and their quirks lightly, with civil inattention. Don't ridicule others who are less developed than you. Learn to see yourself as ridiculous, while smiling at your human shortcomings and at those of others, too. Forgive your enemies if you can. I still say this is mainly good advice. Such nonjudgmental attitudes help reduce conflict and allow for problem solving.

But not all conflict is an illusion, nor can it always be managed perfectly by empathizing instead of blaming. A few conflicts actually must be waged—not destructively so, but definitely head-on. Occasionally, blaming or even anger is appropriate.

Still, the right emotion does not, by itself, guarantee the right action. As Plato suggested, philosophy also matters, for storytellers sometimes make mistakes, and someone must use logos to figure out where they went wrong. The writers of "Northern Lights" hurt countless viewers, though not all of them knew why they felt so bad afterward. The episode needed to end with the Cicelians regretting their cruelty and somehow restoring mutuality with Joel. Nothing short of that message could have justified the painful empathic rupture and the vindictive morality that it promoted.

Northern Exposure is an aesthetic treat and an unsurpassed illustration of emotional appropriateness and moral wisdom. If I have dwelled too long on one painful episode, it is because, ironically, we sometimes learn more from finding mistakes than from enjoying near-perfection.

Chapter 9

The Trouble with Transcendence

Hollywood movies and television dramas are probably the most influential spiritual guides in the world. All around the world, at this moment, people are watching American-made productions—profound or shallow—that tell them about the nature of ultimate reality and their place in it. This used to be a rare topic for dramas, but not lately. These messages, which express the spiritual beliefs and doubts of today's writers, influence local viewers, who may even substitute them for their own traditional beliefs.

And what teachings does Hollywood beam out to the whole of humankind? A mixture of doctrines that have been borrowed from everywhere and reassembled. Our world is in a period of borrowing. When it comes to most other aspects of modern life—rock music, cell phones, the Internet, democracy, Big Macs, private ownership, pierced bellybuttons—the rest of the world eagerly adopts Western ways. That diffusion happens with religions, too, except that the ideas are flowing in both directions. Westerners are eagerly incorporating a variety of foreign theologies.[1]

Not all religions are growing equally. Islamic fundamentalism is spreading fast, but mostly where Muslims already are established. Elsewhere, evangelical Christianity (especially Pentecostalism) is leading, entirely without Hollywood's help. In the educated population of Europe and North America, Buddhism is spreading quickly—definitely with the help of Hollywood. The theological ideas that are discussed in the West are reflected in the stories being created both for export and domestic consumption, for we all keep up with the current spiritual messages of films and television.

This phenomenon is *cultural globalization*—the spread of ideas through entertainment products, trade, and electronic means of communication. The last time when so much religious diffusion was going on may have been during the

Axial Age—the first millennium B.C.E. when the Greeks invented philosophy, the Hindu Upanishads were written, monotheism took root, Siddhartha created Buddhism, Mahavira taught Jainism, K'ung-fu-tzu introduced Confucianism, and Lao Tzu taught Taoism. Ideas traveled great distances. Plato's notions of transcendence and reincarnation probably came from India. Some are calling our own religious ferment a "new Axial Age" because the nature of ultimate reality is so widely discussed.[2]

Earlier I mentioned the Dalai Lama's comment that only one or two of every five people on Earth are religious. I don't think that's entirely accurate. Surveys suggest that a larger proportion have *some* religion and that many who say they aren't believers nevertheless hold notions that are part of a religion. As political scientist Ronald Inglehart has noted, "Although church attendance is declining in nearly all advanced industrial societies, spiritual concerns more broadly defined are not. In fact, in most industrial societies, a growing share of the population is spending time thinking about the meaning and purpose of life."[3] And in the United States, even attendance is higher than in other economically developed societies, especially when it comes to conservative doctrines.

Everywhere, many people get their main spiritual advice from television and film writers. This isn't necessarily bad. It depends on what is being taught and how those beliefs play out in real life. We must ask, As consumers of the global entertainment industry, what theologies are we being taught?

Entertainment for the Soul

You can hear all kinds of theories about the motivations of creative workers in literature and showbiz: that they are only in it for the money and will produce any kind of trash that will sell. That they are ideologues trying to undermine Western civilization by putting forward radical notions that the public cannot swallow. That they are unable to empathize with people of other faiths and—intentionally or not—promote their own traditions while denigrating religions that are far different from theirs. That they crave recognition as artists and will put out whatever is stylish among the arbiters of high culture. That they are atheists who try to make every religion look stupid. And so on.

Probably all of these characterizations are true of a few creative workers, but it's hardly worth trying to substantiate the charges. All we can say is that there are cultural trends, for whatever combination of reasons, and that these variations somehow both reflect and influence the religious sensibilities of the public. Within every culture, there are tensions and contradictions that individuals seek to resolve in their own lives. If a work of fiction can clarify those issues, it can contribute far more meaningful insights than merely by offering an interesting diversion for an hour or two. Still, religion is far from the most common topic of showbiz. As I mentioned in chapter 7, Hollywood producers tend to ignore both education and religion in their storytelling, though perhaps that is changing now.

The faiths that are displayed in Western popular culture are by no means representative of the world's population. You'll see few Hollywood films or novels featuring Hindu swamis or Muslim imams, for example, and the images that do appear may be less than flattering (e.g., *Satanic Verses,* the novel that provoked the fatwa against Salman Rushdie). You'll see few favorable movies about fundamentalist preachers, but occasionally scathing portraits (e.g., *Elmer Gantry*).

Of course, producers quite reasonably expect us not to believe every negative image they create; otherwise they'd have to worry about the anti-Semitism that audiences might pick up from watching *The Merchant of Venice* or the occult beliefs they might absorb from a Harry Potter story. Anxiety over such issues seems misplaced, though it's hard to draw a line between harmless and vicious fiction. One Catholic cardinal has attacked the hugely popular novel *The Da Vinci Code* for convincing readers that Jesus married Mary Magdalene. Is this a reasonable worry? Anyway, pro-Christian films and books generally sell far better than anti-Christian ones. For example, Martin Scorsese's *The Last Temptation of Christ,* which was condemned as antireligious, grossed only $8 million in domestic tickets, compared with Mel Gibson's gruesome but devout *The Passion of the Christ,* which grossed $370 million.[4] We don't know how public opinion was influenced by either.

A fair number of films are advertised as spiritual but lack any religious references at all. For example, *Eternal Sunshine of the Spotless Mind* and *What the Bleep Do We Know?* can be considered pop spirituality or philosophy. The organization Spiritual Cinema Circle sends e-mail reviews to members, organizes viewing groups, and sells DVDs by mail; it explicitly avoids films about organized religions but has made at least one exception in favor of a film about Tibetan yogis. Indeed, Tibetan lama films gained extraordinary popularity in the 1990s—or perhaps the producers are just so impressed by Tibetan Buddhism that they are producing films without regard to profitability.

The messages of Hollywood's proreligious films (I don't know about novels) tend to address external rules and rituals or moral matters rather than theological questions. We have been given extravaganza biblical adventure stories since the days of *Ben Hur,* but the chariot races and stunning sets amount to entertainment in the narrowest sense of the word instead of challenging us to think about ultimate reality. When a popular religious movie does address a problem, it is usually ethical or social reformist in nature. (Bing Crosby in *Going My Way* and Spencer Tracy in *Boys Town* come to mind as examples. An even lighter genre involving pastoral care is the British sitcom of the 1990s, *Father Ted,* which offered more laughs than spiritual insights.)

That, of course, is the problem. In the film or television medium, it is always easier to show than to tell—to let the costumes, stained glass windows, and candles carry us along, rather than write discussions about nonmaterial concerns. Theology can make dull text—whether in print or shown in living color—or it can be moving and intelligent, depending on the talent of the writer. Where analysis is lacking from the dialogue, the audience must find other ways of exploring the story's meaning. They can meet as a club and discuss the plot. And in Toronto, the minister of a large Protestant church preaches a homily every Sunday giving his theological reflections on a film showing locally. He attracts large crowds, and his commentaries are profound and serious.

In the same critical vein, I want to address one single theological issue in this chapter, exploring its significance for the lives of *Northern Exposure* characters. My topic is unsuitable for a Protestant homily and so is my method, for I'm still demonstrating emotional/ethical criticism, which requires me to take my own emotional reactions toward fiction as a starting point for analysis. The topic also requires critics to play theologian in order to dig deeper into the issue than the writers themselves were able to do. I'll address a theme that I've mentioned before: the disagreement between Plato and Aristotle as to whether it is better to concentrate on worldly concerns or on transcendent matters that are not located in space in time. Films and fiction rarely address this question, but *Northern Exposure* did so at the end. A personal experience sets up the problem we'll be considering.

To Accept the Red Strip or Not?

In April 2004 the Dalai Lama came to Toronto and held an eleven-day-long ceremony. Such an event may not be your idea of entertainment, but it appealed to me. Since high school days I've been interested in Buddhism, and this event had wonderful esthetic dimensions. His Holiness and his monks chanted meditatively some ten hours a day. There were dancers wearing weird costumes. There were brass horns ten feet long. Monks spent days painting a big mandala by pouring colored sand and then, displaying nonattachment to the ephemeral, dumped it in the lake. And I got to empathize with a great soul as he lectured on Nagarjuna's philosophy about five hours a day. I had plenty of dopamine but not one adrenaline rush. Zero thrills. Perfect.

Non-Buddhists were allowed to wait until the end to decide whether to take the initiation or just observe. The Dalai Lama does not proselytize. Indeed, he advises *against* changing one's religion. He particularly advised us not to take the initiation unless we intended to practice regularly thereafter. I hadn't made up my mind. I wasn't sure whether I aspired more to transcendence or effective living in this world. I was hung up on the contradiction between Plato and Aristotle, between worldly love and transcendent love.

Transcendence has two conventional meanings: first, the state of excelling or going beyond usual limits (e.g., in a mental or athletic feat) and, second, *a state of existence beyond the limits of material experience.* I had no qualms about excelling, but did I want to live beyond the limits of material experience? To a Buddhist that means overcoming desires to the end of living without a body. That might be wonderful—or not. I remembered my grandmother's Sunday school lesson and how I'd decided against ever going to heaven. I still want this world's problems instead of heaven—or even the Buddhist equivalent to heaven, which nobody understands.

One night I went to dinner with a group, including a Tibetan woman living in Alberta, whom I questioned about her practices. I was amazed. She chants and meditates two hours every morning and two hours every evening—far less than she did as a child in Tibet and less than most of her friends in Canada.

"I'd never get anything done," I said.

"Why do you want to get anything done?" she replied. "If you get to know Tibetans, you'll find that we're extremely happy people. But our level of economic development is low. We're mainly concerned with spiritual matters."

I couldn't answer her. I'm not sure why I want to get anything done, but I do. What I'd like best is to leave the world a little better off for my having been here. She had just helped me decide.

The next day assistants gave long, narrow strips of red cloth to those taking initiation. I declined. I looked around the hall. Of the five thousand people, I seemed to be the only one without a red strip. I calculated: Suppose all of them actually chant or meditate even one hour a day. That comes to 1,825,000 hours during the next year that could be spent instead on getting things done. So I'm still not a Buddhist. Instead of unattached transcendence I've chosen emotion, activism, and writing this book, which I dedicate to the Dalai Lama, who obviously does everything possible to make the world work—and meditates, too.

His activism shows that it's simplistic to consider transcendence as contrary to getting things done. Indeed, meditating helps many people live more wisely. If the audience saved 1,825,000 hours next year, they wouldn't necessarily solve more of the world's problems. They'd spend much of that time taking bubble baths, playing the cello, or watching television—and there's nothing wrong with any of those activities. I choose TV shows and other entertainment specifically that address this question: How should human beings live? However, not all fiction does deal with that issue, nor should it. There's room for escapist fiction and bubble baths—though I prefer grappling with this world's problems, which I can't do if I meditate four hours a day.

But since I actually want both this world and whatever good possibilities lie beyond it, I might have made the opposite decision about taking Buddhist initiation had I not watched *Northern Exposure*'s Joel Fleischman resolve his dilemma by choosing transcendence. As I declined the red strip, I was thinking of him, recalling the day when he chose. He and Maggie were trudging through the snow, completing his quest. He had become a strong, silent man such as Maggie had wanted. Now he saw skyscraper lights ahead—the mythical city of Kiwa'ani—and was eager to press on toward it, but she halted. That was his place, she declared, not hers. She would accompany him no farther. They embraced. Then he walked ahead into fog and dissolved.

This week, exactly ten years after that episode was broadcast, a member of the e-mail list posted an entry. His eyes were still red from weeping, he said. He had just watched the episode and had sobbed for an hour. This was not unusual. Millions of people have cried while watching it. Throughout the sixth season, viewers feel increasing despair over the impending denouement. On our list we call it "SSB"—for "Sixth Season Blues." While we were watching the syndicated show together, members reported SSB illnesses, depressions, quarrels at home. Arguments flared up on the list. Many stopped watching the horrible season after "The Quest." I have a friend who had been an invalid at home during that period, awaiting a heart transplant. He told me later, "I couldn't stop watching it because I had grown to love them. But I couldn't stand to watch it, either, it upset me so." I have never encountered another work of fiction that affected audiences so deeply.

This reaction is not catharsis; we certainly don't feel better for going through it. One woman told me she had cried for hours when Joel left (I did, too) and still weeps whenever she sees it again. She said her husband was surprised because, he said, "I didn't think you even liked Joel."

"I *didn't* like him," she replied. "But I *loved* him."

I did, too. He had been doing soul work for me. But suddenly he had chosen transcendence rather than commitment to the world, and it didn't feel right.

Much later I saw a film about the same dilemma whose ending I did like. It didn't minimize the difficulty of the choice. *Samsara* is a gorgeous 2001 movie by Ron Fricke, shot in the Himalayas. It involves a young Tibetan monk, Tashi, who is coming out of a three-year-long meditation. Everyone knows that he is close to attaining enlightenment. However, within weeks, his sexual longings reawaken. He reminds his mentor, an older monk, that even Siddhartha had experienced a normal human life before giving it up to become the Buddha, whereas he, Tashi, had been a monk since he was a small child. Attracted to a woman named Pema, Tashi slips away from the monastery at night to become a householder. He marries Pema, fathers a son, and becomes a respected farmer. But word arrives that his mentor has died, still uncertain whose choice was better—Tashi's worldly one or his own spiritual quest.

Now Tashi feels drawn back to his transcendent discipline. Just as Siddhartha had slipped away without disturbing his sleeping wife and child, Tashi departs at night, carrying his old robe. At the river, he shaves his hair off and sets forth to rejoin the monastery. But Pema appears in the road, bitter about his selfishness. Whereas the world admires Siddhartha, she can only think of the desolation he imposed on his wife and son by abandoning them. Tashi knows that Pema is right and that their life together had been bliss. Now he is wracked by conflict between his two aspirations: transcendence versus skillful living in the world. He falls to the ground writhing miserably, unable either to turn back or to press on toward the monastery.

The movie ends here, where it *should* end. I can only contrast it to the end of "The Quest," when Joel feels no conflict whatever. It is too easy for him to leave Maggie and his life in Alaska. That, I believe, is the wrong lesson to impart. There's no easy resolution of the conflict between transcendence and this-worldly concerns.

Does It Matter What Religion Your TV Teaches You?

Does it make much difference which religion or spiritual notions are believed in a society? Yes. The doctrines promoted by cinema and fiction influence how we run our lives personally and how our social institutions work. Right now, we see many filmmakers offering movies about Buddhism. What changes could be expected if the West were to adopt Buddhism as its main religion? Historical comparisons offer grounds for some tentative inferences: Buddhist countries generally have been less violent than areas where other religions prevailed. "In all of Buddhist history, there has never been a holy war," explains Buddhist peace worker Sulak Sivaraksa. "Generally, when people think about conflict, they believe that there are only three possible outcomes: victory, defeat, or compromise. From the Buddhist point of view, the end result is less important than the way we work with it."[5]

On the other hand, as an entirely transcendent religion, Buddhism does not have a strong tradition of working collectively toward social reform. Sivaraksa works for social justice and nonviolence, and there are other extraordinary Buddhist conflict workers as well, such as Junsei Terasawa, Thich Nhat Hanh, A. T. Ariyaratne, and of course the Dalai Lama and Aung San Suu Kyi, but such organized activism is less common than in the Judeo-Christian traditions.[6]

Another Buddhist teacher, Ken Tanaka, distinguishes between the "vertical" dimension (spirituality) and the "'horizontal dimension'—the social, worldly, relative dimension, the nitty-gritty world that we live in. Buddhism is considered weak in its involvement with the horizontal.... Buddhism doesn't have a direct pipeline or exhortation as to what one is supposed to do in the world."[7]

Perhaps the best way to show the power of religion in shaping history is to review some studies by the great sociologist Max Weber. He famously showed that the rise of Protestantism led to an ethic conducive to entrepreneurialism, so that capitalism arose largely in Protestant areas. Weber also studied the religions of ancient Judaism, India, and China, always exploring the impact of religious doctrines on the economy. According to the Weberian scholar Robert Bellah, Weber was interested in the ways that religions told their followers to *love*.[8] He had in mind the distinction I introduced in chapter 3 between worldly love and transcendent love, and which we'll explore further in connection with *Northern Exposure*.

Transcendence—the religious abnegation of worldly things—began in India among Hindus, Buddhists, and Jains and spread westward among philosophers (e.g., Socrates and Plato) and religious virtuosos, becoming part of Judeo-Christian theology. A spiritual aspirant was supposed to love everyone and aspire toward a higher kind of consciousness while rejecting the material world. The most fervent believers rejected familial, economic, political, aesthetic, erotic, and intellectual aspects of society. To live this way is to become a homeless beggar or monk, as did the Buddha, Jesus, and St. Francis of Assisi. (If everyone had done so, society could not have functioned.)

Spreading westward, this transcendence-seeking rejection of the world divided into two contradictory orientations, which Weber called *asceticism* and *mysticism*. In India, where people believe in reincarnation and karma, mysticism prevails. There salvation—a distinctive inner illumination—comes from subjective contemplation or meditation, which can be done only if one is free from all everyday interests. Hence mystics flee from the world to sit, looking inwardly in silent stillness and requiring voluntary donations from others for basic sustenance.

On the other hand, the Middle East and, later, European Protestant areas were the centers of asceticism. Judaism, Christianity, and Islam all believe in a single God who created the cosmos and stands outside us, holding us accountable for our deeds. We must serve God soberly by our work in the world, actively obeying His will, even as we renounce the creaturely pleasures of the flesh and of society. Thus, according to Weber, Judeo-Christian world rejection did not exempt one from activity in the world but actually *required* it.[9]

This "worldly asceticism" became especially important in the Protestant sects that believed in predestination. Though the religious founders of these groups by no means intended for their flock to become prosperous businessmen, as Weber explained it, that actually was the outcome of their anxiety about whether they were doomed at birth for hell or destined for heaven. They believed that God gave each person certain assignments—especially a vocation or "calling"—to perform on Earth; the success of this endeavor was taken as a sign of God's favor.

In Weber's metaphor, the ascetic regards herself as an "instrument" in God's hands, whereas the mystic seeks to become a spiritual "container." While in principle both sides reject this world in favor of the transcendent, they do not admire each other's way of seeking salvation.

> The contemplation of the mystic appears to the ascetic as indolent, religiously sterile, and ascetically reprehensible self-indulgence, namely, a floundering in self-created emotions prompted by the deification of the creaturely. From the standpoint of a contemplative mystic, the ascetic appears, by her/his ascetically rationalized conduct within the world, to be forever involved in all the burdens of created things, confronting insoluble tensions between violence and goodness, between matter-of-factness and love.[10]

Both the mystic and the ascetic have this quality in common: an aspiration to transcend the delusion of existing only as a physical body in a material world. This was Plato's attitude, if you'll recall, whereas Aristotle never was oriented toward such transcendent concerns. The disagreement between those two philosophers is still replaying everywhere in modern lives. And, among the seekers of transcendence, some of us are mystics and some are worldly ascetics—and that disagreement is also still being replayed. My grief at the end of *Northern Exposure* occurred because I am (indeed many modern Western people are) predominantly a worldly ascetic, whereas Joel chose mysticism. Is there any way of resolving this contradiction?

Mysticism or Worldly Asceticism?

With the new spread of world religions today, millions of people face a dilemma over whether to pursue a spiritual life seriously and, if so, whether to take the mystical or the ascetic path. We'll explore one such existential drama throughout this chapter.

What difference does it make which theologies Hollywood promotes? Besides influencing the path that viewers take, showbiz has other effects that probably never occurred to Weber. For example, there's the emotional impact on viewers of empathizing with a character who accepts a particular religious conviction that the viewers can't accept. Earlier I tried to show a connection between culture and health, and that's relevant here. If a loved one (including a beloved character) makes a mistake—that is, a choice that you believe won't work out right—you'll worry. And spiritual empathy can hurt a lot more than watching your football hero fumble the ball and lose the game. Such an upset may affect your health. Watching a loved one fail is stressful, and stress is bad for your body. In real life, such experiences may be unavoidable, but in fiction, stress comes from a writer's blunder.

That's what happened at the end of *Northern Exposure.* Every character failed—and my arthritis hurt. Nor was I unique. The pain relief that viewers had derived from the show's joy and erotic playfulness suddenly stopped, and our cortisol levels soared. Lots of us felt unwell. *Northern Exposure* had intelligently addressed the great question, "How should human beings live?" When in the end it gave the wrong answer, we felt it in our bodies. Was it *really* the wrong answer? Well, it seemed wrong to *us*—which is why it hurt. Our beloved Joel made an especially big mistake.

The Cicelians were natural-born philosophers who stimulated Joel's soul work. Their discussions of theology and cosmology were brilliant. If the show hadn't been so wonderful, we would not have felt so let down at the end. I want to review the various theologies presented to Joel in Cicely and their respective implications for his life, for he represents a worldview that is our own.

Joel: A Modern Mystic

Social theorists long believed something called the *theory of secularization,* which predicted that as persons became freed from religious authorities and able to choose spiritual ideas for themselves, they would become less religious until finally modern individuals would lack any interest whatever in spiritual or mystical matters.[11] This prediction was wrong. Joel is a modern, rational, intellectual man—free to choose, yet in touch with his soul all along, which, it turns out, is perfectly normal.

As Rodney Stark has shown with historical evidence, there never was an "age of faith" from which people in Western civilization have fallen away. People in the Middle Ages, for example, were no more religious than modern people. Stark has also disproved other parts of secularization theory, including its claim that modernity decreases the religiousness of individuals and that scientists are less religious than others.[12]

Moreover, there have been numerous surveys of adherence to religious ideas and practices, ranging from belief in God to frequency of attending worship services. Since the American Revolution, the trends in the United States have been more upward than downward.[13] In Europe, religious participation is lower than in the United States, but the differences are minor when comparisons are based on subjective measures of faith. For example, Iceland has been called the most secular country. Only 2 percent of Icelanders attend church weekly, but 81 percent believe there is life after death, 88 percent say human beings have a soul, 82 percent pray, and 40 percent believe in reincarnation. Spiritualism is extremely popular in Iceland, even among intellectuals.[14]

Joel's foray into the wilderness to work on himself is unusual, but we resonate to his concerns. Still, why is his spiritual exploration necessary? As a Jew he has never harbored religious doubts. If his spiritual needs were increasing, why didn't he simply look deeper into Judaism? Instead, he adopts an Eastern religion—evidently learned mostly from Chris.

Yet lots of well-educated individuals are turning to mysticism,[15] especially Buddhism. There are now nearly one million Western-born Buddhists in the United States and an equal number in France.[16] About three times that many foreign-born Asian Buddhists now live in the United States. For Western Buddhist converts, meditation is the main spiritual discipline, with the goal of eliminating suffering by giving up desires and attachments. Buddhists believe in reincarnation and aim ultimately to be released from future rebirths. Theirs is one of the fastest-growing religions in the Western world.

Northern Exposure was produced by Hollywood, and showbiz has always used the Eastern mystic as an archetype of wisdom, usually portraying him as an Oriental monk.[17] In today's movies he's likely to be a Tibetan lama, but previously he might have been a Zen roshi or a wandering Indian sadhu.

Like Joel, an extraordinary number of Jews are attracted to Buddhism. Although only 2 percent of American citizens are Jewish, about 30 percent of American-born Caucasian Buddhists are Jewish.[18] (There is even a name for such a person: a

"JuBu.")[19] However, Judaism is a religion of rationality and "doingness," of mastery in this world, whereas Buddhism encourages nonattachment, disciplined meditation, transcendence, and nonthinking.[20] Meditation is for stilling the discursive mind, creating a blank space for awareness without thoughts. Advanced meditators do experience high, perhaps unique, states of well-being, but material or intellectual skill is irrelevant, or even an impediment, to spiritual enlightenment.

Religious Pluralism in Cicely

Joel's spiritual search begins in Cicely among people who, despite living in the wilderness, are modern intellectuals forever discussing philosophy. They, too, choose the components of their personal faiths from the whole array of world cultures.[21] Most of the religious traditions that are discussed in Cicely can be classified in two categories: those that originated in the Middle East and those from India. But I'll add a couple of faiths that belong in neither category. In the end Joel will shift from his Middle Eastern tradition to an Indian one—a change that today is often promoted by the entertainment industry.

The Middle Eastern group comprises Judaism, Christianity, and Islam. They all envision God as located beyond human beings, creating the cosmos and now addressing us. God is supposedly controlling events, moment by moment, and prayers are petitions for Him to protect oneself or one's group. Each person's challenge is future oriented: to set goals that are consistent with God's plan. For this, one can seek divine guidance and may even receive a "calling."

In Cicely neither Christianity nor Islam is mentioned as often as Judaism, Joel's own tradition. Still, Cicelians often assume that a helpful power is leading them toward purposes that they are "supposed" to do. This notion is found in all three Middle Eastern religions. For example, the most popular religious book today promotes that idea within traditional Christian theology: *The Purpose-Driven Life: What on Earth Am I Here For?*[22] As we've seen, this belief was the basis for the worldly ascetic Calvinist idea of a calling or vocation.

However, not everyone who receives such a summons is particularly ascetic. For example, the TV series *Joan of Arcadia* features a high school girl whom God visits almost daily, giving her tasks to carry out. God always shows up as an ordinary person, but in differing bodies—ranging from a little girl, to a punk with tattoos, to a school janitor. Joan always obeys resentfully, yet she seems to have a free choice; her decisions aren't predestined. I wouldn't call her an ascetic (she doesn't reject the world), and it's not clear that she's Christian, but she certainly is given spiritual vocations—as in Middle Eastern theologies. The outcomes of her assignments are always beneficial to other characters.

In Cicely, the main alternative to the Middle Eastern faiths is the East Indian category: Hinduism, Buddhism, and Jainism. According to these religions, no god confronts human beings from outside. Instead, we must look *within,* where we discover we're part of a vast oneness rather than separate individuals with lasting personal identities. However, as a spiritual discipline, the Indian category is even more individualistic than the Middle Eastern one, since only an individual can meditate, and there is no other portal to salvation. The religious Indian is portrayed as sitting in the lotus position, withdrawn from the world, searching inwardly for ultimate reality. This world-denying orientation resembles the spiritual transcendence toward which Plato aspired. However, he believed transcendence involved discursive thinking, whereas the Indian religions would have us meditate by stilling our mind.[23]

In the East Indian group of religions, no god assigns us goals for the *future* or guides us toward anything. Our own past actions have brought us to our present situation, and now we must freely choose what to do next without divine hints. There is no pull forward, no way of anticipating what we should do. Karma, influence *from the past,* shapes our present opportunities and constraints. Now we freely act and our good or bad intentions will create new karma, which will ripen causally in a future life.

Besides the teachings from India and the Middle East, there's China. People sometimes speak of "Eastern religion," as if they were all similar, but China differs radically from India. It has two antithetical traditions, Confucianism and Taoism, neither of which is world denying. (*Tao* is pronounced "Dow.") Confucianism is a worldly philosophy specifying principles of good conduct, practical wisdom, and proper social relationships. It is not very spiritual but is oriented toward ceremonies and rituals. Whereas Taoism figures prominently in *Northern Exposure* as an influence on Chris, Confucianism never comes up.

Unlike either the East Indian or the Middle Eastern religions, Taoism suggests that people should contain and balance contradictions rather than struggling to eliminate either side. To have good, you have to have evil. To have light, you have to have dark. Thus the Taoist symbol of yin and yang portrays two opposites, black and white, complementing each other, forming a dynamic whole. Taoism taught, for example, that to balance abstract philosophizing, one needed practical on-the-job experience such as craftsmen acquire. The ancient texts of Lao-tzu[24] and Chuang-tzu[25] encourage earthy naturalness and tolerance of ambiguity. Zen Buddhism has adopted elements of Taoism.[26]

Finally, Joel encounters shamanism among the Tlingit Indian tribes, with whom he lives up the river.[27] Shamans leave their bodies and assume animal identities. Tlingits also believe in reincarnation.[28]

Joel's Initial Theology

Joel Fleischman arrives in Cicely as a liberal, presumably Reform, Jew. During Yom Kippur he fasts, examines his soul severely, and prays for the atonement of his sins. Still, his interests do not stray far beyond the empirical. The Jewish faith is not so much transcendent as ethical, emphasizing moral, responsible action in this world. Accordingly, instead of denying the world, he dedicates himself unreservedly to treating his patients and maintaining the competence to do so well.

Joel has not come to terms with impermanence and fragility but regards death as his personal enemy. He likes the fact that one part of the human body—the DNA—can be immortal. Lying in bed with a fever one night, he compares two views that have been expressed that day. Maurice, to all appearances nonreligious, has declared himself a believer in the soul. In fact, he deems the body useful only as a vehicle for delivering the soul on its mission. It makes sense, he states, to jettison the body as soon as its task is complete, just as NASA's boosters are jettisoned after lift-off.

But Joel can't accept the distinction between body and soul. He prefers Holling's view: that we are all genes. Bodies are just a way of spreading DNA around in the gene pool. This idea comforts Joel, the man of flesh. He imagines his adventurous history as genes—flights from Cossacks, hiding in trees, sleeping in the desert of Egypt.

Believing himself to be immortal genes, he does not believe in the immortality of a soul. While reluctantly preparing to be initiated into a Tlingit clan, he and Ed lie on the ground in the forest, watching the moon and waiting for the vision that is supposed to appear before the ceremony. He admits that he has never seen a vision and doesn't believe in spirits. Ed, puzzled by this deficiency, asks what he thinks happens to us after we die. Joel's answer is lame: Maybe what we have done in life will matter to somebody. He usually avoids thinking about it.

Later, on a trip with Maggie to Grosse Pointe for a birthday party, Joel meets her family's young pastor, a shy guy who wants to discuss Joel's religious convictions. He correctly assumes that, as a Jew, Joel does not believe in an afterlife. Most modern Jews don't. Indeed, few Jews know of the wide variety of doctrines about immortality that have prevailed during Jewish history. But, had he known, Joel could have chosen from four Jewish theories about the afterlife: (1) genetic survival through one's descendents—the notion that he does accept; (2) physical resurrection; (3) an immortal soul in heaven; and (4) reincarnation.[29]

Chris's Theology

Of all the Cicelians, Joel is most deeply influenced by Chris Stevens, the New Age combiner of the incompatible. Chris is fascinated by ideas about ultimate reality and can believe all of them at once, even if they contradict each other. He is as intelligent as Joel but doesn't use either/or logic—the scientific method by which mistaken notions are eliminated until only one theory remains. Chris keeps them all.[30]

As the town's ecumenical freelance parson, Chris is always ready with words of wisdom at a wedding or a funeral, always available to his "parishioners" when they show up in his broadcasting booth for advice. Though Cicely's church is a nondenominational Christian one, his perspective is not predominantly Christian. He is more Taoist[31] than anything else, but he mentions such diverse influences as the Sufi poet Rumi, Krishnamurti, Meister Eckhart, Bodhidharma, Mother Teresa, and Nichiren Shoshu Buddhism, and he takes a retreat at a Catholic monastery.

There are advantages to Chris's unscientific ability to embrace contradiction and incongruity. It makes him the most nonjudgmental person in a nonjudgmental town. It also means that he is not of an ethical bent. Ethics appraises behavior as better or worse—a line of thinking that interests Chris not at all. He even favors accepting evil and pain for the sake of deepening awareness. Taoism encourages *balancing*—of yin and yang, of pain and pleasure—instead of asserting one side over the other or eliminating anything. Chris affirms everything—and if something arises that negates what he has affirmed, he simply affirms that, too. His world runs not on the basis of an either/or logic but rather on "both/and."[32] On KBHR he teaches Taoism: that good and bad, dark and light, depend on each other and play against each other dialectically within the soul. You can't get rid of the dark side of yourself, so stare it down. Hug it!

Sometimes Chris explains man/woman love problems as imbalance between yin and yang. But if it isn't balanced, it just isn't. And he quotes the Buddhist Bodhidharma's Taoist-flavored advice: "You can't have a thing until you let it go." (Bodhidharma was a monk who brought Buddhism to China in 470 c.e., where it blended with Taoism, producing Ch'an Buddhism. In about 1200 c.e., Ch'an Buddhism was imported to Japan, where it is known as Zen.)

At other times Chris quotes Jung, who also promoted the paradoxical unity of opposites: "There's no coming to consciousness without pain." If you want consciousness, go lie down with your pain. (Buddhism, by contrast, meant to *eliminate* pain, but instead of contrasting these teachings, Chris accepts them both.)

The insouciance behind these maxims explains why Chris lives alone in a trailer without a committed relationship to a demanding profession or lover. His advice is, If your project is difficult to do, if it requires any struggle to accomplish, let it go. Stop trying. Maybe it will turn out okay and maybe it won't—but in either case, you'll be a free man. (Taoism is not the path for anyone on a career fast track. Nor is it a route to Nirvana. You get to stay human—though of an easy-going type, with the usual pleasures and pains of human existence.)

Northern Exposure writers often quote Joseph Campbell, who expressed similar Taoist attitudes. For example, he made these comments in a chat with Bill Moyers:

> Life is, in its very essence and character, a terrible mystery—this whole business of living by killing and eating. But it is a childish attitude to say no to life with all its pain, to say that this is something that should not have been.... People ask me, "Do you have optimism about the world?" And I say, "Yes, it's great just the way it is. And you are not going to fix it up. Nobody has ever made it any better. It is never going to be any better. This is it, so take it or leave it...."
>
> You yourself are participating in the evil, or you are not alive. Whatever you do is evil for somebody. This is one of the ironies of the whole creation.... Heraclitus said that for God all things are good and right and just, but for man some things are right and others are not. When you are a man, you are in the field of time and decisions. One of the problems of life is to live with the realization of both terms.[33]

Whatever this philosophy may be, clearly it's neither ethics nor *logos*. Nothing can be derived from it to tell you what decisions to make, since every choice you can make is perfect.

But as Campbell knew, in space and time it *does* matter what you choose or reject. When you're subject to the conservation of energy, you have to make either/or choices—and much depends on choosing skillfully. You *can* fix the world up or make it worse, which is why life is such an amazing game. You can win or lose everything.

Still, I admire Chris's ability to affirm opposite opinions at the same time. It's not logical, but it's not just wild irrationality, either. Indeed, I think Joel should have followed Taoism in the end instead of opting for transcendence and detaching himself from emotional engagement with worldly concerns.

Determinism

Certain philosophical contradictions stump even Chris—notably whether the world works randomly or according to plan. Neither answer is satisfying. There's the chilling thought that everything happens by mere chance, and there's no meaning in the universe. We are buffeted by absurd random events with no intentions behind them—nihilism.

The alternative view is the theology of Middle Eastern origin: that the world is run by God's plan. Still, if God created the universe and the laws regulating it, does He sometimes change the plan? Or did He set it going and then go away, leaving it running like clockwork? This latter position holds that the system is inexorable. If so, then it is sheer delusion to suppose we have choices.

Another possibility is that not only does God have plans for the universe but that He/She/It intervenes continually, changing ongoing events, perhaps even in response to our prayers. This "Middle East"–type belief suggests that God has a plan for each of us and that we should trust it and try to follow it. Cicelians will often say, for example, that something "was just not meant to be." Meant by whom? If something is not "meant" to happen, is it possible to do it anyway? If God has a plan for us, is it possible to reject it? The notion of sin suggests that it is all too possible, but the notion of fate suggests that it is not. Chris often thinks about this puzzle, adopting first one view and then another.

For example, early in the series Joel is planning to go to New York on vacation, but Maggie dreams that his flight is doomed. It touches a sensitive nerve for her. Four of her boyfriends have died, and she believes herself cursed, so that every man she loves will die unexpectedly. She is powerfully attracted to Joel, despite denying it. She asks Chris's advice: Should she warn Joel not to go?

At that time, Chris leans toward belief in fate. He urges her to warn Joel to change his flight but then acknowledges that maybe the *new* flight would be the one to crash. Or fate could have determined that Maggie would reach whatever decision she ultimately makes. Maybe nobody has free will. On the other hand, the notion of a random universe run by chance is equally unsettling. At first Chris adopts that explanation when he runs over a dog with his truck and kills it. But later in the day, he switches back to the alternative theory—determinism—after visiting the beautiful woman whose pet he has killed.

Amy invites him in and immediately reveals her passion for transcendental numbers. She is a mathematician writing a dissertation on pi, which is, to her, a spiritual quest. Gazing into his admiring eyes, she explains that the numbers cannot be just a random sequence, as it appears to be, because the sequence stays the same and the relationship between circumference and the diameter stays the same. Chris understands her awe in contemplating this eternal truth. She has a great ambition—to run pi to, say twenty billion digits, where she expects to find order, a pattern—in fact, a sign. They are murmuring to each other now, looking at each other soulfully and whispering in wonder about the truths that God might reveal in such a pattern. He forgets what he has come to tell her. This woman believes that the universe is absolutely orderly and understandable. One just has to look hard to find God's system. At that moment they fall in love.

Later that day, Chris discusses determinism with Joel in the tavern. Now he is reconsidering the dog's death, which no longer seems to him a random accident. Maybe it has been determined by some divine—or perhaps demonic—plan.

Amy's God is a systematic planner who makes no exceptions for anyone. She does not look inward for Him by praying to be enlightened, nor does she petition Him to suspend His natural laws in order to make things work out favorably in a particular instance. Her God sticks by His system, but it is, in principle, understandable. To make life work out right, human beings have to figure His system out and adjust to it. Chris, ever flexible, is willing to go along with this approach and see where it will lead.

But soon their love affair hits a snag. After Chris feeds her parakeet, it also dies. What does it mean? How can they save their relationship? Amy's answer is mathematical. They must balance their equation; he has killed two of her pets, and now they must even the score, for otherwise she would resent him. He consents. The next day they stand on a cliff with his beloved Harley-Davidson motorcycle. It is painful, but together they push it over and watch it smash. Amy feels better. Chris isn't so sure.

That night, in a soliloquy on KBHR, he considers aloud whether life functions randomly or as a perfectly oiled, predictable system. Trying to make sense of the universe, he has tried out the systematic model that day—treating it as a mathematical equation: an eye for an eye. But it can't be like that, he realizes. Both quantum physics and relativity prove that the universe is not the closed-system reversible clockwork that Newton supposed. The cosmos confounds all our notions of it. He picks up a book and reads aloud, "A system is like a lizard; it leaves its tail in your fingers and runs away knowing full well that it will grow a new one in a twinkling."[34]

Amy's relationship with Chris would have benefited more from empathy—mutual caring, rather than balancing equations. According to some scientists, nature is better described by the modern concept of chaos theory or even the Buddhist theory of "dependent origination."[35]

The eclectic Chris combines Middle Eastern and East Indian theologies, plus others. Clearly he believes in God—a tenet of all Middle Eastern faiths but a minority opinion in Asia. His God apparently has issued no particular mission to him. His preoccupation with determinism might have raised the Calvinist notion of predestination, but he lacks any Calvinist sense of vocation. Instead, for him determinism is mainly relevant to the Indian tradition, where time is considered cyclical rather than linear. (Each cycle lasts over four billion years, but eventually we'll go through the whole sequence again, again, again—eternally.) To East Indian theology, the determinism question is, Can you do anything at all differently this time around?[36] (So far as I can see, chaos theory and dependent origination refute eternal recurrence. Nothing will ever recur exactly.)

Karma

Chris combines his Chinese Taoism with a firm (but incongruous) belief in karma, which comes from the religions of India. He attributes his good or bad luck to karma.[37] Without distinguishing in a moralistic way between good and evil, he does believe that somehow "what goes around comes around" and that we reap what we sow. (In *Street Time,* Kevin Hunter probably holds a similar concept of karma.)

As a believer in karma, it would be plausible for Chris to become a Buddhist, Jain, or Hindu yogi, denying the world. However, this never becomes his goal, though his natural personality isn't prone to attachment anyway. And he enjoys life too much to take the Buddhist path: escaping suffering. He is too eclectic to stick to one particular discipline, such as meditation. Once on his vacation he visits a Catholic monastery that observes silence so the monks can pray. Chris finds himself unsuited for that life. He loves to talk.

Ed's Theology

Ed is half Indian, half white. The Indian half is a mystic who sees spirits and tells stories. Ed was raised by his tribe in a town inhabited mainly by whites. He fits into neither culture, which makes him an ideal guide in Cicely for Joel, who never belongs there.

After Ed starts waking up in trees, he consults the healer Leonard, who performs a test and informs him that he has been "called" to become a healer, too—a Tlingit shaman. Ed could refuse the call without incurring retribution from beyond, but he accepts the challenge. His "call" is not a push from the past but a summons toward the future—closer to Middle Eastern theologies than East Indian ones.

The Tlingits believe in rebirth but not karma. Their rebirths are determined by kinship, not their past good or bad deeds. However, their future afterworld contains three "heavens" that are stratified according to the previous morality of the souls inhabiting them. The best heaven, oddly, is reserved for warriors and those who were murdered. It is called *Kiwa'a qawu 'ani,* and the souls there play games all the time. When they play shinny in the sky, it lights up the aurora borealis. Then there is a regular heaven for ordinary people between lives, and a sort of hell called "Dog Heaven" where bad people and suicides go.[38] Inexplicably, Joel will later find "Kiwa'ani"—but to him it will resemble Manhattan.

Maggie's Theology

Though Maggie is not a particularly religious person, she supports Joel in his soul work, preparing a seder for him at Passover, for instance. Her background is Christian, but it is not clear what kind. After her boyfriend Rick dies, she becomes convinced that he has been reincarnated as a stray dog—a theory that fits Tlingit traditions but that no other Cicelians have believed until then. As usual, they are all open to the idea—except Joel.

Maggie frequently allocates blame—preferably to a man and never to herself. Instead of soul-searching, she regularly lies and forgets whatever she regretted. She wants unconditional love—transcendent love—from others without cultivating the capacity for it herself.

Wanting Unconditional Love

Joel discovers this trait of Maggie's early, when her father unexpectedly arrives in Cicely. Maggie needs help covering up her lies. Her real boyfriend, the slow-thinking Rick, is away—fortunately so, because she has told her father that her boyfriend is a certain Dr. Joel Fleischman. That night, Maggie wears a ruffled dress and cooks dinner, while Joel plays his role superbly. He is exactly the kind of guy Frank O'Connell has wanted for his daughter.

But the next day, Joel urges Maggie to tell her father the truth. She does so reluctantly, fearing that it will only reopen his criticisms. Her misgivings prove correct. She can never expect anyone to love unconditionally the tomboyish, reproachful, opinionated pilot and sometime plumber. The only love she knows is worldly love, which must be won by presenting oneself in a form that others will accept.

Joel now understands: Sometimes she will pay the price that vanity exacts for approval but never to win *his* love, which would have to be on her terms. Nevertheless, over time, he develops transcendent love for her. Now he feels protective and tender toward her when she is defensive and hostile; he can see her vulnerability most clearly then. And she softens a bit in response.

One Screwball Romance in a Giant Ecosystem

One day Joel goes to Maggie's house and nervously suggests that they start dating. She is busy vacuuming, trying to rid her house of dust mite allergens, but she stops and smiles. She says yes.

That night, toasting their relationship with red wine, they pledge to begin anew. But she is still obsessed with the mites. He reminds her that we're all part of nature. We eat other creatures and some of them eat us. We're all one ecosystem. He leans forward to kiss her, but she visualizes his pores crawling with bugs and germs. She jumps up, insisting that he leave so she can go take a bath. She has developed a phobia and scratches incessantly.

Later, in the Brick, she announces triumphantly that her new dehumidifier has just annihilated a billion dust mites. Chris muses aloud, imagining the dust mite civilization she has destroyed. Someplace in our galaxy, he supposes, a humongous guy with a gigantic dehumidifier is planning to annihilate *us*. That night, Maggie dreams of chatting with a man-sized dust mite at the bar. He has problems at work, problems at home. His youngest son has just failed carpet navigation. Maggie is sympathetic. She wakes up. Now recognizing her place in the universe, she calls Joel to meet her out in the field. Behind them the mountains glows pink in the sunrise. As he approaches, she stops him and tells him to listen.

"Life! Life everywhere," she says. "The whole earth is throbbing with it. It's like music. All the plants, all the creatures. Ones you see, ones you don't see—it's like this big pulsating symphony. And you and me—we're a part of that. Life is in us, life is on us. We're all in this together." She kisses him. And they kiss again. After this, they are a couple.

So Maggie is also capable of transcendent love, after all; she had felt a rush of it for the whole ecosystem. However, transcendent love doesn't necessarily appear loving, according to the standards of worldly love. Maggie would readily have annihilated billions of more dust mites, despite her newfound love for them. She rightly recognizes transcendent love as compatible with the practical requirements of the world.[39]

Love is one thing. Skillful living in the world is quite another. You can have them both, but you can't translate one into the other because they run on different principles. One obeys the first law of thermodynamics. The other doesn't. Joel will not learn to manage them both but will choose between them.

Meaning, Transcendence, and Immortality

While Chris is away, Bernard substitutes for him at KBHR. Once, when nobody has needed medical care for weeks, Joel is fidgeting from boredom. He goes to see Bernard—a fine fellow in most ways, but a notch lower in emotional intelligence than his "twin" brother. Bernard does not mince words when diagnosing Joel's problem as "existential angst" concerning the *only* question that matters: What is the meaning of my existence?

"Your existence has no meaning," he informs Joel. "None at all. And if you don't come to grips with that, you're going to continue to lead an incomplete, unfulfilled, totally neurotic life. Normally I'm loathe to give advice, but if I were you I'd learn to sit still, to be quiet, to look into the abyss, to do nothing."

I didn't think much of this advice. Joel the antsy antihero seems more attractive than Bernard the judgmental nihilist, who is overly certain of his own wisdom concerning "the *only* question." We all search for the meaning of our existence, and few of us believe that it has none. On the contrary, to revisit chapter 6, Viktor Frankl's logotherapy contrasts sharply with Bernard's philosophy. Frankl saw each of us as having to find meaning in the calls that life issues to us personally, moment by moment.[40]

If Bernard has any spiritual orientation (which seems doubtful), it probably originated in India, where one is not taught to expect assignments from God. Yet it is just such assignments that give us meaning. (Perhaps Bernard just has not been listening.) His bad advice must have impressed Joel, who later will go into the wilderness "to do nothing" and to sever his attachments to the world.

It is not clear why Joel gives up seeking meaning in everyday life. Judaism is not nihilistic. Yet it is true that few Jews still expect God to give them personal assignments. Frankl wrote that "life" calls us, not that "God" calls us, thereby sidestepping the difficulty of authenticating messages from the Creator. Socrates had his *daimon*—a sort of guardian angel who spoke to him aloud, giving advice that was completely reliable. Joan of Arc heard voices, and Joan of Arcadia on television even *sees* God in various disguises, but few of us (except clerics) expect direct calls today.

Bernard notwithstanding, Joel's life isn't devoid of meaning. Freud supposedly was asked once what human beings need. He replied, "To love and to work." Joel has both: medicine as his work and Maggie as his love—a screwball, ambivalent love, but nevertheless meaningful. (If, as viewers believed, his true assignment was to learn the value of community, he never heard that call at all.) A passionate bond, marked by fights and erotic attraction, is a strange mission for a hero's journey, but Joel is obsessed with Maggie for five years, and she with him. They argue about small matters, yet their bickering gives them a sense of playful aliveness. They define themselves as "mutually desirous incompatibles." Life has summoned them to worldly love—to experiment with relatedness, with consent and reciprocity.[41] Despite this call, Joel will eventually abandon it and his medical practice, giving up everything that lent meaning to life—his work and his lover—for a way of being beyond material existence.

Wanting Immortality

Aspirations toward immortality are not limited to India's religions. Martha Nussbaum, who has written about Plato's search for the eternal, considers it a perfectly understandable goal for human beings—one that almost everyone would choose if they had a chance.

Nevertheless, Nussbaum herself would choose this-worldly mortality, as she explains in *Love's Knowledge*.[42] Certain joys are possible, she observes, only because of the limitations built into us. Immortality is boring. The Greek gods couldn't experience excellence, as we can. Take an athlete, for example. A god could outrun any mortal, so any race between them would be pointless. Only our finite nature creates the possibility of surpassing our usual limits and achieving something extraordinary. Gods never have to strive, so they can't understand our striving. Yet it's the striving and the possibility of failing that make our lives meaningful. We want challenges and obstacles, but then we try to overcome them. Mortality is more interesting than immortality, but each death makes us sad. We choose a life with the possibility of suffering and then organize our lives to minimize it.

Still, Nussbaum reminds us that transcendence has several meanings, some of which one can rightly favor. She does not wish for transcendence as immortal existence, beyond human experience, but mortal beings have other means of transcendence: to surpass limits, achieve excellence, flourish, and contribute to society.

I have alluded to yet another kind of this-worldly transcendence: the ability to coexist with contradictions instead of eliminating either side. This was Chris's kind of transcendence, and it has much to recommend it.

The Risk Junkie and the Control Freak

Now Maggie and Joel are a couple. But love does not make anything easy, and they keep fighting. After one blow-up, Joel asks her to marry him. She says yes.

Yet he wonders whether she will be able to stand married life with him, so they try living together first. This is the experiment life has assigned them.

He brings his clothes over. They negotiate an agreement about rinsing out the bathtub. She seduces him away from scrubbing the frying pan. He opens his prized bottle of cognac to share while they cuddle.

But oddly, whenever they come close to making love, a gun goes off someplace. First it's Maggie's shotgun. Next Haydon Keyes is walking by while they are engaged erotically. His rifle blast breaks their window. Next it is an antique gun on somebody's wall. This situation is making Joel too nervous for sex, whereas Maggie finds it an aphrodisiac. He catches her hiding the loaded rifle again, this time under the couch. She giggles and admits that she likes thrills and surprises. He is appalled, but Maggie hates the way he tries to control everything. She stomps off angrily, announcing that he needn't worry about explosions tonight because there will be no sex.

The next day Joel consults Chris, whose advice is classic Taoism: Joel should give up and go with the flow. So he resolves to tell Maggie that he will become a less controlling person, but when he gets home, he finds that she has been crying. She tells him to move out. Joel is devastated. He has worked toward this union for so many years! But then he goes on a house call to Manonash, a Tlingit village up the river.

Renouncing the World for Wisdom

Manonash[43] is just a few shacks without electricity or running water. That, Joel decides, is what he needs. Here he will work on himself. He will learn to let go of his desires and become nonattached. He stays there, living in a corrugated tin shed.

Maurice sends Ed in a canoe to fetch him, but Joel is no longer the expressive man Ed has known. He is a calm, shabby guy who shows little emotion while recounting his breakup with Maggie. Leaving, Ed asks whether Joel will ever come back.

"Well, if that's the way, that's the way I'll go," replies Joel, in his new manner of surrendering to the Tao.[44] He and Ed hug good-bye.

Yet Joel is becoming more Buddhist than Taoist, whether or not he knows the difference. He hunts, spear-fishes with the men, and tans hides. But he mainly seeks transcendence beyond material human experience. He has no guru, but one old Tlingit man teaches him to think like a salmon.

Life continues in Cicely. Maurice hires Joel's replacement, a competent but wooden doctor with a blonde journalist wife who settle into Joel's old cabin. But the mood of Cicely has turned negative. It is no longer a magical, nonjudgmental society. Maurice and Holling resort to fisticuffs. Chris, the wisest man in town, becomes a goofy simpleton. Maurice hires Haydon Keyes to steal for him. Chris refuses to sell back a keepsake to Maggie that she has mistakenly donated for auction. Shelly steals the tapes that Joel had recorded in Cicely. Chris starts pursuing Maggie. Class and gender conflict emerge, with an exclusive all-male club blackballing Holling. Shelly and Holling go to Maggie for marriage counseling. No one worries about Joel's departure except Maggie. Viewers hate to watch anymore.[45]

The Self as a Mushroom

Because Joel's birthday is approaching, Maggie asks Holling to decorate a cake, which she takes to Manonash to give him. He greets her casually, as an old acquaintance instead of his soul mate. She is shocked by his scruffy appearance and his wretched little shack, but he tells her that he's happier than ever before. Still, she begs him to leave, for he will surely die here. She keeps visualizing his death—by quicksand, by fire, by a falling boulder. But he speaks lightly as he gathers mushrooms.

"All the tension between you and me—it's based on an illusion of separateness. It ain't so," he says, pointing at the ground. "These are honey mushrooms. They look like they're individual mushrooms, but they're all connected. They are outcroppings of one mushroom that runs underground as far as the eye can see. This incredible fungus is spread over at least thirty-five square miles. It's the same with human beings. There's no separateness here. There's no 'other.' Really, we're just one. We're part of the same big mushroom. What I'm trying to tell you is, I never left you. I'm always there."

Maggie can't understand this perspective, of course (who could?), but she can see that he is deepening inwardly. He has recognized the mystics' oneness. That night, sitting companionably together in his hut, they share his birthday cake.

The Quest

Later, before dawn one winter morning, Joel knocks at Maggie's door. He has found a French explorer's 1785 map showing the location of Kiwa'a Ani—"the Jeweled City of the North."[46] He wants her to go with him to find it. Maggie is amazed at this new Joel. She knows Kiwa'a Ani is a myth, but she consents to fly there with him.

Soon they land in the snow and set off on their dangerous hike. First they encounter an aged Japanese dressed as a World War II soldier who provokes a tussle with Joel. He claims his first name means "dragon." That fits nicely: Joel needs to fight a dragon on his hero's journey.

Next they come upon a luxurious resort, where they spend days. Joel has lost interest in Kiwa'a Ani, Maggie realizes. This must be where the sirens lure men to their death. But this search is something Joel is supposed to do! She pulls him toward the door.

Later, walking through the snow, he starts talking like Plato. "I've always had the sense there's a whole other reality—a *real* reality—that we can't see," he says.

Next they come to a gated bridge. To cross it Joel has to answer a riddle: How do you keep the one you love?

"You don't," Joel tells the gatekeeper. "Love is selfless—nonpossessive. So if you truly love someone, you have no desire to possess them. You *don't* keep them." That is the right answer.

That night Joel and Maggie lie in their pup tent talking about why they have met. Maggie says she used to wonder how, out of all the people in the world, she could ever find the right ones to be her friends and her husband. Now, she says, "I think you meet the people you're supposed to meet." Maggie and Joel now share a belief in a benign force that summons them toward a particular future. They have assignments that they are "supposed" to do, and they meet the people they are "supposed" to meet. Plato's vision of a reality beyond this one combines with the archetypal hero's journey, and with the "Middle East" theology of a responsibility to God. Here we see modern pluralistic syncretism.

The couple walk into the snowy night with the map, counting their paces. Joel stares into the distance. Shimmering lights are visible. Skyscrapers! Kiwa'a Ani is Manhattan! He walks ahead and then stops to wait for her. She doesn't follow. That, she says, is *his* place. She belongs here. He accepts her decision. They embrace and he heads off to the Jeweled City. Maggie watches him until he disappears in mist.

Later she receives a postcard of the Staten Island ferry. It reads, "New York is a State of Mind. Love, Joel."

Why We Wept

Why did viewers weep at this ending of *Northern Exposure*? Because it was the *wrong* ending. (Yes, there is such a thing.) Not only did we have to lose characters whom we loved, but their deeds did not culminate in fitting outcomes. These were good people whose worst mistakes occurred in the denouement. They all failed, evidently without even realizing it.

We like people, not only on narrow moral grounds but for their emotional intelligence. The Cicelians lost their superb emotional appropriateness—so much so that we had to break empathy with them. Fine people came to a tragic end. Aristotle would have joined Plato in criticizing these writers now.

Joel and Maggie especially lost their way. For five years they had fought harm-lessly—the kind of play fighting that puppies do. Their real summons had been obvious: to invent a lively and mutually autonomous union. But suddenly the conflict stopped being playful. Fights had to be resolved, win or lose. Why was that scenario necessary? Maggie had been a risk junkie all along, and Joel had been a control freak, but they had lived with the conflict and even enjoyed it. Suddenly one of them had to give way to the other—either/or. Joel would try to change, though every viewer took his side in that particular dispute—gunshots are not fun and not aphrodisiacs. This new, painfully serious insistence on resolving, normalizing, and taming their screwball relationship disappointed viewers. Some conflicts are too charming to end that way.

Audiences want dramatists to answer this question: How should we live? Yet we don't expect flawed characters to reform and become models for us to emulate. In the case of the ending of *Northern Exposure*, we simply wanted Maggie and Joel to show us how to live together well with all their flaws. These two people are antiheroes; we love them for their foibles, and we want them to love each other in the same way. Worldly love needs frequent interventions by transcendent love—the love that is given without being deserved. A screwball comedy must end with the marriage of two Superego IIs, each supplied with an abundance of faults to overlook in the other. The viewers had a right to expect this conclusion, for they, too, must manage conflict and imperfection. The only guidance that can help is instruction in good-humored forbearance.

Transcendent love is not enough. When Joel informed Maggie that they, like parts of the big mushroom, were never really separate, this was a spiritual insight. But it's inadequate compensation for living apart. When he went to Manonash, the man of flesh became a man of spirit—as if he had to choose between the two—while Maggie stayed corporeal.

He pretended to be happy in Manonash, but the viewers disbelieved him. After such a rejection, happiness would have been pathological. The old expressive Joel became abnormally unemotional, ethereal instead of lively. In the end, he acquired all the traits that Maggie had demanded of him, including an eager-ness for such risks as the quest for Kiwa'a Ani. Nevertheless, when she finally had to choose, she didn't go with him to the Jeweled City. The viewers saw that she had not really wanted him to become nonattached. Instead, she had always wanted him to love her passionately, without ambivalence. He had cultivated the wrong traits for a screwball romance. Influenced by Chris's quotation from Bodhidharma, Joel concluded that "love is nonpossessive; you *don't* keep the one you love." With transcendent love, maybe you don't, but you certainly try to when it comes to worldly love—which both he and Maggie wanted. Life had given them an assignment—to invent a way of being together well as "mutually desirous incompatibles"—but they didn't complete it.

And so they parted almost casually. Though they had been engaged, they had never even discussed where they would live. Neither of them had ever uttered the word *love*. Only on his postcard from New York would Joel at last say that word to Maggie.

The hero completed his journey and returned home. He had always been an effective person in the conserved space-time world, for Jewish culture supports *doing*—mastery of matter and logos. Now he had acquired an awareness of *being*, which is not confined to particular physical events. He left Alaska with an enlarged capacity for transcendence but a diminished concern for ordinary life. He grew to understand transcendent love well. Unfortunately, he considered it incompatible with worldly love, which presents a whole different array of problems that he gave up trying to solve. This is a common mistake of mystics.

Attachment is required to make the world work. You have to care enough to perform all the necessary doingness. Life won't get easy. That's what makes it a perfect game. Meaning comes from contributing to a purpose larger than oneself.[47] Joel's life had meaning before Monanash; it was his attachment to Maggie and medicine. Cultivating nonattachment up the river, he abandoned his patients and the meaning that came from caring about them. He left them and the other Cicelians without even saying good-bye, diminishing the community that had been his home and leaving some of them bereft—especially Chris, who wept bitterly over the loss of his friend. Joel was professionally unethical and personally disloyal. He also relinquished Maggie unemotionally. Did he gain meaning for his life, overall?

How far can one travel, living simply on the purity of transcendent awareness? And is that an ethical way to live? Perhaps so, for those who believe that this world is a place of suffering and that Nirvana is the goal—or, as Plato did, that this world is less real than the invisible one beyond. But for millions watching *Northern Exposure* around the globe, it's the wrong message. They want to see the hero flourish in ordinary life, while also attaining harmony with the universe. Both.

Could Joel have attained great wisdom by practicing Judaism exclusively? Probably not, for he would have learned little about transcendence that way. Yet he could have retained his passions while learning transcendence. Through him the audience could have received a great teaching—an illustration of how to combine work and love with clarity of soul.

Chris's Taoist philosophy might have helped him, showing him how to unite opposites—good with evil; spirit with flesh; transcendence with skillful living, and especially mysticism with worldly asceticism. Irreconcilable oppositions play together in the Tao's constantly changing dynamic, without destroying either of them, for they each require the other. Contradictory elements coexist, complementing each other. The conflict worker Johan Galtung, who uses the Taoist model in his work, has offered a light-hearted example of how mysticism and worldliness might coexist. "In Norway there used to be a saying, he who has 'given himself to the world' and he who has 'given himself to God,' and a conflict between those two lifestyles. But not in California. There you can meditate on a skateboard or in a Porsche. Material things are trivialities for many and for that reason not necessarily in contradiction with the spiritual."[48]

The *Northern Exposure* writers now have taught their syncretic religious beliefs to many millions of viewers. I wish they had taught us to prize our problems. Unwisely, Joel abandoned his problems for the sake of a boring heaven: Kiwa'a Ani, the warrior's heaven, where souls have nothing to do but play shinny in the sky. By offering only an incomplete solution to Joel's dilemma, the writers failed to deliver the most important message they could have contributed to the world: The conservation of energy is a good thing. So is love. Enjoy them both.

Yet we thank Joel for what he did give us. We celebrate his partial success, we learn from his life, and we still miss him.

Conclusion

Every theology is a particular way of explaining how the universe works, and so is every scientific theory. The two domains are similar, except that science requires empirical evidence and an either/or logic that can sometimes create unnecessary conflict. Yet there is theological evidence, of a sort, in the way that people live when they follow a particular faith. Such evidence does not prove the truth of religious propositions, but it indicates the results that a believer may expect from following them. Theological beliefs make a difference and critics can contribute by exploring them.

Cicelians are mystics and philosophers grappling with the big question: How should we live? They draw their answers from pluralistic array of world cultures, without achieving coherence. But perhaps that does not matter. "Middle East"–based beliefs about what we are "supposed" to do can be combined with

Taoist admonition to "go with the flow" and with a resigned "India"-based acceptance that "what goes around comes around." Such New Age concoctions work for some Cicelians.

The transcendent Joel left, but the eclectic Taoist Chris stayed—and became Maggie's new lover.

Chapter 10

Conclusion

We began with this challenge from the UN General Assembly and the Dalai Lama: How can we create a culture of peace and compassion? My answer: with entertainment—especially long-running stories in installments that make you fall in love with characters or at least care about them—*really, really, really* care. Love can change your way of thinking completely. I don't have survey data, but I've asked around.

It even happened to that austere, head-in-the-clouds, rational philosopher, Plato—the same guy who had excluded poets from of his utopian city-state[1] and advised everyone to transmute their erotic love into a transcendent appreciation of beauty.[2] Apparently he finally fell in love. Straight through his middle dialogues, Plato had kept saying that all emotions were irrational and that poets and playmakers should not be given free access to audiences, lest they stir up passions and undermine clear, cold reasoning.

Then, in *Phaedrus,* he recants that view. In fact, he makes Socrates explicitly renounce such an attack on Eros. Socrates had just stated his usual point of view to a young man and was about to leave when his daimon stopped him. This invisible guardian spirit often stopped Socrates when he was about to make a mistake but never told him what he should do instead. In this case, the daimon told him that he had committed a sacrilege by insulting Eros, who was supposedly a god and who therefore deserved respect. Socrates halted and then made a completely different kind of speech to the young man, Phaedrus, telling him that the madness of love was actually a powerful and valuable force: It was in fact the source of human motivation. He finally got it right.

Rationality works well for judging the best way to work toward your goals, but the goals themselves enter your soul when you are seized by irrational attachments. The energy to pursue goals comes from emotions. Max Weber later made the same point when he noted the importance of charisma in world history. When a new religion or social movement emerges, its leader is usually someone whose wisdom and insight seem almost superhuman and whose personal magnetism sweeps people away. This charisma resembles what I've called "limerence."

What made Plato change his mind? Martha Nussbaum and some other classics scholars speculate that he had fallen in love with a guy named Dion and that the experience caused him to revise his views about the importance of irrational emotions.[3] I won't go into the story, but it's plausible, and I'll put a link to Dion's amazing biography on www.twoaspirinsandacomedy.com, this book's Web site.

But my point here is to mention the other shift that accompanies Plato's recanting of his views about love. He had always criticized poets for being emotional and drawing their audience into emotions, too—a state of mind that he saw as a form of madness. Now he acknowledges the value of passion and even sees some of it in philosophy. Nevertheless, he never concedes that poetry (or, what concerns us, drama) can, by itself, provide an adequate grasp of truth. Always it needs the additional insights yielded by philosophy, though he supposes that the two may be combined.

Plato's new position narrows to insignificance the gap between his and Aristotle's views of drama and poetry. Both men recognize a place for emotional storytelling in our lives. And we can acknowledge the validity of Plato's insistence that this poetic, emotional storytelling needs the support of additional, critical rationality.[4] To me, this seems to settle the "ancient quarrel."

Emotion Is the Source of Our Motivation

It's useless to argue against love and charisma. You may hate the people whom I love, and there's no getting around that. But skilled writing can create stories and imaginary characters who move millions of people (though not everyone) deeply. We can put that art to good use. Though eros and charisma are irrational by their very nature, they can cooperate with rationality and serve purposes that make excellent sense. Intuition and creativity are "semirational." They live on the border between emotion and intellect,[5] and we should pay attention to them, without necessarily acting on every hunch. I'm promoting the use of stories to motivate work toward urgent social change.

Sometimes everyone needs a motivational boost—at least everyone who has decided, as I have, against denying this world and who intends to love it instead.

Our planet needs our protection, and, fortunately, doing so gives wonderful satisfaction. Hedonism—the pursuit of personal pleasure—does not satisfy. As Einstein said in the passage that Chris quotes in a *Northern Exposure* episode, "Man is here for the sake of other men—above all for those upon whose smiles and well-being our own happiness depends, and also for the countless unknown souls with whose fate we are connected by a bond of sympathy."

That bond of sympathy goes beyond one's intimate friends and family; it includes all of humankind. Psychologist Martin Seligman specializes in studying the causes of happiness. He has described happiness as "the *pursuit of meaning,* [which] … consists in attachment to something bigger than you are. The self is not a very good site for meaning, and the larger the thing that you can credibly attach yourself to, the more meaning you get out of life."[6] Fortunately, the world is offering some huge projects today.

Ask yourself: Do you believe that the planet is approaching a life-or-death crisis? That global warming is going to wreak havoc but could perhaps still be limited?[7] That suburbanites may have to crowd back into cities because of the impending energy shortage?[8] That the nuclear arms race has revived, with the possibility still existing that weapons could be launched accidentally?[9] That wars leave environmental and social scars that can poison generations of human beings and animals?[10] That millions of refugees around the world are learning hatred more than hope?[11] That our society may collapse like Easter Island unless we learn to manage our resources within a couple of decades?[12] That large teams of civilian peacekeepers, armed only with surveillance equipment such as video cameras and Internet access, may be able to forestall acts of genocide such as those that happened in Rwanda and Srebrenica?[13] That twenty thousand people die every day from preventable hunger or malnutrition?[14] That the world needs to conserve the increasingly scarce fresh water, share it humanely, and stop polluting our aquifers?[15] That HIV/AIDS can be controlled?[16] That our criminal justice system can be replaced, largely with restorative justice?[17] I do.

Do you believe that everyone needs to work on some of these problems? I do.

But most people aren't engaged in social movements, research, or political action—because they haven't a clue how to make a difference. To work on these enormous issues may seem as futile as commanding the tides to stop.

Still, these are *our* problems, and we should be thankful for them. They're a source of meaning for everyone who owns them, and they're superb problems, because they're solvable. Our challenge is to show others how to help solve them. How can we motivate people to care about solving them—*really, really, really* care?

Through storytelling. Not around the campfire but on TV, radio, DVD, and the Internet. Stories whose lovable characters are fully engaged in solving these problems. (Stories can make you do things. *Northern Exposure* made me write this book.)

Stories that instigate social change come in countless forms. There are comic books that straighten out kids' heads—some of which are even designed by other kids.[18] There's a computer game, *Pax Warrior,* that forces players to confront issues that General Roméo Dallaire faced in Rwanda, trying to prevent genocide. There are improvisational plays directed by a Brazilian dramatist-politician, Augusto Boal, who stops the show in the middle and invites spectators onstage to tell the characters how to handle the situation.[19] There are political protests staged as satirical street theater. During the Communist era, the Poles were masters at this, improvising dramas to "celebrate" the 1917 Russian Revolution. (The cops didn't dare break these up.)

All stories educate—even ones that only *mis*educate. When you tell a story, you can't help sending a message, any more than you can help speaking prose. And your audience will get it. For example, Dr. Neal Baer, who used to be a producer for the medical series *ER,* recounts a time when an episode dealt with human papilloma virus. Researchers questioned the viewers before and after the episode. About 50 percent had learned from it that the HPV virus causes cervical cancer—which translates into forty million viewers. That's a lot of disease prevention. Baer added:

> Many producers hide behind the notion that we're just "entertaining." So, because we're just entertaining, that means that if it's lightweight, it doesn't really matter. The show is to take your mind off things and that excuses any responsibility for portraying these issues accurately and responsibly. Others feel that if we educate them, they'll turn off the dial because we'll be giving them all these facts and figures.... I [look for a] great story and that way I'll be able to integrate information naturally, as it comes through our characters. It's always about our characters.[20]

Evidently Baer is already halfway there. He understands that he's educating, and he has even designed programs specifically to expose the truth about some medical fact that is generally taboo. He combines rationality with drama, as Plato proposed. What more does he need to consider? The motivational factor. He could get us so worked up about problems that we'd take action to solve them. The best way to do that is with the messages in great stories that are "always about our characters." It's the characters who get our emotions going.

Film and television producers have developed certain ethical norms, such as not portraying attractive characters smoking, not seeming racist, and usually showing homosexuals in a positive light. But they can do far more to educate with gripping, emotionally searing stories. Call it "edutainment."

Edutainment

This approach is being used in foreign countries with enormous success—especially in addressing development issues, such as family planning, HIV/AIDS prevention, adult literacy enrollments, and female employment. (I described the case of Tanzania in chapter 2.) Edutainment is especially successful in demonstrating personal behavior that viewers will want to emulate. In one Mexican soap opera, an old man is gradually coming around to enrolling in a literacy course. The last episode ends showing him reading a letter from his granddaughter. My American friend wept while watching it. The next day, the entire Mexican adult education program was swamped with applicants.

Two remarkable organizations are engaged in developing radio and television serial dramas on human reproductive issues: Population Media Center[21] and Population Communication International.[22] They have shown that drama induces people to do things, whereas public service announcements and billboards do not. And a series can be remarkably cost-effective. For example, the radio soap opera folks in Tanzania calculated that for each new person they persuaded to adopt HIV prevention, the cost was only eight cents.[23] They don't preach to the audience about what to do but rather show them the consequences of particular actions.

I mentioned in chapter 2 Miguel Sabido's innovative soap operas that informed the public about population issues in Mexico from 1975 to 1982. Since then, others have adopted his approach with excellent results. His shows are melodramas; that is, there are good guys, bad guys, and people in between, and with no ambiguity about who is whom. Good people start off with conventional opinions, but new situations make them consider, say, family planning. If this presentation is done slowly and credibly, showing the characters debating the matter in private, public opinion will go along with their decisions—and often adopt the same practices themselves. What works best is for viewers to get together and discuss each episode. This outcome often happens in India and Africa, where not everyone owns a radio or television, and the neighbors like to come over in the evenings to have a look.

Several factors influence the success of these episodic dramas. First, the series should last for a year or longer, and viewers must come to care about the characters. You can't form deep attachments quickly. Second, the audience must discuss the characters' predicament among themselves—the more, the better.

We used to do that. Think back several years to speculations "around the water cooler" about who killed J. R. Ewing on *Dallas*. Or when we laughed together about Lucy's silly shenanigans last night. Everybody talked about those shows. Today, with hundreds of different channels and with a digital video recorder in lots of homes, people usually don't watch or read together. To share opinions, they have to plan ahead or post e-mails on a list to other fans.

Episodic Television to Save the Planet

Consider all the impending global calamities that I listed earlier. They make fabulous themes for television stories. If, as we have considered, tales can increase or reduce smoking as a cultural habit, lower the birthrate enough to decrease global population growth by one billion, make homosexuality socially acceptable, start a civil war, abolish slavery, prompt citizens to overthrow repressive regimes around the world by applying nonviolent resistance, raise the average IQ of whole societies by three points per decade, or double the use of condoms in HIV-infected countries within one year, then why in God's name aren't we using this tool more effectively and consciously to improve life on our planet? Well, let's do so!

Here's my idea: I want a whole bunch of television series featuring ensembles of smart, likable characters (always including at least one sexy, unattached male and female) who are working on these social problems. One series for each of these issues, please. One show about scientists—maybe resembling the *M*A*S*H* ensemble—studying the polar ice cap and global warming. Another series about a good-looking international team of unarmed civilian peacekeepers in a conflict zone. A third show about American volunteers educating Afghan girls and women in a refugee camp. One about an Oxfam group helping land-hungry Brazilian farmers make a living without burning down their rain forest. One with two protagonists—a military officer down in a nuclear weapon silo, trained to launch a ballistic missile at a moment's notice, and his antinuclear activist brother. And so on. The characters should have interpersonal conflicts, intelligent conversations, thrilling adventures, love affairs, and fun, and they shouldn't be saints. The writers should make us laugh (intelligently, without jokey lines or canned laughter) and feel vicarious love and joy. We need our dopamine and oxytocin. And please use music; half the purpose is to give us intense feelings. Saving the world should be good for our immune systems.

Some shows can be cliffhangers for viewers with the thrill-seeking gene, but their dangers should never be resolved by violence. Our characters must manage their predicaments like civilized people, teaching us a lesson or two about what a culture of peace looks like. We must love them—or at least really, really, really care about them.

Though the world is fragmented—different cultures, different languages, thousands of different channels—we want large audiences to follow our shows and discuss them as they unfold. As the TV industry is organized now, a new series appears first on a U.S. network and, a few years later, begins showing abroad in syndication. That's no way to get a global discussion going. We want the whole world to watch our shows during the same week. This is a big challenge. The television moguls can do it for special events—say, the Academy Awards—but not for a series. *Uncle Tom's Cabin* would not have been influential had it not appeared in prolonged, popular installments. Still, we have advantages that Harriet Beecher Stowe lacked: the Internet, e-mail, and blogs to keep discussions alive.

Plato was right. Stories are not enough, by themselves. Philosophers are required, too. Stories can stimulate our interest and motivate us, but discussion and participation are also necessary, to make our world a democratic *polis*. For example, Richard Stratton could have told you about restorative justice, but he didn't; *I* did. *Street Time* motivated me to look for solutions, and, as a sociologist, I found some good ones. (In Plato's day there were no sociologists, so he would have called me a philosopher.) If one of our proposed shows deals with the criminal justice system, it must illustrate possible improvements and stimulate public discussion. But how?

The television network should maintain a moderated Web site for each series, where viewers can send serious comments. Only the most intelligent letters will be posted, but some of them can be developed into future episodes, exploring how this or that solution might look and how it might affect the characters' lives. The writing and discussions should be interactive over time. That will motivate and empower citizens. Let viewers know that their suggestions carry weight, just as Boal does by inviting critics in the audience onstage to propose changes. The Web site is where civil society organizers can connect with viewers to work out practical proposals and recruit participants to a campaign. After the show motivates people, they need to be shown how to help their beloved characters solve problems. Otherwise, we'll fail to achieve our objective.

Let me give a concrete illustration of the sort of show we need. Green Cross International is an organization that Mikhail Gorbachev founded after the Soviet Union came apart. Intended as a counterpart to the Red Cross, which addresses the health and social problems resulting from war, Green Cross mainly addresses war's *environmental* consequences. Experts working for this group inspected the effects of the Kuwaiti oil fires, for example. Their mission is not primarily peace building, but when a Green Cross team encounters conflicts in the course of their work, they naturally try to solve them.

I want a television series about a Green Cross team. The team's members could be research scientists of various nationalities and their staff, and Gorbachev could make occasional guest appearances and help publicize the show. I happen to know the president of Green Cross International, Dr. Alexander Likhotal, formerly the press spokesman for Gorbachev, who continues to work closely with him. I have suggested my idea to Likhotal and Gorbachev, even listing some possible topics for treatment in specific episodes.[24] They like the idea but are at a loss as to how to make it happen. Well, that's the challenge. We need new ways of getting the shows and other cultural products that we want.

Fortunately, we are not alone. Precisely as this book was ready to go to the typesetter, I discovered the emergence of a new production company that is already enacting many of the innovations that I have suggested here. An immensely rich man, Jeffrey Skoll, who made billions as the president of eBay, is spending much of his wealth on an imaginative type of philanthropy. His new organization, Participant Productions, teams up with Hollywood companies to produce movies that deal with urgent social issues. His funding guarantees his partners that they will not lose money by addressing global problems. Skoll's main goal is to inspire people to become social activists. After watching one of his films, audiences are invited to visit his company's Web site, www.participantproductions.com/, to learn more and to participate in discussions on blogs. There are always suggestions there about how individuals can help solve the problem. So far, Skoll funds primarily feature films (which is wonderful!) but perhaps he will soon sponsor the creation of episodic television dramas (which can be even better).

While rejoicing in Skoll's wonderful contribution, we realize that the main solutions must come from ourselves. If we want culture to flower globally, we have to become mindful consumers of it, and we must address the serious structural obstacles hampering its improvement.

Addressing Structural Challenges to Create a Great Culture

Our challenge is to transform global culture, making it a source of inspiration and wisdom to support human flourishing. This requires a restructuring of entertainment globally to make the most valuable elements more accessible. In chapter 2, I mentioned Ann Swidler's metaphor of culture as a tool kit. Since people choose tools partly on the basis of accessibility, what we need to do is rearrange our tools to make the most useful ones conspicuously available. This doesn't involve censorship. It isn't necessary to ban particular fictional products (except for children or perhaps prisoners) but instead to allocate the public venues for displaying them with regard to the common good. Already adult television programming is often restricted to hours when children are presumably in bed. The same principle could be extended. Unfortunately, decisions about such matters are made today not in a democratic way by citizens but by business interests—especially advertisers.

Superficially, our present arrangements seem entirely reasonable. After all, each of us is a consumer. We pay only for the entertainment (magazines, cable TV, hockey games) that we personally want. We have an enormous array of options—including hundreds of television channels at any moment. If you don't like something, you can just do something different. What's wrong with that?

Turn on your TV, and you will answer that question yourself. With two hundred channels to choose from, there is little worth watching. That's what's wrong. Your interests and tastes don't influence the decision makers who produce the array of options from which you choose. Yes, they try to find out what you want. They watch the Nielson ratings with fierce attention and imitate the shows that are most successful. They are even attaching monitors to individuals now that pick up the sounds of programs and ads around us as we go through the day.[25] But the whole premise is that entertainment is a commodity sold to individuals, rather than a culture that surrounds us and affects our minds, bodies, and way of thinking collectively. This premise is never challenged, yet it determines the quality of our experiences.

I have interviewed numerous actors, writers, and producers who worked on *Northern Exposure*. Without exception they all said that the show was an accident—a fluke—that could never happen again. They knew how wonderful it was (some of them told me that they, too, had wept when finally watching touching scenes on which they had worked), but they insisted that such a brilliant series couldn't be produced today. Yes, it was financially successful, but the money managers in Hollywood don't understand why. They are constrained by short-term competition and cannot allow the creative workers enough freedom for artistry to emerge. The industry is entirely oriented toward making money, not satisfying our cultural concerns.

Journalist Christopher Hitchens has described an experience that reveals what is missing. He was asked to join a focus group of about 250 persons previewing two television pilot sitcoms to determine whether they would be broadcast to the entire country. He found the event a sham. The audience was required to evaluate products—denture adhesives, douches, laxatives, and nasal sprays—in addition to the shows, both of which were unfunny insults to the intelligence. Still, only two people walked out. The others, though appearing depressed, dutifully ticked off the boxes of the loaded questions, for the questionnaires allowed no way of expressing their true opinions. Hitchens waited outside and talked to people as they left. Their comments were invariably intelligent, but the survey had not sought to find out what they really thought. Instead, wrote Hitchens, "by the simple expedient of asking stupid questions, the organizers of the evening had successfully factored all this out and walked off with an enormous pile of stupid answers and a load of free market research."[26]

It would be unfair to call the people running this event malevolent. They are simply and reluctantly part of a "system" that is set up for the sole purpose of making money for advertisers and the big entertainment companies, such as Viacom, Disney, and Sony. What is discouraging is that nobody can see a clear exit from this system. That's what we have to figure out.

A solution begins, I think, with an awareness that cultural products are not commodities in the same sense as clothing and food, which we choose and consume individually. Our culture is our shared resource. Whatever others "consume" changes them in ways that affect us, so we all must care about it. For example, I don't go to the ballet very often (I find myself worrying that a dancer may fall), and I probably will never visit the Everglades. Yet I gladly contribute tax money to support the ballet and the Everglades because I want them to exist in my world—not for my personal consumption but to preserve the richness of our shared environment. Some things can only exist when they are owned collectively rather than individually. Culture is like that.

In fact, most cultural activities are subsidized by the public. I edit a magazine that survives only because of government grants and low postal rates—which almost all magazines receive. Radio and television broadcasters depend on the use of an assigned spectrum of the airwaves—a resource that is owned by the public and allocated by the government, nowadays without charge—with the expectation that the programming should meet society's cultural needs. That expectation is not enforced, but it should be.

Culture not only is but *must* be subsidized. The founders of the United States recognized the connection between media subsidies and a diverse marketplace of ideas in which citizens could engage.[27] Such decisions are political and should be reached democratically in the context of open, ongoing public discussions. Moreover, the receipt of public funding should entail greater self-restraint than might be expected of other kinds of businesses. For example, our magazine is run almost entirely by volunteers as a public service, though all of us surely would demand to be paid if it were, instead, a restaurant or a shoe store. Showbiz, on the other hand, lacks any sense of responsibility to repay society by providing cultural excellence or limiting its profits. And citizens, for their part, rarely realize that they are subsidizing these immensely wealthy, but unaccountable, production and distribution companies. Subsidies are made in the name of the public, but without public consent or even consultation.

Robert McChesney and John Nichols have proposed some media reforms that might overcome the worst of these problems. They suggest expanding funding for noncommercial, public service broadcasting and making it democratically accountable. They would set far stricter standards for commercial broadcasters as a condition for granting them broadcast licenses. They would allow citizens to redirect $150 or $200 per year from their tax payments to any nonprofit medium of their choice. This could move $25 or $30 billion into the American nonprofit media and create healthy competition among independent producers of culture. Without involving any government censorship or control of media content, this plan would keep Wall Street and Madison Avenue from dominating culture.[28] I have a couple of other, more ambitious suggestions to add: that the decision making of corporations must be transparent for public scrutiny and that each corporation's board of directors be required to include representatives of environmental civil society organizations, as well as workers and consumers of the products. We need to make our economy more responsive to human needs through democratic reforms.[29]

Freedom To and Freedom From

The only real defense against overly powerful social forces (such as wealthy entertainment corporations) comes from the strength of numbers—notably social movements and mass protests. Media reform is not yet really a social movement, but it will become one if people come to realize how crucial it is for solving other social problems, such as environmental issues. There is already a growing view that communication is a *right* that must be protected.[30]

This perspective actually is a promising one—at least if we consider communication rights as more than access to advanced technology. This notion can be a way of framing a number of disparate issues within a single concept. For example, communication includes both freedom of speech and privacy. It includes not only the right to communicate but also the right not to be pestered by those with whom one does not wish to communicate.

Advertising is one form of communication that everyone often wants to avoid. It is too powerful simply because the public has not organized politically to limit it—a move that is entirely practicable. In the early 1940s, the U.S. Supreme Court had to determine whether advertising should be exempt from government regulation on the grounds that it was protected by the First Amendment to the U.S. Constitution—freedom of speech. The Court decided that selling something for a profit was not entitled to the same kind of protection as political speeches. Over time, however, this position has changed, so that now the Supreme Court largely accepts that advertising is covered by the right to free speech and therefore can be thrust into your face, whether you like it or not. This change has resulted from the growing power of corporations, and it can be reversed if the public gains renewed power and articulates its objections.[31]

Not all media reforms have to be legislated or determined by the Supreme Court. Many improvements can be made if the public organizes to demand it, even at the grassroots level. This involves haunting producers and networks and forcing them to pay attention. They don't actually *know* what we want them to produce. They resort to a lot of guesswork. To be sure, they know what shows are being watched, but they don't know what the viewers get from the experience. For example, they don't know why viewers turned to reality shows instead of dramas. Sometimes Hollywood's money managers are astonished when ticket sales take off unexpectedly, allowing a product to influence public opinion, as, for example, Michael Moore's documentaries have repeatedly done. He showed what is possible, and now we need for others to show us through *fiction* how to preserve the world.

We have to remind writers that we're reading and watching their work. Understandably and even excusably, they forget us. For example, *Northern Exposure* writer Jeff Melvoin was assigned to write an episode called "Kaddish for Uncle Manny," in which Joel's uncle dies and he has to find ten Jewish males in Alaska to constitute a minyan—a precondition for saying the traditional prayer for the dead. Joshua Brand spelled out the plot for Melvoin to write: The Cicelians would all help find Jews, but in the end Joel would abandon the whole idea of collecting strangers to pray with him. Instead, he would invite the townspeople together for this purpose, since they were his community.

As a Jew himself, Melvoin had some qualms about this plot, but he went along with it because it made good sense and good drama, even though it violated his own religious practices. It provoked a great debate among Jewish viewers, most of whom accepted the change. As Melvoin recalled during our interview:

> One of my friends said, "Do you realize you are changing American culture?" The magnitude of the statement shocked me. When we writers were in the room working, mostly we were thinking of a dozen people at most who were going to watch that show. If I had thought about the larger groups of people who were

going to see it, it would have paralyzed me. While we were writing it, I think it's a good thing that we were not aware of the impact we were having.

On the defensive side, if we want freedom of choice, that also means freedom *from*—not only freedom from excessive advertising but also from distressing images. As matters stand, everyone is allowed to put almost anything into the common cultural space where others can't avoid seeing it. Instead, we need *separate* spaces for people who crave shows that the rest of us find deleterious. One theater for horror and gratuitous violence, for instance, and one for the rest of us. Separating venues is not censorship. Actually, however, we already have censorship: the control by financial interests over what gets produced. You have no say in the matter, but you are exposed to the results, unless you live in a cave with a blanket over your head. Democracy should give you more control over the circumstances of your own life, plus a say in organizing our common cultural experiences.

Take violent programming, for example. Evidently *all* kinds of people are harmed physiologically by watching scenes such as the opening battle in *Saving Private Ryan,* which has been proven bad for the cardiovascular system. (Recall chapter 3.) If you have a heart attack, your physician will tell you to stress your heart with *physical* exercise but to avoid *emotional* stress such as watching edgy or angry movies. Adrenaline and cortisol can cause arrhythmia and a lopsided enlargement of the heart. Healthy people should follow the same advice and avoid the same stress hormones, but no one can do so. If you watch TV at all, however selectively, you'll be exposed to advertising clips from violent or suspense shows. If you go to movies, you'll be subjected to trailers of the kind you should avoid. When Janet Leigh died, every newscast showed the shower scene from *Psycho,* a movie that surely was rated as unsuitable for children—and was unsuitable for me, too. That's the kind of thing our freedom of choice should prevent.

Just as smokers no longer are allowed to pollute the air that we all must share, anxiety-provoking images should be excluded from sites that we all must share. If thrill seekers want adrenaline and cortisol, it should be a private activity enjoyed in seclusion. It may not be good for them, but that is their right. It is my right to stay away. A social movement oriented toward the protection of communication rights must include the right to freedom *from* unnecessary and potentially harmful communication.

Pressure to "Clean Up Television"

My top priority involves demanding more constructive shows, rather than protesting against bad ones, but some people do emphasize that, and they have a right to do so—as private citizens. For a while there was an organization dedicated to lobbying to improve television.[32] There have also been numerous interventions by private organizations to block the showing of stories that they consider offensive. Sometimes their disruptive demands have succeeded in getting programming changed. The networks have sometimes tried to develop a less antagonistic relationship with advocacy groups. For example, in 1986 NBC met representatives of twenty organizations, including the National Gay and Lesbian Task Force, the PTA, the Southern Baptist Convention, and the American-Arab Anti-Discrimination Committee. At the end, they were all invited to keep in touch for regular feedback. Noting that the success of advocacy groups has varied from one period to another, Kathryn Montgomery writes, "Groups concerned about alcohol and drug abuse found the television industry most receptive to their suggestions when that issue became important as a major public health concern."[33] If Montgomery is right about the alcohol and drug abuse argument, then the emerging evidence that exposure to stressful films harms the cardiovascular and immune systems may convince public health authorities to exclude such programming from the common space. Clearly the health research on secondhand smoke was decisive in getting smoking banned from areas sharing a common source of air.

Another approach involves the use of the boycott against advertisers. This takes work to organize, but it's effective and does not depend on the government. During the O. J. Simpson trial, a Toronto television station, CITY TV, presented a celebratory Simpson film festival, much to the disgust of some citizens, who organized a response. One woman, Valerie Smith, contacted the companies whose ads were to be broadcast during that show. She reported, "Every company we called took immediate action to make sure their advertisements did not run during the Simpson festival. There was no hesitation and no argument. It was quite an education.... Anti-social television programs do not exist without advertisers."[34]

In a similar display of feminist solidarity, some women at the University of Toronto at Mississauga visited the campus bookstore manager en masse, protesting against the display of a pornographic magazine with a cover showing a naked woman being shoved through a meat grinder. These women were vigorously opposed to government censorship, but they had no qualms about insisting, as private citizens, on the removal of this piece of cultural rubbish from the public space.

Government control is a different matter. However, it is government regulatory agencies that allocate airwaves to particular broadcasters, holding them to standards that supposedly reflect community values. Strengthening the democratic responsiveness of these agencies, and giving them stronger teeth, would be entirely appropriate. However, as the number of satellite channels and cable companies proliferate, this mechanism of public accountability is weakening. While airwaves are public property, cables are not, and hence they are not held accountable.

Still, rather than pursuing primarily the elimination of junk, I am more interested in fostering excellence—which is made difficult by the lack of astute, trustworthy criticism. Naturally, all criticism is subjective (none more so than this book), but it is still an essential service that deserves our recognition when it is insightful. It also should be criticized when it is not.

Criticism

In choosing whether to watch or stay away from a show, we need to know a good deal about its content. A simple rating system is inadequate. We need sensitive critics who pay attention to their own emotions and tell us what to expect. It is inadequate to say merely whether sex or violence is shown. What perspective do the writers take on their topic? For example, do we see the violence through the eyes of perpetrators or their victims? Are a plurality of contrasting moral views expressed during a single episode or film? Do the writers induce us to love characters and then turn them into such horrible people that we must break empathy with them? Are a character's admirable or loathsome qualities recognized in the end? Critics should tell us about all of these factors.

When sex is shown, the quality of the couple's relationship colors everything. Is crude or impersonal or exploitive sex shown gratuitously—or to make a point in the story? Is the sex tender? Ridiculous? Pitiable? Funny? Obscene? Cruel? Such complexities cast meanings on each image, each action. Critics should tell us about the shades of meaning in such acts.

What is the violence like? Amusing, light, and playful (as in Charlie Chaplin's boxing match)? Harsh, but supposedly adventurously fun (as in *Raiders of the Lost Ark*)? Terrifying (as in *The Blair Witch Trial* and *Psycho*)? Vicious (as in *Pulp Fiction* and *Kill Bill*)? Dreadful, but creating tragic pity (as in *Gandhi* and *Schindler's List*)? I enjoyed Chaplin's "play violence" and was moved by the tragic films, but all of those in the middle range, including the Indiana Jones type, seemed dehumanizing. An extensive checklist rating system may be helpful, but mostly we must depend on the perceptiveness of critics, who, unfortunately, tend to become desensitized through overexposure to pain. (Their job must be terrible for the immune system.) But we can tell them what to watch for.

Ambiguity

I began this lengthy meditation with one objective: to seek standards by which to judge the excellence or even acceptability of various types of entertainment. I took the Roman gladiatorial contests as absolute zero. Everything else would be better than that and I expected to find some clear logic underpinning my judgments. But I was too optimistic. Reasonable criteria for appraisal did emerge, to be sure, but for each such standard there was often an equally reasonable *opposing* one. Contradictions emerged, so that it became hard to take unequivocal positions.

Now I find that I admire both Plato and Aristotle as much as at the beginning—and still for their contrasting concerns. Plato was right to worry about mimesis. People do imitate; empathizing makes it more likely; and there are dangers involved in exemplifying evil behavior, even on the part of clearly unattractive characters whom we ourselves would never emulate. Someone else will.

Yet without conflict, a story is boring and colorless. We require wrongdoers in dramas. Aristotle saw the value of learning to pity them, for often they are victims of bad "moral luck"—not necessarily blameworthy for their evil intentions. Tragedy teaches compassion for human failings. Yet in *The Poetics* he rightly insisted that characters receive their just deserts, though we may pity them and consider justice itself too cruel. We gain moral insights from empathizing and from persisting in doing so even when it is hard. Hence we must love "gray" characters, as Aristotle suggested, though they are dangerously seductive moral models. There is no easy solution to our conundrums. Empathy is good for us, yet it can hurt and lead us astray morally. And if our morality requires us to break empathy, that can hurt even more.

Can ethical writers resolve these contradictions? No, but they can balance them thoughtfully. Writers must coexist with moral antinomies, balancing yin and yang, rather than sticking to consistent, clear principles. At least, I have no principles to offer.

Well—a few. Here they are:

A writer can contribute more by illustrating possible ways of *solving* a problem than by allocating blame to those who create it.

In the end, every character should recognize the good or bad that has been done.

We can bear seeing tragedy overcome the people we love, we can even bear losing them, but we cannot bear losing love itself. We must never have to convert our love into hatred.

The emotional appropriateness of others is as important to us as the morality of their actual deeds. Yet for ourselves, appropriateness can be a hazardous judgment. It requires that we be true to different loyalties: to our own principles, to the feelings of others, and to the objective reality that we confront. Often these requirements are contradictory, irreconcilable. We must balance them.

As an audience, we are always learning how to live. Compassion is the most challenging virtue to learn—compassion, forbearance, or even affection for the very flaws of another. Loving an antihero is a valuable lesson in that moral project, especially if we can *laugh* at him lovingly. Empathizing with him, we may vicariously seek transcendence, even while finding ourselves ridiculous and modestly accepting the limitedness of the human condition.

May these reflections contribute to a culture of peace and compassion.

Notes

Chapter 1

1. Benedict Carey, "What Makes People Happy? TV, Study Says," *New York Times*, December 2, 2004, referring to an article in *Science*.

2. Richard Rorty, "Redemption from Egotism: James and Proust as Spiritual Exercises," www.stanford.edu/~rrorty/redemption.htm.

3. Rorty, "Redemption from Egotism."

4. Brander Matthews, *The Development of the Drama* (New York: Scribner's, 1912), 107–46.

5. Sissela Bok, *Mayhem* (New York: Perseus, 1999), 15.

6. The Dalai Lama, in *Healing Emotions: Conversations with the Dalai Lama on Mindfulness, Emotions, and Health*, ed. Daniel Goleman (Boston: Shambhala, 1997), 18.

7. Daniel Goleman, *Healing Emotions*, 33–34, 44.

8. Vinay Menon, "Why We Like to Watch," *Toronto Star*, August 3, 2002.

9. Karl Popper, *Objective Knowledge: An Evolutionary Approach* (Oxford: Oxford University Press, 1972), 147.

10. Steven Johnson, *Everything Bad Is Good for You: How Today's Popular Culture Is Actually Making Us Smarter* (New York: Riverhead, 2005).

11. Johnson, *Everything Bad Is Good for You,* 139–56. Evidence to the contrary is often cited—for example, that literacy rates are not improving around the world. However, as I read that evidence, it is problematic, too, since the literacy measurements are set to test individuals' ability to read at the level required for functioning well in everyday life. Because everyday life is increasingly complex, these tests also are made increasingly difficult, which makes comparisons across time questionable. People need higher and higher reading skills in order to handle everyday matters. What is clear is that people who use computers have higher prose reading skills than those who do not. See *Literacy in the Information Age: Final Report of the International Adult Literacy Survey* (Paris and Ottawa: Organisation for Economic Co-operation and Development and Statistics Canada, 2000).

12. Simon Baron-Cohen, *The Essential Difference: The Truth about the Male and Female Brain* (New York: Perseus, 2003).

13. Howard Gardner, *Changing Minds: The Art and Science of Changing Our Own and Other People's Minds* (Boston: Harvard Business School Press, 2004), 27–48.

14. Lee Siegel, "Freud and His Discontents," *New York Times Book Review,* May 8, 2005, 29–30.

15. Karl Jaspers, *Origin and Goal of History,* trans. Michael Bullock (London: Routledge and Kegan Paul, 1953); Shmuel N. Eisenstadt, "The Axial Age: The Emergence of Transcendental Visions and the Rise of Clerics," *European Journal of Sociology* 23 (1982): 292–314.

16. Jaspers, *Origin and Goal of History.*

17. Andre Gunder Frank, review of *Maps of Time,* by David Christian, *International History Review,* forthcoming.

18. Thomas McEvilley, *The Shape of Ancient Thought: Comparative Studies in Greek and Indian Philosophies* (New York: Allworth, 2002).

19. McEvilley, *The Shape of Ancient Thought,* 197.

20. The lost second book of Aristotle's *Poetics,* which dealt with comedy, may have contained a polemical response to Plato. See Stephen Halliwell, "Aristotle's Poetics," in *The Cambridge History of Literary Criticism,* vol. 1, *Classical Criticism,* ed. George A. Kennedy (Cambridge: Cambridge University Press, 1989), 150.

21. *Katharsis* meant "purification," though not always by the same means. To Plato in *Laws, katharsis* meant purification of the soul through successive reincarnations. See McEvilley, *The Shape of Ancient Thought,* 99. But Martha Nussbaum translates the word as "clarification"—a more cognitive term. See her *The Fragility of Goodness* (Cambridge: Cambridge University Press, 1986), 388–90.

22. I should mention briefly a related opinion held by some critics today: that it's not modern stories but modern *technology* that harms people. Jerry Mander, notably (and in stark contrast to Steven Johnson), argues that television is always bad for people, regardless of the content of the programming. He says it is hypnotic, inducing alpha waves in the viewers' brains. I am not perturbed by this effect. Occasionally I even try to get into an alpha state by meditating. To me the important issue instead concerns the moral and social consequences, positive or negative, of imitating fictive characters. See Jerry Mander, *Four Arguments for the Elimination of Television* (New York: HarperCollins Quill, 1978).

Chapter 2

1. Here and throughout the book, I change the names and identifying traits of people whose personal lives I discuss, but I generally acknowledge their contributions in the preface.

2. Extensive contemporary evidence demonstrates many negative effects of television on children. I cannot report it adequately here, but see, for example, Alicia Wittmeyer's report of three studies in 2005 showing that too much television leads to poor academic performance. One study by scholars from Stanford and Johns Hopkins universities found that children with TVs in their bedrooms scored lower on standard-

ized tests than those who watched the same amount of TV but did not have bedroom sets. A second study at the University of Washington found that watching TV before age three can hurt children's reading skills by age six. A third study tracked one thousand people in New Zealand for nearly thirty years and found that whose who watched the most television between ages five and fifteen were the least likely to graduate from high school or college by age twenty-six. However, Professor Deborah Linebarger of the University of Pennsylvania claims that studies should not focus on the amount of time children spend watching TV but, rather, on the content of what they are watching, for good programs are beneficial. See Alicia Wittmeyer, "Children's TV Use Linked to Poor Academic Performance," *Los Angeles Times,* July 5, 2005. Or see www.commercialfree childhood.org/news/tvpooracademicperformance.htm. Educational programs are beneficial. There seems to be an incompatibility between the research suggesting that certain aspects of IQ are *improved* by TV and the research reported above. Theoretically, however, both conclusions could be valid. Some forms of intelligence might improve while school performance actually declines.

3. The man was convicted of this offense on June 18, 2004. The *Globe and Mail* reported he "literally went from his computer, where he was looking at child pornography, to grabbing a real little girl off the street." When the police asked him whether child porn made him do it, he said, "With time, and I don't know how it is for other people, but for myself, I would say that yes, viewing the material does motivate you to do other things. In my case, for sure. The more I saw it, the more I longed for it in my heart." *Globe and Mail,* June 19, 2004, A15.

4. Ulric Neisser, "Is Intelligence on the Rise?" *American Scientist* (September–October 1997); James R. Flynn, "Massive IQ Gains in 14 Nations: What IQ Tests Really Measure," *Psychological Bulletin* 101 (1987): 171–91.

5. Barbara Crossette, "Population Estimates Fall as Poor Women Assert Control," *New York Times,* March 10, 2002, International Section, 3.

6. Harriet Beecher Stowe, *Uncle Tom's Cabin* (Boston: Jewett, 1852).

7. *London Times* review of "Uncle Tom's Cabin," September 3, 1852.

8. For this account of Garcia's influence, I am indebted to Victor Sumsky, who recounted these events to me in Moscow in 1992. For two of Garcia's books, see *The Filipino Quest: A Just and Lasting Peace* (Quezon City, Philippines: Claretian, 1988) and *The Sovereign Quest: Freedom from Foreign Military Bases* (Quezon City, Philippines: Claretian, 1988). I was later able to interview Garcia.

9. This training program was led by the International Fellowship of Reconciliation's Richard Deats, whom I have interviewed.

10. His acceptance of Gandhi's ideas was reflected in a famous defense speech, *Testament from a Prison Cell* (Manila: Benigno S. Aquino, Jr. Foundation, 1984).

11. Peter Ackerman and Jack DuVall, *A Force More Powerful: A Century of Nonviolent Conflict* (New York: St. Martin's, 2000), 375–76. Other writers have portrayed Aquino's commitment to nonviolence as intermittent. See Mark R. Thompson, *The Anti-Marcos Struggle: Personalistic Rule and Democratic Transition in the Philippines* (New Haven,

Conn.: Yale University Press, 1995), 112. However, Sandra Burton discusses the great impact of the film *Gandhi* before Aquino's return home in *Impossible Dream: The Marcoses, the Aquinos, and the Unfinished Revolution* (New York: Warner, 1989), 107–14.

12. Ackerman and DuVall, *A Force More Powerful,* 291.

13. For other evidence that the movie renewed worldwide interest in the Mahatma, see Sandford Krolick and Betty Cannon, eds., *Gandhi in the "Postmodern" Age: Issues in War and Peace* (Golden: Colorado School of Mines Press, 1984), xiii, 3, and passim.

14. Gene Sharp, *From Dictatorship to Democracy* (Boston: Albert Einstein Institution, 1993).

15. Jane Rosenzweig, "Can TV Improve Us?" *The American Prospect* (online edition) July 1, 1999, at www.prospect.org/print/V10/45/rosenzweig-j.html.

16. Howard Gardner, *Changing Minds* (Boston: Harvard Business School Press, 2004), 128–29.

17. William N. Ryerson, "The Effectiveness of Entertainment Mass Media in Changing Behavior." Ryerson is president of the Population Media Center, Shelburne, Vermont. His paper can be obtained by sending an e-mail to pmc@populationmedia.org or visiting the center's Web site at www.populationmedia.org.

18. Ryerson, "The Effectiveness of Entertainment Mass Media in Changing Behavior." See also Arvind Singh and Everett M. Rogers, *Entertainment-Education: A Communication Strategy for Social Change* (Mahwah, N.J.: Lawrence Erlbaum, 1999), 148–79.

19. Ryerson, "The Effectiveness of Entertainment Mass Media in Changing Behavior." See also Singh and Rogers, *Entertainment-Education.*

20. Johann Wolfgang von Goethe, *Die Leiden des jungen Werther* [*The Sorrows of Young Werther*] (Hamburg: Asmus, 1970), originally published in 1774.

21. David P. Phillips, "The Influence of Suggestion on Suicide: Substantive and Theoretical Implications of the Werther Effect," *American Sociological Review* 39 (June 1974): 340–54.

22. David P. Phillips, "Suicide, Motor Vehicle Fatalities, and the Mass Media: Evidence toward a Theory of Suggestion," *American Journal of Sociology* 84 (1979): 1150–74.

23. David P. Phillips, "The Impact of Fictional Television Stories on U.S. Adult Fatalities: New Evidence on the Effect of the Mass Media on Violence," *American Journal of Sociology* 87, no. 6 (1982): 1340–59.

24. Phillips's findings initially received less notice than they deserved. However, other scholars have confirmed his discoveries. Evidently suicide coverage in the mass media does substantially affect suicide rates. Phillips's innovative research methods had advantages over previous experimental research that also had demonstrated imitative behavior. Still, critics complained that he was not proving any relationship between *individual* behavior and exposure to the press, but only proving *aggregate* effects, without offering any explanation for the mechanisms by which individuals were influenced. See J. N. Baron and P. C. Reiss, "Same Time Next Year: Aggregate Analyses of the Mass

Media and Violent Behavior," *American Sociological Review* 50 (June 1985): 347–63. See also Paul Marsden, "Operationalizing Memetics—Suicide, the Werther Effect, and the Work of David P. Phillips," available from PaulMarsden@msn.com and pespmc1.vub. ac.be/Conf/MemePap/Marsden.html. Marsden's research is oriented toward a new theory called *memetics*, as described in Susan Blackmore's book, *The Meme Machine* (New York: Oxford University Press, 1999). However, these theorists have the same problem as Phillips in providing any rigorous theory by which to explain social contagion. See S. Stack, "Media Impacts on Suicide," in *Current Concepts of Suicide,* ed. D. Lester (Philadelphia: Charles, 1990), 107–20.

25. Marsden, "Operationalizing Memetics."

26. Male subjects were brought together in pairs and told they were subjects in a study of physiological reactions to stress. Actually, one of the pair was a confederate of the experimenters. His task was to annoy the real subject by giving him mild but uncomfortable electric shocks as punishment for a supposedly poor performance on the task. Then the subject had a chance to shock the fellow who had mistreated him. Naturally, he was somewhat angry. Some of the subjects were in a room with a gun on the table, among a pile of papers. Some were in a room with two badminton racquets instead of a gun. The control group's room had neither gun nor racquets. When subjects had a chance to punish the annoying confederate, those in the room with the gun administered more shocks than those not exposed to the gun. See Leonard Berkowitz and A. LePage, "Weapons as Aggression-Eliciting Stimuli," *Journal of Personality and Social Psychology* 7 (1968): 202–7. Also see L. Berkowitz, "Impulse, Aggression, and the Gun," *Psychology Today* 2 (1968): 19–22. This kind of study has been replicated many times, though in about half of the instances the results have fallen short of statistical significance.

27. Of all 14-year-old boys, 9 percent of those who watched less than one hour per day had engaged in aggressive acts by age sixteen or twenty-two, whereas 32 percent of those who watched one to three hours per day, and 45 percent of those who watched more than three hours per day, had subsequently engaged in aggressive acts. André Picard, "Study Links Violence to Daily TV Viewing," *Globe and Mail,* March 20, 2002, A1, A6. Picard was reporting research by Jeffrey Johnson, published in the journal *Science* on the same date.

28. Many of these findings have been widely reported elsewhere. Nevertheless, by omitting them, I may be biasing the evidence in favor of Aristotle's side, for the omitted research overwhelmingly substantiates Plato's complaints about the harmful effects of imitating immoral plots. (My review appears on the book's Web site, www.twoaspirin-sandacomedy.com. Both Plato and I will be pleased if you read it there.)

29. George Gerbner is the creator of *cultivation theory,* which explains viewers' perceptions of social reality in terms of their exposure to media. Heavy viewers were far more likely to overestimate the amount of violence in society. See George Gerbner, "Violence in Television Drama: Trends in Symbolic Functions," *Television and Social Behavior,* vol. 1, *Media Content and Control,* ed. G. A. Comstock and E. A. Rubinstein (Washington, D.C.: U.S. Government Printing Office, 1972), 28–187.

30. Melvin L. DeFleur and Margaret H. DeFleur, *Learning to Hate Americans: How U.S. Media Shape Negative Attitudes among Teenagers in Twelve Countries* (Spokane, Wash.: Marquette, 2003).

31. Keith Oatley and E. Duncan, "Structured Diaries for Emotions in Daily Life," in *International Review of Studies in Emotion*, ed. K. T. Strongman, vol. 2, 250–93 (Chichester, England: Wiley, 1992).

32. Keith Oatley, "A Taxonomy of the Emotions of Literary Response and a Theory of Identification in Fictional Narrative," *Poetics* 23 (1995): 1–2, 53–74.

33. "Watch Soaps," *Globe and Mail*, October 5, 1998, A13. See also Peter Hills and Michael Argyle, "Positive Moods Derived from Leisure and Their Relationships to Happiness and Personality," *Personality and Individual Differences* 25 (1998): 523–35.

34. See Andrea L. Press, *Women Watching Television: Gender, Class, and Generation in the American Television Experience* (Philadelphia: University of Pennsylvania Press, 1991).

35. Jonathan Cohen, "Parasocial Break-up from Favorite Television Characters: The Role of Attachment Styles and Relationship Intensity," *Journal of Social and Personal Relationships* 21, no. 2 (2004): 187–202.

36. I corresponded with Michael Argyle to ask whether he knew of any research on the health and well-being of bereaved fans of a defunct soap. He said he did not, but he also felt sure that there are significant health effects.

37. Luc Brisson, *How Philosophers Saved Myths: Allegorical Interpretation and Classical Mythology* (Chicago: University of Chicago Press, 2004), 36–37.

38. Brisson, *How Philosophers Saved Myths*, 162.

39. Brisson, *How Philosophers Saved Myths*, 45. He points out, however, that Plutarch rejected this Stoic approach as impious and atheistic.

40. Brisson, *How Philosophers Saved Myths*, 163–65.

41. Nicholas Reeves, *The Power of Film Propaganda: Myth or Reality?* (New York: Cassell, 1999), 239–40.

42. Robert Coles, *The Call of Stories: Teaching and the Moral Imagination* (Boston: Houghton Mifflin, 1989), 38–39, 163–67.

43. Joanna and her colleagues have written a book for Afghan children. The stories deal with the typical traumas of war for a refugee family, exemplifying ways of coping with the stress. These books are being published in Farsi and Pushto languages and used in schools.

44. Gary Solomon, *Reel Therapy: How Movies Inspire You to Overcome Life's Problems* (New York: Lebhar-Friedman, 2001).

45. Solomon, *Reel Therapy*, 4.

46. Solomon, *Reel Therapy*, 7.

47. Martha C. Nussbaum, *The Therapy of Desire: Theory and Practice in Hellenistic Ethics* (Princeton, N.J.: Princeton University Press, 1994), 484.

48. Leo W. Jeffres, *Mass Media Effects*, 2d ed. (Prospect Heights, Ill.: Waveland, 1997), 24.

49. Julie Winstone, a psychologist at Southampton University, studied aging bingo players, noting that their mental fitness is kept up by the game. *BBC Report*, February 26, 2001.

50. Robert D. Putnam, *Bowling Alone: The Collapse and Revival of American Community* (New York: Simon & Schuster, 2001).

51. Wayne C. Booth, *The Company We Keep: An Ethics of Fiction* (Berkeley: University of California Press, 1988), 72.

52. Kate Taylor, "Can We Judge Art on Moral Grounds?" *Globe and Mail,* January 31, 2002, R7, R8.

53. John Gardner attributes the "first great evasion" of moral criticism to New Criticism in his book *On Moral Fiction* (New York: Basic Books, 1977). However, in his wonderful book *The Company We Keep,* Booth has also offered an explanation for the downgraded status of ethical criticism, without blaming it on New Criticism. He attacks some common academic ideologies instead, such as the (presumably unbridgeable) fact/value split and notions about what kind of proof is necessary to establish "knowledge."

54. New Criticism was dominant in the United States. (W. K. Wimsatt, Cleanth Brooks, and John Crowe Ransom were leaders.) In Britain, on the other hand, F. R. Leavis was the most influential critic during that period, and in his essays moral factors were always relevant.

55. Erich Fromm, *The Sane Society* (New York: Holt, 1995), and *Escape from Freedom* (New York: Holt, 1994).

56. Margaret Walker Urban, "Moral Repair and its Limits," in *Mapping the Ethical Turn: A Reader in Ethics, Culture, and Literary Theory,* ed. Todd F. Davis and Kenneth Womack (Charlottesville: University Press of Virginia, 2001), 112.

57. Elaine Scarry, *On Beauty and Being Just* (Princeton, N.J.: Princeton University Press, 1999), Part II.

58. Martha C. Nussbaum, *Upheavals of Thought: The Intelligence of Emotions* (Cambridge: University of Cambridge Press, 2001), especially chap. 14.

59. Carl J. Charnetski has shown that listening to some kinds of background music—classical music, jazz, or light rock—for half an hour increases levels of immunoglobulin A (IgA), a protein that defends one from upper respiratory infections. However, listening to some annoying tone clicks causes a decrease in IgA. See Carl J. Charnetski and Francis X. Brennan, *Feeling Good Is Good for You: How Pleasure Can Boost Your Immune System and Lengthen Your Life* (Emmaus, Pa.: Rodale, 2001).

60. Sandra E. Trehub, Department of Psychology, University of Toronto, personal communication.

61. Ann Swidler, "Culture in Action: Symbols and Strategies," *American Sociological Review* 51, no. 2 (April 1986): 273. See also her book *Talk of Love: How Culture Matters* (Chicago: University of Chicago Press, 2001).

Chapter 3

1. Aristotle, *Nichomachean Ethics,* Book II.

2. For a fuller discussion of the nervous, immune, and endocrine systems, see the appendix for this chapter on the book's Web site, www.twoaspirinsandacomedy.com. You will find appendixes for other chapters there as well.

3. Psychologists who specialize in this field distinguish among various affects or feelings: *emotions* (which tend to come and go within seconds or minutes), *moods* (which may last all day or even longer), and *temperament* (the enduring affective tendencies of an individual). They also distinguish between affect and sexuality, which is considered to be a biological process more comparable to eating, drinking, and breathing than to emotions. I will not attempt to observe all these distinctions here.

4. Ruut Veenhoven, ed., *How Harmful Is Happiness? Consequences of Enjoying Life or Not* (Rotterdam: Universitaire Pers Rotterdam, 1989), chaps. 6, 8, and 9.

5. The Dutch Longitudinal Study among the Elderly sampled 3,149 persons aged sixty-five and over from 1955 to 1957 and measured their happiness or satisfaction. By 1983, the subjects who had been satisfied earlier had lived longer. See Dorly J. H. Deeg and Robert J. van Zonneveld, "Does Happiness Lengthen Life?" chap. 5 in Veenhoven, *How Harmful Is Happiness?* Unfortunately, the study did not quantify pleasure or happiness. It did not differentiate between satisfaction and frequent intense pleasure. Indeed, few studies do make such comparisons, which are important.

6. David Lykken, *Happiness: What Studies on Twins Show Us about Nature, Nurture, and the Happiness Set-Point* (New York: Golden, 1999), 58.

7. Lykken, *Happiness,* 84–85.

8. Researchers measure the activity of various areas of the brain with electrodes attached to the scalp. Subjects with more right-sided brain activation display more negative and less positive moods than their more left-side activated counterparts. Also, when shown a short film clip designed to elicit fear and disgust, those subjects with right-sided activation respond with more negative emotion. Moreover, such right-sided persons have less natural killer cell activity than their left-frontal counterparts, and they show less immune reactivity to stress. (See the book's Web site for a summary of immune functions: www.twoaspirinsandacomedy.com.) Richard J. Davidson, "Honoring Biology in the Study of Affective Style," in *The Nature of Emotion: Fundamental Questions,* ed. Paul Ekman and Richard J. Davidson (New York: Oxford University Press, 1994), 323–24. Asymmetry of brain activation may even be present in the fetus.

9. The Dalai Lama and Daniel Goleman, *Destructive Emotions: How Can We Overcome Them?* (New York: Bantam, 2003), 337–44.

10. E. A. Maguire et al., "Navigation-related Structural Change in the Hippocampi of Taxi Drivers," *Proceedings of the National Academy of Science of the United States of America* 97, no. 9 (2000): 4414–16.

11. The relationship seems bidirectional. People with small hippocampi are more susceptible to posttraumatic stress disorder (PTSD), which in turn may diminish the size of the hippocampus. See Robert M. Sapolsky, "Chickens, Eggs, and Hippocampal Atrophy," *Nature Neuroscience* 5 (November 2002): 1111–13.

12. Arlie Russell Hochschild, *The Managed Heart: Commercialization of Human Feeling* (Berkeley: University of California Press, 1983).

13. See Viktor E. Frankl, *Man's Search for Meaning: An Introduction to Logotherapy* (New York: Simon & Schuster, 1959), for the story of life in a Nazi concentration camp;

and S. Folkman, J. T. Moskowitz, E. M. Ozer, and C. L. Park, "Positive Meaningful Events and Coping in the Context of HIV/AIDS," in *Coping with Chronic Stress,* ed. B. H. Gottlieb (New York: Plenum, 1997).

14. The Dalai Lama in *Healing Emotions: Conversations with the Dalai Lama on Mindfulness, Emotions, and Health,* ed. Daniel Goleman (Boston: Shambhala, 1997), 5.

15. D. N McIntosh, R. C. Silver, and C. B. Wortman, "Religion's Role in Adjustment to a Negative Life Event," *Journal of Personality and Social Psychology* 65 (1993): 812–21. See also Harold G. Koenig and Harvey J. Cohen, *The Link between Religion and Health: Psychoneuroimmunology and the Faith Factor* (New York: Oxford University Press, 2002).

16. For example, the immune system produces *cytokines,* chemicals that can pass through the blood–brain barrier, changing central nervous system functioning and personal behavior. If cytokines are administered to a person, they can influence her temperature, sleep, moods, and ways of moving.

17. Cousins founded the Dartmouth Conferences to bring together high-level Soviet and American citizens. U.S. President Kennedy once asked him to carry out a diplomatic mission with Soviet First Secretary Khrushchev, and he would have succeeded had the American U2 spy plane not been shot down during the negotiations.

18. Hans Selye, *The Stress of Life* (New York: McGraw-Hill, 1956).

19. In fact, Selye's explanation for these negative effects was mistaken. The problems resulting from stress are not due, as he supposed, to the depletion of certain chemicals but instead to the surplus of stress-induced chemicals—especially cortisol. Still, he was right in showing that stress does have harmful health effects.

20. Norman Cousins, *Anatomy of an Illness as Perceived by the Patient: Reflections on Healing and Regeneration* (New York: Bantam, 1979), 35.

21. Cousins, *Anatomy of an Illness,* 41–43.

22. Robert Ader and Nicholas Cohen, "CNS–Immune System Interactions: Conditioning Phenomena," *Behavioral and Brain Sciences* 8 (1985): 379–94. This experiment built on work that the two researchers had been doing in the 1970s. See also Candace B. Pert, *Molecules of Emotion: Why You Feel the Way You Feel* (New York: Touchstone, 1997), 190. Actually, Ader's and Cohen's conditioning experiment should not have been surprising. Russian scientists had made similar discoveries early in the century, while exploring the phenomenon of conditioning, which Pavlov and his famous dogs had demonstrated. (The dogs were fed while a bell was rung; eventually they would salivate when the bell was rung but no food was presented.) Western scientists simply had not paid attention to some other Russian discoveries about the conditioning of the immune system.

23. One study has already shown this possibility by treating a woman with lupus whose drug was administered along with cod liver oil and rose perfume. After a few such occasions, the taste of cod liver oil and the smell of the perfume were administered alone, in between the regular treatments. The patient's health improved steadily, though she had only half as many "real" treatments, the others lacking any genuine medication.

See K. Olness and Robert Ader, "Conditioning as an Adjunct in the Pharmacotherapy of Lupus Erythematosus," *Developmental and Behavioral Pediatrics* 13 (1992): 124–25. Also see Shelley E. Taylor, *Health Psychology,* 3d ed. (New York: McGraw-Hill, 1995), 545.

24. Pert, *Molecules of Emotion,* 191.

25. Pert, *Molecules of Emotion,* 23–25.

26. For example, acetylcholine, norepinephrine, dopamine, histamine, glycine, GABA, and serotonin.

27. Pert, *Molecules of Emotion,* 67.

28. Pert, *Molecules of Emotion,* 70. Many protein substances have unexpectedly turned out to be peptides, including insulin and most of the hormones, but not the steroid sex hormones.

29. Notably the amygdala, hippocampus, and other components of the limbic system, which had been thought to generate emotions.

30. Taylor, *Health Psychology,* 31.

31. Alan Watkins, "Mind-Body-Pathways," in *Mind–Body Medicine: A Clinician's Guide to Psychoneuroimmunology,* ed. Alan Watkins (New York: Churchill Livingston, 1997), 12.

32. Paul Martin, *The Healing Mind: The Vital Links between Brain and Behavior, Immunity, and Disease* (New York: St. Martin's, 1997), 35–37.

33. Martin, *The Healing Mind,* 158–59. Likewise, a nine-year California study took into account a number of health-related risk factors and found that having close ties with friends, a spouse, and/or relatives was the best predictor of good health and reduced mortality. (That study did not ask about soap opera watching!)

34. For example, one study showed that widowed or divorced parents who had lost a child had a higher rate of mortality during the next ten years, whereas married bereaved parents seemed to be statistically protected by the comforting presence of their spouses; they had no greater risk of premature death than nonbereaved parents. See Martin, 164.

35. Martin, *The Healing Mind,* 168.

36. Martin cites this lovely epigram, *The Healing Mind,* 164.

37. Martin, *The Healing Mind,* 171.

38. E. Friedmann and S. A. Thomas, "Pet Ownership, Social Support, and One-year Survival after Acute Myocardial Infarction in the Cardiac Arrhythmia Suppression Trial (CAST)," *American Journal of Cardiology* 76 (1995): 1213–17. Dean Ornish reviews other studies of pet ownership in his book *Love and Survival: The Scientific Basis for the Healing Power of Intimacy* (New York: HarperCollins, 1998).

39. A. McGrady et al., "The Effects of Biofeedback-Assisted Relaxation on Immunity, Cortisol, and White Blood Cell Count," *Journal of Behavioral Medicine* 15 (1992): 343.

40. Tomio Hirai, *Zen and the Mind* (Tokyo: Japan Publications, 1978).

41. Robert R. Provine, *Laughter: A Scientific Investigation* (New York: Penguin, 2000), 40.

42. Sensibilities change. In early Greek comedy, dramatists also employed a lot of toilet humor. See Erich Segal, *The Death of Comedy* (Cambridge, Mass.: Harvard University Press, 2001).

43. A. J. S. Rayl, "Humor: A Mind–Body Connection," *The Scientist* 14, no. 19 (October 2, 2000): 1. See the project's Web site, www.rxlaughter.com. Oddly, comedians do not seem to live longer than others, as one might expect. One laughter researcher speculates that it is because comedians do not usually laugh at their own jokes—but this is only his untested theory.

44. L. S. Berk et al., "Neuroendocrine and Stress Hormone Changes during Mirthful Laughter," *American Journal of Medical Sciences* 298 (1989): 390–96; and L. S. Berk et al., "Eustress of Mirthful Laughter Modifies Natural Killer Cell Activity," *Clinical Research* 37 (1989): 115A.

45. Kathleen M. Dillon, Brian Minchoff, and Katherine H. Baker, "Positive Emotional States and Enhancement of the Immune System," *International Journal of Psychiatry in Medicine* 15, no. 1 (1985–1986): 13–18.

46. William F. Fry, "The Physiologic Effects of Humor, Mirth, and Laughter," *Journal of the American Medical Association* 267, no. 13 (1993): 1857–58.

47. Michael Miller, M.D., of the Center for Preventative Cardiology, University of Maryland, in a presentation to the American Heart Association in New Orleans, November 16, 2000.

48. Nicholas Bakalar, "Laughter as Good Exercise," *New York Times*, March 10, 2005.

49. University of Maryland Medical News, November 15, 2000, www.umm.edu/news/releases/laughter.html.

50. Keiko Hayashi, M.D., University of Tsukuba, reported in *Diabetes Care* 26 (2003): 1651–52.

51. Hayashi, report in *Diabetes Care*.

52. Matisyohu Weisenberg, Inbal Tepper, and Joseph Schwarzwald, "Humor as a Cognitive Technique for Increasing Pain Tolerance," *Pain* 63 (1995): 207–12.

53. Dolf Zillmann, Minet de Wied, Cynthia King-Jablonski, and Stefan Jenzowsky, "Drama-Induced Affect and Pain Sensitivity," *Psychosomatic Medicine* 58 (1996): 341.

54. In the *Symposium,* Plato depicts transcendent love as more than a dichotomy distinguishable from everyday worldly love, but rather as extending in stages from worldly love. We begin, he says, by loving the beauty in particular individuals, but then we can love the beauty that is unseen in them—their beautiful souls. Increasingly we love beautiful thoughts and ideas, coming to recognize ourselves in an ocean of beauty, until eventually we see beauty in itself—eternal and absolute. This recognition brings us close to God.

55. Conservation of energy (the first law of thermodynamics) states that energy can be converted from one form to another and from matter, but it cannot be created or destroyed.

56. Hanna Newcombe, *How Things Come Together* (Dundas, Ontario: Peace Research Institute–Dundas, 1998). Or see her Web site, hwcn.org/~aq053.

57. Robert N. Bellah, "Max Weber and World-Denying Love: A Look at the Historical Sociology of Religion," Humanities Center and Burke Lectureship on Religion and Society, University of California, San Diego, October 30, 1997. Bellah is elaborating a paper by Max Weber, "Religious Rejections of the World and their Directions," which was published in *From Max Weber: Essays in Sociology,* trans. and ed. Hans H. Gerth and C. Wright Mills (New York: Oxford University Press, 1946). I draw on this work heavily here.

58. Ornish, *Love and Survival,* dust jacket.

59. D. C. McClelland, "Motivational Factors in Health and Disease," *American Psychologist* 44, no. 4 (1989): 675–83.

60. S. Cohen, "Psychosocial Models of the Role of Social Support in the Etiology of Physical Disease," *Health Psychology* 7 (1988): 269–97.

61. J. G. Verbalis, M. McCann, C. M. McHale, and E. M. Stricker, "Oxytocin Secretion in Response to Cholecystokinin and Food Differentiation of Nausea from Satiety," *Science* 232 (1986): 1417–19.

62. Ronald de Sousa, *The Rationality of Emotion* (Cambridge, Mass.: MIT Press, 1990), 315.

63. Arthur Aron, Helen E. Fisher, Debra J. Mashek, Greg Strong, Hai-Fang Li, and Lucy L. Brown, "Reward, Motivation, and Emotion Systems Associated with Early-Stage Intense Romantic Love," *Journal of Neurophysiology* (July 2005). For a summary, see www.the-aps.org/press/journal/05/9.htm.

64. Dorothy Tennov, *Love and Limerence: The Experience of Being in Love,* 2d ed. (Lanham, Md.: Scarborough House, 1999), 23–24.

65. Tennov, *Love and Limerence,* 23.

66. Tennov, *Love and Limerence,* 213.

67. Tennov, *Love and Limerence,* 148.

68. Tennov, *Love and Limerence,* 257.

69. Helen Fisher, *Why We Love: The Nature and Chemistry of Romantic Love* (New York: Holt, 2004), 18.

70. Tennov, *Love and Limerence,* x.

71. Tennov, *Love and Limerence,* 41.

72. See also Michel Odent, *The Scientification of Love* (New York: Free Association Books, 1999), 51.

73. Richard Owen, "Men Cannot Help Falling in Love at Fifty," *The Times* (London), August 24, 2000. Owen is citing a survey of four thousand men in their early fifties by Giuseppe La Pera, a psychologist at San Vincenzo Hospital in Rome.

74. Tennov, *Love and Limerence,* 107.

75. Tennov, *Love and Limerence,* 111.

76. Helen Fisher, *Anatomy of Love: The Natural History of Monogamy, Adultery, and Divorce* (New York: Norton, 1992).

77. Roy F. Baumeister and Sara R. Wotman, *Breaking Hearts: The Two Sides of Unrequited Love* (New York: Guilford, 1992), 191.

78. Tennov, *Love and Limerence,* 142.

79. Fisher, *Why We Love,* 24.

80. Blaise Pascal, "No. 147," in *Pensées* (Garden City, N.Y.: Doubleday, 1961), originally written in 1660.

81. Tennov, *Love and Limerence,* 74–75.

82. Tennov, *Love and Limerence,* 64.

83. Doc Childre, Howard Martin, and Donna Beach, *The HeartMath Solution* (San Francisco: HarperSanFrancisco, 1999).

84. Donatella Marazziti, Hagop S. Akiskal, A. Rossi, and G. B. Cassano, "Alteration of the Platelet Serotonin Transporter in Romantic Love," *Psychology in Medicine* 29, no. 3 (May 1999): 741–45.

85. Pert is quoted by Nina Amir Lacey, "Love + Loving = Better Health," *Conscious Choice,* February 1999, www.consciouschoice.com/1999/cc1202/healthoflove.html.

86. This work is by Andreas Bartels and Semir Zeki at University College in London and reported by Matthew Herper, "The Science of Love," June 28, 2004, forbes.com/maserati/singles2004/cx_mh_0624love_04single.html.

87. There are several variants of this theory, not all of which are compatible. See Stanton Peele with A. Brodsky, *Love and Addiction* (New York: Taplinger, 1975). Also see R. L. Solomon and J. D. Corbit, "An Opponent-Process Theory of Motivation I: Temporal Dynamics of Affect," *Psychological Review* 81 (1975): 119–45.

88. Anthony Walsh, *The Science of Love* (New York: Prometheus, 1999). See also Helen E. Fisher, *Why We Love: The Nature and Chemistry of Romantic Love* (New York: Holt, 2004), a study that assigns highest causal significance to dopamine, perhaps especially when accompanied by adrenaline.

89. Aron, Fisher, Mashek, Strong, Li, and Brown, "Reward, Motivation, and Emotion Systems Associated with Early-Stage Intense Romantic Love."

90. Chocolate contains PEA and also useful antioxidants called *phenols* that extend longevity. I-Min Lee and Ralph Paffenburger at the Harvard Medical School found that men aged sixty-five and older who regularly ate chocolate lived nearly a year longer than those who did not.

91. However, Mario Beauregard at the University of Montreal is studying the neurobiology of mystical experiences, which include transcendent love of God. He invites nuns from a contemplative order to pray and meditate while his instruments measure their brain activity, especially when they sense contact with God.

92. "Ooh La La! Pain Relief That's a Fantasy," *Johns Hopkins Magazine,* June 2000, www.jhu.edu/~jhumag/0600web/health.html#pain.

93. Barry R. Komisaruk and Beverly Whipple, "The Suppression of Pain by Genital Stimulation in Females," *Annual Review of Sex Research* 6 (1995): 151–86; also, Komisaruk and Whipple, "Love as Sensory Stimulation: Physiological Consequences of Its Deprivation and Expression," *Psychoneuroendocrinology* 23, no. 8 (1998): 927–44.

94. Odent, *The Scientification of Love,* 38; Komisaruk and Whipple, "The Suppression of Pain by Genital Stimulation in Females."

95. In hamsters, blood endorphin levels increase by about 200 percent from the beginning to the end of the sex act, according to Candace Pert, *Molecules of Emotion.*

96. Carl J. Charnetski and Francis X. Brennan, "The Effect of Sexual Behavior on Immune System Function," paper presented at the Eastern Psychological Association Convention, Providence, R.I., 1998. However, according to this research, increasing the frequency of sex beyond this level did not offer any further immune advantage.

97. See David Weeks and Jamie James, *Secrets of the Superyoung* (New York: Berkley, 1999). In Scotland, Weeks found in a study of 3,500 people aged 30 to 101, that sex helps one look four to seven years younger. See also Cindy M. Meston, "Aging and Sexuality," *Western Journal of Medicine,* October 1997.

98. E. B. Palmore, "Predictors of the Longevity Difference: A 25-Year Follow-up," *Gerontologist* 6 (1982): 513–18; and L. Abramov, "Sexual Life and Frigidity among Women Developing Acute Myocardial Infarction," *Psychosomatic Medicine* 38 (1976): 418–25.

99. G. Davey Smith, S. Frankel, J. Yarnell, "Sex and Death: Are They Related? Findings from the Caerphilly Cohort Study," *British Medical Journal* 315 (1997): 1641–45. These findings seem to refute an ancient theory of Oriental medicine—that ejaculations deplete a man's level of energy and overall health. Tantric sex advises the cultivation of an ability to have sex without reaching orgasm, at least on the part of males.

100. Thomas W. Laqueur, *Solitary Sex: A Cultural History of Masturbation* (Boston: MIT Press, 2003).

101. George G. Gellup Jr., Rebecca L. Burch, and Steven M. Platek, "Does Semen Have Anti-depressant Properties?" *Archives of Sexual Behavior* 31, no. 3 (June 2002): 289–93. For the prostaglandin speculation, see Theresa L. Crenshaw, *The Alchemy of Love and Lust* (New York: Putnam, 1996), 304.

102. Kenneth Mah and Yitzchak M. Binik, "The Nature of Human Orgasm: A Critical Review of Major Trends," *Clinical Psychology Review* 21, no. 6 (2001): 829.

103. Odent, *The Scientification of Love,* 75. Also, I asked Erick Janssen, a researcher at the Kinsey Institute, about this phenomenon. He replied:

> Many reports, indeed, are known of men and women describing how they became or stayed sexually aroused in a situation that was dangerous. Car accidents are a well-known example,... but from a biological point of view it cannot be considered very adaptive to become sexually aroused under conditions that are life threatening (unless you know there is nothing you can do to rescue or save yourself). Another factor that complicates the analysis is that sexual arousal involves bodily and subjective responses, and they do not always coincide. Women may show genital responses (become lubricated) during a rape—but that doesn't mean they want to be in that situation or that they feel sexually aroused.

104. Tom Lutz, *Crying: The Natural and Cultural History of Tears* (New York: Norton, 1999), 35–38.

105. Similarly, a 1950s study in England showed that most men who cried at films claimed that heroism, patriotism, and bravery were most likely to make them cry. See Lutz, *Crying,* 65.

106. Provine, *Laughter,* 111.

107. Gerald C. Cupchik and Stephen Kemp, "The Aesthetics of Media Fare," in *Media Entertainment: The Psychology of Its Appeal,* ed. Dolf Zillmann and Peter Vorderer (Mahwah, N.J.: Erlbaum, 2000), 259.

108. Dolf Zillmann, "Humor and Comedy," in Zillmann and Vorderer, *Media Entertainment,* 51.

Chapter 4

1. Neal Gabler, *Life the Movie: How Entertainment Conquered Reality* (New York: Vintage, 1998).

2. Shakespeare's *As You Like It.*

3. Eric Klinger, *Daydreaming: Using Waking Fantasy and Imagery for Self-Knowledge and Creativity* (Los Angeles: Tarcher, 1990), 214.

4. Antonio Damasio, *The Feeling of What Happens: Body and Emotion in the Making of Consciousness* (San Diego, Calif.: Harcourt, 1999), 203.

5. Klinger, *Daydreaming,* 59–60.

6. Because this view is so commonly shared, philosopher and novelist Iris Murdoch felt proof unnecessary when she wrote, "The chief enemy of excellence in morality (and also in art) is personal fantasy: the tissue of self-aggrandizing and consoling wishes and dreams which prevents one from seeing what is there outside one" (Iris Murdoch, *The Sovereignty of Good* [London: Routledge, 1970 and 1996], 59). I know of no evidence that daydreaming robs people of their ability to recognize reality.

7. Klinger, *Daydreaming,* 101.

8. Klinger, *Daydreaming,* 102.

9. Klinger, *Daydreaming,* 113.

10. Adam Smith, *The Theory of Moral Sentiments* (London: Millar, 1759), 1.

11. Important contributions to this debate include M. T. Davies and T. Stone, eds., *Folk Psychology* (Oxford: Blackwell, 1995); and Andrew Meltzoff and Alison Gopnik, "The Role of Imitation in Understanding Persons and Developing a Theory of Mind," in *Understanding Other Minds,* ed. S. Baron-Cohen, H. Tager-Flusberg, and D. J. Cohen (Oxford: Oxford University Press, 1993).

12. Charles Darwin, *The Expression of the Emotions in Man and Animal* (New York: Appleton, 1896).

13. J. Decety, T. Chaminade, J. Grèzes, and A. N. Meltzoff, "Rapid Communication: A PET Exploration of the Neural Mechanisms Involved in Reciprocal Imitation," *NeuroImage* 15: 265–72; T. Chaminade, A. N. Meltzoff, and J. Decety, "Does the End Justify the Means? A PET Exploration of Imitation," *NeuroImage* 15: 318–28.

14. Lee Alan Dugatkin, "Interface between Culturally-Based Preferences and Genetic Preferences: Female Mate Choice in *Poecilia Reticulata,*" *Proceedings of the National Academy of Sciences USA* 93 (April 1996): 2770–73.

15. Lee Alan Dugatkin, *The Imitation Factor: Evolution beyond the Gene* (New York: Free Press, 2000).

16. Robert M. Gordon, "Sympathy, Simulation, and the Impartial Spectator," in *Ethics* 105, no. 4 (July 1995): 728.

17. This approach, originally called *social learning theory*, was promoted most notably by the psychologist Albert Bandura. See his book *Social Learning Theory* (Englewood Cliffs, N.J.: Prentice Hall, 1977).

18. The concept of empathy originated in Germany, where the term *Einfülung* (in-feeling) was applied in aesthetic theory. The notion was that you appreciate a painting or statue by "feeling yourself into it." I doubt that you can really empathize with a painting of a nonhuman object. However, you may construct an impression of the *artist's* experience and that would probably qualify as empathy, though you couldn't check the validity of your impressions.

19. James Elkins, *Pictures and Tears* (London: Routledge, 2001), 196–97.

20. John Sloboda, "Music Structure and Emotional Response: Some Empirical Findings," *Psychology of Music* 19, no. 2 (1991): 110–20.

21. However, I once did fall in love with the concertmaster of the Boston Symphony for one whole concert. He seemed to enjoy playing immensely. Probably the music, combined with his expression of bliss, was what evoked my unusual empathic fascination.

22. James H. Billington, *The Face of Russia* (New York: TV Books, 1998), 48.

23. Elkins, *Pictures and Tears,* 184–85.

24. Elkins, *Pictures and Tears,* 4.

25. Elkins, *Pictures and Tears,* 202.

26. Elkins, *Pictures and Tears,* 212.

27. Elkins, *Pictures and Tears,* 217.

28. French brain researcher Jean Decety's studies show that perspective taking is a key mechanism allowing people to distinguish between self and other. His team has identified the part of the brain involved in imagining oneself or another person in a situation: the premotor cortex, an area usually devoted to planning action. Whenever you imagine action of any kind, your brain is planning that move. If you imagine *yourself* carrying out the action, that part of the brain that connects with your muscles gets ready to move physically, stopping just short of actually acting. If you imagine *another* person's action, the same area of the brain is engaged, but there is no increased blood flow.

29. Marshall McLuhan, *Understanding Media: The Extensions of Man* (New York: McGraw-Hill, 1964).

30. Charles McGrath, "The Triumph of the Prime-Time Novel," in *Television: The Critical View,* 6th ed., ed. Horace Newcomb (New York: Oxford University Press, 2000), 246.

31. T. J. Scheff, *Catharsis in Healing, Ritual, and Drama* (Berkeley: University of California Press, 1979).

32. K. D. Craig, "Physiological Arousal as a Function of Imagined, Vicarious, and Direct Stress Experiences," *Journal of Abnormal Psychology* 73 (1969): 513–20.

33. John L. Caughey, *Imaginary Social Worlds: A Cultural Approach* (Lincoln: University of Nebraska Press, 1984), 32.

34. Caughey, *Imaginary Social Worlds,* 33.

35. Caughey, *Imaginary Social Worlds,* 41.

36. Caughey, *Imaginary Social Worlds,* 49–51.

37. Caughey, *Imaginary Social Worlds,* 54.

38. The fourth one came later, after this chapter was written, and constitutes an exception to my generalizations. It was from a prison inmate who had been obsessed with the narrator, Humbert Humbert, of Nabokov's novel *Lolita.* It was the most depressing novel he had ever read, and, along with Humbert, he fell hopelessly in love with little Lolita. He kept reminding himself, "It's just fiction," trying to suppress his thoughts. He obtained two novels written from Lolita's perspective and kept them on his shelf for months before reading them. "Eventually I decided to get it over with. I read quickly, with the goal of just getting through them as soon as possible. Fortunately, I didn't experience the sorts of obsessive thoughts that *Lolita* had brought about.... On reading *Lo's Diary,* my identification shifted to the girl, whereas with *Lolita,* I'd been rooting for Humbert. With *Lo's Diary* I came to loathe him. I'm now very glad I read it." He never said whether the obsession was related to the charge for which he was incarcerated.

39. Written between 1927 and 1958 by Walter R. Brooks, the series enthralled the writer Adam Hochschild, whose 1994 review of his porcine hero revealed how deeply his own moral sensibility had been shaped by the stories. Adam Hochschild, "Paragon of Porkers," in his book *Finding the Trapdoor: Essays, Portraits, Travels* (Syracuse, N.Y.: Syracuse University Press, 1997), 235–40.

40. The "Friends of Freddy" have a Web site: www.freddythepig.org. I asked them what Freddy had meant to them. Three successful male writers or professionals answered. One, a playwright, said, "Freddy left his imprint. I am fond of writing about community and social justice issues. And I cannot bring myself to write a one-sided character—again, everyone in Freddy has good and bad qualities." And the CEO of a famous software corporation wrote, "The effects of the books I read were profound. No other factor better explains who I am today." He also writes and publishes stories in his spare time.

41. Talcott Parsons and Robert F. Bales, *Family: Socialization and Interaction Process* (Glencoe, Ill.: Free Press, 1955), 56–57.

42. Object relations psychoanalysts don't all agree about the degree of coherence and unity of the self. However, there must be *some* unity in a normal personality; otherwise, one would suffer from the strange disorder of persons with multiple personalities that pop in and out of awareness.

43. Before that happened, object relations theorists say that you, the newborn infant, could not distinguish between your mother's breast and yourself. While this may be true, I wonder how they know. No one remembers that period of life.

44. Parsons and Bales, *Family,* 73–74. Philip Slater was a member of the team authoring this book, and he was strongly influenced by object relations theory. This emphasis was presumably largely his contribution to the book. Also see D. W. Winnicott, "The Capacity to Be Alone," in *Maturational Processes and the Facilitating Environment: Studies in the Theory of Emotional Development* (New York: International Universities Press, 1958), 29–36.

45. But there is also something called fraud, and imposters who cannot substantiate their claims with material evidence may be sent to jail. As sociologist W. I. Thomas famously proclaimed, "If men define situations as real, they are real in their consequences." However, sociologist Erving Goffman cautioned against believing in that maxim too confidently. "All the world is not a stage," he wrote. "Certainly the theater isn't entirely. (Whether you organize a theater or an aircraft factory, you need to find places for cars to park and coats to be checked, and these had better be real places, which, incidentally, had better carry real insurance against theft.)" Erving Goffman, *Frame Analysis: An Essay on the Organization of Experience* (New York: Harper Colophon, 1974), 1.

46. Kirk Douglas, *The Ragman's Son: An Autobiography* (New York: Pocket Books, 1988), 243.

47. Michael W. Rodriguez, "John Wayne Lied to Us," mikerod.home.texas.net/Stories/johnlied.html.

48. Eric Bentley pinned much of the blame for the United States' involvement in the Vietnam War on Wayne. See Garry Wills, *John Wayne's America: The Politics of Celebrity* (New York: Simon & Schuster, 1997), 14.

49. Robert Warshow, *The Immediate Experience: Movies, Comics, Theatre, and Other Aspects of Popular Culture,* enlarged ed. (Cambridge, Mass.: Harvard University Press, 2001), ix.

50. The classic use of this meaning is applied in Erich Auerbach, *Mimesis: The Representation of Reality in Western Literature* (Princeton, N.J.: Princeton University Press, 2003).

51. Keith Oatley, "Shakespeare's Invention of Theatre as Simulation That Runs on Minds," in *Artificial Intelligence and Simulation of Behavior 2000* (Birmingham, England: Ontario Institute for Studies in Education), 1–9.

52. Plato, *The Republic* Book X (originally written in 360 B.C.E.).

53. Plato was not unique in his misgivings about the contagious effects of mimesis. German playwright Bertold Brecht wrote dramas that tried to break the audience's empathy at frequent intervals during the show, to help them keep their critical judgment. He wanted audiences to keep thinking, even if their feelings had to be interrupted repeatedly. But his approach has never gained much popularity among playwrights.

54. Immanuel Kant, *Metaphysics of Morals,* trans. Mary J. Gregor (Cambridge: Cambridge University Press, 1996), 576. See also Wolfgang Palaver, "Mimesis and Scapegoating in the Works of Hobbes, Rousseau and Kant," a paper presented at Colloquium of Violence and Religion, Antwerp, May 31, 2001; and Helmut Schoeck, *Envy: A Theory of Social Behavior,* trans. M. Glenny and B. Ross (New York: Harcourt, Brace & World, 1969).

55. Robert J. Shiller, *The New Financial Order: Risk in the 21st Century* (Princeton, N.J.: Princeton University Press, 2003).

56. Thomas Hobbes, *The Elements of Law Natural and Politic,* ed. G. C. A. Gaskin (Oxford: Oxford University Press, 1994), 78.

57. René Girard, *The Scapegoat,* trans. Yvonne Freccero (Baltimore: Johns Hopkins University Press, 1986), 44.

58. Of course, at a global level we still live in a primitive way, for there is no international government that holds a monopoly on the legitimate use of violence, as there is *within* countries.

59. René Girard, *Deceit, Desire, and the Novel: Self and Other in Literary Structure,* trans. Yvonne Freccero (Baltimore: Johns Hopkins University Press, 1961), 19.

60. Marxists treat this vicarious method of evading conflict as "false consciousness," for they regard resentment in situations of inequality as normal and desirable. I, on the other hand, consider *mudita* a wonderful solution to a common human problem.

61. I wish Girard had developed and documented this part of his theory.

62. Here I invent names for the characters and actors, as Gwen requested. This interview was emended in consultation with Gwen.

Chapter 5

1. N. J. Frijda, "Aesthetic Emotions and Reality," *American Psychologist* 44 (1989): 1546–47.

2. T. Binkley, "Piece: Contra Aesthetics," *Journal of Aesthetics and Art Criticism* 35 (1977): 265–77.

3. Phoebe Ellsworth, "Levels of Thought and Levels of Emotion," in *The Nature of Emotion: Fundamental Questions,* ed. Paul Ekman and Richard J. Davidson (New York: Oxford University Press,1994), 194.

4. Steven Johnson, *Everything Bad Is Good for You: How Today's Popular Culture Is Actually Making Us Smarter* (New York: Riverhead, 2005).

5. Peter Vorderer and Silvia Knobloch, "Conflict and Suspense in Drama," in *Media Entertainment: The Psychology of Its Appeal,* ed. Dolf Zillmann and Peter Vorderer (Mahwah, N.J.: Erlbaum, 2000), 69–70.

6. Sissela Bok, *Mayhem: Violence as Public Entertainment* (Reading, Mass.: Addison Wesley, 1998), 15.

7. Bok, *Mayhem,* 18–19.

8. Bok, *Mayhem,* 20.

9. J. H. Goldstein, "Why We Watch," in *Why We Watch: The Attractions of Violent Entertainment,* ed. J. H. Goldstein (New York: Oxford University Press, 1998), 212–26. Young males are especially frequent filmgoers, and some of them see the same action film several times; as a demographic segment they are especially attracted to violent entertainment. However, the top ten films ever produced by the end of 1998, based on

revenue and adjusted for inflation are, according to Abraham Ravid, *Gone with the Wind, Snow White and the Seven Dwarfs, Star Wars, Bambi, Fantasia, Pinocchio, The Sound of Music, Jaws, ET,* and *101 Dalmatians.* Of these, only three, *Star Wars, Jaws,* and *ET,* are rated PG in the United States.

10. Joanne R. Cantor, "Children's Attraction to Television Programming," in Goldstein, *Why We Watch,* 88–115.

11. George Gerbner in a 1994 video, *The Killing Screens,* and a lecture in Toronto, 1997.

12. E. L. Palmer, A. B. Hockett, and W. W. Dean, "The Television Family and Children's Fright Reactions," *Journal of Family Issues* 4 (1983): 279–92; G. G. Sparks, M. M. Spirek, and K. Hodgson, "Individual Differences in Arousability: Implications for Understanding Immediate and Lingering Emotional Reactions to Frightening Mass Media," *Communication Quarterly* 41 (1993): 465–76.

13. Mary Beth Oliver, "Respondent Gender Gap," in Zillmann and Vorderer, *Media Entertainment,* 222.

14. Glenn G. Sparks and Cheri W. Sparks, "Violence, Mayhem, and Horror," in Zillmann and Vorderer, *Media Entertainment,* 80.

15. Sparks and Sparks, "Violence, Mayhem, and Horror," 86, citing Dolf Zillmann and J. B. Weaver, "Effects of an Opposite-Gender Companion's Affect to Horror on Distress, Delight, and Attraction," *Journal of Personality and Social Psychology* 51 (1986): 586–94.

16. Sparks and Sparks, "Violence, Mayhem, and Horror," 84.

17. P. E. Hoon, J. P. Wincze, and E. F. Hoon, "A Test of Reciprocal Inhibition: Are Anxiety and Sexual Arousal in Women Mutually Inhibitory?" *Journal of Abnormal Psychology* 86 (1977): 65–74.

18. S. A. Wolchik, V. E. Beggs, J. P. Wincze, D. K. Sakheim, D. H. Barlow, and M. Mavissakalian, "The Effect of Emotional Arousal on Subsequent Sexual Arousal in Men," *Journal of Abnormal Psychology* 89 (1980): 595–98.

19. James B. Weaver III, "Personality and Entertainment Preferences," in Zillmann and Vorderer, *Media Entertainment,* 39.

20. Weaver, "Personality and Entertainment Preferences," 241–44.

21. Richard Depue, personal communication.

22. S. Finn and M. B. Gore, "Social Isolation and Social Support as Correlates of Television Viewing Motivations," *Communications Research* 15 (1988): 135–58.

23. See Diane D. Ashe and Lynn E. McCutcheon, "Shyness, Loneliness, and Attitude Toward Celebrities," *Current Research in Social Psychology* 6, no. 9 (May 4, 2001). The term *parasocial* was introduced by D. Horton and R. R. Wohl in "Mass Communication and Parasocial Interaction: Observations on Intimacy at a Distance," *Psychiatry* 19 (1956): 215–29. Again, the authors conclude that parasocial relationships normally affirm real social relationships, rather than replace them. So does Jonathan Cohen in "Parasocial Break-up from Favorite Television Characters: The Role of Attachment Styles and Relationship Intensity," *Journal of Social and Personal Relationships* 21, no. 2 (2004): 187–202.

24. Ann Burnett and Rhea Reinhardt Beto, "Reading Romance Novels: An Application of Parasocial Relationships Theory," *North Dakota Journal of Speech and Theater* 13 (2000).

25. John T. Cacioppo, Gary G. Berntson, Jeff T. Larsen, Kirsten M. Poehlmann, and Tiffany A. Ito, "The Psychophysiology of Emotion," in *Handbook of Emotions,* 2d ed., ed. Michael Lewis and Jeannetta M. Haviland-Jones (London: Guilford, 2000), 186. The authors review research showing the deleterious effects of negative emotions on susceptibility to infection, response to vaccine, wound healing, and the declines of aging.

26. The findings also depend on how emotions are elicited (e.g., whether by triggering memories of previous real events or by showing film clips of emotional scenes) and how they are identified empirically (e.g., whether by asking the subject what she is feeling or by measuring her facial expressions). Researchers cannot be satisfied to measure the effects of the autonomic nervous system alone, but they should also take account of their subjects' endocrine reactions, PET brain scans, and production of neuropeptides as they experience various emotions. Such complex studies are only beginning to be done.

27. E. Harmon-Jones and J. J. B. Allen, "Anger and Frontal Brain Activity: EEG Asymmetry Consistent with Approach Motivation Despite Negative Affective Valence," *Journal of Personality and Social Psychology* 74 (1998): 1310–16.

28. Robert W. Levenson, "The Search for Autonomic Specificity," in Ekman and Davidson, *The Nature of Emotion,* 256–57.

29. Joseph E. Ledoux, "The Degree of Emotional Control Depends on the Kind of Response System Involved," in Ekman and Davidson, *The Nature of Emotion,* 270.

30. Robert W. Levenson, "Emotional Control: Variation and Consequences," in Ekman and Davidson, *The Nature of Emotion,* 276–78.

31. Levenson, "Emotional Control," 278–79.

32. Researchers have found that petting a dog for eighteen minutes raises immunoglobulin A levels 12 percent. See Carl J. Charnetski and Francis X. Brennan, *Feeling Good Is Good for You: How Pleasure Can Boost Your Immune System and Lengthen Your Life* (Emmaus, Pa.: Rodale, 2001), 128.

33. Phoebe C. Ellsworth, "Levels of Thought and Levels of Emotion," in Ekman and Davidson, *The Nature of Emotion,* 195. Carl Charnetski and Francis Brennan have established these effects of music even in busy office settings.

34. Antonio Damasio, *Descartes' Error: Emotion, Reason, and the Human Brain* (New York: Grosset, Putnam, 1996).

35. *Katharsis* meant "purification," though not always by the same means. To Plato in *Laws,* katharsis meant purification of the soul through successive reincarnations. See Thomas McEvilley, *The Shape of Ancient Thought* (New York: Allworth, 2002), 99.

36. Stephen Halliwell suggests that Aristotle's notion of catharsis may not have rested on the notion of "purging" or reducing negative emotions but on *augmenting our capacity* to feel the negative emotions (pity and fear) "in the right way and towards the right objects." If, indeed, the cultivation of an attitude of pity toward the flawed protagonist

was the value that Aristotle saw in catharsis, I can't argue against it. However, that is not the traditional definition, which does imply a discharge of built-up negative emotion. You should just be aware that certain disagreements about catharsis research may be semantic rather than substantive. See Halliwell's "Aristotle's Poetics," in *The Cambridge History of Literary Criticism,* vol. 1, *Classical Criticism,* ed. George A. Kennedy (Cambridge: Cambridge University Press, 1988), 164.

37. Some psychoanalysts today hold a somewhat different theory—that people often feel a compulsive need to repeat and review experiences similar to their old traumas, mainly for the purpose of mastering their own emotions. See Judith Guss Teicholz, Daniel Kriegman, and Susan Fairfield, eds., *Trauma, Repetition, and Affect Regulation: The Work of Paul Russell* (New York: Other Press, 1998).

38. R. G. Geen and M. B. Quanty, "The Catharsis of Aggression: An Evaluation of a Hypothesis," in *Advances in Experimental Social Psychology,* vol. 10, ed. Leonard Berkowitz (New York: Academic Press, 1977), 1–37.

39. T. J. Scheff, *Catharsis in Healing, Ritual, and Drama* (Berkeley: University of California Press, 1979), 18.

40. Scheff, *Catharsis in Healing, Ritual, and Drama,* 138.

41. Roger J. Booth and James W. Pennebaker, "Emotions and Immunity," in Lewis and Haviland-Jones, *Handbook of Emotions,* 563. This essay summarizes the entire body of research on this topic.

42. Wendy Ellen Davis, as reported by Tom Lutz, *Crying: The Natural and Cultural History of Tears* (New York: Norton, 1999), 131.

43. Sophocles's *Ajax* was an exception. However, not to glorify the Greeks, I should say that their actual military behavior was hardly gentle. For example, they took the town of Melos for no defensive reason, put to death all males of military age, and enslaved the women and children.

44. Nicholas Bakalar, "Laughter as Good Exercise," *New York Times,* March 10, 2005. Bakalar was reporting on a paper presented by Michael Miller, M.D., University of Maryland, on preventive cardiology at the American College of Cardiology conference, Orlando, Florida.

45. Susan Feagin, "The Pleasures of Tragedy," *American Philosophical Quarterly* 20 (1983): 97.

46. Robert J. Yanal, *Paradoxes of Emotion and Fiction* (University Park: Pennsylvania State University Press, 1999), 158.

47. Yanal, *Paradoxes of Emotion and Fiction,* 158.

48. Richard B. Sewall, *The Vision of Tragedy: Tragic Themes in Literature from the Book of Job to O'Neill and Miller* (New York: Paragon House, 1990).

49. Sewall, *The Vision of Tragedy,* 5.

50. See Sewall, *The Vision of Tragedy,* chap. 2, "The Book of Job."

51. Stanley Schachter and Jerome E. Singer, "Cognitive, Social, and Physiological Determinants of Emotional State," *Psychological Review* 69 (1962): 378–99. Ethical critiques of the experiment have been made. For one thing, it is now unacceptable to administer adrenaline without the subject's permission and knowledge.

52. Dolf Zillmann, "Coition as Emotion," in *Alternative Approaches to the Study of Sexual Behavior,* ed. D. Byrne and K. Kelley (Hillsdale, N.J.: Erlbaum, 1986), 173–99.

53. Zillmann does not say so, but this probably also explains the use of obscene or power-oriented fantasies as a stimulus to blocked sexuality. However, such a means of arousal evidently has the unfortunate consequence of interfering with oxytocin ("cuddle hormone") production, and therefore it might well be self-defeating.

54. Dolf Zillmann, "The Psychology of the Appeal of Portrayals of Violence," in *Why We Watch: Attractions of Violent Entertainment,* ed. Jeffrey H. Goldstein (New York: Oxford University Press, 1998), 207.

55. Zillmann, "The Psychology of the Appeal," 208.

56. An enzyme, MAO, is negatively related to sensation seeking; MAO in the brain regulates monoamine neurotransmitter systems. Cortisol, a stress responsive hormone, is negatively related to sensation seeking, which suggests that sensation seekers' low cortisol levels may explain the tendency for them to have fewer deleterious physiological effects from stress. Testosterone also tends to increase sensation-seeking tendencies. See Marvin Zuckerman, *Behavioral Expressions and Biosocial Bases of Sensation Seeking* (Cambridge: Cambridge University Press, 1994), 318–19.

57. The DRD4 gene, more specifically, is dopamine receptor number D4. It encodes for one of the five dopamine receptors in the brain. People who have attention deficit disorder and hyperactivity and who are highly risk taking all have a variant form of the DRD4 gene. See Y. C. Ding, H. C. Chi, D. L. Grady, A. Morishima, K. K. Kidd, P. Flodman, M. A. Spence, S. Schuck, J. M. Swanson, Y. P. Zhang, and R. K. Moyzis, "Evidence of Positive Selection Acting at the Human Dopamine Receptor D4 Gene Locus," *Proceedings of the National Academy of Sciences USA* 8, no. 99 (January 2002): 309–14.

58. Frank Farley, "The Type T Personality," in *Self-Regulatory Behavior and Risk Taking: Causes and Consequences,* ed. L. P. Lipsitt and L. L. Mitnick (Norwood, N.J.: Ablex, 1991).

59. Zuckerman, *Behavioral Expressions,* 201, citing A. F. Furnham and M. Bunyan, "Personality and Art Preferences," *European Journal of Personality* 2 (1988): 67–74, and other sources.

60. Zuckerman, *Behavioral Expressions,* 220–21, citing F. J. Held and W. Ruch, "The Location of Sense of Humor within Comprehensive Personality Spaces," *Personality and Individual Differences* 6 (1985): 703–15, and other sources.

61. Zuckerman, *Behavioral Expressions,* 256–57.

62. Zuckerman, *Behavioral Expressions,* 176.

63. Zuckerman, *Behavioral Expressions,* 150, citing J. J. Sciortino, J. H. Huston, and R. W. Spencer, "Perceived Risk and the Precautionary Demand for Money," *Journal of Economic Psychology* 8 (1987): 339–46.

64. Zuckerman, *Behavioral Expressions,* 211.

65. Zuckerman, *Behavioral Expressions,* 148, citing R. I. Brown, "Arousal and Sensation Seeking Components in the General Explanation of Gambling and Gambling Addictions," *International Journal of the Addictions* 21 (1986): 1001–16.

66. Zuckerman, *Behavioral Expressions,* 374. This relationship does not necessarily hold true for professional criminals, whose motivations are oriented toward money,

but it does apply to people who act out primarily for the excitement. See chap. 10 in Zuckerman, *Behavioral Expressions.*

67. Zuckerman, *Behavioral Expressions,* 374.

68. Zuckerman, *Behavioral Expressions,* 211, citing R. Tamborini and J. Stiff, "Predictors of Horror Film Attendance and Appeal: An Analysis of the Audience for Frightening Films," *Communications Research* 14 (1987): 415–36, and other sources.

69. Apter's theory involves several sets of antithetical states, which I will not discuss here. See his book *The Dangerous Edge: The Psychology of Excitement* (New York: Free Press, 1992).

70. Apter, *The Dangerous Edge,* 3.

71. Sven Svebak has shown physiological differences between serious-minded people (who are arousal avoiding) and play-oriented individuals (who are generally arousal seeking). Serious-minded people have greater muscle tension, faster heart rates, and more rapid and deeper breathing. They also have different kind of muscle fibers from arousal-seeking persons. See Sven Svebak, "Personality and Sports Participation," in *Sports, Medicine, and Health,* ed. P. H. Hermans (Amsterdam: Elsevier, 1990), 87–96. Also see Frank Farley, "The Big T in Personality," *Psychology Today,* May 1996, 44–50.

72. P. Caputo, *Rumor of War* (New York: Ballantine, 1977), 218.

73. Apter, *The Dangerous Edge,* 78.

74. Actually, Canada does maintain a small disaster assistance team, which has been dispatched to such places as a tsunami-stricken region of Asia, but much larger units are sometimes required.

75. Norbert Elias and E. Dunning, *Quest for Excitement: Sport and Leisure in the Civilizing Process* (Oxford: Blackwell, 1986).

76. Jeffrey Goldstein, "Why We Watch," in *Why We Watch: The Attractions of Violent Entertainment,* ed. Jeffrey Goldstein (New York: Oxford University Press, 1998), 214.

Chapter 6

1. Azar Nafisi, *Reading Lolita in Tehran: A Memoir in Books* (New York: Random House, 2003), 122–35.

2. Another negative effect is that the quality of sex instigated by pornographic arousal is unsatisfying, since no oxytocin is stimulated by such imagery, and the balance of other peptides is probably skewed.

3. Christopher Reed, "Searching for a Hollywood Ending," *Globe and Mail,* December 31, 2002, R1. Reed reports that the Hollywood studios have blocked the showing of this documentary so far. (Why? Are they ashamed of their products?) However, Livingston is suing for the right to use the relevant film clips.

4. Alexandra Benis Molloy, "Watching What We Watch," *Harvard Public Health Review,* Fall 2000.

5. Molloy, "Watching What We Watch."

6. Aristotle, *The Poetics.*

7. What about comedies? *The Poetics* did not explore the question of justice in regard to comedy. However, Aristotle probably would have advised that all good characters have good luck and all bad ones bad luck, so that the audience of a comedy will experience delight instead of fear and pity.

8. James P. Hammersmith, "Shakespeare and the Tragic Virtue," *Southern Humanities Review* 24, no. 3 (Summer 1990): 245–54.

9. For example, Hammersmith points out that ordinarily nothing is wrong with being a contemplative person such as Hamlet. Indeed, Hamlet's friend Horatio has the same temperament, which is actually a virtue, but Horatio does not happen to be in the predicament that Hamlet faces—having to act decisively. Thus Hamlet tragically fails to act, whereas in other circumstances he might have been an exceptionally fine and able person.

10. Dolf Zillmann, "Mechanisms of Emotional Involvement with Drama," *Poetics* 23 (1994): 33–51.

11. Those children (usually younger) who were still reasoning at the level of "expiatory retribution" were glad to see any amount of punishment imposed. In fact, they inferred the magnitude of the transgression from the severity of the punishment, so they tended to enjoy witnessing especially harsh punishment because they supposed that it was correcting a more serious transgression. See Zillmann, "Mechanisms of Emotional Involvement with Drama," 47.

12. Zillmann, "Mechanisms of Emotional Involvement with Drama," 48.

13. I spent all day once channel hopping to get an up-to-date overview of daytime television. About one-fourth of the shows were dramas involving some blameworthy character or group (e.g., an enemy army). One-fourth were comedies (albeit rarely funny ones) or soap operas, and the remaining half of the shows were "miscellaneous" (e.g., religious homilies, dubbed foreign-language dramas, *The Iron Chef,* public affairs, and John Edwards's *Crossing Over*). The culture of blame is important, in both violent shows and such shows as *The People's Court.*

14. E. R. Dodds, *The Greeks and the Irrational* (Berkeley: University of California Press, 1951).

15. Mary Lefkowitz has explained the logic of the Greek gods' ethics in her book *Greek Gods, Human Lives: What We Can Learn from Myths* (New Haven, Conn.: Yale University Press, 2003).

16. The plays are *Agamemnon, The Libation Bearers* (*Choëphoræ*), and *Eumenides.*

17. See Richard Seaford, "Historicizing Tragic Ambivalence," in *History, Tragedy, Theory: Dialogues on Athenian Drama,* ed. Barbara Goff (Austin: University of Texas Press, 1995), 208.

18. Isaac Ray Corner, "A History of Justice: Origins of Law and Psychiatry," *American Academy of Psychiatry and Law* 24, no. 2 (April 1999): 12–14.

19. The Archaic Age is usually defined as 750 to 500 B.C.E., when the Classical Age began.

20. Dodds, *The Greeks and the Irrational,* 31.

21. Dodds, *The Greeks and the Irrational,* 33.

22. Dodds, *The Greeks and the Irrational.*

23. Scholars differ on this matter, but their disagreement seems partly semantic. Compare Thomas McEvilley, *The Shape of Ancient Thought* (New York: Allworth, 2002), and Gananath Obeyesekere, *Imagining Karma: Ethical Transformation in Amerindian, Buddhist, and Greek Rebirth* (Berkeley: University of California Press, 2002). McEvilley sees karma in Greece where Obeyesekere would not, in that there is no systematic payoff for virtue in subsequent rebirths. The closest the Greeks came to karma was in Plotinus, as late as 204–70 C.E.

24. Stephen Halliwell, "Aristotle's Poetics," in *The Cambridge History of Literary Criticism,* vol. 1, *Classical Criticism,* ed. George A. Kennedy (Cambridge: Cambridge University Press, 1989), 175.

25. Dodds, *The Greeks and the Irrational,* 7.

26. Karen Ridd, "Resistance," *Peace Magazine,* November/December 1991, 18, www.peacemagazine.org/archive/v07n6p18.htm.

27. You may recognize a similar plot in Victor Hugo's *Les Misérables,* where a bishop pretends to have given Jean Valjean what he had stolen. This kindness evokes a lifelong moral redemption in Valjean.

28. Ruth Morris and Colleen Heffren, "The Practice of Peace," *Peace Magazine,* December 1986, 33–34, www.peacemagazine.org/archive/v02n6p33.htm.

29. Ron Rosenbaum, *Explaining Hitler: The Search for the Origins of His Evil* (New York: Random House, 1998).

30. The Tokyo and Nuremberg trials did declare that soldiers cannot be exonerated because of simply following orders, but in fact the courts did not punish low-level subordinates for war crimes.

31. One of my friends disapproved of his lenience, just as the children disliked the good prince if he did not impose sufficiently harsh punishment on the bad prince. Tit-for-tat is a strong norm, often for a good reason.

32. A line of psychological research compares the morality of justice seeking with the morality of care. This perspective often elaborates on the distinction made by Carol Gilligan, *In a Different Voice: Psychological Theory and Women's Development* (Cambridge, Mass.: Harvard University Press, 1982). See, for example, Joan Tronto, *Moral Boundaries: A Political Argument for an Ethic of Care* (New York: Routledge, 1994).

33. Unlike the war crime tribunals in Nuremberg and Tokyo, the new court excludes capital punishment, even for those found guilty of genocide. Almost all modern societies accept that capital punishment is a violation of human rights.

34. Between 1160 and 1270, English common law emerged, replacing church jurists with an adversarial system of justice. By the sixteenth century, the notion of legal insanity had been established. In 1843, Daniel McNaughton was acquitted of killing the secretary to British Prime Minister Robert Peel. The verdict was met with widespread outrage; as a result, the McNaughton Rules were formulated to spell out the concept of legal insanity. The rules, which are still generally binding today, allow the jury or judge

to establish that a defendant is incapable of understanding the charges against him, or was unaware of the difference between right and wrong when committing the offense, or is mentally unable to contribute to his own defense. See Isaac Ray Corner, "A History of Justice: Origins of Law and Psychiatry," *AAPL Newsletter* [American Academy of Psychiatry and the Law] 24, no. 2 (April 1999): 12–14.

35. Hannah Arendt, *Eichmann in Jerusalem: A Report on the Banality of Evil* (New York: Viking, 1963).

36. Arendt, *Eichmann in Jerusalem,* 277.

37. Arendt, *Eichmann in Jerusalem,* 277. Her opinion, though deviant within current jurisprudence, is not unique. Justice Oliver Wendell Holmes wrote in 1881, "It may be said, not only that the law does, but that it ought to, make the gratification of revenge an object.... The first requirement of a sound body of law is that it should correspond with the actual feelings and demands of the community, whether right or wrong. If people would gratify the passion of revenge outside of the law, if the law did not help them, the law has no choice but to satisfy the craving itself, and thus avoid the greater evil of private retribution" (*The Common Law* 46).

38. Trudy Govier, *Forgiveness and Revenge* (New York: Routledge, 2002), 77.

39. Mary-Wynne Ashford, "Boredom as a Neglected Issue in Violence Prevention Programs in Schools," Ph.D. diss., Simon Fraser University, 1996.

40. Paul T. P. Wong and Prem S. Fry, eds., *The Human Quest for Meaning: A Handbook of Psychological Research and Clinical Applications* (Mahwah, N.J.: Erlbaum, 2001). See also Douglas V. Porpora, *Landscapes of the Soul: The Loss of Moral Meaning in American Life* (Oxford: Oxford University Press, 2001). Porpora attributes this ennui to the lack of religion.

41. As reported by Irving D. Yalom, *Existential Psychotherapy* (New York: Basic Books, 1980).

42. Yalom, *Existential Psychotherapy.*

43. Chris Hedges, *War Is a Force That Gives Us Meaning* (New York: Public Affairs, 2002), 3, 5.

44. Hedges, *War Is a Force That Gives Us Meaning,* 13–15.

45. Hedges, *War Is a Force That Gives Us Meaning,* 22.

46. He did not deal with melodrama—intense, dramatic stories about all-good and all-bad characters. Such stories provide a rigorously fair payoff for everyone in the end. Writers with artistic aspirations tend to prefer more nuanced stories involving morally ambiguous characters, but that is partly a matter of aesthetic fashion.

47. Joseph Campbell with Bill Moyers, *The Power of Myth* (New York: Doubleday Anchor Books, 1988), 3.

48. Arne Vetlesen poses a version of this question (*Perception, Empathy, and Judgment: An Inquiry into the Preconditions of Moral Performance* [University Park: Pennsylvania State University Press, 1994], 216) and answers it, not by calling emotions a "duty" but by saying that "feelings are required in the sense that there can be no successful act of moral perception, or of moral judgment, without the participation of the faculty of empathy." In fact, I think we actually do expect particular emotions of each other and

ourselves as a matter of obligation. That is the import of Arlie Russell Hochschild's book *The Managed Heart: Commercialization of Human Feeling* (Los Angeles: University of California Press, 1983).

49. I have subsequently heard of another possible case: Michael Corleone in *The Godfather*.

50. Interview with John Hiscock, cited on IMDb, 11 May, 2001, www.imdb.com/name/nm0001254/news.

51. Mervyn Rothstein, "Time for Joey Pants to Take His Off," *New York Times*, January 5, 2003, AR3.

52. Michael Bardo, Lewis Donohew, and N. G. Harrington, "Psychobiology of Novelty-Seeking and Drug-Seeking Behaviour," *Brain and Behaviour* 77 (1996): 23–43.

53. Lewis Donohew and Michael Bardo, "Designing Prevention Programs for Sensation Seeking Adolescents," in *Increasing Prevention Effectiveness* (in press). The authors show that novelty-seeking and drug-seeking behaviors, which activate the mesolimbic dopamine reward pathway, tend to become addictive behavior. However, alternative activities that stimulate the same pleasurable feelings can be used as substitutes.

54. Viktor E. Frankl, *Man's Search for Meaning* (New York: Simon & Shuster, 1984), 152. The version that I first read in the 1950s was titled *From Death Camp to Existentialism*.

55. Frankl, *Man's Search for Meaning,* 57.

56. Ashford, *Boredom as a Neglected Issue,* 42.

57. As I write, only *The West Wing* provides such drama regularly on television.

Chapter 7

1. Main cast: Rob Morrow plays Kevin Hunter; Scott Cohen plays James Liberti; Erika Alexander plays Dee Mulhern; Michelle Nolden plays Rachel Goldstein; Christopher Bolton plays Peter Hunter; Kate Greenhouse plays Karen Liberti; Jack Knight plays Sean Hunter; Terrence Howard plays Lucius Mosley; Jeffrey James plays James Liberti Jr.; Simon Reynolds plays Steven Goldstein.

2. Ben Stein, *The View from Sunset Boulevard: America as Brought to You by the People Who Make Television* (New York: Basic Books, 1979).

3. Stein, *The View from Sunset Boulevard,* 127.

4. Stein, *The View from Sunset Boulevard,* 32.

5. For one exception, see George Gerbner, Larry Gross, Michael Morgan, and Nancy Signorelli, "Charting the Mainstream: Television's Contributions to Political Orientations," *Journal of Communication* 32, no. 2 (Spring 1982): 100–27.

6. The conflict between realism and morality has troubled writers at least since they began writing novels. Henry Fielding and Samuel Richardson were rival English novelists, and it was said (including by Samuel Johnson) that in pursuing realism, Fielding courted immorality. See Michael McKeon, *The Origins of the English Novel, 1600–1740* (Baltimore: Johns Hopkins University Press, 1987), 416.

7. Thomas Kuhn, *The Structure of Scientific Revolutions,* 3d ed. (Chicago: University of Chicago Press, 1996 [1962]).

8. U.S. Department of Justice, Bureau of Justice Statistics, "Recidivism of Prisoners Released in 1994," www.ojp.usdoj.gov/bjs/abstract/rpr94.htm.

9. Bernard Williams, *Moral Luck: Philosophical Papers, 1973–1980* (Cambridge: Cambridge University Press, 1981).

10. Steven Johnson, *Everything Bad Is Good for You* (New York: Riverhead, 2005).

11. Bruce Lenman and Geoffrey Parker, "The State, the Community, and the Criminal Law," in *Crime and the Law: The Social History of Crime in Western Europe since 1500,* ed. V. A. C. Gatrell, Bruce Lenman, and Geoffrey Parker (London: Europa, 1979).

12. Howard Zehr, *Changing Lenses: A New Focus for Crime and Justice* (Scottsdale, Pa.: Herald, 1995).

13. A justification for the penal system is its deterrent effect. The harshness of punishment should be foreseeable and serve as a disincentive to would-be criminals. There are, however, methodological problems involved in demonstrating any such deterrence, and some studies have failed to find any at all. See David S. Lee and Justin McCrary, "Crime, Punishment, and Myopia," Working Paper 11491, National Bureau of Economic Research, June 2005, www.nber.org/papers/w11491. See also Richard Freeman, "The Economics of Crime," in *Handbook of Labor Economics,* vol. 3C, ed. Orley C. Ashenfelter and David Card (New York: Elsevier, 1999).

14. The solicitor general of Canada has reviewed recidivism rates and in one Winnipeg comparison concludes:

> The offenders who participated in the restorative justice program had lower recidivism rates than the matched group of probationers. With each year during the follow-up the differences in recidivism rates for the two groups widened. At the first year, the restorative justice offenders had a recidivism rate of 15% compared to 38% for the probation group. At the second year the respective rates were 28% and 54% and by the third year the rates were 35% and 66%.

See J. Bonta, S. Wallace-Capretta, J. Rooney, and K. McAnoy, "An Outcome Evaluation of a Restorative Justice Alternative to Incarceration," *Contemporary Justice Review* no. 5 (2002): 319–38. For a comparison of several studies see "Restorative Practices and Re-offending," www.restorativejustice.org/editions/2002/July02.

Chapter 8

1. If Simon Baron-Cohen is right, there should be corresponding gender difference in preferences for the two shows, but I have no evidence that this is the case.

2. Less so in his old age. Eventually, in his final work, *Laws 10,* no longer mentioning Socrates, he endorses policies that can only be called totalitarian.

3. Martha C. Nussbaum, *The Therapy of Desire: Theory and Practice in Hellenistic Ethics* (Princeton, N.J.: Princeton University Press, 1994), 93–95.

4. Aristotle, *Nichomachean Ethics,* 1126.

5. Arlie Russell Hochschild, *The Managed Heart: Commercialization of Human Feeling* (Berkeley: University of California Press, 1983).

6. "Civil inattention" is a concept that sociologist Erving Goffman introduced. It refers to the politeness that emotionally intelligent individuals employ by seeming not to notice another person's social gaffe.

7. Simon Critchley, *On Humour* (London: Routledge, 2002).

8. Critchley, *On Humour,* 95, 101–2. The italics are mine.

9. Critchley, *On Humour,* 103.

10. Sigmund Freud, "Humor," in his collected works, *Standard Edition,* vol. 21, ed. J. Strachey (London: Hogarth, 1961), 161–66, as cited in Critchley, *On Humour,* 103, 105, 119.

11. Jane Feuer, "MTM Enterprises: An Overview," in *MTM "Quality Television,"* ed. Jane Feuer, Paul Kerr, and Tise Vahimagi (London: BFI, 1984), 4–6, 40.

12. Joshua Brand took the main responsibility for production. Then, after masterminding 66 of the 110 episodes, he left. The new executive producer, David Chase, is highly talented, but his sensibility was not suited to *Northern Exposure.* Nevertheless, the fifth season was not sharply different from the previous ones.

13. Joseph Campbell's *The Hero with a Thousand Faces* (Princeton, N.J.: Princeton University Press, 1949) is mentioned several times in the series, and there are explicit comparisons of Joel's journey to Campbell's heroes, such as Odysseus. Campbell draws upon Carl Jung.

14. Joseph Campbell with Bill Moyers, *The Power of Myth* (New York: Doubleday, 1988), 186.

15. See D. Byrge and R. Miller, *The Screwball Comedy Films: A History and Filmography, 1934–1942* (Jefferson, N.C.: McFarland, 1991).

16. Stanley Cavell, *Pursuits of Happiness: The Hollywood Comedy of Remarriage* (Cambridge, Mass.: Harvard University Press, 1981). Also see his *Cities of Words: Pedagogical Letters on a Register of the Moral Life* (Cambridge, Mass.: Harvard University Press, 2004), which revisits these old films and explores the supposed connections between them and Emerson, Locke, Mill, Kant, Rawls, Nietzsche, Ibsen, Freud, Plato, Aristotle, Henry James, Shaw, Shakespeare, and Plato.

17. Cavell, *Pursuits of Happiness,* 182.

18. Cavell, *Pursuits of Happiness,* 183.

19. Christine Scodari, "Possession, Attraction, and the Thrill of the Case: Gendered Myth-Making in Film and Television Comedy of the Sexes," in *Critical Studies in Mass Communication* 12 (1995): 23–29.

20. Erich Segal, *The Death of Comedy* (Cambridge, Mass.: Harvard University Press, 2001), 453–56.

21. Campbell, *The Hero with a Thousand Faces,* 28.

22. The following books have been identified as an incomplete list of the works from which Chris reads to us, mentions, or quotes—some of them several times: *The Complete Works of Walt Whitman*; *Where the Wild Things Are,* by Maurice Sendak; *War and Peace,* by Tolstoy; *A Midsummer Night's Dream,* by Shakespeare; *Remembrance of Things Past,* by Marcel Proust; *The Divine Comedy,* by Dante; something unidentified by Søren Kierkegaard; *A Portrait of the Artist As a Young Man,* by James Joyce; *Leaves*

of Grass, by Whitman; *Lincoln: The President,* by J. G. Randall; *Call of the Wild,* by Jack London; *Oedipus Rex*; something unidentified by Albert Einstein; *Don Juan,* by Lord Byron; *A Joseph Campbell Companion*; *Renascence and Other Poems,* by Edna St. Vincent Millay; *The North Pole,* by Robert Peary; *Paddle to the Sea,* by Holling Clancy Holling; *The Tempest,* by Shakespeare; *Zen and the Art of Motorcycle Maintenance,* by Robert Persig; *Pilgrim's Progress*; *House of Mirth,* by Edith Wharton; *Billy Budd,* by Herman Melville; something unidentified by Carl Jung; *Tales of Kipling*; *Slouching toward Bethlehem,* by Joan Didion; *The Sound and the Fury,* by William Faulkner; *The Hero with a Thousand Faces,* by Joseph Campbell; *Charlotte's Web,* by E. B. White; Genesis in the Bible; something unidentified by Henry David Thoreau; *Being and Time,* by Martin Heidegger; something unidentified by Raymond Chandler; *The Maine Woods,* by Thoreau; something unidentified about the history of medicine; something about gulls by Robert Ardry; *The Double,* by Dostoyevsky; *The White Goddess,* by Robert Graves; *One Hundred Years of Solitude,* by Gabriel García Márquez; "The Meaning of Psychology for Modern Man," by Carl Jung (an essay from the *Collected Works of Carl Jung*); *The Poetry of Robert Frost*; *Collected Sonnets,* by Edna St. Vincent Millay; *Interview with a Vampire,* by Anne Rice; *The Masks of God,* by Joseph Campbell; *Rhymes of a Red Cross Man,* by Robert Service; *Rhymes of a Rolling Stone,* by Robert Service; *Moby Dick,* by Herman Melville; *The Sum of All Fears,* by Tom Clancy; *The Stranger,* by Albert Camus; *Fear and Trembling* and *The Sickness unto Death,* by Kierkegaard; *The Conduct of Life,* by Ralph Waldo Emerson. Thanks to Kevin Wright.

23. Albert Einstein, as quoted by James A. Haught, ed., *2000 Years of Disbelief: Famous People with the Courage to Doubt* (Amherst, N.Y.: Prometheus, 1996), 241.

24. Herman Melville, *Billy Budd and Other Stories* (London: Lehmann, 1951).

25. Daniel Goleman, *Emotional Intelligence: Why It Can Matter More Than IQ* (New York: Bantam Books, 1997), 44–45.

26. Edmond Rostand, *Cyrano de Bergerac* (New York: Applause Theatre Books, 1996).

27. Susanne K. Langer, *Philosophy in a New Key: A Study in the Symbolism of Reason, Rite, and Art* (Cambridge, Mass.: Harvard University Press, 1942), 176.

28. Bruno Bettelheim, *The Uses of Enchantment: The Meaning and Importance of Fairy Tales* (New York: Random House, 1989), 26.

29. A classicist can make a good living trying to explain away Plato's inconsistency. See, for example, Susan B. Levin, *The Ancient Quarrel between Philosophy and Poetry Revisited: Plato and the Greek Literary Tradition* (Oxford: Oxford University Press, 2001); and Richard R. Buxton, ed., *From Myth to Reason? Studies in the Development of Greek Thought* (Oxford: Oxford University Press, 1999). This much is clear: He thought selective myth telling might be helpful in educating children, and he believed that a myth telling a "noble lie" might be useful. But there are still abundant contradictions. In fact, modern logicians have also disagreed about whether myths and other evocative artistic productions are rational. My impression is that the best resolution of this problem (which is even more complex than Plato realized) may have been proposed by Susanne

K. Langer, who distinguished between "discursive" and "presentational" symbolism. The former seemingly corresponds to logos and the latter to mythos—at least to poetry. To Langer, myths are neither; rather, they are raw material from which poetic compositions can be assembled. See her books, *Philosophy in a New Key: A Study in the Symbolism of Reason, Rite, and Art*, 3d ed. (Cambridge, Mass.: Harvard University Press, 1957), and *Feeling and Form: A Theory of Art* (New York: Scribner's, 1953).

30. G. E. R. Lloyd, *Polarity and Analogy: Two Types of Argumentation in Early Greek Thought* (Cambridge: Cambridge University Press, 1979), 259.

31. Carl Jung, *Psychology and Religion,* in *Collected Works,* vol. 11 (New York: Pantheon, 1958). Campbell says (in *The Hero with a Thousand Faces,* 18) that Jung cites Friedrich Nietzsche as defending the same notion in connection with the myth of eternal recurrence.

32. Joshua Brand told me that he had never read Campbell, which astonished me, for *Northern Exposure* was profoundly mythic, from start to finish.

33. Bettelheim, *Uses of Enchantment,* 25.

34. The Day of the Dead has some features of Halloween, but it is primarily a day for families to spend together remembering their departed loved ones. Though it is a real custom in Central America, it is not indigenous in Alaska and is presented here with poetic license.

Chapter 9

1. Robert Wuthnow, *America and the Challenges of Religious Diversity* (Princeton, N.J.: Princeton University Press, 2005).

2. Yves Lambert, "Religion in Modernity as a New Axial Age: Secularization or New Religious Forms?" *Sociology of Religion* 60 (Fall 1999).

3. Ronald Inglehart, "Religious Services?" worldwide data from a 1998 survey, Institute for Social Research at the University of Michigan.

4. Michael Medved, "Oscar Bids Reflect Industry's Discomfort with Religion," *USA Today,* January 25, 2005, www.usatoday.com/news/opinion/editorials/2005–01–25–medved_x.htm.

5. Sulak Sivaraksa, *Seeds of Peace: A Buddhist Vision for Renewing Society* (Berkeley, Calif.: Parallax, 1992).

6. Metta Spencer, "Buddhist Peacemakers," *Peace Magazine* (April–June 2004): 11, www.peacemagazine.org/archive/v20n2p11.htm.

7. Ven. Ken Tanaka quoted by Judith Linzer, *Torah and Dharma: Jewish Seekers in Eastern Religions* (Northvale, N.H.: Aronson, 1996), 246.

8. Robert N. Bellah, "Max Weber and World-Denying Love: A Look at the Historical Sociology of Religion," Humanities Center and Burke Lectureship on Religion and Society, University of California, San Diego, October 30, 1997.

9. Max Weber, *The Sociology of Religion* (Boston: Beacon, 1993), 166–84.

10. Weber, *The Sociology of Religion,* 169.

11. Max Weber, "Science as a Vocation," in *From Max Weber,* ed. C. Wright Mills and Hans H. Gerth [1919] (New York: Oxford University Press, 1946). See also Eliezer Schweid, "The 'Post-Secular' Era," *The "Middle East" Post,* Letter/Viewpoints, No. 440, 16 Tishrei, 5761 [October 15, 2000], for the history of secularization.

12. Rodney Stark, "Secularization, R.I.P.," *Sociology of Religion* 60, no. 3 (Fall 1999): 249.

13. For a summary and discussion of these trends, see William H. Swatos Jr. and Kevin J. Christiano, "Secularization Theory: The Course of a Concept," *Sociology of Religion* 60, no. 3 (Fall 1999): 209–20.

14. Stark, "Secularization, R.I.P.," citing R. F. Tomasson, *Iceland, the First New Society* (Minneapolis: University of Minnesota Press, 1980).

15. Philip Wexler, in his book *Mystical Society: An Emerging Social Vision* (Boulder, Colo.: Westview, 2000), 3, points out that 43 percent of Americans and 48 percent of British people have had one or more mystical experiences. He argues that mysticism is becoming a major religion for educated Western persons.

16. All such Buddhist sects in the West appeal predominantly to well-educated Caucasians except for Soka Gakkai, which has a large working-class membership.

17. The Oriental monk first appeared in films in 1919, when D. W. Griffith produced *Broken Blossoms, or The Yellow Man and the Girl.* That monk and the wise gurus of later films displayed the calm demeanor that has come to typify the monk as a pop cultural icon. See Jane Naomi Iwamura, "The Oriental Monk in American Popular Culture," in *Religion and Popular Culture in America,* ed. Bruce David Forbes and Jeffrey Mahan (Berkeley: University of California Press, 2000).

18. Linzer, *Torah and Dharma,* 277.

19. See Rodger Kamenetz, *The Jew in the Lotus: A Poet's Rediscovery of Jewish Identity in Buddhist India* (Toronto: HarperCollins Canada, 1995).

20. Linzer, *Torah and Dharma,* 247–49.

21. Peter Berger, *The Heretical Imperative: Contemporary Possibilities of Religious Affirmation* (New York: Anchor Books, 1980), 28.

22. Rick Warren, *The Purpose-Driven Life: What on Earth Am I Here For?* (Grand Rapids, Mich.: Zondervan, 2004).

23. Linzer, *Torah and Dharma,* 228–29, drawing on Berger, *The Heretical Imperative.*

24. Ellen Marie Chen, trans., *Tao Te Ching: A New Translation with Commentary* (New York: Paragon, 1989).

25. Burton Watson, trans., *The Complete Works of Chuang Tzu* (New York: Columbia University Press, 1968).

26. Julia Ching, *Chinese Religions* (London: Macmillan, 1993), 141, 216.

27. Frederica de Laguna, *Under Mount St. Elias: The History and Culture of Yakutat Tlingit* (Washington, D.C.: Smithsonian Institution, 1972).

28. Antonia Mills and Richard Slobodin, eds., *Amerindian Rebirth: Reincarnation Belief among North American Indians and Inuit* (Toronto: University of Toronto Press, 1994).

29. Rabbi Yonassan Gershom, *Beyond the Ashes: Cases of Reincarnation from the Holocaust* (Virginia Beach: A.R.E Press, 1992), chap. 3.; Simcha Paull Raphael, *Jewish*

Views of the Afterlife (Northvale, N.J.: Aronson, 1996). See the book's Web site, www. twoaspirinsandacomedy.com, for a history of Jewish notions of the afterlife.

30. For this scientific method, see Karl Popper, *The Logic of Scientific Discovery* (London: Routledge, 2002).

31. Ching, *Chinese Religions,* chap. 5.

32. The *Star Wars* series of films represents Taoism. "May the Force be with you" refers to "The Tao," an eternal force (but not a personal God) that pervades the universe. Joseph Campbell, the inspiration to the films' creator, George Lucas, imported both Taoism and the hero's journey myth into the plot.

33. Joseph Campbell with Bill Moyers, *The Power of Myth* (New York: Anchor Doubleday, 1988), 80–82.

34. Although the show does not disclose authorship of this quotation, it was actually Ivan Turgenev's advice to Leo Tolstoy.

35. See the discussion between two scientist-Buddhists, Matthieu Ricard and Trinh Xuan Thuan, *The Quantum and the Lotus: A Journey to the Frontiers Where Science and Buddhism Meet* (New York: Crown, 2001), especially 63–64. See the book's Web site, www.twoaspirinsandacomedy.com, for information on chaos theory and dependent origination.

36. *Groundhog Day* is a 1993 film starring Bill Murray as a grouchy TV weatherman much like the young Joel Fleischman. His assignment: to cover a groundhog emerging to see its shadow. The day is unpleasant. He pursues a girl who has no interest in him, and a snowstorm forces them to stay over in the little town. Every morning thereafter he awakens, still in that town, replaying the same miserable day. (He alone realizes that it is recurring; everyone else forgets.) Eventually he realizes that he can learn from his mistakes of the previous day. He becomes a better man and learns to please the woman until, finally, he wins her heart and the day stops repeating itself. He is liberated from the wheel.

Before and during the Axial Age, this "eternal recurrence" notion was a standard theory from India to Europe. Unlike the writers of *Groundhog Day,* some philosophers assumed that one cannot change anything on any new replay. According to Aristotle's pupil Eudemus, "If one may believe the Pythagoreans, the same things will recur exactly, and I shall be holding my pointer and talking to you as you sit there, and everything else will be exactly as it is now" (as cited by Thomas McEvilley, *The Shape of Ancient Thought* [New York: Allworth, 2002], 72). The Stoics later held the same belief, and so did Friedrich Nietzsche (*Thus Spake Zarathustra* [New York: Prometheus, 1993]). To him, this recurrence theme was a way of avoiding nihilism, the lack of meaning or direction in life. All you have to do, moment by moment, is decide which of the options before you is the one you'd prefer to keep repeating over and over for eternity. This makes you responsible for your own actions, even if you believe, as Nietzsche did, that "God is dead." Bill Murray's character has more wiggle room than most ancient theorists; he can experiment with new ways of behaving every day until he has developed the virtues that he originally lacked.

Another drama that is, I think, about eternal recurrence is Samuel Beckett's *Waiting for Godot.* However, we all see different things in that play.

37. Nowadays people around the world increasingly do so as well. In a survey of more than 1,000 Canadians of all ages and backgrounds in 2003, 55 percent said they believe in "karma or destiny." (Both terms imply inevitability, rather than freedom of choice.) (See Gabrielle Bauer, "Gods and Other Mysteries," *Canadian Reader's Digest,* November 2003, with data from an Ipsos-Reid survey.) Surveys in the United States show that 25 percent of the population believes in reincarnation. (See Russell Chandler, *Understanding the New Age* [Grand Rapids, Mich.: Zondervan, 1993].) Most of the respondents are presumably Christian, though according to Christian eschatology, the afterlife is supposed to involve resurrection on Judgment Day, not rebirth. See the book's Web site, www.twoaspirinsandacomedy, on the ethicization of karma.

38. De Laguna, *Under Mount St. Elias,* 770; George Thornton Emmons, *The Tlingit Indians,* edited and with additions by Frederica de Laguna (Seattle: University of Washington Press, 1991), 289.

39. In this regard, Maggie shows more insight than the historic religions that Weber compared. Historically, it has generally been assumed that transcendent universal "brotherly" love must have a "cash value" that can be claimed by the needy—an assumption that brings love into contradiction with the first law of thermodynamics. (See Newcombe in chapter 3.) In his studies of religion's economic consequences, Weber explores the endless ways of attempting to manage this incompatibility. See Max Weber, *The Sociology of Religion* (Boston: Beacon, 1991).

40. Viktor E. Frankl, *Man's Search for Meaning* (Boston: Beacon, 2000).

41. Stanley Cavell, *Pursuits of Happiness: The Hollywood Comedy of Remarriage* (Cambridge, Mass.: Harvard University Press, 1981).

42. Martha C. Nussbaum, *Love's Knowledge: Essays on Philosophy and Literature* (New York: Oxford University Press, 1990), 365–91.

43. Diane Frolov, who wrote this and many other episodes, had studied both theology and dance. With wide interests in Eastern religion, she participated in retreats with the followers of a deceased guru from India, Meher Baba. The name *Manonash* refers to a lengthy period of seclusion when Meher Baba lived in solitude and silence, carrying on his spiritual quest for transcendence. Likewise for Joel, the Manonash place and period are marked by concentrated soul work.

44. *Tao* means "the way or the path." Taoism encourages ease and naturalness. You don't struggle; you just follow the path.

45. Barry Corbin, the experienced actor who played Maurice, told me he had been so troubled by this trend that he flew down to Los Angeles several times to warn the producers that the show would be cancelled if this kind of writing continued. They did not believe him. I interviewed several people on the production team, none of whom would identify by name the source of the problems, which they had all recognized as serious. One hinted that when problems arose in the script, it became impossible to reach higher-level producers by phone; they were busy lining up new jobs for themselves.

Ultimately, I concluded it was David Chase who had altered the spirit of Cicely. He had found the show too "precious" for his tastes, which would find full expression only later in his own creation, *The Sopranos,* a show that was absolutely antithetical to *Northern Exposure.*

46. Kiwa'a Ani? Why did Diane Frolov and Andrew Schneider send Fleischman to the Tlingits' heaven? Was this some kind of code? Did they disagree about whether to let him live or die? Or does this imply that he *did* die and go to a better place than New York City? Unfortunately, Frolov has declined to answer my queries, so we'll never know what they meant.

47. Martin Seligman, *Authentic Happiness: Using the New Positive Psychology to Realize Your Potential for Lasting Fulfillment* (New York: Simon & Shuster, 2004).

48. Johan Galtung, *Transcend and Transform: An Introduction to Conflict Work* (Boulder, Colo.: Paradigm, 2004), 17.

Chapter 10

1. Plato, *The Republic,* especially Book X.

2. Plato, *The Symposium,* especially Socrates's recounting of Diotima's advice.

3. Martha Nussbaum, *The Fragility of Goodness: Luck and Ethics in Greek Tragedy and Philosophy,* rev. ed. (Cambridge: Cambridge University Press, 1986), chap. 7.

4. Nussbaum, *Fragility,* 224–27.

5. Johan Galtung, *Transcend and Transform: An Introduction to Conflict Work* (Boulder, Colo.: Paradigm, 2004), 160. Also see Malcolm Gladwell, *Blink: The Power of Thinking Without Thinking* (Boston: Little, Brown, 2005).

6. Martin E. P. Seligman, *Authentic Happiness* (New York: Simon & Shuster, 2004). This quotation is drawn from an interview at www.edge.org/3rd_culture/seligman04/seligman_index.html.

7. James Howard Kunstler, *The Long Emergency: Surviving the Converging Catastrophes of the Twenty-First Century* (New York: Grove, 2005). Also see dels.nas.edu/ccgc.

8. See Paul Roberts, *The End of Oil: On the Edge of a Perilous New World* (Boston: Houghton Mifflin, 2004).

9. Nuclear Age Peace Foundation, www.wagingpeace.org.

10. Green Cross International, gcinwa.newaccess.ch/index.htm.

11. UN High Commissioner for Refugees, www.unhcr.ch/cgi-bin/texis/vtx/home.

12. Jared Diamond, *Collapse: How Societies Choose to Fail or Succeed* (New York: Viking Adult, 2004).

13. Carl Stieren, "Civilian Peace Service," *Peace Magazine,* April 2005.

14. The Hunger Project, citing a UN FAO report. See www.thp.org/faq.html.

15. Green Cross International, gcinwa.newaccess.ch/index.htm.

16. TakingITGlobal, understanding.takingitglobal.org/health/HIVAIDS.

17. See www.restorativejustice.org.

18. The Breman produces Holocaust-related comics; see www.willeisner.com/index normal.html. Dark Horse Comics has urban youths create comics; see services.darkhorse. com/education/index.php.

19. Augusto Boal, *Theatre of the Oppressed* (New York: Theatre Communications Group, 1979); Augusto Boal, *The Rainbow of Desire: The Boal Method of Theatre and Therapy* (New York: Routledge, 1995).

20. Neal Baer, M.D., executive producer, *Law and Order SVU*, in a panel discussion, Entertainment Summit West, Los Angeles, October 2003. See Population Communications International at www.population.org/index.shtml.

21. See www.populationmedia.org.

22. See www.population.org/index.shstml.

23. Arvind Singhal and Everett M. Rogers, *Entertainment-Education: A Communication Strategy for Social Change* (Mahwah, N.J.: Erlbaum, 1999), 170.

24. Here's what I wrote: "Alexander, let's imagine a weekly one-hour-long drama, lasting two or three years, about a Green Cross International team in an unnamed Middle Eastern Islamic country (which should not closely resemble any particular real country). The team is examining the effects of a recent war on the environment and health. The writers must be instructed to avoid preaching, joke machine humor, formulaic plots, and the display of violence. Whenever violence is seen to be impending, the excitement of the story must arise from the activities of the team as they try to prevent it, not resort to it. Let's have them living in a small family-run hotel where other foreigners (journalists, salesman, etc.) also stay, so there can be regular interaction with an international ensemble and traditional locals. Within ten minutes, I could think of twenty serious issues that might be addressed in the show—each one providing no more than one of the three storylines that make up a typical episode. (The other two storylines should be entertaining—humorous, romantic, adventurous, or touching.) Viewers could certainly come up with a better list, but here's mine:

- The water system is wrecked. What are the health consequences?
- Corruption. How should the team handle demands for bribes?
- Islam. It is not a unitary thing, for there are conflicts among Sunnis, Shiites, and Sufis. (One Green Cross guy can be an Arabic-speaking poet yet also a modern, Westernized scientist—and a Sufi, to challenge stereotypes.)
- The effects of depleted uranium
- Separatist demands for, say, an independent Kurdistan versus the development of a nationwide democracy
- The offensiveness of Hollywood culture to conservative Islamic sensibilities
- Gender relations and the attitude of the international characters toward Sharia law
- A suspicion that certain local people may be terrorists (Have one character be a glamorous Russian journalist with a taste for risk who loves to investigate such suspicions. What will she do after she finds out the truth?)
- The power of a local oligarchical family

- The practice of suppressing reportage of news
- The plight of refugees
- How to support a local group of citizens in their nonviolent resistance against the undemocratic regime or against an unfair but powerful economic interest group
- What political actions should be taken toward people who have caused the social problems resulting in war? Forgive them? Blame them? Bring them to justice? What kind of justice? Sharia?
- Can targeted sanctions by foreign governments have a decisive influence on the policies of a tyrannical regime? What price does this impose on the poorer citizens?
- Does the U.S. government seek economic control (e.g., over oil), and how does this intention influence its policies toward dictatorship?
- Do trade barriers (especially agricultural subsidies) by Europe, Japan, and the United States harm poor people abroad?
- Can an outsider contribute to the protection of women and children by demonstrating conflict management processes? By promoting awareness of human rights?
- Is war satisfying to people with the thrill-seeking gene, giving their lives meaning? If so, what substitutes can satisfy those needs in this particular culture?
- Which is more satisfactory after a war: a truth and reconciliation commission with amnesty for repentant persons, or the International Criminal Court? Are the two approaches compatible? How does the unequal access to water interact with the politics of the country and its neighbors?

25. Jon Gertner, "Our Ratings, Ourselves," *New York Times Magazine,* April 10, 2005, 34–41, 56.

26. Christopher Hitchens, "Free to Choose," *The Nation* 267, no. 2 (July 13, 1998): 9.

27. Robert W. McChesney and Robert A. Hackett, "Beyond Wiggle Room: American Corporate Media's Democratic Deficit, Its Global Implications, and Prospects for Reform," in *Democratizing Global Media: One World, Many Struggles,* ed. Robert A. Hackett and Yuezhi Zhao (Lanham, Md.: Rowman & Littlefield, 2005).

28. Robert McChesney and John Nichols, "Platform for Media Reform," *MediaFile* 20, no. 1 (January–February 2001). From their book, *It's the Media, Stupid* (New York: Seven Stories Press, 2000).

29. David Held, *Models of Democracy* (Palo Alto, Calif.: Stanford University Press, 1997).

30. Sean O. Siochru, "Finding a Frame: Towards a Transnational Advocacy Campaign to Democratize Communication," in Hackett and Zhao, *Democratizing Global Media.*

31. Robert W. McChesney in his article with John Nichols, "The Making of a Movement," *The Nation* (January 7, 2002).

32. Dorothy Swanson, *The Story of Viewers for Quality Television: From Grassroots to Prime Time* (Syracuse, N.Y.: Syracuse University Press, 2000).

33. Kathryn C. Montgomery, *Target, Prime Time: Advocacy Groups and the Struggle over Entertainment Television* (New York: Oxford University Press, 1990).

34. Valerie Smith, "Television Advertisers Reject Violence," *Peace Magazine,* September–October 1994, 22, www.peacemagazine.org/archive/v10n5p22.htm.

Index

About the Author

Metta Spencer received a Ph.D. in sociology from the University of California, Berkeley, in 1969 and joined the faculty of the University of Toronto in 1971. She taught courses for and coordinated an interdisciplinary program in peace and conflict studies for thirteen years at the Mississauga campus. She wrote ten editions of an introductory textbook, *Foundations of Modern Sociology*, coauthored *Adolescent Prejudice* (1975), and edited several books, including *Research in Social Movements, Conflict, and Change* (1991), *World Security* (1994), *Women in Post-Communism* (1997), *Separatism: Democracy and Disintegration* (1998), and *The Lessons of Yugoslavia* (2000). Since 1997 she has been professor emeritus, but she continues her engagement with social issues.

Both professionally and as an activist citizen, her work focuses primarily on problems of war and peace—nowadays mostly the search for alternatives to war. This book explores the possibilities of a culture of peace, including public education for nonviolent ways of addressing conflicts. To the same end, Spencer participates enthusiastically in civil society organizations and since 1985 has edited *Peace Magazine*, which is now published quarterly in Toronto (see www.peacemagazine.org/). She has written hundreds of articles, often for the latter publication. Her ongoing research explores the influence of the international peace movement on Soviet and Russian military policy. Her personal Web site is metta.spencer.name; her Weblog, which is updated three times weekly, is metta-spencer.blogspot.com; the Web site for this book, on which readers can find expanded discussions of some of the material in this book, is www.twoaspirinsandacomedy.com.